THE LAW AND PRACTICE OF THE KIRK

A GUIDE AND COMMENTARY

by

ANDREW HERRON

First edition published 1995 by Chapter House Ltd
26 Bothwell Street, Glasgow G2 6PA.

First Edition March 1995
Reprinted March 1995

ISBN 0-948643-13-7

Printed in Scotland by Bell and Bain Ltd, Glasgow

CONTENTS

PREFACE

THE FOLLOWING PAGES are designed to provide a simple presentation of how the affairs of the Kirk are managed. They do not aspire to be an ordnance survey map of the field of Kirk Law; neither are they meant to be a replacement of, but merely a substitute for, an updated Cox, however urgently needed that may be. That is not my field. I have tried to keep clearly at the front of my mind the ordinary reader be he or she member, office-bearer, probationer, parish minister, or even presbytery clerk. I have deliberately kept to a minimum lengthy extracts from Acts and Regulations, trying rather to indicate the appropriate legislation, so that, with the aid of Dr Weatherhead's admirable reprint of "Acts of the General Assembly from 1929" at hand, the legal researcher should readily have the necessary authority before him.

The book is designed as a Guide. A guide tells you not only where exactly you will find a particular landmark it gives you some description of what the thing looks like, how it came to be there, and maybe even tells the odd ghost story from its past. As Clerk for over twenty years to the Presbytery of Glasgow I enjoyed unique opportunities of seeing the various Acts not just in print but in operation and have thus been able, I hope, to clothe the bare bones of legality with some kind of human tissue. The book is also intended as a Commentary. Where I have digressed — as has happened quite often — to comment upon some aspect of a particular statute (in not a few instances even to be critical of it) I have made it perfectly clear that the views are my own, and the reader is at perfect liberty to disagree.

I have been inspired to produce this work partly to fill to some extent the vacuum until a "proper Cox" is available, but even more because the success which attended the appearance some years ago of my little "Guides" (for copies of which I am constantly being asked to this day) has convinced me of how desirable it is that a book taking a practical as well as a popular approach to this subject should be available.

There is a convention that the General Assembly attracts a plural verb —

a kind of "Royal We." To this custom I have adhered fairly faithfully though in cases where it produced a grammatical nonsense ("Thinking of the General Assembly we must remember that they consist of ....") I have not hesitated to ignore it. In the same spirit, to avoid the dreary repetition of "he or she", "him or her" ("When a member approaches his or her minister he or she is likely to ask him or her about his or her....) I have employed the masculine form throughout. If this gives offence I can only express regret and say that none is intended. In an age when new words, many of them unutterably ugly, are being coined daily I do wish someone would produce a set of inter-sex pronouns.

I have been indebted to a great many people both in and out of 121 George Street for reading over parts of the work and raising questions, correcting errors and offering comments. It would be pointless to print a long list of names and invidious to select idividuals for special mention, so I shall not identify any but hope that one and all they will accept a most sincere Thank You.

I must, however, express my very deep indebtedness to Lord Davidson for encouragement and help while the work has been awriting and concluding with his gracious and more than generous commendation of the end-product in his Foreword. It is with pleasure and gratitude that I recall the days between 1973 and 1978 that we spent together in what is popularly known as "the playpen" (see Glossary) in the Assembly Hall.

My ignorance of the whole business of publishing and marketing is nothing short of abysmal, and had it not been for the skill and guidance of Nicholas Gray of Chapter House, Ltd, this would still be a manuscript. For the patience and the faith he has shown throughout the process of converting it into an attractive sales-product I cannot ever be too grateful.

Finally may I wish my readers helpful and interesting as well, I hope, as informative reading — the book was written with a view to being read, not just to being set, however prominently, on a shelf as a work of reference.

ANDREW HERRON
January 1995

FOREWORD

By The Hon Lord Davidson, Senator of the College of Justice

The Committee of the United Free Church, which compiled the Manual of Practice and Procedure for that Church nearly a century ago, expressed the hope in their Preface that the volume would prove a sufficient guide both to the courts and the individual members in the discharge of their duties, and continued as follows: "It will serve also to exhibit the developed working of the Presbyterian System, which our forefathers established on the great fundamental principles laid down in the New Testament for the Church of Christ. The Christian Society throughout the world was to be a brotherhood of mutual service, according to the gifts bestowed on each member of it. There was to be no exercise of lordship or authority by individuals; no blind deference to be paid to any one on earth as teacher, or father, or master. On these principles Presbyterianism was founded, and what was claimed for it at first, and may be claimed for it still, is that it conserves on one hand the unity, order, and discipline of a well-constituted Church, and on the other hand the rights and privileges of an intelligent and spiritually-minded Christian people." These words are no less apt today because they remind us that one of the most distinctive features of Presbyterianism is its system of government through courts, a system to be contrasted with the imperial structure of Church government which in Scotland was displaced at the Reformation.

Today many Churches throughout the world have adopted the ideals of a Christian society based on the Presbyterian System, but all of these recognised the debt they owe to those who over the past four centuries have fashioned and refined that system in Scotland. It is therefore entirely appropriate that this contemporary guide to the practice and procedure of the Kirk should be prepared by Dr Andrew Herron who, in the course of a long and distinguished life of service to the Kirk, was for more than twenty years Clerk to the Presbytery of Glasgow, a court which has a strong claim to be called the largest in the Presbyterian spectrum. In addition his experience as a parish minister, as Convener of important Assembly committees, as a General Trustee, and as Moderator of the General Assembly, makes him superbly well qualified to describe the Kirk's contemporary practice and procedure.

This book contains much more than a statement of the Kirk's laws and practices. The reader will derive a double benefit. The first is that he will be given a clear and accurate account of a particular law or practice. Secondly, in many instances he will find out the reason for the rule. In some cases Dr Herron will explain why he does not agree with the reasoning on which the rule is based. I believe that this accompanying commentary is invaluable. Many within and outwith the membership of the Kirk are critical of its practices and procedures. These are alleged to be obscure, antique and inefficient. This book gives the answer to such criticisms. To those who complain of obscurity Dr Herron states the relevant rules with luminous clarity. The supporting commentary explains, where appropriate, the origin of the rule. If the explanation is convincing, the critic may be content with suggesting that the rule could with advantage be rewritten in simpler terms. But if he still seeks abolition of the rule he will not be able to plead ignorance of the implications of the proposed change for the Kirk.

In many places Dr Herron's exposition draws attention to the fact that, as a result of the unions achieved in this century, current practices and procedure incorporate several traditions. This mixture of traditions reminds the reader of the significant contribution that sound procedures can make to the unity of the Kirk. The would-be reformer has to recognise that for his proposals to succeed there has to be broad agreement reflecting differing standpoints, and that an existing rule which to some seems to be merely obstructive is regarded by others as a valuable protection. Throughout his life-long service to the Kirk Dr Herron has been acutely aware of the delicate balance that has to be maintained between the claims of tradition and the need to develop soundly-based innovations appropriate for a Church which proclaims that it is reformed yet always in need of reformation.

I therefore confidently recommend this book in the hope that it will be widely read. The industry that Dr Herron has invested in mastering the immense detail of the subject together with the wisdom so evident in his commentary entitle this book to a respected place in the literature of the Presbyterian system.

C K DAVIDSON

Chapter 1

CONGREGATIONAL AFFAIRS

WHAT IS A CONGREGATION? According to the dictionary it is a number of people gathered together for worship. For legal purposes, though, we want something a little more specific. The most recent official definition is that found in Act iv 1984 — "a company of persons associated together in a Parish whose names are on the Communion Roll and who are under the pastoral oversight of a Minister or Ministers and a Kirk Session, for Christian worship, fellowship, instruction, mission and service." This definition is "for purposes of the Act" (anent Readjustment) which, presumably, is why it confines itself to those whose names are on the Roll. In ordinary usage adherents and children are regarded, very properly, as part of the congregation, which may therefore be defined as a group of members, adherents and children gathered in a particular area under a Minister and Kirk Session for Christian worship, instruction, fellowship, mission, and service.

Members — The Members of the congregation are those persons who have been admitted by the Kirk Session (a) by profession of faith, (b) by certificate of transference, or (c) by special resolution (p 296) and whose names appear on the Communion Roll. They are entitled to vote on all matters affecting the work and witness of the congregation, including the election of a Minister in a vacancy, and excluding only those matters which fall within the exclusive preserve of the Kirk Session (*q v*). According to Cox, "It is the duty of members to be faithful in attendance on Gospel ordinances, to accord to their Minister all due honour and respect in the Lord, to submit to the Kirk Session as over them in the Lord, to cherish a spirit of brotherly love among themselves, to give of their means for the maintenance of the Christian ministry and the furtherance of the Gospel, and to share with their Minister the responsibility for Christian witness and service." Some part of these obligations are included in questions put to entrants at admission to full communion (p 3), and some to questions put to the congregation at the induction of a minister (p 89).

Adherents — I cannot find any official definition of this term in its normal application, but I think it is generally understood to refer to persons who are not in full communion with any branch of the Church, or who are members of some other congregation, yet are regular worshippers in the congregation to which they "adhere". They are found principally in Highland parishes and are people who believe in all sincerity that they are not worthy to commit themselves to full Church membership and come forward to the Lord's Supper. There is provision whereby during a vacancy Adherents of the former class may have their names added to the Electoral Register, but it should be noted that they have no say whatever on any issue of readjustment. Adherents may not take any part in the management of the congregation's affairs and cannot be elected to Congregational Board, Deacons' Court or Committee of Management. In 1963 an Overture presented to the Assembly by the Presbytery of Caithness sought clarification of the position of Adherents and it was remitted to the General Administration Committee "to consider the place of adherents in the life and work of the Church and, if so advised, to suggest proposals to grant adherents a definite status within the Church."

The Committee reported the following year (Repts 1964, p 14) that the tendency prevalent in some areas to decline the commitment involved in Church membership, however sincere its motive, was one not to be encouraged, and that to grant status and recognition to such adherents would merely establish more firmly a tradition from which the Church should be seeking to break away. Besides, if people genuinely felt unable to accept the responsibility of membership of a congregation they could scarcely be expected to undertake the responsibilities of rule within that congregation. So, apart from the exception noted above, there is no official status for adherents.

In response to a request in 1993 that the Committee (on Mission and Evangelism Resources) should consider the question of Adherents a report was submitted to the following Assembly (Repts 1994, p 396). This was approved and has been sent down to Presbyteries and Kirk Sessions for "consideration and implementation as appropriate to their parishes." It has, as I see it, no relevance in the present context.

Children — The baptized families of believers are members of the congregation though not yet in full communion.

Until 1985 the Kirk Session was required in terms of a deliverance of 1930 to keep a Roll of Baptized Persons not Communicants. This was a carry-over of a position held in the former U F Church that "all baptized young persons in the congregation ... have special claims to supervision and care.

"Their names should be entered in a Roll ... and each Elder should endeavour to make himself acquainted with the young in his district and to promote their spiritual welfare." (U F Manual p 7). The need to keep such a roll was departed from in 1985, but not the need for caring oversight by Elders.

For the question of the admission of children to the Lord's Supper see p 301.

Supplementary Roll — The Kirk Session is required also to maintain a roll of persons whose names have been removed from the Communion Roll without their having sought or been given a Transference Certificate and who are still resident in the district. Such people, while continuing to be the responsibility of the Kirk Session in some limited sense, do not form part of the congregation, have no voting rights whatever and may not have their names put on the Electoral Register in a vacancy. They may, however, take communion if they so request.

Question on Admission — On being admitted to full membership of the Church the candidate has to answer questions relating to his Christian faith and commitment and promising to support the work of the Church.

There is no statutory form for this latter. The 1940 Book of Common Order suggests, "Do you promise to make diligent use of the means of grace, to share dutifully in the work and service of the Church, and to give of your substance, as the Lord may prosper you, for the advancement of His Kingdom throughout the world?"

This is considerably expanded in Common Order (1994) which exacts a promise to join regularly with fellow Christians in worship on the Lord's Day, to be faithful in reading the Bible and in prayer, to give a fitting proportion of their time, talents and money for the Church's work in the world, and to profess publicly their loyalty to Jesus Christ, to serve Him in their daily work, and to walk in His ways all the days of their lives. It is, I take it, for each Kirk Session to determine what vows should be required of those coming forward.

Response to Induction of Minister — When a Minister has been inducted or introduced to a charge the Moderator of Presbytery puts to the congregation(s) a question in these terms — "Do you, the members and adherents of this congregation, accept Mr A B whom you have called to be [who has been introduced as] your Minister, and do you promise him all due honour and support in the Lord; and in view of the pastoral and missionary obligations of this congregation do you each now agree to share with your Minister the responsibility for Christian witness and Christian service, and will you give of your means, as the Lord shall prosper you, for the maintenance of the Christian ministry and the furtherance of the Gospel?" (Act ix 1958). The congregation are invited to signify their assent by standing. (This question is put after the induction [introduction] of the Minister has been completed lest an affirmative answer be thought to be a condition of such induction [introduction]).

Status of Congregations

Apart from the cases of Church Extension charges and Mission Stations the matter of the status of congregations is largely governed by Act iv 1984 and reference is made to the Chapter on Reappraisal where the subject is dealt with at length.

No Change — A congregation may be involved in linking, it may have its choice of Minister restricted or the tenure of its ministry made terminable, or it may be transferred or transported without in any way affecting its enjoyment of full status as a congregation of the Church. A congregation may be declared a Continued Vacancy and be deprived altogether of the right to call a Minister without its status as a congregation being in any way affected.

Change — Where a congregation has agreed to transport with its assets in people and funds to, for example, a new housing estate it may be found advantageous for it to adopt the status of a Church Extension charge, and this it will be allowed to do on application to the Extension Projects Committee. The change will be made a condition of the Basis of Transportation.

The Act of 1957 (xvii) included a form of readjustment omitted from the new Act — it was called "reduction" and it consisted in a congregation being reduced to the position of a Mission Station. While this Act was repealed in 1984 it would still be in order, I imagine, for a Presbytery so minded to resort to this expedient and to claim as its justification for doing so the terms of Para 19 of the new Act. Were a congregation to be reduced in this way its status would be vitally affected, for, while it would still be a congregation it would no longer have a Kirk Session and no longer be a charge.

Dissolution — When a congregation is no longer able to continue its individual existence and no form of readjustment commends itself it may be appropriate to consider dissolution whereby on an agreed date the life of the congregation comes to a full stop, its parish area having been reallocated to other congregations.

Name of Congregation

In 1961 the General Assembly approved a recommendation of its General Administration Committee in the following terms (Repts 1961, p 15) — "As a result of representation made to it the Committee took up consideration of the past and present custom of naming congregations 'X Street Church of Scotland'. In 1929 the Commission of the General Assembly authorised the use of the word 'parish', and the Committee is strongly of opinion that the correct designation of a congregation should be 'X Street Parish Church'. There is only one Church of Scotland, and the Committee recommends that the General Assembly discourage the use of such a title as 'X Street or X Church of Scotland' and urge the use of the word 'parish', and authorise any such change where necessary." The Committee might have gone further and said that to call a linked charge — as has been done — "Brown Street and St John's Churches of Scotland" is an obvious nonsense.

To me it has always seemed that the word "parish" as an adjective goes with "Church" and not with "congregation" and that while it is correct to speak of X Parish Church we should refer simply to "the congregation of X". Failure to appreciate this distinction has led on occasion to difficulty and ill-feeling arising in a case of readjustment where the Basis of Union had clearly stated, "The name of the united congregation shall be 'Oldburgh'" but later a Notice-Board had appeared at the Church door headed "Oldburgh Parish Church." There is no essential contradiction, but one can understand how claims of breach of faith came to be made by those unaccustomed if not actually hostile to this terminology. It would have been nonsense to say, "The name of the united congregation shall be Oldburgh Parish Church" — for whatever a congregation is it is not a Parish Church! I would suggest that the simplest and fairest way to avoid hurtful confusion is to write into the Basis, "The united charge shall be known as Oldburgh Parish Church."

There is today a noticeable tendency to incorporate the word "Kirk" into the name of a congregation — the East High Kirk. It should always be proper to add the word Church after the distinctive title of a congregation, but clearly East High Kirk Church does not make sense. People are at liberty — maybe should be encouraged — to speak of Kirk rather than Church, but not for purposes of distinguishing one congregation from its neighbours.

Charge — One sometimes finds the terms "charge" and "congregation" treated as alternatives, but this can lead to confusion for they do not mean the same thing. A charge may be defined as "a sphere of pastoral duty normally fulfilled by a Minister and centred on a congregation or congregations." The definition given in Act iv 1984 is "a sphere of pastoral duty to which a Minister is or Ministers are inducted." The definition is for purposes of the Act (anent Readjustment) and does not conform to normal usage. Where more than one Minister is inducted the charge, admittedly, is called one collegiate charge, but each Minister is inducted to a separate charge within it. And even under conditions of Continued Vacancy a charge remains a charge, even if a vacant one. It is important too to note that the linking of two or more congregations creates one charge without affecting the independence of the separate congregations of which it is composed.

Linked Charge — Where two congregations have been linked to form one charge it is usual to designate the result as A *with* B and there is much to said in favour of putting them in alphabetical order — the "with" in italics being abbreviated "linked with" and the alphabetical order being to emphasise that they are there on terms of equality.

Constituting a Congregation

The constituting of a congregation is largely governed by the provisions of Act iv 1984 to which reference should be made. The information supplied below is of the briefest.

A congregation of the Church of Scotland may be constituted in any one of four ways — (a) by Church Extension where no congregation had existed before; (b) by reception of an existing congregation from another denomination or from some other existing society; (c) as a result of Union; or (d) as a consequence of Severance.

(a) Church Extension Charge

In the pre-Union Church of Scotland a new charge began as a Chapel of Ease. In the churches of the Secessions it was generally Praying Societies that came to be "congregated", though in later times it was not unusual in the cities for part of a UP congregation to hive off and create a charge in a new area. Quite often in the U F Church a cause would begin as a Preaching Station. Since 1929 a charge begins as a Church Extension charge under regulations, amended from time to time, and presently as follows.

In normal circumstances it will lie with the Minister and Kirk Session of a parish within which extensive housing development is occurring to approach the Presbytery with a view to having a new charge erected there, though in this the Presbytery may itself take the initiative. When satisfied that a case exists the Presbytery reports accordingly to the National Mission's Committee on Extension Projects which in conjunction with the Reappraisal Committee has to decide whether a new charge is called for or whether other ways can be devised for dealing with the situation. If it is decided to proceed towards a Church Extension project the Presbytery next confers with the local authority or other developer with a view to securing a suitable site, transmitting its findings to the Assembly Committee which may authorise negotiations for purchase. Though there is no rule governing this the Local Authority will usually give land to the Church at a price lower than the market value fixed by the District Valuer, but will write conditions into the title restricting the use to Church purposes. Consultation must also be held with Ministers and Kirk Sessions of contiguous parishes and a provisional parish area has to be defined.

If the population of this is or will be sufficient to justify a charge (a minimum of around eight thousand is generally accepted) the Extension Projects Committee will take steps towards the appointment of a Minister and of an architect, the former to get to work among the people in some makeshift accommodation which it is for the Presbytery to secure, the latter to prepare plans for the erection of buildings. A provisional Kirk Session will be appointed by the Presbytery, consisting of the Minister along with Assessor Elders from neighbouring charges. Before plans for the building have been finally approved cosultation should be had with the General Trustees in whose name they will finally be registered.

Full Status — Any time after its fifth anniversary a Church Extension charge may itself apply for full status, or the Presbytery may take the initiative, as it will do after at latest the eleventh anniversary.

When application is thus made the Presbytery reports the matter to the Assembly Committee along with its views on the following — (a) adequacy of numbers; (b) availability of leadership; (c) suitability and condition of place of worship, halls, and manse; (d) whether an "effective role" is being played in the parish; (e) adequacy of stipend provision proposed; (f) prospect of repayment of its share of building costs; (g) whether it has met its allocation to Mission and Aid; (h) "general progress and harmony." The Committee will then (after local consultation if deemed desirable), decide whether or not to support an approach to the General Assembly for full status.

Assuming it is agreed to go forward, a scheme is prepared setting forth the arrangements for stipend and including application for Initial Endowment Grant (p 201) to which there shall be attached the nucleus of a Fabric Fund. When a manse is to be purchased or built application may be made to the Maintenance of the Ministry Committee for a Manse Grant. Any heritable property already held shall be transferred to, and any to be acquired shall be taken in name of, the General Trustees.

It requires an Act of Assembly to create a new charge, and this is passed on the strength of a deliverance in the Report of the Board of National Mission, the new congregation being represented at the bar when the matter is dealt with. A draft Act is submitted in terms as set out in the Regulations. If the Assembly pass the Act a Deed of Constitution is immediately prepared by the Solicitor of the Church who has to be satisfied that all the regulations have been complied with, and this is then issued by the Delegation of Assembly. It is usual for the Presbytery to arrange for the Deed of Constitution to be handed over by its Moderator along with an expression of congratulation and good wishes at Morning Worship on a convenient Sunday. The whole expenses of the Act and of the conveyance of property as well as all other outlays will be shared equally by congregation and central funds.

The Act (unless it itself provides otherwise) becomes operative on the day of issue of the Deed. On that day, therefore, the charge becomes a Parish *quoad sacra*, it acquires the right to appoint a Kirk Session of its own, all Assessor Elders being thanked and discharged, though some of these may continue for a spell, and the area delineated in the Act is disjoined from its previous connection to become the parish of the new charge.

(b) By Reception

The second method — that whereby an existing congregation comes into the Church of Scotland — is naturally of fairly rare occurrence. In 1954 all the congregations of the United Original Secession Church acceded to the Church of Scotland and a Basis was prepared and mutually agreed that covered the whole situation. Then in 1972 when the Presbyterian Church of England united with the Congregational Union of England and Wales to become the United Reformed Church in England and Wales two of her congregations — in Jersey and Guernsey — petitioned for admission and were received into the Church of Scotland; as had been the congregation of Berwick-on-Tweed Wallace Green by petition the previous year.

I am not aware of any other case of this type.

A parallel situation has, however, been created by Act iii 1973 anent Congregations of the Deaf. There are in Scotland a number of congregations of deaf persons formed under the auspices of local Welfare Societies for Work among Deaf and Dumb (now referred to as Deaf People), the bulk of the members being Presbyterian in background, and the government being in the hands of Ministers and Kirk Sessions. The Ministers have been ordained in the Church of Scotland (since 1969) and the Elders have been ordained according to Church of Scotland practice.

The Act of 1973 enunciates the steps to be taken for acceptance.

Application is to be made to the Presbytery at the instance of the Kirk Session with the approval of a majority of the Presbyterians (of whom there must be at least fifty) called to a meeting after two Sundays' notice. There must also be obtained agreement of the Directors of the local Society who hold (and will continue to hold) the titles to the property and who are (and will continue to be) responsible for the payment of stipend. The Presbytery may then petition the General Assembly in name of the congregation. It would clearly be inappropriate for such a congregation to be erected into a parish *quoad sacra*, to have a parish area delimited for it, or to be given a Deed of Constitution — it is merely "admitted" by the Assembly and as soon as convenient thereafter "received" by the Presbytery at a service at which also the Minister is "introduced". The Minister and an Elder have seats in Presbytery, all become subject to the supervision of Presbytery, and the congregation is expected to make such contribution as it feels able to the funds of the Church of Scotland. The ministry is terminable in character — it may be terminated by the Society, but only with concurrence of Presbytery.

A comparable process was adopted in 1985 when what had been an independent Church at Quarrier's Homes at Bridge of Weir was admitted as the congregation of Mount Zion Church, Quarrier's Homes — though in this case the Petition was in name of the Council of Management of the Homes and the Vestry Committee of the Church, with concurrence of the Presbytery of Greenock, and a parish area was assigned.

Very shortly afterwards the new congregation united with Kilmacolm St Columba's.

(c) By Union

In the third case two or more congregations have united, and unless stipulated otherwise in the Basis of Union, this will have involved the uniting of Parishes, Kirk Sessions, Financial Boards, property and funds, and all congregational agencies and organisations. We say, quite properly, that a new congregation has been formed and it is most desirable that a new name should be adopted, and that new minute-books, registers, and so on should be brought into use. At the same time it has to be recognised that the new congregation is a continuation of the life of its components (as a river is of its tributaries). A beqest made to one of the uniting congregations which had not vested by the date of union (because, for example of a life-interest which had not yet exhausted) is payable to the new congregation and that in spite of the change of name. Named office-bearers who are *ex officiis* trustees of heritable property continue to hold in name of the new congregation (Conveyancing (Scotland) Act 1924 Sect 26). In the case where a Mission Station united with its parent body it would scarcely be true to say that a new congregation had been created, for the Station had been under the direction and control of the parent charge and the names of its members had been entered on the Communion Roll of that body.

(d) By Severance

A union once effected is indissoluble, but there is nothing to prevent part of a parish being broken off to form the base of a new charge and some of the congregation having their names transferred to the roll of that new charge. It may also be appropriate to transfer some part of the funds to the new cause. This will not often happen, but recourse has been had to it in a case where a long-established congregation in serious straits united with a Church Extension congregation on a Basis which provided that they would physically unite within the new buildings when these were ready for occupancy. In the interval the fortunes of the older congregation revived and they wished to resile from the bargain continuing as a separate entity. A severance was effected.

MANAGEMENT OF CONGREGATIONAL AFFAIRS

The Kirk Session is the body having overall responsibility for the life of a congregation — a responsibility which extends beyond the membership to all the people of the parish. There is a Kirk Session in every parish of Scotland, so that every person resident in this land is the spiritual responsibility of some Kirk Session. Act xvii of 1931 defines the duty of the Session as in general terms "to maintain good order, to cause Acts of Assembly to be put into execution, to administer discipline, to judge and determine causes, and to superintend the religious and moral condition of the parish." It is interesting to note that their responsibility extends only to Acts and does not include Regulations of Assembly. Whatever may be the method of administering the temporal affairs of a congregation the Kirk Session has an over-riding authority. For full particulars regarding the constitution, powers and duties of the Kirk Session see the Chapter under that title (p 279).

Meetings for Ecclesiastical Purposes

From time to time a meeting of a congregation may be called "for ecclesiastical purposes". Any business other than the day-to-day finances and the ordinary care and maintenance of the property is an ecclesiastical purpose, and the term includes the erection of new, or substantial alterations to existing, buildings, the purchase of a new manse, the installation of an organ, or any other major change or addition.

Who Calls — Such meetings are normally called by order of the Kirk Session. In a vacancy the Interim Moderator has power to call a meeting for the appointment of a Vacancy Committee and later for the election of a Minister, besides which he may in certain circumstances be requisitioned to call a congregational meeting. The Presbytery may at any time call a meeting of the congregation. When Presbytery appoints a Committee to confer with a congregation on any matter, including reappraisal, the Convener is invested with power in name of the Presbytery to summon congregational meetings.

Who Presides — Normally the Moderator or Interim Moderator of Session presides, but he may authorise in writing any other Minister of the Church. When the meeting is called by order of Presbytery the body instructing the calling of the meeting nominates a Chairman. In the case of a meeting to discuss reappraisal this is constituted by the Moderator or Interim Moderator who then relinquishes the chair in favour of the Presbytery representative (p 72).

How Recorded — The Session Clerk is responsible for taking the minute which is engrossed in the Session records. In his absence a Clerk *pro tem* is appointed by the meeting (Act xviii 1932). A draft minute is taken and is approved and initialled by Chairman and Clerk before the meeting rises.

How Called and Constituted — Act xvii of 1956 ordains that all congregational meetings are to be called "by intimation to the congregation on the Lord's Day by the officiating Minister or Session Clerk." The intimation should set forth clearly the business to be transacted. After each reading it should be duly attested as having been served, and it should be laid on the table at the opening of the meeting. In all normal cases intimation has to be made on two separate Sundays, though it, is generally accepted that the meeting may be held on the day of the second calling. The citation of a congregation whose Minister has received a Call requires only one Sunday's notice. All congregational meetings are opened and closed with prayer, in this context the pronouncing of the benediction being regarded as the closing prayer. The sufficiency of the notice calling a congregational meeting can be challenged only by a petition specifying clearly the nature of the objection and lodged with the Moderator or Interim Moderator, or the Moderator of Presbytery if the meeting was called by that court. (It is unusual to require that a petition be lodged with the Moderator — I imagine it would suffice if it were addressed to the Moderator and lodged with the Clerk.)

Voting — Unless expressly provided otherwise voting is by standing up. There is no provision whereby on any matter of union (presumably readjustment generally though the Act does not say so) a plebiscite or referendum can be taken (Act xxii 1932). In the election of Elders, however, the congregation may resolve to use voting-papers (p 63). When the business before the meeting is a question of union it may be moved, seconded and agreed that a vote be taken by ballot. For the highly complicated machinery involved see p 63. The Act claims that this is available "in case of union", and it would seem therefore that it is not available in case of linking, terminable appointment or other form of readjustment.

Dissent — It is always in order for any member present at a congregational meeting to record his dissent against any decision reached. He should not do so, however, unless he has taken all steps competent for him to have the decision opposed — by moving against it at the least. He may also bring the matter dissented from under review of the Presbytery by Petition (p 269). Such Petition, with its reasons, should be lodged with the Presbytery Clerk without delay.

Meetings for Temporal Purposes

The regulations governing the calling and conduct of congregational meetings for temporal purposes vary according to the history and constitution of the congregation and depend largely on what body is responsible for the management of temporal affairs. For a full statement regarding these bodies reference should be made hereunder to the passage concerned with "Its Constitutional Character" (p 16). Briefly the situation is as follows.

Kirk Session — (*quoad omnia*) — The principle to be kept in mind here is that the Kirk Session is not answerable to the congregation but only to the Presbytery, and that therefore it is not under obligation to call congregational meetings for any purposes other than the conduct of a vacancy. Since, however, it is nowadays the congregation that will have to foot the bill incurred there is a great deal to be said for enlisting their interest and support in any temporal project of significance, and that as early as possible. The Session is always at liberty to call such a meeting and will do so under the same conditions as if it were a meeting for ecclesiastical purposes, the main point to be observed being that while the meeting may tender advice it cannot issue orders to the Kirk Session. Act iii 1994 anent the Calling of Congregational Meetings to Approve the

Annual Accounts of Congregations in Certain Cases requires that in every congregation there shall be held an annual, meeting to approve the accounts. The rules governing this are substantially those set forth in the Model Deed (see hereunder) except that the notice calling the meeting is to be "made from the pulpit on a Sunday giving at least one week's notice." Since it does not require "one week's clear notice" I take this to mean that the meeting could be held at the close of the service the following Sunday.

Congregational Board — (*quoad sacra*) — In terms of the Model Deed of Constitution (Act xxi 1965 as amended as Act ii 1989, and again as Act ii 1994) the Stated Annual Meeting of the congregation, called on two Sundays' intimation, is to be held in the Church, Church-hall or elsewhere as intimated not later than 31st March for the purpose of electing members to the Board. The chair is taken by the Moderator or Interim Moderator of Session, by another member of Presbytery authorised by him, or by a person appointed by the meeting — in that order. The Clerk of the Board keeps the minute which he enters in the Board records. Even although the Minister has elected not to act as Chairman of the Board he is entitled to take the chair at this meeting. So far as the Model Deed is concerned it would appear that the only reason for the Stated Annual Meeting is to make appointments to the Congregational Board. In terms, however, of Regulations anent congregational finance it is required that after the annual accounts have been approved by the Financial Board they have to be submitted by that body to the Stated Annual Meeting for congregational approval. Oddly, the Model Deed makes no provision for the calling of any congregational meeting apart from the Stated Annual Meeting. Were a serious emergency to arise — in regard to fabric, for example — it would be in the first place a matter for report to the Kirk Session who would then, if so advised, call a congregational meeting for ecclesiastical purposes. It is suggested that this would be the wise course to follow were the Board anxious to take the mind of the congregation on any matter affecting their (the Board's) affairs.

Deacons' Court (former Free) — Latterly the Deacons' Court was often replaced by a Congregational Board (U F style). All that follows applies equally in either case. An annual congregational meeting is to be called as soon as possible after the close of the financial year. It is presided over by the Moderator of Session, whom failing by an office-bearer chosen by the meeting (Act xviii 1932). Special meetings for temporal purposes are called by the Kirk Session and presided over by the Moderator or by a Minister authorised by him in writing (F C xiv 1847; xviii 1932). The Clerk of the Court or Board acts as Clerk at all meetings for temporal purposes and the minute is entered in the records of the Court or Board as the case may be.

Committee of Management (former U P) — In terms of Act xviii 1932 ordinary meetings are those held periodically in terms of the constitution, presided over by the Preses or in his absence by a member of the congregation (who may be the Minister or an Elder) chosen by the meeting, and the minute is taken and recorded in the Committee minute-book by the Clerk of the Committee. The Annual Congregational Meeting is held as soon as possible after the close of the financial year, with at least one Sunday's, notice, and it is presided over by the Preses of the Managers. No special business can be transacted at that meeting, but a special meeting may be called for the same day to allow of extraordinary business being dealt with. A Special Meeting is called by the Managers, but only with consent of the Kirk Session specifying clearly the nature of the business. Such a meeting is presided over by a chairman chosen by the meeting, who may be the Preses, the Minister, an Elder, or any member of the congregation. The minute is taken by the Clerk of the Committee and engrossed in the Committee records.

Special Cases — In any case where a congregation operates under a special constitution the provisions of that constitution must be observed in regard to the holding of congregational meetings.

Meetings to Appoint Trustees

In certain congregations congregational meetings are held from time to time as provided for in the constitution for the purpose of electing trustees to hold the congregational property and for other matters connected therewith. In cases where these matters are not covered in the provisions of the local constitution the appointment of trustees is to be regarded as an ecclesiastical matter to be dealt with at a meeting called for ecclesiastical purposes. In whatever manner it is dealt with it is most important that there should at all times be a sufficient number of trustees surviving and active — and wise that there should be a good safety margin.

ITS CONSTITUTIONAL CHARACTER

The constitional character of the Church of Scotland springs from an intensely complicated story of fraction and of re-union extending over all of two centuries, and the congregations of today continue to reflect aspects of the historical roots from which they have sprung. It is important, therefore, to know something of this history. For our purposes the main divisions are those identified conveniently by the terms Old Parish, Parish *quoad sacra*, Free, and U P, and we shall look at these in some detail. Then to bring things up-to-date there has to be added a fifth group — Post 1929.

Old Parish

Parish quoad omnia — The old parish is properly known as a parish *quoad omnia*, and it is important to understand the distinction between this and the parish *quoad sacra*. The structure of Church government which we call Presbyterianism adopted after the Reformation in 1560 and perfected by Andrew Melville in 1592 is a kind of pyramid erected on the parish as its base. Knox's ideal was that every parish should have a Church with a Minister and Kirk Session and a School with a Dominie. The parish of those early years had its quasi-civil commitments in that the Kirk was the instigator and supporter of things like education and the care of the poor, and in this state it continued for many years with little change. The various secessions, beginning in 1731, led to the creation of new congregations and the hiving off of many members, but the parish and its parish church was always there. When the civil aspects of the Church's work began gradually to be taken over under an elementary system of local government the idea of the parish as the unit of administration was maintained with a Parish School Board looking after education, a Parish Council taking care of the poor, and so on. The parish being adopted as the unit of local government the term inevitably came to have both a civil and an ecclesiastical connotation. The, population upheaval that followed on the Industrial Revolution created for the national Church problems many and varied. The national economy had been based on agriculture and the Church had been geared to serve a farming community. The base of the economy had now moved over to industry, the population-pattern had changed dramatically, the whole face of the country had become near unrecognisable — and how was the Church to cope? By an odd quirk of fate the emergence of the Secession congregations went some way towards meeting the challenge of the time by creating additional places of worship, but the old Church if it were to retain its claim to be a national Church had to provide for the needs of the people wherever they might be, and for this purpose the original parish churches were both inadequate and often ill-placed. Even more inadequate were the resources for sustaining what we should now call the charitable work to which the Kirk was committed in the civil sphere.

New Parishes Act 1843 — It was in those days a highly complicated affair to create a new parish. The last Parliamentary Act designed for this purpose was in 1843. At that date there were 924 parishes in Scotland and as a result of the new legislation the number increased to 933, including Maryhill and Springburn in Glasgow, and the "youngest" being Coll erected on 15th March 1865.

The Collegiate Charge — The first expedient resorted to in the effort to cope with the expanding population in the towns was the creation of collegiate charges — two ministers were appointed to a First and Second charge within the one building and serving the one congregation. In some cases — Hamilton, Ayr, Elgin come to mind — a second church came to be built, but that was a later development and in the original design they were, like St Cuthbert's in Edinburgh and The Abbey in Paisley, confined within the one building. Apart from the very real and quite serious strains and tensions which such an arrangement created at the personal level it went only a very little way towards solving the growing problem of Church Extension. It is worth recording that there are today no collegiate charges surviving from those times.

The Burgh Church — The next effort at keeping abreast with the population explosion took the form of legislation which obliged the burghs out of funds at their disposal to erect and maintain Churches and to pay the stipends of their Ministers. (The Paisley provision for stipend is to be found in a Cart Navigation Act!) In all, forty-five Burgh Churches are still extant, most of them in what are now the four cities, as well as Dumfries, Greenock, Kilmarnock, Paisley, Perth, Queensferry, and Stirling.

The Parish Quoad Sacra

The ultimate answer to the problem of providing for the new communities was found in creating parishes exclusively for religious purposes.

The Chapel of Ease — It was always possible for a group of people to band themselves together, rent or build some sort of meeting-place, and by their own freewill offerings engage the services of a Minister. For a long time now the Secession congregations had been showing just how successfully this could be done. Hence the appearance of the Chapel of Ease. If such a congregation was to have a Minister (as opposed to making do with preachers, students, etc) it had to have a constitution and this could be granted only by the General Assembly. It may seem odd that this power should have been reserved for the supreme court, and there had been considerable controversy over the point, for there were those who wanted the power vested in Presbyteries. There was a hidden complication. This was a day when opposition to patronage (whereby the chief of the heritors had the right to choose the new minister in a vacancy) was growing in intensity and disputed settlements were becoming only too common. In such a situation there was always a temptation for people dissatisfied with the Minister inducted against their wishes to leave the parish church, setting up in opposition as a Chapel of Ease. However convenient and attractive this might be as an immediate way of escape from a difficulty it was no long-term solution of a problem and in the long run must be to the hurt of the Church. It was felt that in considering applications for the erection of Chapels the General Assșembly would be able to take a more balanced and detached view than a Presbytery deeply and intimately embroiled in the local troubles.

The growth of the Chapels of Ease created a kind of two-tier ministry, for the Minister of the Chapel had no Kirk Session, no parish, and no seat in Presbytery or Synod. In 1834 the Assembly made an attempt to rectify this by the passing of the Chapels Act which purported to give to the new causes status and independence, which carved out parishes for them, and which awarded their Ministers seats in the courts. In fact for all ecclesiastical purposes they became parishes in the full sense of that term — that is to say, they were parishes *quoad sacra* (in respect of sacred things). Some eight years later, in the Stewarton Case, the Court of Session decided that the General Assembly had no power of itself to pass the Chapels Act — thereby, incidentally, contributing a major factor towards making the Disruption inevitable.

Quoad Sacra — As explained above, the Parish *quoad sacra* grew out of the Chapel of Ease. Ats of Parliament of 1854, 1868, and 1876 enabled the Teind Court to erect Parishes *quoad sacra*, and in 1903 it was reported to the Assembly that at that time the number of them was 426. For all the ordinary purposes of a congregation such a charge was complete and independent. the things distinguishing it from the *quoad omnia* variety being that it had no teind to provide a stipend, no heritors to maintain church and manse buildings, they did not read banns of marriage and had no obligations of a civil nature. And prior to the abolition of patronage in 1874 there was the marked distinction that the Minister of such a charge *was chosen by the congregation*.

The U Ps

The United Presbyterian Church which combined with the Free Church in 1900 to form the United Free Church had itself come into being in 1847 in consequence of the union of the United Secession and Relief Churches. A considerable number of congregations, largely in the Highlands and Islands, felt unable on grounds of conscience to join the union and continued as the Free Church, the body commonly referred to today as "The Wee Frees". It is perhaps easier, though, if we approach the matter from the other end, that is, from the beginning historically. First, Ebenezer Erskine and others left the Church in the First Secession, establishing in 1733 what they called the Associate Synod, a denomination which grew very considerably in the next few years but which from, its earliest days was torn by dissension. As early as 1747 its ranks were split in the most bitter conflict over the attitude to be adopted towards the Burgess Oath, a division that came to be known as "The Breach" and that led to the appearance of a Burgher and an Antiburgher denomination. A theological issue, very similar in character in these two branches split each of them into Auld Lichts and New Lights — the Burghers in 1799 and the Antiburghers seven years later. In 1820 the New Light sections from each side found it possible to come together as the United Secession Church. There was a second and completely separate group of Seceders. In 1761 Thomas Gillespie, along with two others, established the Presbytery of Relief "for the relief of Chistians oppressed in their Christian privileges." This body, the Church of the Second Secession, gained considerable strength without, strangely enough, undergoing any of the internal dissension that had characterised the Church of the First Secession, and manifesting a spirit of good will not so common at the time in welcoming to their Table all who were in love with the Lord Jesus Christ irrespective of denominational affiliation. These were the two bodies which in 1847 came together to form the United Presbyterian Church — the U P's. According to Professor

M'Ewan "the union was a natural, if not an enthusiastic, one. Its influence upon both churches was in all respects beneficial, resulting not only in greater corporate strength, but in the removal of tendencies which had limited the work of each when separate." The new denomination claimed at the time of union to have 518 congregations. An important characteristic of the U P congregations was that in every case they were "gathered" and had no territorial commitment and no feeling of territorial responsibility. They were, of course, without endowments — had, in fact, a bitter hatred of the very idea — and were therefore bound to areas where they could find the necessary financial backing. It was not unusual for a congregation to move from an area of a city which had gone down in the social scale to another where the financial prospects were brighter.

The Frees

The Disruption of 1843 can be traced to a variety of causes, the principal one being the long-festering sore of patronage. An upsurge of democratic aspiration which in England led to a demand to elect Members of Parliament expressed iself north of the Border in a demand to choose their own Minister. What actually triggered off the event was the judgment of the House of Lords in the Second Auchterarder case followed by the decision in the civil courts that the Church had no power to pass, as it had purported to do in 1834, the Veto Act and the Chapels Act. No fewer than 451 Ministers walked out of the Establishment to set up a new and independent Church — the Free Church because it was to be free from all State interference. The new body flourished greatly. The crying need for Church Extension at that time provided it with at once a challenge and an opportunity — an opportunity of which it was well qualified to take advantage because of its markedly evangelical bent. In 1876 the cause was strengthened by the accession of the bulk of the Reformed Presbyterian Church which, as far back as 1690, because of its opposition to the terms of the Revolution Settlement, had set up its independent banner.

From the day of its inception the Free Chuch had, due in no small measure to the leadership which Thomas Chalmers supplied, a profound sense of territorial responsibility such as had never been felt by any of the earlier break-away groups.

Post-1929

The year 1929 saw the union of the Church of Scotland with the United Free Church of Scotland to become a renewed Church of Scotland. Again there was a group within the United Free Church who could not see their way to come in and who continued apart as the United Free Church (Continuing), though the "Continuing" was later dropped from the name.

Since 1929 all charges created of new are, on achieving full status, erected by Act of Assembly into parishes *quoad sacra.* In most cases where new congregations come into being as a consequence of a local union it is a term of the Basis that the new body will function as a parish *quoad sacra* under the Model Deed (Act ii 1994). The General Assembly of 1965 "recommended and urged those congregations which have not yet decided to adopt the Model Deed of Constitution to adopt the Model Deed now in its amended form." Before 1965 it had been a pre-condition of becoming a parish *quoad sacra* that a congregation should transfer its heritable property into the name of the General Trustees, and this had proved a serious obstacle particularly in the case of former U P congregations which have all along prided themselves upon holding their own titles. This condition was removed in the amended Deed approved in 1965 and a cocerted effort was made, with some success, to persuade congregations voluntarily to adopt the Model Deed and so become parishes *quoad sacra.*

The advantages that would accrue from the acceptance of one standard constitution and one pattern for administering the affairs of all congregations of the Church must be apparent. When in the past two denominations have united this whole aspect has been glossed over in the hope that once united the two bodies would grow together. What has actually happened is that congregations discover they can live together perfectly well with their differences and new generations are brought up in the separate traditions — of which they may come to be rather proud. It is certain that any attempt to compel uniformity would be bitterly contested, on the one side from the parish *quoad omnia* supporters and on the other from the former U P's.

CONGREGATION'S RESPONSIBILITIES

Quite apart from its spiritual obligations and the responsibilities that the members owe to one another, and its duties as a body corporate *vis-a-vis* the parish generally, a congregation has certain quite specific responsibilities of a financial and material kind in respect of provision for its Minister in the matters of stipend and of retirement prospects, and of outlays incurred in travelling in respect of attendance at meetings, its share of Assembly and Presbytery expenses, in respect of a contribution towards Mission and Aid, and in respect of the maintenance of its property — all in addition to meeting the costs incurred in the provision of services of worship and the support of its own agencies.

Ministerial Support — The obligations in respect of stipend are today covered in terms of a Vacancy Schedule completed and approved before the induction of every Minister, showing the amount of the stipend, the sources from which it is to come, the expenses that are to be met, whether a manse is to be provided and if not what arrangements are to be come to (payments in lieu being now forbidden), and also indicating the amount that will be contributed to or received from the Aid to the Ministry Fund. There is also an obligation to contribute to the Ministers' Main Pension Fund a sum in ratio of the stipend for the current year (at present 20% and, see Reports 1994 p 325, likely to remain at that figure until the end of the year 2003), and to meet the employer's contribution in respect of National Insurance. In all cases the congregation is responsible for payment of the Council Tax on the Manse. The Minimum Stipend Fund of an earlier day has been superseded (1986) by the creation of a Mission and Aid Fund which embraces a congregation's obligations in respect of the General Purposes Fund, the Mission and Service Fund and the Aid to the Maintenace of the Ministry Fund. It is accepted that the Schedule does not constitute an enforceable contract, but it was reported to the Assembly in 1994 that the Committee on Maintenace of the Ministry had taken a decision "to depart from the policy of writing off Shortfalls in Stipend Payments and will, from now on, accumulate these and take account of the total accumulation when considering future Vacancy and Revision Schedules." One might have thought the solution here was to reduce the amount asked from the congregation, but I am afraid that is not what is in mind in this case!

Assembly and Presbytery Dues

The superior courts of the Church have no direct source of income, but they incur considerable expenditure and this they have to recover by a direct charge on congregations.

Assembly Dues — Though called simply Assembly Dues this item used to include the General Purposes Fund and represented a very considerable burden, involving as it did the cost of maintaining and running the Offices and the Assembly Hall as well as the cost of the Assembly itself — a very large sum since the introduction in 1962 of meeting the expenses of commissioners. The whole of these costs are now met out of the Mission and Aid Fund.

Those Committees which are involved in spending money meet their own outlays and include these in their annual budget, but there are many committees which have no income — "committees without funds" such as the Board of Practice and Procedure, the Committee on Church and Nation and the like — and the expenses incurred by these bodies have to be met from central sources. This too comes from the General Purposes section of the Mission and Aid assessment.

Ecumenical Contributions — From time to time there has been debate regarding the proper way in which the cost of the Church's affiliation to bodies such as the World, the British, and the Scottish Councils of Churches, the World Presbyterian Alliance and, more recently, ACTS, CCBI and so on should be met. Denominations which are members of these bodies are expected to pay what is in effect a membership fee since the bodies have no other means of support. The amount to be contributed is fixed by the recipient not by the donor. As the years have passed activities in the ecumenical field have expanded considerably so this year the involvement of the Church of Scotland was £206,000. The Assembly of 1984 decreed that while the Board of World Mission and Unity would recommend payment of the various amounts it would do so as part of a budget and it would be for the Assembly Council "to take into consideration the question of ecumenical contributions when it advises the Board of Stewardship and Finance on matters of priority, resources, and co-ordination of Board policies." This has now been departed from, the present position being that the Boards of World Mission and of Finance confer and reach agreement on the level of these contributions. The sums are then reported to the General Assembly by the Board of World Mission, but the contributions come from the General Purposes Fund, that is, from outwith any Departmental Budget.

Schemes of the Church

It was as late as 1800 or thereby that the Church first became conscious of obligations beyond its own borders. Until that time all collections taken at parish churches had been for support of the poor, while the Secession bodies were faced with the claims of their own upkeep. Thus when the idea of, for example, sending a missionary abroad first took hold of the popular imagination there was no machinery to cope with the situation. So Assembly Committees were created to deal with things like Foreign Missions, Highlands and Islands, Jewish Missions and so on, and special collections were taken at Church services in support of these. These took the form of "retiring collections" and for long after the Union continued to be uplifted at Church doors on leaving the service — hence the "retiring". (It was the great John White who on one occasion characterised them as being "very retiring!")

Weekly Freewill Offering — The introduction of the W F O system brought in a new factor, for it enabled the member not only to contribute methodically but to designate his offering between "ourselves" and "others". Not that everybody did that, so that at the close of the year the financial board of the congregation had the job of allocating this income among the various schemes concerned. Latterly to assist them in this a simple division of a pound sterling on the ratio of the budgets of the various Committees was made available. Despite the fact that many congregations were exceedingly generous — usually to some "pet scheme" — the system was sadly deficient as a means of support for work which was growing both in extent and in intensity. Further, since each Committee was free to pursue the elusive "extra" in the way that seemed to it best an utterly unhealthy spirit of competition was developing among Committees which were inclining to mount special "appeals", to impose "targets" and what have you with a view to acquiring a larger slice of a cake of strictly limited proportions.

Co-ordinated Appeal — The Assembly of 1959 accepted a proposal that was to come into effect as from the beginning of 1961 for the introduction of a Co-ordinated Appeal. This was designed in the first place to substitute one all-embracing appeal in place of the multitude of demands that had become self-defeating. It had been hoped that Maintenance of the Ministry would have been included, but this was going to raise so many complications that the demands of the ministry, active and retired, were excluded from the appeal. A second objective of the Appeal was to impose some restriction on Committees by securing from them budgets of their coming requirements to enable the General Finance Committee to ensure they would not get themselves involved in projects however praiseworthy for which funds were not available.

Mission and Service — However accurate as a description the name "Co-ordinated Appeal" had little to commend it as a selling-point, so the fund was given the name of Mission and Service and the body which took charge of its administration was called the Stewardship and Budget Committee. Every Commitee was to submit a budget of its anticipated commitments for the coming year and these were carefully scrutinised and on occasion pruned. They were then added together and a sum added to cover contingencies (though it seemed to me the principal contingency was a shortfall in the total income) and in this way there was reached a grand total of what was required. This was now broken down among congregations and Presbyteries were informed, their duty being first to make any adjustments which with their local knowledge they might think appropriate, and secondly to convince congregations of their duty to meet the sums asked for, and if they fell significantly short to discover what was amiss.

Board of Stewardship and Finance — The Stewardship and Budget Committee was merged in 1983 with the General Finance Committee to form the Board of Stewardship and Finance, and this body now has the duties of — (a) promoting Christian stewardship, (b) preparing a co-ordinated budget, (c) allocating the said budget, and (d) administering the financial services of the Church (which had previously been the business of General Finance). A scheme has since been introduced that unites the demands of Ministry, Schemes, and General Purposes into one single appeal — or, perhaps more accurately, demand. What inevitably happened in the past was that congregations in financial straits have paid up in full for Ministry and General Purposes and have trimmed Mission and Service to conform with what was available. Obviously there will still be congregations which will fall short — no new method of book-keeping is going to alter that. In such cases the question of priorities must arise and here presumably the Assembly Council will be called in since one of its functions is "to advise the General Assembly on the relative importance of work in various fields."

Maintenance of Property

Increasingly the heritable property of the Church is coming to be vested in the General Trustees — more than five hundred properties of the UF Church have been transferred — but the Trustees merely hold for behoof of the congregation, and while they are trying to build up a Central

Fabric Fund from which to make grants it is with the congregation that the responsibility for maintenance and insurance wholly lies. A great deal of the Church's property is now fairly old and in need of constant and costly repairs while much of the more recent building having been put up at a time when the demand was great and finance was limited is already revealing its many deficiencies, much of it being in city areas where vandalism is a way of life and where money is scarce. The business of maintaining its property in a sound and serviceable condition is one of the most urgent problems confronting the Church today. It represents a very large subject and is dealt with at some length in Chapter 4.

The Deed of Covenant

This may be a convenient point at which to say a word about the Deed of Covenant, or Bond of Annuity, a concession made by the Inland Revenue from which the Churches profit considerably. The principle is that where a taxpayer is prepared to bind himself for a period of more than three years (until 1980 it was six) to pay to a specific charity a certain sum by way of annual contribution the amount of Income Tax paid on that sum will be repaid direct to the charity. The Church is regarded as a charity in this context and the Deed may be granted in favour of the Church of Scotland or of the local congregation — per its Treasurer in either case. Normally such a Deed is a "Net Deed" — that is to say the grantor fixes the amount which he will pay irrespective of what may be the basic rate of tax. Suppose the grantor is proposing to contribute £3 a week (which he may do through the WFO) he will give a deed for £156 and, at the 25% rate the Church will recover £52. Alternately he might opt for a "gross deed" fixed upon what the Church is ultimately to receive, but advantage is rarely taken of this today. Normally the contribution is terminable on death.

As from 1983 those paying Income Tax in excess of 25% on part of their income can obtain relief in respect of their Deed at the highest rate to which they are liable, though the Church can recover still only at the 25% rate. Such a tax-payer, however, can at no extra cost to himself, pass the benefit to the Church by increasing the payments under his deed — which, indeed, appears to be the intention of the Government. Take, for example, a person liable to tax on part of his income at 40% and who has granted a Deed for £300, he could grant a new Deed for £375, thus benefitting the Church by 25% at exactly the same cost to himself.

The *Gift Aid Scheme* allows single payments to charities by individuals or limited companies in the UK to qualify for tax relief provided such payments are made out of income which is taxed at the basic rate, the minimum limit being £250. The *Payroll Giving Scheme* allows individuals to make tax-free donations of up to £900 per annum provided their employer is willing to participate in the scheme. Particulars of these two Schemes, as well as Deeds of Covenant and other information is available from the General Treasurer. Congregational Treasurers should also acquire a copy of the "Charity Tax Pack" from FICO (Scotland), Trinity Park House, South Trinity Road, Edinburgh EH5 3SD. (This, I believe, is a contraction for "Financial Intermediate Claims Office" — formerly called "Claims Branch").

ADMINISTERING ITS TEMPORAL AFFAIRS

In the Unions of 1900 and 1929 freedom was left to congregations to continue the management of their temporal affairs in the way to which they had been accustomed. In the Church of Scotland there had been a difference between the practice of the old parishes and that of the *quoad sacra* charges. Thus four quite separate and distinct methods continued to operate — and do to this day. In general terms these may be described as management by a Kirk Session, by a Congregational Board, by a Deacons' Court, or by a Committee of Management. Again in general terms these may be said to belong respectively to a parish *quoad omnia*, to a parish *quoad sacra*, to a Free Church congregation, and to a congregation of the UP tradition. Before examining these in detail a word should be said about how the idea of "temporal affairs" first emerged in the history of the Church of Scotland.

Heritors — Heritors figured very prominently on the temporal side of the life of the early Scottish Church. The heritors of a parish were the owners of land within the parish in virtue of which they had a duty to erect and maintain a church capable of seating two-thirds of the examinable persons (those not under the age of twelve) resident in the parish, to provide and maintain a manse with suitable offices and garden, to provide a glebe, and from the fruits of their land to pay a stipend. The heritors met as a body, kept minutes etc, but they formed no part of the ecclesiastical system. These various obligations continued almost unchanged until the whole affair was revolutionised by the Property and Endowments Act of 1925 (passed to smooth the way towards the Union of 1929). In effect all the lands and heritable property were made over to the Church, being transferred into the name of the General Trustees who had, of course, to assume responsibility for them and to hold them for behoof of the congregations concerned. At the time of handing-over all property was required to be in good order, failing which a sum had to be paid sufficient to put it to rights. The system of stipend was completely changed in consequence of the 1925 Act so that now the heritors' obligations have either been written off, wholly redeemed, or become a standard charge. For all practical purposes the heritors may be said to have completely disappeared from all but the history books.

From all of which it will be apparent that the economics of the parish of those distant days were vastly different from those of the congregation of today. All the buildings of both church and manse were erected and maintained by the heritors who also out of teind had to pay the stipend, the needs of heating and lighting were met (however inadequately) by the sun, even the provision of Communion Elements was taken care of. Through the Parish Church, in short, the services of religion were made available absolutely free of charge for all who wished to avail themselves of them. The only money asked for from those who attended the services was the collection taken at the door (sometimes at the kirkyard gate and sometimes by bag or ladle during the service) and this was for the relief of the poor. Looking after the poor being manifestly a spiritual exercise the collection came under the direction of the Kirk Session. When for the first time contributions were sought from congregations to support causes like Foreign Missions, Highlands and Islands and so on these were made the subject of additional collections but were still under control of the Kirk Session. That is how it has come about that until recently under all but the Free Church constitution the Poor Fund and giving to Schemes of the Church were the affair of the Kirk Session.

Seat Rents — It is not strictly accurate to say that the Church door collection was the sole contribution made by the worshipper, for rents were charged for sittings in the Church. These began as a charge under the heritors, but under *quoad sacra* administration they came to represent a substantial item of income and were to be used to defray "the necessary expense of a precentor, a beadle or Kirk officer, and other expenses necessarily incurred in dispensing the ordinances of religion and not otherwise provided for." The introduction of the Weekly Freewill Offering led in most cases to the discontinuance of the practice of seat-letting and there can be but few instancess of its being still in operation today. Evidence of its one-time prevalence is to be found in most Churches in the little brass frames affixed to the book-board at the end of each pew in which the names of the seat-holders used to be entered, now usually containing some words of welcome to the service.

CONGREGATIONAL CONSTITUTIONS

When around the middle of the 18th century Secession congregations set up their independent banner they found themselves faced with the problem not only of raising a great deal of money of which they had known nothing within the establishment but also with the problem of how this aspect of the congregation's life was to be directed and controlled. So each congregation equipped itself with a document known as a "Constitution", a document which did two things — first it set forth the arrangement for the holding of the heritable property by trustees, and secondly it made detailed provision as to how the temporal affairs would be administered by a Committee of Management answerable to the congregation. This new body was in a way taking the place of the missing heritors and it saw itself as being completely free from direction by Kirk Session just as the heritors had been. It was the business of this Committee to see to the maintenance of all Church property, to pay the stipend, and to look after all other temporal affairs.

While all this was happening in the Secession ranks the number of *quoad sacra* parishes was rapidly increasing. In the early days each of these too had its own constitution determining how affairs were to be managed. Before a parish *quoad sacra* could be erected, however, the Presbytery had to be satisfied that there were endowments adequate to provide a certain stipend, that there were buildings, and that there was an acceptable constitution. So constitutions, while they began in varying shapes and sizes, came more and more to conform to a standard pattern.

When the Free Church began in 1843 it had a very vivid realisation of the temporal commitments its congregations were taking upon themselves. To equip them for this it revived the New Testament office of Deacon and the management of its temporal affairs was put in the hands of Deacons' Courts, though after the 1900 Union these were inclining to be replaced by Congregational Boards (UF style).

All congregations which have adopted the Model Constitution are, of course, in the matter of temporal affairs administered by Congregational Boards. Immediately the Delegation of Assembly has resolved to grant full status to a Church Extension charge it is issued with a Deed of Constitution, prepared by the Solicitor of the Church.

These, then, are the four systems — let us look in detail at how they are constituted and how they work.

(a) The Kirk Session

In a decreasing number of *quoad omnia* parishes which have not adopted the Model Constitution all the affairs of the congregation, spiritual and temporal, are under the direction of the Kirk Session, and the procedure followed by that court is the same no matter what the nature of the business before it.

Property — All the heritable property of such a charge is likely to be vested in the General Trustees, but it should be noted — (a) that the responsibility for its maintenace and insurance lies with the congregation, (b) that no extraordinary repairs, improvements or additions are to be made without prior consent of both Presbytery and General Trustees, (c) that when the actual church building is affected consultation with the Advisory Committee on Artistic Matters should be sought at a very early stage, certainly before the proposals have become hard and fast, and (d) that no part of the property may be sold, let, or otherwise disposed of, nor can it be given in security for debt, without the same consents. While it is useful that informal discussion with a possible purchaser should be conducted at local level Presbytery and Trustees must be brought in before any missives are prepared. Only in a very few exceptional cases are local parties in a position where they can grant a valid disposition.

Congregational Meeting — Reference has been made earlier to the conduct of a congregational meeting for ecclesiastical purposes (p 11). Under the *quoad omnia* regime the Kirk Session is not under obligation to call any congregational meeting except in filling a vacancy. At the same time if, for example, an extension to the halls was being contemplated a Kirk Session would seem peculiarly ill-advised to proceed without reference to the full membership who, after all, are going to have to pay the accounts. There are, too, cases where a Kirk Session feels there is an advantage in holding an Annual Congregational Meeting at which reports may be given and discussion engaged in on the year's work. Difficulty may arise at such a meeting, for it is quite possible that someone will make a proposal about something he thinks ought to be done and this may become the subject of lively discussion and of a motion and call for a vote. It is for the Moderator to be careful here to ensure that such a motion is framed as a recommendation and not as an instruction. For the Kirk Session not being answerable to the congregation does not take instruction from it. When effect is given to the proposal — if it is given — it will be in consequence of a Kirk Session resolution and not of a congregational vote.

Churchyard — The Kirk Session may, if it so wishes, take over the management of a churchyard no longer in use. It may also retain the custody and management of old ecclesiastical buildings within a churchyard which has been transferred to the Local Council. In neither case can it be compelled to do so and should hesitate to shoulder the added responsibility unless for some adequate reason. In the case where a church is situated in a churchyard which has been transferred to the Council the right of access is retained by the congregation (Property and Endowments Act 1925, Sec 32).

Audit — It is recommended that whether it is responsible for all congregational finances or only for a limited number of funds the Kirk Session should keep regular accounts and have these duly audited. It should also record in its minutes that this has been done.

(b) The Congregational Board

In former *quoad sacra* parishes, in newly erected parishes, in united congregations where different methods had obtained in the uniting bodies, and in cases where the congregation has voluntarily agreed to adopt the Model Constitution the temporal affairs are in the hands of a Congregational Board consisting usually of the Minister, the Elders, and a number of Elected Members from the congregation. Rather more than seventy per cent of congregations now operate under this system.

Normally all Elders on the Kirk Session are members of the Board. Provision is made, however, that a congregation may resolve that the number of Elders is to be restricted to not fewer than five for a congregation of 200 or fewer, eight when between 200 and 400, and twelve when over 400. Intimation of the proposal for such a change must be included in the notice calling the Stated Annual Meeting and the motion must be approved by at least two-thirds of those present at the meeting (not just those voting). Following the same procedure such a resolution may at a later time be rescinded. When it is agreed to reduce in this way it is for the Session to determine which of its number are to act and for how long.

At the Stated Annual Meeting each year the *Elected Members* are appointed. These are members in full communion with the congregation, men or women, of eighteen years or more, up to a number equal to but not exceeding the number of Elders, and they are elected for a period of three years after which they may be re-elected. In a congregation where there are fewer than six Elders the Presbytery may authorise the election of six members to the Board. Should an Elder die, resign or be disqualified in course of the year the Kirk Session may take steps to have him replaced. If on the other hand it is to an Elected Member that one of these things happens during the year the Board itself may co-opt someone to complete his term subject to ratification at next Stated Annual Meeting.

The provision for reducing the Session representation on the Board was one of the changes effected in 1965 and had in mind the case of the congregation having a large Session. Seventy is not at all unusual, yet a Board of 140 is unwieldy, whereas to restrict the Elected Members to say a dozen puts the Session in complete control. It is suggested that when a Kirk Session exceeds twenty-five serious thought should be given to adopting the arrangement for restriction. It will generally be found that there are Elders keen enough on the work of the Session but more than happy to be relieved of the additional duties entailed by the Board.

Chairman — The Board is presided over by a Chairman (not a Moderator) and the Minister or Interim Moderator is *ex officio* holder of this office. Should he not wish this position the Board will appoint one of its own members to preside. I am of opinion that the Minister could change his mind in this matter, but if this is done I think he should wait till the Stated Annual Meeting either to step down or to take over. After a vacancy it is to be presumed that the new Minister will wish to take the chair whatever may have been the case under his predecessor. In the temporary absence of the Chairman the Board elects one of its number to act *pro tempore*. The Chairman has a casting vote only.

Clerk — At its first meeting after election the Board appoints a Clerk who keeps regular minutes of all Board meetings, of the Sated Annual Meeting, and of any other meeting held for temporal purposes. He need not necessarily be a member of the Board.

Treasurer — The Board has also to appoint a Treasurer to take charge of the congregation's finances. The Deed also requires (this is not optional) that a member of the Board should be appointed to countersign cheques drawn by the Treasurer and must on no account sign a few blank ones "just to be handy". For practical convenience it is usual — and wise — to appoint two persons either of whom may act in this way.

Auditors — Annually the Board appoints two Auditors (who may not be of their number and need not even be members of the congregation) to examine the books and accounts of the Treasurer. There is nothing to prevent the appointment of professional auditors and a great deal to be said in its favour, and in this case only one Auditor need be appointed.

Quorum — The number of the quorum varies with the size of the Board — three if fewer than 9, five if from 10 to 20, seven if more than 20.

How Called — Generally the Board makes its own arrangements about regular meetings. Constitutionally it is to be called by the Chairman either by pulpit intimation or personal notice, and on written request from a quorum he must call a meeting within ten days. In terms of the Deed a first meeting of the Board must be held within a month of the Stated Annual Meeting and is to be called by the Minister. For details regarding the conduct of meetings reference may be made to the chapter on the Kirk Session (p 279).

Its Business — The first duty of the Board is to see to the ingathering of all funds due to the congregation (except the Poor Fund and any other fund under Session control). At the Annual Meeting it is to provide members with an estimate of anticipated income and expenditure for the current year. It has also to see to the maintenance and insurance of all fabric whether held locally or by the General Trustees, nor may it launch upon any alterations to or improvements upon fabric without having in hand or guaranteed sufficient funds to meet the cost without encroaching on normal income, and for expenditure (at the moment of over 15,000) it must also have the approval of Presbytery, of the Advisory Committee on Artistic Matters and of the General Trustees.. Further it has to provide opportunity for the congregation to contribute to funds for which the General Assembly has enjoined special collections to be taken.

Contracts of Employment — Church Officer and Organist or Choirmaster are appointed by the Kirk Session which defines their duties and they are subject to the direction of the Minister. It is the Board which enters into Contracts of Employment with the persons appointed.

Stated Annual Meeting — A meeting of the congregation for temporal purposes (the Stated Annual Meeting) is to be held not later than 31st March in each year after two Sundays' notice (which must clearly specify the venue, not necessarily Church or Church Hall). Permission may be given by the Presbytery on cause shown for a meeting to be held on a later date; but in the absence of such permission if the meeting has not been held by the end of March it is for the Kirk Session to report the matter to the Presbytery which will take steps to ensure that such a meeting is held without delay. The chair is taken by the Minister (or Interim Moderator) or by a member of Presbytery appointed by him, whom failing by someone elected by those present. The record of the meeting is taken by the Clerk of the Board and entered in his minute-book. Two items of business fall to be transacted at this meeting — first elections have to be made to the Board and secondly the accounts have to be approved.

Review of Decisions — Should a question be raised regarding the legality or propriety in terms of the constitution of anything done it is open to any person or body having an interest to approach the Presbytery by petition and the judgment of the Presbytery on the matter is final, except that any party may at a meeting of Presbytery held not less than twenty-one days after judgment was given produce a certificate over the signature of the Procurator saying he regards the matter as one suitable for appeal to the superior courts, in which case appeal may be taken to the General Assembly then and there.

If in some particular the Board has contravened the terms of the Constitution and has persisted in so doing in spite of the fact that "their attention has been called to the matter" the Presbytery may remove from the Board those who have been guilty of such contumacy (contempt for the higher court and its rulings), declaring them ineligible for re-election for three years, and may take steps to fill the resulting vacancies. If the offence is so serious as to constitute contumacy I take it that the way in which "attention has been called to the matter" must have been of a quite formal kind, such, probably, as an injunction by the Presbytery following upon a judgment by it, and would not arise in consequence of, say, a letter addresssed to the Board by a member. If, then, a member of a congregation is unhappy about the way the Board is acting he should bring this to the attention of the Board and if this does not lead to amendment he should petition the Presbytery. The Deed does not indicate what is to happen to Elders who are *ex officiis* members of the Board should they be guilty of contumacy in this way. It will therefore be for the Presbytery to decide what kind of disciplinary action it considers appropriate.

Other Congregational Meetings — The Model Deed makes no provision for the holding of any congregational meeting in addition to the Stated Annual Meeting. Were a critical situation to arise,in regard to fabric for example, that would seem to be a matter for the Board to report to the Kirk Session who might then be expected to call a congregational meeting for ecclesiastical purposes. In my own view this would be the wise course for the Board to follow were it anxious to take the mind of the congregation on any issue which seriously affected its (the Board's) affairs.

(c) The Deacons' Court

In a former Free Church congregation one is likely to find a Deacons' Court made up of the Minister, the Elders, and a considerable number of Deacons who, in the early days were ordained for life on the principle that however much the duties of Session and Court might differ the character of the appointments was the same. So the Deacon, elected by the congregation, was, in face of the congregation, ordained by the Kirk Session, and he (or she) held office for life. The matter was covered by Free Church Assembly Acts of 1846 and 1847.

How Constituted — The Minister (or Interim Moderator) is *ex officio* a member of the Court, as are all the Elders, it being held that "the higher office scripturally includes the lower" and that accordingly the Elder is not excluded from the exercise of the Deacon's function." There are also Deacons, men or women, over eighteen years of age, in full communion, elected by the congregation at the annual meeting or at a meeting called for the purpose, the Kirk Session having determined how many are required and when. The method of election is as with Elders (p 31) but it is recommended that the two should not be elected at the same meeting.

Tenure — The Deacon once ordained held office until death, resignation, or disqualification, which could overtake him if he was absent from meetings for a year without cause known, but it was in the hands of the Session that such action was taken, after due notice given. The pattern more widely adopted latterly was that Deacons were appointed for three years, after which they could be re-elected; but they were not ordained, being commended to God in prayer at Morning Worship on the first convenient Sunday after their election. It is open to a conggregation at any time, two Sundays' notice having been given, to resolve to change from the old to the new pattern, and if this is done those Deacons who are already ordained may elect either to relinquish that status or to retain it, and in the latter case they will continue on the Court without their names at any time being submitted for re-election. Likewise in a case where a congregation with ordained Deacons unites with another and the united congregation adopts the Model Constitution the ordained Deacons may, if they so wish, become life-members of the Congregational Board, the other deacons joining the Board on the usual terms.

Officials — The Minister (or Interim Moderator) presides over the Deacons' Court as *Chairman*, and in his absence the Court appoints one of its members to act *pro tempore*. The Chairman may not move a resolution, but he can introduce business and address the Court on it, and he has a casting vote (only). A *Clerk* is appointed by the Court to keep a record of its proceedings. The Court also appoints a *Treasurer* who is responsible for all congregational funds, including the Poor Fund. The Church Officer in virtue of holding that post is *Officer* of the Court with the duty of being in attendance at its meetings if required. At the Annual Meeting each year the congregation appoint two persons to act as *Auditors*.

Meetings — It is usual for meetings to be held monthly — this was originally prescribed as a minimum. They may also be called by pulpit intimation or personal notice, with this speciality that while it is normally the Minister who convenes, during a vacancy it is the Clerk and not the Interim Moderator who has this duty. The *quorum* is three (with no need that one be a Minister) and meetings are normally in private. Any three members may requisition a meeting by giving notice to the Chairman. For particulars about the conduct etc of meetings reference should be made to Chapter 11 on the Kirk Session.

Its Business — The Deacons' Court has the management and charge of the whole property, heritable and moveable, of the congregation, and is required to apply spiritual principles in the conduct of its affairs. Heritable property is generally held on titles which include what are called "the Free Church clauses" — this being a reference to the Model Trust Deed of the Free Church of Scotland, in which it was *inter alia* declared that the Trustees holding the properties had no power to burden them with debt, or to sell, alienate or dispose of the same or any part thereof unless for the purpose of providing another place of worship or manse, and then only with consent of the General Assembly. Following upon the famous Free Church Case of 1904 the Government appointed a Commission in terms of the Churches (Scotland) Act 1905 to allocate the property of the former Free Church, and this was done under Orders of Allocation which substantially continued the earlier position, in particular the subjection of all alienation of property to the consent of the General Assembly.

It is for the Deacons' Court to ensure that the church, halls and manse are kept in a proper state of repair, and it has too the duty of raising the funds necessary for this purpose. Extraordinary repairs or additions to buildings must not be put in hand without prior consent of Presbytery, Advisory Committee on Artistic Matters and General Trustees.

The Kirk Session appoints and dismisses Organist and Church Officer, but it is the Deacons' Court which determines as well as pays their salaries. The Kirk Session may confer with the Deacons' Court about the appointment of the Organist as also about his terms of service. In the case of others employed in connection with the convenience of worshippers the Deacons' Court has full powers and engages and dismisses, defines the terms of service, and fixes and pays salaries.

In former Free Church congregations it is the Deacons and not the Kirk Session who are responsible for the care of the poor of the congregation with power to appoint special collections to raise funds for this purpose. For many years after 1843 the Deacons' Court had a special responsibility in connection with the Sustentation Fund (their version of Maintenance of the Ministry) and it was usual for a Deacon to share with an Elder the care of a district and to visit therein in pursuit of this very important matter. Today the business of stipend is on the same footing as in all other congregations.

The original Free Church Act set very strict bounds to the powers of the Deacons' Court which "has no power of discipline over its own members. It can neither admit to the office of Deaconship nor depose from it. Nor can the resignation of a Deacon be competently received by the Deacons' Court nor dealt with by them in any way. But the Deacons' Court is entitled to certified extracts from the minutes of Kirk Session insofar as by admission, removal, suspension or deposition of office-bearers these minutes affect its membership, and any change of which the Court thus obtains evidence ought to be recorded.

Congregational Meeting — An Annual Congregational Meeting is called by the Deacons' Court as soon as possible after the end of the financial year. It is presided over by the Moderator of Session, whom failing by an office-bearer chosen by the meeting (Act xviii 1932). Special meetings for temporal purposes are called by the Kirk Session and presided over by the Moderator or by a Minister appointed by him in writing (FC xiv 1847; Act xviii 1932). The Clerk of the Court acts as Clerk at all meetings for temporal purposes and the minute is entered in the records of the Court. At the Annual Meeting the Court presents a report of its proceedings during the previous year, giving such information and explanation as may be asked for, and receiving any suggestions which may be offered for its consideration with reference to the future administration of the funds. It would appear that the Court is not bound to accept instructions from the congregation in relation to the managing of its affairs. It is, however, answerable to the Presbytery insofar as it may take any step, or adopt any resolution, which the Presbytery can pronounce to be of a censurable nature, or in violation of any enactment of an Act of the General Assembly (FC 1846 xiv).

Congregational Board (Free Church Pattern)

In some Free Churches latterly and in the United Free Church quite frequently the Deacons' Court came to be replaced by a body called the Congregational Board and consisting of the Minister, Elders, and a number of members of the congregation elected for a three-year period by the congregation which also determined how many of them there should be. Their sphere of activity and their *modus operandi* are essentially those of the Deacons' Court.

(d) Committee of Management

In former UP congregations there is usually a Committee of Management, sometimes called a Board of Managers, and commonly referred to simply as "the Managers", differentiated from the other types by the fact that it finds no necessary or preferential place for the Minister, has little or no connection with the Kirk Session, and is very much under direction and control of the congregation in the discharge of all its affairs.

The Constitution — Each congregation of the former UP Church had its own constitution, though latterly these came to conform very closely to a standard pattern. The constitution itself contains provision for its being altered, but only after a proposal to change has been "entertained" at one congregational meeting and approved at the next and has subsequently obtained the approval of the Presbytery. So although all conform to a pattern there is considerable diversity in detail — particularly in the extent of the liberty allowed to the Managers in the spending of money without reference to the congregation. Act ix 1970 requires that a copy of the local constitution is to be supplied to any candidate in a vacancy immediately on his being nominated.

The Managers — The Committee of Management consists of Managers to a number fixed by the congregation (not fewer than six and rarely more than fifteen) elected by them at the Annual Meeting (in some cases the election is by voting papers distributed beforehand and returned at the meeting), and serving for a period of three years but being eligible for re-election thereafter. Managers must be members in full communion, and if women are to be eligible a resolution to this effect must have been approved at a congregational meeting called for that purpose. I have not myself seen a constitution which lays it down that neither the Minister nor Elders are to be eligible, but I imagine the traditional bar against the Minister is all but universal while that against Elders is very general indeed, the usual drill being that an Elder will not be elected a Manager and that if a Manager is ordained as an Elder he will resign from the Management. In case of a vacancy occurring in the Committee a replacement can be found only at a congregational meeting called for the purpose and the person elected undertakes only the unexpired period of service.

As with Deacons it is recommended that on the first convenient Sunday the names are read over by the Minister who then commends them to God in prayer.

Preses — The chairman of the Committee of Managers is known as the Preses. The term is not a common one (it is not found in the Oxford English Dictionary). It is pronounced "preesis", not "praysee" as one occasionally hears these days. It comes from the same root as the verb "to preside" and it is to be found in at least one other context — when the creditors in a bankruptcy meet to look after their affairs they appoint a preses. The ecclesiastical variety is, I believe, properly called Preses of the Managers. I have in my hand a Constitution dated 1894 which draws a distinction between the Preses of the Congregation and the Preses of the Managers. In this case the congregation itself elects a Preses, a Treasurer, a Clerk, and twelve "elective managers". It goes on to provide that "the

Managers shall out of their own number elect a Preses — who may or may not be the person chosen as congregational preses — and he shall preside at meetings of managers." The only sense I can make of this is that the Preses elected by the congregation presides over meetings of the congregation while the Preses of the Managers presides over those of the Managers — and that does not sound very sensible. I have not come across a case but I am told by one who has had direct experience of the system in operation that "the Congregational Preses was not Preses of the Managers but was regarded as the congregation's 'shop steward' who would guarantee to raise in the Managers matters of interest to the congregation or any part of it. He then chaired the congregational meetings and was able from the chair to report, without fear or favour, on what the Managers had said or done in response to the issues he had raised on behalf of the congregation." The Preses of the Managers carries all the normal responsibilities of a chairman, ensuring that the business is orderly conducted and properly recorded. He has a casting as well as a deliberative vote and he can introduce business and speak to it.

Other Officials — The congregation also itself elects, or it empowers the Managers to elect, from their own number, a *Clerk* who is to keep a minute-book recording the doings of the Committee and of congregational meetings for temporal purposes and to make this accessible to Managers at all reasonable times. The *Treasurer* is appointed in exactly the same fashion. Two persons, not Managers, are appointed at the Annual Meeting to act as *Auditors* for the ensuing year.

Meetings — Regular meetings of the Committee are held — quarterly at least. They are called by the Preses, or in his absence by the Clerk, by pulpit intimation or by personal notice. A meeting may be requisitioned by one-third of the Managers. The *quorum* if it is not fixed by the constitution is three, or one-third where there are more than nine.

Business — The Managers are fairly confined in what they may do. A limit is generally set upon what they may spend on repairs without calling a special congregational meeting. They may attach the congregational property in security for debt provided they have the authority of the congregation secured at a special meeting called for that purpose, and also, if the titles require it, the authority of the Presbytery. From the other side they may be restrained by the Kirk Session. It is expressly affirmed that they have no jurisdiction over the conduct of public worship, and while they are to apply spiritual principles to the management of temporal affairs they have no degree of spiritual rule and no authority to review the actions of Minister or Kirk Session. They have, however, wide jurisdiction in how they run the temporal affairs and are, in many cases, very jealous of their rights in this regard. The Church Officer is appointed by a joint meeting of Session and Managers presided over by the Moderator of Session and recorded in the Session minutes. Minor officials are appointed by the Managers It used to be that the stipend was fixed on the recommendation of the Managers at the Annual Meeting and was paid in advance, but in all matters of stipend they now act in uniformity with the general rules.

Congregational Meetings — An Annual Business Meeting is held as soon as possible after the close of the financial year; it is called on the strength of at least one Sunday's notice, and is presided over by the Preses. It is customary to invite the Minister to open this meeting with prayer, after which he is expected to leave. No extraordinary business can be transacted at this meeting, but this can conveniently be got round by calling a special meeting for the same time. Special meetings of the congregation for temporal purposes are called by the Managers on two Sundays, specifying the nature of the business and only with consent of the Kirk Session. Such a meeting is presided over by a chairman chosen by the meeting, who may be the Minister, the Preses, an Elder, or any other member of the congregation. The minute is taken by the Committee Clerk and engrossed in his records.

(e) Special Cases

In any case where a congregation operates under a special constitution (a Burgh Church, for example) the provisions of that constitution must be observed in respect of the management of temporal affairs and of the holding of congregational meetings.

Changing the Method

It is always in order for a congregation no matter what its historical affiliations to resolve to adopt the Model Deed of Constitution. A congregation in the former Free or UP tradition may adopt any one of the other methods except the old *quoad omnia* system.

When a union is effected involving two or more congregations which had been operating under different forms of constitution it is usually written into the Basis of Union that they will adopt the Model Deed of Constitution, and in such a case the Delegation of Assembly is held authorised without further formal action to issue a Constitution accordingly. When the two congregations had been operating under the same constitution (other than the Model) the Presbytery may agree that that constitution will continue to operate in the united congregation. There may be difficulty when two former UP's unite because, as has been pointed out, constitutions differ as between one and another. In a case of this kind it would be for the Presbytery to produce a version acceptable to both sides. In the case of a former United Free Church resolving to adopt the Model Constitution it is no longer necessary for it to make over its property into the hands of the General Trustees, though, of course, it is at liberty, and is strongly encouraged to do so.

Procedure — The movement towards a change in the method of administration of temporal affairs begins at the level of the Kirk Session which if it thinks this should be done calls a congregational meeting (for ecclesiastical purposes) on two Sundays' notice, and if the congregation concur the matter is reported to the Presbytery. That body may then authorise the change, and it will notify the Delegation of Assembly which proceeds to issue a Deed of Constitution.

The Case for Uniformity — As has been stated, the Model Deed was produced in revised form in 1965 with a view to making it easier for all cogregations to accept it as a standard pattern. It was the opinion of the Special Committee which looked into the matter that the Model Constitution had much to commend it, the other methods being defective in one way or another. It was further updated in 1994.

The old *quoad omnia* pattern has many very ardent supporters especially among Ministers. It is, however, utterly undemocratic and suffers gravely through its failure to involve the ordinary membership in decision-making at any point. In a day when so many of the material requirements of the congregation were being provided for it by outsiders this might not have mattered too seriously. But today it is the ordinary membership that has to foot the bills and which, therefore, if it does not like the Session's way of handling things has a quick and easy — and effective — way of showing its disapproval — even if they can't do so at a meeting. It is most important today that the voice of the membership should be heard in determining congregational policy, and for this the *quoad omnia* constitution makes only the least provision.

The old UP method stands at the opposite extreme from the democratic point of view and when it works well it works extraordinarily well. There are not wanting Ministers who will tell how wonderful it is to be freed from all those irksome financial chores and to be able to get on with their proper job. The other side of the story is that when the system works badly it can do so quite disastrously badly. Difficulties are bound to arise, for the system is based on a neat clear-cut distinction between the spiritual and the temporal, and never the twain shall meet — a distinction not reflected in reality. The system, not surprisingly, works best where there is constant contact and conference between Elders and Managers. And that, of course, is precisely what the Model Deed is designed to provide.

The Deacons' Court has inclined over the years to work itself towards a pattern almost indistinguishable from the Model Constitution and it should never be difficult for a congregation in this tradition to change over.

As has been indicated, the Assembly in 1965 went no farther than to "recommend and urge" the adoption of the Model Deed of Constitution. Pressure has not been brought to bear, but the change has much to to commend it.

The Amended Model Deed

The General Assembly of 1994 amended the Model Deed in certain particulars, as it is entitled to do in terms of Act ii of 1989 which claims that the provisions of the Act are "subject to any Regulations or Directions which may hereafter be enacted by the General Assembly." A copy of the new Deed, to be known as the Amended Model Deed, is being supplied to all congregations operating under the Model Deed.

Substantially the Deed is as it was except in two respects. First of all there has been added after "the minister" in the *ex officio* membership of the Board, "or ministers of the congregation, any associate minister, or assistant minister, deacon or deaconess appointed to serve with the congregation". The Report (p 5) had included also "or Probationer Minister", which is apparently a mistake for, presumably, "Probationer Assistant." In any case he is not included in the Act. Neither is an Auxiliary Minister seconded to work in the parish. These may, of course, at the Stated Meeting be elected to places.

Secondly certain changes have been rendered necessary in view of Government legislation affecting charitable institutions and the keeping of their accounts. I quote the Reports (page 5) — "The amendments are necessitated by changes being made in the Church's accounting procedures. As compared with the existing Deed the proposed new Deed simply makes general reference to the Accounts and accounting procedures of the congregation, and leaves the detail of that matter to the separate Regulations anent Congregational Finance approved by the General Assembly from time to time.

"In the past detail on accounting procedures has traditionally been in the Model Deed. Procedures for accounts and audits, however, are constantly developing, and the fact is that Model Deeds have tended to become out of date fairly rapidly on this score.

"The new Deed, therefore, it is hoped will be in force for a substantial period of time, and any changes required in accounting procedures will simply be made through amendments to the Regulations anent Congregational Finance. Whenever a Model Deed is issued in the future a copy of these Regulations will be issued with it."

Chapter 2

PARISH REAPPRAISAL

WHEN THE CHURCH OF SCOTLAND became re-united in 1929 one of the most pressing tasks confronting the new body was that of readjusting its agencies. The periods of population explosion in Scotland had more or less coincided with times of secession, and in its own peculiar way the divisions of the age had contributed enormously towards meeting the demand for Church extension. Inevitably, though, it had done so in a quite random and haphazard fashion so that by 1929 the situation was crying out for rationalisation. In almost every village in Scotland at that time there were three charges of the Church of Scotland — near the geographical centre of the parish there would be the Old Kirk, in the heart of the village would be the Free Kirk, and at a point determined by some accident of history you would find the U P Kirk. The union of Free and UP in 1900 had gone some way — but not very far — towards reducing this number.

By 1929 the population was shrinking — dramatically in the rural areas — so that in very many parts of the country three congregations were functioning where one would have more than sufficed. Everyone agreed that this was so — at least until it came to affect their particular congregation!

As the 'thirties advanced the need for readjustment took on a fresh urgency in consequence of the great schemes of house-building being undertaken by local authorities on the outskirts of the built-up areas and resulting in depopulation of the over-crowded central districts. About the same time, too, the situation in the country areas had reached that stage where even after the three-in-a-village had been dealt with the communities had become too small to justify even a single ministry either economically or in any other way, so that the concept of linking took its place alongside that of uniting as a way of making a shrinking supply of ministers serve to fulfil the Church's obligation of maintaining a territorial ministry throughout every corner of the land. Then came the great post-war housing sprawl of the late 'forties.

The first thirty years after 1929 saw some 800 unions and 100 linkings effected. Twenty-seven years later the numbers had risen to 1230 and 520 respectively.

A national Church is bound to ensure that the needy and deprived districts are not left churchless because of local financial stringency, and this can be achieved only by preventing needless duplication and overlapping in more prosperous areas; and while it is true that examples of meaningless duplication have now been fairly nearly eradicated there are still cases, especially in the cities and larger towns, where there is room for further readjustment — even if now we call it reappraisal. The most recently published figures for the Presbytery of Glasgow, for example, reveal that of the 124 congregations within the city boundaries 53 have fewer than three hundred members and 27 between three and five hundred. So that every time a vacancy occurs in any charge the question of possible readjustment has to be looked into and probably pursued. The procedure was considerably revised in recent times and is now covered by the provisions of Act iv 1984 as amended by Act iii 1988, Act iii 1989, and Act ii 1992. The matter is under the direction of the Assembly Committee on Parish Reappraisal (within the Board of National Mission) which in 1990 took over from the Committee on Unions and Readjustmets ("U and R" for short) which had been a branch of the Department of Ministry. In either case it will be referred to hereunder simply as "the Assembly Committee".

FORMS OF READJUSTMENT

Readjustment may take any one of a variety of forms and it is well to have a clear picture of these before considering the mechanics of how readjustment is achieved.

(a) Union

Union occurs when two or more congregations agree to unite, with all their agencies, to form one congregation. Union is effected by the Presbytery with concurrence of the Assembly Committee and it has to be reported to the Maintenance of the Ministry Committee. There are cases (very few) where union can be effected only by the General Assembly or their Commission, these being cases which involve some modification of arrangements set up by and existing under a decree of the Court of Teinds, or some modifiction of an Act of Assembly, or of a Scheme of the Scottish Ecclesiastical Commissioners. In such cases only the General Assembly can effect the union except that where it is a Court of Teind decision that is involved the Commission of Assembly has the necessary power. Where the congregations involved are in neighbouring Presbyteries an Act of Assembly is called for to adjust Presbytery bounds.

Basis of Union — A Basis of Union has to be prepared which in the end will be submitted to the congregations for their approval. This deals with the choice of a name, the fusion of property and funds, the choice of a building as the place of worship where that is called for and the future use or disposal of the remaining property, how the temporal affairs are to be managed and by whom, the delimitation of a parish area, the choice of a manse and the disposal of the redundant manse, and decides what is to happen about a Minister. Almost any of these issues can prove controversial, and the last can be highly complicated.

Minister Retiring — The usual case is that one charge is vacant and the other full, and it may be that the Minister concerned is prepared to consider retiring in the interest of union (for terms etc see pp 65 ff). The united congregation would then in such a case be vacant and would normally be given power to call in the usual way. It could be, however, that even after union the charge was not thought capable of supporting a full ministry and in that case any conditions to be imposed would be written in to the Basis. Where a vacancy is going to have to be filled it is wise to indicate either in the Basis or in an Annexation, an allocation of places on the Vacancy Committee as between the components and it is good that the congregations should meet separately before union for the purpose of electing these.

The Minister instead of retiring immediately may agree to carry on in the united charge for a year or two years or until his xth birthday, when he will demit and a new Minister will be chosen in the usual manner. This can prove a most satisfactory arrangement, helping over what can be a difficult period by having at the helm someone intimately familiar with the problems and personalities involved yet not going to have to live on indefinitely in the midst of it all. Although his date of retirement does not coincide with the date of union he will still be regarded as retiring in the interest of union.

When a Minister demits his charge in the interest of union it is not in my view necessary for the Presbytery to go through the normal process for a demission — the acceptance by him, by the congregation, and by the Presbytery of the Basis of Union is to be seen as fulfilling all that is required. It is important, though, that he should be cited to a meeting of Presbytery close to his time of departing so that suitable notice may be taken of the close of his ministry. And, whatever his age, he will, if he is prepared to continue to take his part in the business of the court, retain his seat in Presbytery — subject to the conditions to be imposed on all retired ministers in terms of an Act of 1995.

Date of Union — In a case of union a question may arise as to the date when the union should take place. There is no rule on the subject and normally an early date is desirable. Where, however, a new Minister is being chosen there is much to be said for allowing the congregations to continue on their own until a nominee has been chosen and then for uniting and inducting in one service. The enthusiasm associated with beginning a new ministry may well help to smooth out some of the problems connected with the launching of a union.

Minister Continuing — The Basis may provide for union being effected under the Minister of one of the charges. Under the earlier legislation this could be done only with consent of both congregations. In terms of Para 4(e) of the new Act the Presbytery may in such a case proceed in face of congregational disapproval provided it has the agreement of the Minister and the concurrence of the Assembly Committee — the Presbytery is, however, "to make every effort to secure the approval of the congregations involved." It is not necessary that such a Minister should be inducted either into the charge with which his congregation is uniting, or into the united charge, but the Presbytery will mark the occasion by holding a "Service of Declaration of Union and of Introduction of Mr A.B."

There is no automatic financial recognition of the additional responsibility undertaken by the Minister, but in every case a Revision Schedule is issued for completion by the united congregation and this may well result in an increase in stipend. At one time an additional £100 per annum was paid to a Minister who took on a linking, but this is no longer so, though again there will be Revision Schedules.

Deferred Union — Where the Minister is not prepared to retire and the other congregation is not willing to accept him, and the Presbytery does not want to force the issue, recourse may be had to Deferred Union, an arrangement whereby the vacant congregation is allowed to call and a

Minister is inducted as their Minister on an undertaking that, on the occurrece of a vacancy in the other charge, union will automatically take place with him as Minister. To conserve the rights of that other congregation they will be fully represented on the Joint Vacancy Committee and they will vote in the election of the nominee. When the vacancy actually occurs no further voting or formality is required — it remains only for the Presbytery to proceed to a "Service of Declaration of Union and of Introduction of Mr A.B."

Should a second vacancy occur before it has been possible to implement the terms as above, this will normally mean that the agreement is accepted as still being in force and the procedure for election etc will be repeated. On the other hand it is open to the Presbytery to regard that piece of readjustment as having exhausted itself and to examine the whole situation afresh in light of prevailing circumstances. And if the Presbytery can take that line of its own will then presumably it is in order for any party having an interest to petition the Presbytery to do just that.

Place of Worship — One of the subjects likely to cause most heart-burning will be the choice of buildings to be retained for the work of the united congregation and the decision on the fate of redundant property. In recent times there has been an increasing willingness to submit this question to arbitration and in the meantime to get ahead with the business of uniting. In many ways this is the fairest solution. The Assembly Committee on Extension Projects is always ready to arrange a panel of arbiters. But if, as often happens, professional surveys are required (in addition to those already available in the normal way) the cost of this falls on the united congregation and will constitute a first charge on any funds accruing from the sale of redundant property.

Arbiters' Decision — The finality of the Arbiters' decision on use of buildings is an issue that has recently given cause for trouble in a number of cases. Congregations A and B have agreed to unite on terms of a Basis of Union which obliges them to accept as final the decision of Arbiters on the use of buildings. The Arbiters declare that Church A is to be the place of worship while Church B is to be sold or otherwise disposed of. The union is duly effected, Church A is in regular use for worship and Church B is on the market but with no immediate takers. Certain minor slating repairs seem to be called for at A and these are put in hand. The slater reports that he finds the woodwork on the roof to be in a dangerous condition of disrepair etc, etc, that the masonry at wall-heads has been affected, and so on, and that the total bill he estimates at around x thousand pounds — adding cheerfully that it might be a bit more. A professional survey shows building B to be structurally sound.

Can the congregation set aside the judgment of the Arbiters and move the place of worship to B? Former members of Congregation A may well claim — and that with some vehemence — that they cannot. My own view is that they can. Every Basis of Union ends with a clause which says that while the above articles are an instrument to effect the union of Congregations A and B the united congregation shall be free, like other congregations, to arrange its affairs under authority of Presbytery as the need may arise. Clearly this is a case where a need has arisen. I am not blind to the fact that this might seem to suggest that in a case where X had a massive numerical preponderence over Y the officers of XY could depart from those provisions in the Basis designed to secure the rights of the weaker group, claiming justification in the clause quoted. The protection against such sharp practice lies in the phrase "under authority of the Presbytery", for I am sure that court could be relied upon to ensure that underhand manoevring of that kind was not permitted. At the same time I think the Presbytery could be counted on to support a realistic approach to the situation envisaged above. The Basis of Union is an instrument designed to bring two congregations into one: it does not bear the stamp of the law of either Medes or Persians. See also "Power to Readjust" hereunder.

Preparatory Work — The Basis of Union (whether immediate or deferred) confines itself very properly to general directions and makes no provision for delicate matters such as which of the Session Clerks will act in the united Kirk Session, how the Woman's Guild branches will function after union, what will be the position of the Boys' Brigade Officers, who will be Organist — so you can go on and draw a list of quite terrifying choices. These choices have to be made and, make no mistake, it is largely upon the degree of tact and wisdom and patience — and firmness — with which these questions are faced that the success or otherwise of the union will to no little extent depend. It is important, therefore, that, any time after the principle of union has been accepted, and certainly not later than when the Basis has been approved by both sides, a steering committee of some sort should be appointed to smooth the way for the merging of the two bodies. It is most unwise to allow the union to occur before these issues have been explored and resolved as far as possible. This is a field where the Presbytery can be of little help, and the Assembly Committee of even less, for everything here depends upon local knowledge, initiative and goodwill.

Power to Readjust Basis — As has been commented upon above every Basis of Union has a closing paragraph in some such words as – "While these terms and conditions shall form a basis of union for the two congregations now uniting, the united congregation shall be free, like other congregations, to adjust arrangements under authority of the Presbytery as need may arise." This to me clearly implies that the Basis is primarily an instrument for fusing the congregations into one, and, the said union having been effected, the new united congregation is on all fours with other congregations so far as the management of its affairs is concerned.

Suppose, for example, that at the time of union some highly complicated name was devised and a couple of years later the Kirk Session felt that a new and simpler title should be substituted, then, as I see it, it is for the Session to secure the approval of congregation and Presbytery and that will be that. I cannot see that any Assembly Committee has an interest — apart from being informed. And equally I cannot see that the Basis of Union should be altered to take account of this change. Indeed I am satisfied that after the union has taken place the Basis cannot be altered. Unlike a Basis of Linking it is not a contract of partnership. The union once effected the Basis becomes an historic document. In agreeing to a change such as I have instanced the Presbytery might care to frame its resolution in some such terms as "Notwithstanding the terms of Paragaph 1 of the Basis of Union of date ..... the name of the congregation shall henceforward be ....." But this is merely to acknowledge the existence of the Basis, not to change it. And what I have said about Name would apply equally to Place of Worship, Management of Temporal Affairs, or any other of its clauses.

Power to Impose — A completely new feature of the 1984 Act is contained in Para 4(e) which states "while it shall be the duty of the Presbtery to make every effort to secure approval of the congregations involved, the right of the Presbytery to effect readjustment in terms of this Act is hereby affirmed, subject to the consent of any minister or ministers whose rights are involved, and subject also to the concurrence of the Assembly's Committee." This is in face of the opinion of the then Procurator some years ago that a vacant congregation could not be forced to unite under a "sitting minister". In the last resort I imagine the

Presbytery has power to dissolve a recalcitrant congregation that adopted this position — I am not so sure they have, or indeed could be given, the power to "impose". I am not aware of any case having arisen and would be happy to think that none would.

(b) Severence

This is an instrument which enables one congregation to become two congregations, and obviously is not often resorted to. In fact its principal use is in dealing with a case where for some reason a union has not proved satisfactory and it is desired to separate the two elements. It is generally accepted that the omelette is incapable of unscrambling, but it can be divided into two small omelettes. An agreement to sever involves a Basis providing for the erection of a new parish, for the establishment of a Communion Roll, for the allocation of property and funds, and probably for questions of ministry, for if the charge is full the Minister will have either to go with one group or to stay with the other. It is perhaps worthy of comment that a method not dissimilar to this seems commonly to have been employed in the United Secession Church in the creation of new charges in developing areas of the cities — a bit of an established congregation (including a group of members, some office-bearers and certain funds) were broken off and transplanted.

Severance is effected by the General Assembly passing an Act in response to a petition from the Presbytery with concurrence of the Assembly Committee, the matter having been reported to the Maintenance of the Ministry Committee.

(c) Linking

The effect of linking two or more congregations is that they share the services of one Minister who will conduct worship in each of the parishes, and coming to terms regarding the division of the cost of stipend and of providing a manse, but in every other regard retaining their identity and their autonomy. At one time the two Kirk Sessions had to meet jointly once a year to appoint a Representative Elder to Presbytery, but Act ii of 1977 gave the right to each Kirk Session to have its own Representative Elder, and joint meetings are now held only as deemed appropriate.

The procedure towards linking is, with obvious modifications, the same as that for union and concludes with the acceptance by both or all congregations of a Basis of Linking. It is effected by the Presbytery with the same restrictions as apply in the case of Union.

For a variety of reasons linking may be the answer to a readjustment problem. In a case where union is thought to be desirable but cannot as yet be achieved linking may be resorted to as an interim measure. This will be done in the belief that it will bring union nearer though such a hope can well prove illusory. The normal and proper use for linking is that you have two or more congregations too far apart to function as one but not strong enough to carry on effectively as independent units. It should never be resorted to when two close-neighbouring congregations in a town ought to be united but neither will give way on the question of buildings.

A linking may be "Deferred" in precisely the same way as a Union (p 48).

The distinction once recognised between permanent and temporary linking has been departed from and under the new Act any linking may be dissolved by the Presbytery with concurrence of the Assembly Committee. This will normally be done with a view to effecting some other linking arrangement either immediately or within the foreseeable future.

Manse — Generally speaking one of the manses will be chosen, the other being sold and the price invested to form a fund the first charge on the income of which will be to meet the agreed share of Council Tax and cost of upkeep. In determining what these shares should be it should be borne in mind that one of the congregations is already making a large contribution via the capital value of the house. Alternatively, of course, both houses may be disposed of, a completely new one purchased and a plan approved for sharing both the price and the costs of maintaining what is now a joint asset.

While, as has been said above, a linking is no longer officially described as temporary there are occasions when it is clear that it is of a purely provisional nature to keep things going until another vacancy opens the way for the establishment of a more acceptable pattern. A + B and C + D is the obvious answer, but it is A and C that are vacant, so it is they that are linked — but only for the present. In such a case the manse question must be considered very seriously and care taken not to dispose of a house which may be the ideal one once the long-term solution has been achieved.

Basis of Linking — In the case of linking the Basis is a most important document, for it, like a contract of partnership, is a deed which not only brings the two parties together but determines the nature of their ongoing relationship. Any proposal, therefore, to amend or depart from its provisions would seem to require the agreement of both congregations, of the Presbytery, and of the Assembly Committee — that is to say, of all who had approved of it in the first place. In this it differs completely from a Basis of Union (p 51). It contains, of course, the usual clause giving power to amend as need may arise.

While they remain two congregations they constitute together one charge, and they are generally designed "the linked charge of A *with* B".

(d) Transportation and Transference

There are three separate and distinct ways in which a congregation may move geographically — first, without in any way disturbing its parish boundaries it may move its place of worship within these boundaries from one site to another; secondly it may move to a new parish in a different part of the same Presbytery; and thirdly it may move from the bounds of one Presbytery to those of an adjoining one.

The first of these is a straightforward affair requiring the approval of the Presbytery, but not raising any question of readjustment and not involving any Committee of Assembly unless financial assistance is involved. This, obviously, is effected by a simple resolution of Presbytery, subject to the usual rights of appeal. That at least is my view, though it may not be universally accepted.

The second is known as *Transportation*. It arises in an unusual kind of situation — where a congregation near the heart of a town or city has acquired a considerable sum of money in respect of its buildings (these having been sold for commercial development, or conveyed under a Compulsory Purchase Order, or destroyed by fire being well insured) and where it would be indefensible to rebuild within the already over-churched parish area. In such circumstances the congregation may be persuaded to "transport" to a completely new district, carrying with it its assets and its traditions. This also I see as being effected by a simple resolution of Presbytery, though I imagine the concurrence of the Assembly Committee would have to be obtained and, of course, if it involved any of the exceptions set forth under Union an Act of Assembly would be required.

The third is known as *Transference*. Here it is said that the congregation is transferred from the bounds of one Presbytery to those of another, but what in fact happens is that the Presbytery bounds are redrawn to include/exclude the transferred parish. It is essential, therefore, that it be adjacent to the Presbytery border. In this way the congregation is moved while staying put! The case arises where it is desired to effect a union or linking between two congregations on opposite sides of a Presbytery boundary. Transference can be effected only by the General Assembly or the Commission of Assembly and that on petition by the Presbytery desiring the change. A copy is served on the other Presbytery which indicates whether or not it consents. If contested the case is heard, naturally, by the Assembly or their Commission.

(e) Restricted Choice

A vacant congregation may be given permission to call but have their choice restricted in some way — usually to a person over a certain age, occasionally to a probationer. These are quoted merely as examples and the Presbytery may restrict in any way which to it seems proper. An age-restriction will incline to be imposed for one of two reasons — because it is felt the work is of such extent as may well be undertaken by an older person, or because it is desired that a vacancy should again occur in the charge within a fairly short time. In restricting to a probationer the Presbytery is deliberately taking a risk — what is in mind is that this is the kind of charge where a young person could well exercise a fruitful ministry but would be unlikely to stay much longer than five years — and it is the hope of the Presbytery that he won't! But it need not work out that way for he has been inducted *ad vitam aut culpam.*

In terms of Act xvii 1957 a charge in certain circumstances might be "suppressed", in which case it would be ministered to by a Minister Without Charge appointed by the Presbytery and capable of having his ministry terminated by that body at any time. From the point of view of the congregation the choice of the term "suppressed" was, to say the least, unfortunate, and it was later replaced by the idea of a Terminable Appointment, the appointee being chosen by the congregation and introduced by the Presbytery. For this the 1984 Act has substituted the concept of Terminable Tenure. The Minister is elected in the usual way and is inducted, not *ad vitam aut culpam* but on the understanding that the Presbytery may for any reason terminate his tenure on giving six months' notice in writing. Lest there should be any misunderstanding the person elected is required, before his appointment is sustained, to sign an acceptance of a written Basis of Terminable Tenure setting forth at length and with great precision the conditions of the appointment.

Sometimes a specific time is mentioned in connection with such an appointment — say "for three years". This is unfortunate and can lead to needless difficulty by creating the impression that a minimum of three years is being guaranteed for the new ministry when in fact that period is meant to be a maximum with the possibility of being terminated even sooner. The Presbytery is at liberty to intervene at any time during terminable tenure to re-assess the situation and the incumbent has no rights to be conserved apart from the right to six months' notice.

The sense of inferiority created by the use of "suppression" lingers on and congregations generally incline to feel the imposition of terminable tenure puts them in a second-class category. If the new ministry proves at all successful they can be counted upon to approach the Presbytery, not now for restoration of status, but to have the Minister inducted without limit of time. This is quite commonly granted and in that case a fresh Service — one of Induction — is held.

(g) Dissolution

Dissolution is all that the name implies — it marks the end of the road for a congregation. As such it is to be avoided if at all practicable. It may be, however, that a situation arises where a gathered congregation cannot continue its independent life and where any union that could be contrived would be a wholly artificial affair, and the former members would in any case attach themselves to congregations nearer their doors. In such circumstances dissolution may be the proper answer, though even there consideration should be given to the possibility of a nominal union with a neighbour.

Dissolution will be effected by the General Assembly or by their Commission consequent upon a petition of Presbytery with annexed to it a Basis of Dissolution making provision for the issue of certificates of transference to all members, for the allocation of the parish area (including, it may be, an interim arrangement), for the destination of property and funds and probably also for the appointment of trustees to hold the heritable property until it can be conveyed to its ultimate owners — and all with concurrence of the Assembly Committee and the Presbytery.

Property — It is important that steps be taken timeously to deal with all property. A Committee should be appointed to take firm hold (more or less literally) of all moveables, for these can have a way of proving themselves "removeable" at the instance of members wanting "keepsakes". Steps should also be taken to protect against vandalism. Oddly enough the most effective of these last-named is to give the premises the appearance of still being in use. And if, as will probably be the case, there is no immediate prospect of disposing of the heritable property care must be taken that it is not left vested in trustees *ex officiis*, for when the congregation ceases to exist such trustees will cease to exist as legal entities and will be incapable of granting a valid disposition in favour of a buyer. Such trustees should at least convey the property to themselves as individuals for the purpose of holding till a purchaser can be found. Conference should also be had with the insurers to make certain that adequate cover is still in force.

Memorials — The question of the future of memorials raises problems in every case where a building becomes redundant, but this is particurarly so in a case of dissolution where there is no other building to which they can be transferred. Circumstances vary so enormously that no general rules can be laid down except to say that we here tread on very delicate ground, that relatives of the person commemorated should be consulted and that it is often possible to find a home for quality stained glass and that in this context the Advisory Committee on Artistic Matters should be consulted.

Members — Members of the congregation should be encouraged to take Certificates of Transference and lodge them right away with other congregations. Immediately after the closing service has been held the Session Clerk should pass to the Presytery Clerk such a certificate in respect of every member on the Communion Roll who has not personally collected one, and the Presbytery Clerk has the responsibility of distributing these, with a note of explanation, to the Ministers of the various parishes within which the persons reside. It is most important that old people (and a congregation facing dissolution has a lot of these) should not be left to take the initiative in forming a new congregational allegiance but that active steps be taken, and taken without delay, to bring them within the care of some other Minister and Kirk Session.

Date — Once it has been agreed that a congregation is to dissolve it is a great pity for its death throes to be needlessly protracted. Yet the business of winding up can take a long time. The difficulty can be got round by the Presbytery fixing a date for dissolution sufficiently remote to allow for all necessary steps to be taken and all formalities observed, and at the same time granting permission to the Kirk Session to discontinue public worship as from a date in the immediate future. In this way the congregation can have the satisfaction of going out on a note of some strength and triumph instead of just fading away over a period of some months.

(h) Continued Vacancy

When the Presbytery is not prepared to grant leave to call and yet all attempts at readjustment have failed, the charge may, with concurrence of the Assembly Committee, be declared a Continued Vacancy. The congregation is not allowed to take any steps towards finding a Minister, the Interim Moderator continues as Moderator of Session and ensures that ordinances are maintained, and the congregation is served either by a *locum tenens* or by pulpit supply. While it is convenient in many ways that a retired Minister should act as both interim moderator and locum such an arrangement can lead to complications and it is probably wise to keep the two offices in different hands.

The creation of a Continued Vacancy (which stems from a Presbytery resolution with concurrence of the Assembly Committee) must never be seen as a long-term solution — for it marks, in fact, the failure to find a solution. At best it is a device for keeping a congregation in being until some change in the neighbouring circumstances opens the way for proper long-term readjustment. The Act requires that once every three years the situation is to be reviewed by the Presbytery.

(i) Joint Ministry — 1984

A new feature of the 1984 Act was that it made provision whereby a union that would create a charge too large to be served by one Minister but desirable for other reasons might be effected "and the charge will be served by two or more Ministers one of whom shall be Minister of the charge and the other or others his associate or associates." The Presbytery is to set forth in the Basis of Union a definition of the respective duties of each of the Ministers. Should it be that a Minister was already serving in each of the charges united these two may act as colleagues within the united charge — that is to say, they will jointly share both duties and responsibility and will take turn of presiding at meetings of Kirk Session. But when one of them demits the other will become sole Minister and an associate will be appointed to work with him — on a quite different footing.

Shared Ministry — So much for the Act of 1984. In 1994 the Committee reported to the Assembly that in its view there were envisaged here two entirely different situations and that it would be helpful to have these separately designated "Shared Ministry" and "Joint Ministry." The former of these, *Shared Ministry*, is defined as the case where two Ministers share one ministry in a single charge, as in Falkirk Old for example. The Report goes on to point out that where there is to be a Shared Ministry care must be taken in the Basis to cover (a) Stipend, (b) National Insurance and pension arrangements, (c) Pension entitlements, (d) Respective duties, (e) Sick Leave, (f) Holidays, (g) Position where a vacancy occurred in either, (h) Procedure to be followed in the event of a breakdown in working arrangements, (i) Occupancy of Manse, (j) Relation to the courts, (k) Review.

Joint Ministry — 1994 — This is defined as "one in which a charge has within it another Church appointment." Examples of this are at Alvie and Insh whose Minister is also Warden of the Badenoch Christian Centre, and Bridge of Allan Chalmers carrying responsibility for the Chaplaincy at Stirling University. The Report goes on to outline steps that should be taken in such a case to avoid a conflict of interest — such as a clear definition of the duties and hours for the non-parochial appointment, steps to prevent the vetoing of a sole nominee, the appointment of a Presbytery committee to monitor and support (Repts 1994 p 370).

Part-Time Ministry — When we have got as far as Joint Ministry as defined above we have got very close to the idea of a Part-time Ministry. The Committee has, in fact, given considerable thought to the implications of this and has consulted Presbyteries in regard thereto. The proposal advanced was that such a charge might be created when either (a) such a charge was necessary for a territorial purpose, *e g* in a remote area, or (b) where such a charge could be joined to another Church appointment for the benefit of the Church. The Committee was not unaware of the danger of small congregations within cities contriving to survive in independence by use of this device. In the event the Assembly accepted a Deliverance approving the creation of such charges as from 1st July 1994. I should myself have thought that so radical a change in the traditional pattern of ministry would have required Barrier Act procedure.

(j) Other Forms

A further feature of the 1984 Act is the statement that the forms of readjustment set out are not to be treated as exhaustive and that a Presbytery may "devise" a new form to deal with a new situation and that unless this is at variance with the law of the Church it is likely to attract the concurrence of the Assembly Committee.

QUESTION OF READJUSTMENT

On the death of a Minister in a charge, or on his being deposed from office, or at the meeting of Presbytery at which the translation or demission of a Minister in a charge is agreed to the Presbytery appoints one of its Ministers to be Interim Moderator in the vacancy or anticipated vacancy as the case may be, and in the latter instance he will act for purposes of readjustment as Moderator of Session even though the Minister is still in office. The Assembly Committee is informed of the vacancy and the question of readjustment is deemed to have been raised.

Not to Pursue the Question — The Presbytery may take the view that it is so obvious that no question of readjustment arises that it can there and then resolve accordingly. Or it may reach that conclusion after it has conferred with local parties, and if so again it will resolve accordingly. It then agrees to grant the congregation permission to call a Minister without restriction, subject to the concurrence of the Assembly Committee, and the congregation may immediately get busy with the preparation of its Electoral Register. Should the Assembly Committee not see its way to concur procedure is sisted and the question is pursued (Act v 1984, Para 3). Since the Presbytery cannot be expected to press the readjustment issue with conviction after going on record that the question should not be pursued the Act provides that from the outset it shall have the active participation of representatives of the Assembly Committee.

It has to be emphasised that a decision not to pursue taken by the Presbytery at this early stage has the effect of allowing the vacant congregation to proceed without delay towards the filling of the vacancy. But this is provisional, and they should be cited to hear the response of the Assembly Committee even if that is favourable, for a member of Presbytery would be in order in dissenting and the congregation should be there to defend their interest. In the event of the Assembly Committee not concurring, procedure (which at that stage cannot have proceeded beyond the preparation of the Electoral Register) will be sisted until the issue is resolved.

Pursuing the Question — The Presbytery may, and generally will, resolve that the question should be pursued. This, of course, is without prejudice to its right at a later stage when the possibilities have been fully explored to argue that there is no case for readjustment and that the congregation should be permitted to call without restriction.

Let it be, on the other hand, that Presbytery has resolved that the question should be pursued it remits to its own Reappraisal Committee to arrange for a group to meet with the local office-bearers, that is elders and members of the financial court. The Interim Moderator may, and in my opinion should, attend such meetings, but they are presided over by a member of the Presbytery deputation. It is likely that ere long it will be necessary to carry the discussion into other quarters and to meet with office-bearers of some other congregation or congregations. This the Presbytery Committee has authority to do. Assuming the other congregation has a Minister he, obviously, has to be consulted and his permission given before approach is made to his office-bearers. No discussion whatever in which the interest of the Minister is involved can take place in his absence without his specific permission given in writing.

Basis of Union — Let it be that the situation looks hopeful, the next stage is to prepare a Basis of Union. To this end both sets of office-bearers appoint a small group — say six from each side — to meet with the Presbytery deputies and hammer out the terms of a Basis. It should be kept clearly in mind that at this stage there is no commitment to unite but only an agreement that if union is to take place these are reasonable terms. Until such a document has been finalised it would be unfair to expect anyone to commit himself to a decision For or Against union.

Having prepared a draft Basis the Committee has now to take this to a full meeting of both sets of office-bearers. While it is desirable not to have to amend the Basis it is at this stage still in order to do so should feeling be strong on some point. But clearly this will involve a further meeting of the joint group and then again of the two full groups. Once agreement has been reached in both groups and the consent of the Minister, if involved, has been obtained, the stage is set for taking the matter to the congregations. Before doing this the Presbytery deputies will be wise to discover just how far they can count on the support of the office-bearers for the proposal to unite and not merely for the Basis as a workable formula. It is good if the chairman is able to tell the congregation that their office-bearers are unanimously (or nearly so) in favour.

Congregational Meetings — For the purpose of considering the Basis of Union meetings of both congregations have to be held. They are called by the Presbytery after two Sundays' notice, stating the business in some such terms as "to consider and if so resolved to accept a Basis of Union with the congregation of X." In each case this meeting will be presided over by a member of the Presbytery. Presytery has to arrange that copies of the Basis should be available to members before the date of the meeting, preferably on the days when the intimation is read, and it is the duty of the chairman to go through this, clause by clause, answering questions and seeking to clarify any matter in doubt as well as to hear comments, critical or otherwise. It is not, however, in order for him to accept amendments on detail or counter-proposals on general matters — the deal is up for acceptance or rejection as it stands. It is then for the chairman to ask the meeting whether they are prepared to unite on the terms discussed — he must on no account call for motions. The vote must be counted even if the result is obvious. With the exception noted hereunder there is no machinery for any kind of plebiscite or for recording the votes of absent members. The vote is taken by standing up.

One or two points regarding these meetings call for comment.

It is highly desirable that the two congregational meetings should take place simultaneously or at least that one should follow immediately on the heels of the other. Incalculable harm can be done if a sufficient interval is allowed to let gossip develop. The notice calling the meeting should state clearly that its purpose is to consider and if so advised to adopt a Basis of Union with the congregation of X. Any other business is incompetent. Should it become clear as the discussion proceeds that there is no hope for the acceptance of the proposed union but that they might be happy to transport to a Church Extension area the wise course is to persist in putting the Basis to a vote and closing the meeting. This new possibility can be examined in a proper and orderly fashion thereafter — enough for the moment to dispose of the proposed union.

It is most important that the Presbytery should have arranged for copies of the Basis to be distributed well in advance — it is quite unfair to hand them out as people are gathering for the meeting. Further, the chairman should remember that while the terms of the Basis are familiar to him — possibly to the point of exasperation — they are not so to most of those present and he must be patient and painstaking in going through the document and in dealing with questions.

It is important too that the chairman should put the question quite simply For or Against when it comes to the vote. It is quite wrong to call for motions. It is unreasonable to expect that even the most convinced office-bearer is going to make a passionate speech in favour while there is every likelihood of an intensely effective speech being made on the other side. This could be both unfortunate and unfair. It would appear that the law allows for a ballot vote to be taken at a meeting such as the above, but only in the case of a union — this in terms of Act xxii 1932 and Ballot Regulations 1934 (Reg App D). These regulations include the requirements that it shall be moved and seconded at the meeting that the vote be taken by ballot, that the voting take place before the meeting adjourns or ends, and that voting-papers supplied by the Committee are alone to be used. Unless the latter two requirements can be complied with the chairman is not to accept the motion — and it would seem to be easy to have it occur that it was not possible to comply! Unless advance notice had been given of an intention to move for a ballot I take it the chairman is entitled to go to the meeting not having made the considerable and expensivc preparation for an eventuality most unlikely to arise.

The position of a retiring minister can be an awkward one. If he is retiring to facilitate the union he would be wise to take no active part in the congregational meeting. The Interim Moderator may also find himself in a difficulty in that the office-bearers may want him to act as their spokesman and advocate and that in a way which does not coincide with his own inclinations. There is no reason, however, why he should not do this, for it is important if a wise decision is to be reached that both sides of the case should be clearly and convincingly presented and it may well be that he is the person best qualified to act as advocate. *Note*: While I have spoken throughout in terms of a case of union the identical considerations apply *mutatis mutandis* in the case of any of the other forms of readjustment, except as hereunder and except where the ballot possibility applies (see above).

No Basis Required — In the case of a Restricted Choice or of of a Continued Vacancy no Basis of Readjustment is required and no meetinmg of the congregation is necessary. It is probably wise, however, to hold a congregational meeting and to explain to them what is involved and why the step has been taken. The Presbytery may well come in for some hostile comments, but it is good that an opportunity should be given both to make these criticisms and to have them answered. Only one Sunday's notice is required for a meeting of this kind.

At the Presbytery

The matter has now to go to Presbytery. It used to be that, on occasion and with a view to saving time, Presbytery might approve a Basis provisionally subject to its being accepted by both congregations at a later date; but under the new procedure (see hereunder) no time-saving is achieved by this. When the Presbytery is going to deal with a readjustment situation at this stage — that is say to reach a final and determinative conclusion upon it — the congregation or congregations should on two Sundays' notice be cited to appear for their interest. The Presbytery Committee reports with its recommendation and the congregational representatives are given an opportunity to speak and to answer questions, after which they are "removed" from the bar. A decision is then reached by the Presbytery and procedure is immediately sisted. Parties are recalled and the judgment intimated. Because of the sist it is not in order for any kind of appeal to be taken at this point — either dissent from within the Presbytery or appeal from the congregation. But the latter is summoned *apud acta* to the next regular meeting. In these circumstances there is no call for edictal intimation to the congregation. The relevant minute is then adjusted and approved and an extract forwarded to the Assembly Committee.

Seeking Concurrence — The Assembly Committee now consider the matter and may decide to concur in the Presbytery judgment, in which case an extract minute to this effect is sent to the Presbytery Clerk and its receipt is reported at next meeting of the court, congregational representatives being present. It is at this point that anyone having an interest may appeal or dissent and complain and this will go direct to Assembly or Commission.

The Act is not very clear on the point, but it would seem that if the Assembly Committee does not concur there is not yet any effective decision against which the congregation could competently appeal and that so far as they are concerned they must attend once more when the disagreement has been resolved and a clear and effective resolution has been arrived at. If I am right in all of this there can be no right of appeal at this stage but the Presbytery appears to be enjoined to resolve to take the whole matter to the Assembly by way of Reference. Or the Presbytery may decide to hold conference — as they may well have been invited to do — with the Assembly Committee, or the Presbytery may invite that Committee to appear at one of its meetings or to meet with its own Committee.

Complicated Procedure — This cumbersome and time-consuming procedure has to be seen as an attempt to avoid an awkward situation that has been known to arise under the earlier regime when any appeal went in the first instance to the Synod. Since the Synod is no longer with us some alteration might be made to simplify and expedite procedure.

RETIREMENT IN THE INTEREST OF READJUSTMENT

For a very long time there has been a widespread feeling of dissatisfaction, if not of resentment, about the terms given to Ministers retiring in the interest of readjustment. When a Minister sacrificed what could be quite a few years of stipend-earning and satisfaction-giving service he was entitled to be recompensed, but the way the affair worked out created a feeling that for no obvious reason different people were faring very differently. For example, Messrs A and B in neighbouring charges are both well into their sixties. Mr A decides the time has come when in the interest of his congregation he should seek retirement, and without fuss or ado he informs the Presbytery Clerk of his intention to demit. This is accepted, Mr A is granted the usual retirement annuity and goes forth with his modest life-savings to look for a house. Having met with the congregation thus rendered vacant the Presbytery Committee now approaches Mr B, possibly much less fit than Mr A had been, and learns from him that retiring had been the last thought in his mind; but, of course, he would want to be accommodating. So terms are offered to induce him to demit — terms which involve preferential treatment in the matter of pension and which include the life-occupancy of the manse for himself and his widow. A and B started off in an almost identical position — most emphatically that is not how they ended up. How can you justify such a disparity? Obviously you cannot. So occasion was taken when the 1984 Act was framed to design provisions which would produce a more equitable end-product. Hence Para 22, "When the demission of a Minister facilitates readjustment such demission may be regarded as a demission in the interest of readjustment, providing the procedure, terms and conditions are in accordance with the following povisions." In these terms A's demission facilitates readjustment every bit as much as does B's.

Procedure — When a Minister has intimated to the Presbytery Clerk his intention of demitting on the grounds of age or infirmity the Clerk is to inform the relevant Committee of Presbytery and they, even at this early stage, are to confer with the Minister concerned and with any other Minister who they think may be affected. If there appear to be possibilities approach is to be made to the Secretary of the Parish Reappraisal Committee with a view to formulating draft terms for retirement. Such terms, if approved by the appropriate sub-committee, are to be conveyed to the Minister or Ministers concerned, and to the Presbytery Clerk, and if acceptable they are to be "incorporated in the Basis of Readjustment before that is presented to the cogregation or congregations involved" — though clearly at this stage they are still a long way from such a Basis.

It is specifically laid down that a Minister who has declined to demit to facilitate readjustment will not have his subsequent demission regarded in this light even although readjustment is achieved as a result of it.

Para 21(g) of the Act states that "an offer by any minister to demit in the interest of readjustment by any procedure other than that outlined above shall be disregarded." The significance of this is not obvious, but it might appear to mean that initiative in any matter of retiring in the interest of readjustment must come from the side of the Presbytery and not from that of the Minister. But if a Minister were to approach the Presbytery Clerk saying he had it in mind to retire within the next year or so, but if his going immediately were to facilitate union he would do so, surely such an approach would not have to be "disregarded."

Terms and Conditions — Financial — Financial provision is made by the Assembly Committee and by the Maintenance of the Ministry Committee on the advice of their Joint Sub-Committee on Retirements in the Interest of Union as follows —

(a) No provision is made for a Minister who has not reached his 60th birthday.

(b) If between 60 and 65 the Minister may receive up to, but not exceeding an allowance at the rate of the Minimum Stipend then obtaining until his 65th birthday — that is to say, the amount of his annual payment is fixed at the time of retirement and remains at that level, not increasing with rises in the Minimum Stipend. After his 65th birthday he will qualify as in (c) hereunder.

(c) If he has reached his 65th birthday, or when he reaches it, he will receive either all, or what would have been for him the appropriate proportion of, the Standard Annuity of the Retirement Scheme Committee five years earlier than he would otherwise have done.

(d) Local parties are at liberty to supplement these terms, but they can do so only under the conditions generally governing such supplementary payments (p 195).

Terms and Conditions — Housing — Housing or an allowance in lieu may be made available as provided hereunder, but, of course, only with consent of the local congregation whose property is involved, and that no matter in whose name are the titles:

(a) A redundant manse may be given on terms of life-occupancy to the Minister and surviving spouse (male or female) so long as remaining unmarried — all subject to agreement with local parties as to payment of Council Tax, repairs and maintenance.

(b) A redundant manse may be sold and an alternative house purchased and life-occupancy given on terms as above.

(c) A redundant manse may be sold and from the income from the proceeds the Minister may be paid a sum at the rate fixed from time to time by the Assembly Committee.

(d) When two or more Ministers have to be taken care of no housing will be provided but a redundant manse or manses may be sold and at the discretion of local parties, both or all Ministers may be paid an allowance from the proceeds.

One hopes that these terms will not be too strictly adhered to or that every bargain made with a retiring minister will be required to conform completely to them. For instance, suppose the Minister involved were in his sixtieth year and were agreeable to some adjustment to the total to be paid him overall provided he could go, must this offer be rejected? Or where two ministers are retiring and both manses are to be disposed of it is difficult to see how "the discretion of local parties" is to be obtained before both ministers had committed themselves to retiring. Or a case in my own experience where the local office-bearers were very happy that the Minister should have life-occupancy of the Manse but flatly refused to consider any continuing interest for his widow. Both Minister and wife considered this to be acceptable. But would it be possible with the regulations as they stand? Situations vary so greatly it is good to have some room in which to manoevre.

There is, it seems to me, the over-riding difficuty that the last word in any bargain lies with the party having something to sell which you are anxious to purchase. So long as *ad vitam aut culpam* remains the Kirk has no power to require a demission, and it seems a pity to lose some urgent piece of readjustment for the sake of some trifling demand even if it does not strictly conform to the regulations.

Chapter 3

VACANCY PROCEDURE

THE ENTIRE BUSINESS of the choosing and installing of a Minister in a vacant charge is today governed by the provisions of Act v 1984 anent the Settlement of Ministers.

VACANCY

So long as a charge has a Minister inducted or introduced to it it is said to be "full" (though the term is rarely heard). At all other times it is held to be "vacant".

How Caused — A vacancy may be caused in any one of the following ways, and in no other:
a) by the death of the Minister;
b) by the translation of the Minister;
c) by the demission of the Minister;
d) by the termination at the instance of the Presbytery of an appointment under Terminable Tenure;
e) by the dissolution of the pastoral tie in terms of the Act anent Congregations in an Unsatisfactory State or that anent Congregations in Changed Circumstances; or
f) by the deposition of the Minister by the Presbytery or by the General Assembly.

Patronage — With the exception of one brief spell (1680–1712) all appointments to vacant parishes in the Kirk were made under a system called "patronage" whereby the chief heritor (or patron) had the right to "present" the living to a Minister of his own choosing. The person chosen had to be fully qualified, and after being presented he was taken on trials by the Presbytery which had to satisfy itself as to his "life, literature and doctrine" before settling him in the parish. Acceptability to the parishioners was held not to be a relevant consideration. Once inducted the Minister was established *ad vitam aut culpam*, and in virtue of this the stipend vested in him. He was not in any sense or degree under control of the patron whose rights began and ended with the presentation. It is probably true that the system produced no more, and no more serious, misfits than any later system of popular selection, but in a day of increasing democratic awareness it was bitterly resented, and for more than a century and a half most of the troubles that vexed the Kirk could be traced to its baneful influence. Patronage was responsible for the Secessions of 1733 and 1771, and, of course, for the Disruption of 1843. It goes without saying that other factors were at work and doubtless the split would have arisen in any case, but patronage provided a point around which the differences could centre. It was as comparatively recently as 1874 that an Act of Parliament finally abolished the right of patronage and vacant congregations acquired complete freedom within limits set by the Kirk itself to choose their Minister.

Free Election — It is not to be wondered at that a right so hardly won should be treasured and that its exercise should be hedged about with regulations and restrictions. These can prove exasperating, particularly when they appear to achieve nothing but a needless waste of precious time, but they all have their reasons and in the long run it will be found that time is saved rather than lost by a scrupulous observance of the rules.

Very soon after the Union there was passed in 1932 the Act anent the Election, Settlement and Translation of Ministers (to bring together the practice of the two branches of the Church in this field) and this Act, amended many times over the years, continued to operate for the next half-century. Then, as has been said, came the Act of 1984 representing essentially a tidying-up of the position and introducing some new features. It is this Act which the following pages attempt to set forth in simple terms, but for details reference should be made to the Act itself (v, 1984).

Interim Moderator

The key figure in the life of the vacant congregation during the months of the vacancy is the Interim Moderator who represents at once the missing Minister and the authority of the Presbytery.

Appointment — At the first opportunity after the occurrence of a vacancy caused by death or deposition the Presbytery appoints one of its Ministers (not a member of the vacant congregation) to act as Interim Moderator of Kirk Session during the vacancy. In other cases at the Presbytery meeting at which steps are finally taken to create a vacancy under any other of the conditions outlined above, the Presbytery appoints a Minister to act, this time first of all in the prospective vacancy and thereafter in the actual vacancy. Such a Minister enjoys full power as Moderator of Session in respect of all vacancy business, including readjustment, although the Minister is still responsible for all ordinary Session business. When the charge is a linked one the Interim Moderator holds office in both (or all) of the constituent congegations. The name of the Interim Moderator has to be forwarded without delay to the Department of Ministry.

Prospective Vacancy — Before 1960 no single step could be taken towards the filling of a vacancy until that vacancy was an established fact. It was felt, however, that vacancies were needlessly protracted to the considerable hurt of the congregation when, for example, weeks passed awaiting the actual date of demission, weeks or even months during which much at least of the preliminary work could have been advanced. An Act (xxiii) of that year accordingly provided for the appointment of an Interim Moderator in the anticipated vacancy and for his taking certain preliminary steps which might include the entire readjustment negotiations. Under the 1984 Act progress may go on up to and including the election of the Vacancy Committee, and even at that point request may be made to the Presbytery to proceed further, that court being at liberty, if satisfied this would be in the best interest of the congregation (which it need not be), to grant such permission. But in no circumstance is a nomination to be reported to the Kirk Session before the charge has actually become vacant.

While there is obvious advantage in being able to get the formal preliminaries out of the way while the sitting Minister is still "sitting" it can be dangerous to proceed too far in such a set-up. Each case has to be judged on its merits — hence the prohibition of advancing beyond the appointment of the Vacancy Committee without specific approval of Presbytery.

His Duties — It is the duty of the Interim Moderator to preside at all meetings of Kirk Session and of all congregational meetings at which the

Minister would have presided had the charge been full. When such a meeting has been called by order of the Presbytery in connection with readjustment the Interim Moderator constitutes the meeting, relinquishing the chair to the Presbytery representative, but he has the right to speak, though not to propose a motion, at such a meeting. The arrangements for the supply of the pulpit during the vacancy are the responsibility of the Interim Moderator in consultation with the Kirk Session and (in respect of payment) with the financial court. Insofar as he can do so consistently with his other duties he will seek to supply the want of a settled Minister throughout the period of the vacancy.

Date and Declaration of Vacancy — The date of the vacancy is the day when the Minister (a) dies, (b) is deposed, (c) is inducted to another charge, (d) demits office as agreed with the Presbytery, (e) comes to the end of his terminable tenure, or (f) has the pastoral tie binding him to the congregation dissolved. On the first convenient Sunday after the occurrence of the vacancy pulpit intimation has to be made that on a certain date the Church became vacant and for what reason — the traditional "preaching the Kirk vacant." It is not necessary for the Interim Moderator to do this in person, though it may well provide him with an admirable opportunity to introduce himself to the vacant congregation. In the case of a prospective vacancy this intimation should not, I am quite sure, be made until the vacancy has actually occurred.

Question of Readjustment

In every case where a pastoral charge becomes vacant it is to be presumed that the question of readjustment automatically arises, and the Presbytery has therefore immediately to consider whether the question, having arisen, should be pursued or whether the congregation should be allowed to proceed without restriction. The question is as simple as that, the form which readjustment, if any, might take being at this stage quite irrelevant. Should the decision be in favour of granting unrestricted right of call the Presbytery will go on to give such permission subject to the concurrence of the Assembly Committee. If that latter body does not see its way to concur this will have the effect of sisting procedure and the question will be pursued in face of the Presbytery's decision to the contrary. Any decision to pursue the question will have the effect of halting procedure at the point of finalising the Electoral Register. (For full details anent readjustment procedure see previous chapter, on Parish Reappraisal).

PRELIMINARIES

The Electoral Register — The Electoral Register of a congregation consists of a consecutively-numbered list in alphabtical order of the names and addresses of all persons, members and adherents, who are entitled to vote in the election of a Minister and includes the names of any on the Supplementary Roll who have applied to be so included (p 3). An up-to-date register is a "must" before any effective steps whatever can be taken towards filling the vacancy. But note that for purposes of voting at congregational meetings in connection with readjustment the right to vote is confined to members whose names are on the Communion Roll, and the Electoral Register should not be used in this connection.

As soon as conveniently possible after the appointment of the Interim Moderator (not waiting for the occurrence of the vacancy) intimation is made that the Kirk Session is to meet in connection with the preparation of an Electoral Register, and that anyone whose name is not already on the Communion Roll and who wishes his name to appear on the Register should lodge a Certificate of Transference with the Session Clerk without delay, and that anyone wishing to register as an Adherent should submit a claim on the appropriate form. The term Adherent (p 2) is used in a variety of senses, but for this purpose it is clearly confined to a person not under eighteen years of age who, not being a member of any other congregation in Scotland, is a regular worshipper in the vacant charge. Act vi 1951 provides that a person whose name is on the Supplementary Roll may "on application" be added to the Register. A meeting of Kirk Session is held within fourteen days of this intimation to consider claims and to prepare the Register, which is then made available for inspection at times and places deemed suitable, and intimation to this effect is given from the pulpit on one Sunday, the intimation stating also when the Kirk Session is to meet and citing any who have an interest to appear then. At that meeting the Session finally adjusts the Register which is attested in its name by Moderator and Clerk. In all matters concerning the right to be included in the Register the decision of the Kirk Session is final. It should be borne in mind that in many congregations today the Communion Roll is a loose-leaf affair and that in others the practice is to keep the Communion Roll in Elders' Districts and not in alphabetical order. It is wise, therefore, that the Interim Moderator should have early consultation with the Session Clerk or Roll-keeper regarding the Register so that what may prove a quite considerable task may be put in hand without delay.

The Register duly attested by the Session is now transmitted to the Presbytery Clerk for attestation in name of the court, and a duplicate copy is lodged with him for retention.

Any member wishing to move to another congregation — and it is surprising how many do so move during a vacancy — must make written application for a Certificate of Transference and the Session Clerk retains the letter and informs the Interim Moderator who deletes and signs the relevant entry in the Electoral Register. There is thus provision for taking names off the Register, but there is no way in which the names of new members may be added. When, as a consequence of readjustment negotiations, there has been delay, and a period of longer than six months has elapsed between the attestation of the Register and the congregation receiving permission to call, the Kirk Session may, if it so desires, revise and update the Electoral Register by means of an Addendum.

Permission to Call — This, sometimes referred to in papers of an earlier day as the *conge d'elire*, will be given by the Presbytery when agreement has been reached with the Assembly Committee —

a) that the congregation is to be allowed to call (with or without restriction or on terminable tenure); or
b) that some form of readjustment has been, or is about to be, effected which will result in the creation of a vacant charge to which a Minister is to be called (with or without restriction or on terminable tenure); or
c) that there has been a deferred union or deferred linking one of whose terms is that the vacant congregation is to call a Minister who will ultimately be Minister of the united or linked charge; or d) that an Associate Minister is to be appointed.

Presbytery Advisory Committee — One of the new provisions of the 1984 Act is that at the same time that permission to call is given the Presbytery is to appoint a Committee of three (at least one an Elder), the Presbytery Advisory Committee, which will in the first place meet with the Kirk Session of the vacant charge (with Kirk Sessions jointly in case of linking or deferred union or linking), then with the Vacancy Committee when that has been appointed, to consider together, in light of the whole circumstances of the parish, what kind of ministry would be best suited to their needs. It is conceded that in the case of island and other remote charges it is enough if Interim Moderator and one member of the Vacancy Committee meet with the Presbytery Committee.

Vacancy Schedule — As soon as agreement is reached that a charge is to be allowed to call there is forwarded to its Congregational Treasurer from the Assembly's Maintenance of the Ministry Committee a Vacancy Schedule which is to be completed by the financial court in conference with representatives of the Presbytery's Maintenance of the Ministry Committee setting forth the proposed stipend arrangements. If endowments are involved a recommendation will havc been made by the Assembly Committee as to whether any question should be raised regarding their future use. It should be noted that until the Vacancy Schedule has received approval of the Assembly Committee an induction of a Minister to the vacant charge cannot take place.

THE VACANCY COMMITTEE

Election — The Electoral Register complete and permission to call having been duly received the next business is *to* elect a Vacancy Committee. Intimation is made on two Sundays that a congregational meeting will be held (normally at the close of the principal — not necessarily first — diet of worship) for the dual purpose (a) of electing a Vacancy Committee, and (b) of determining whether the election of a Minister is to be by ballot or by open vote. The Interim Moderator presides at this meeting and the minute is engrossed in the Session records. The first question to be resolved is, How many? It is recommended the number should not exceed thirteen for a Roll under 500, nineteen between that and 1000, and twenty-five thereafter. These figures are given as maxima but they are, I think, generally accepted as the norm. When two or more congregations are involved the number which each is to provide is stipulated in the Basis of Union or Linking or will be fixed by the Presbytery.

This question duly disposed of, the Moderator calls for nominations when any name may be proposed which appears on the Electoral Register, the only restriction being that if the nominee is not present the proposer must be able to assure the meeting of his or her willingness to act. Attention might be drawn by the Moderator to the importance of bearing two things in mind in choosing the Committee — first that as far as possible it should reflect every aspect in the life of the congregation (youth and age, the Session, the Guild, the Choir, Youth Organisations, etc), and secondly that their duties will take most members of the Committee away on many Sundays and the home front must not be denuded of responsible office-bearers. For obvious reasons it is usual to hope that when nominations up to the agreed maximum have been received this may satisfy the meeting. If, however, more names are forthcoming then a vote has to be taken among all those nominated, each person present having votes up to the number agreed as the total for the Committee. This represents a complicated exercise (for the voters) and it is not unknown if the nominations are only one or perhaps two in excess of the agreed total to enlarge the Committee to include them. I imagine the legality of this is highly questionable, and it is at best a short-cut device to be sternly discouraged. It is only too easy for an unscrupulous party to get someone on to the Committee as such an "extra" who would not stand a chance in a straight election.

In the case where two congregations are uniting it is advisable for the Committee to be appointed before the union has taken place, each congregation meeting as a separate unit.

Method of Voting — A decision has then to be taken on whether the election is to be by ballot or at an open meeting. When the vacancy embraces two or more congregations the election must of necessity be by ballot. A decision on this point duly recorded has to be adhered to.

First Meeting — The Vacancy Committee should meet as soon as convenient after its election so as to appoint a Convener, a Vice-Convener, and a Clerk. The Interim Moderator will always be available to act as assessor should the Committee wish advice, and he should certainly take the chair at this first meeting. Should the Committee so desire, and he is agreeable, he may act as Convener, but he has no vote either deliberative or casting. If, on the other hand, a member of the Committee occupies the chair he exercises both a deliberative and a casting vote. If thought appropriate a Clerk may be appointed who is not a member of the Committee, and in that case, of course, he or she takes no part in the deliberations.

Choice of Courses — The remit of the Vacancy Committee is "to nominate one or more persons to the congregation with a view to the election and appointment of a Minister", and in fulfilment of this they have a choice of four courses —

(a) They may follow the established course of looking around, advertising, letting it be known that they are in the market for suggestions, and in these and other ways preparing a list of candidates whom they will "hear" — first in their own pulpits. The Department of Ministry compiles and has available a list of all Probationers and Ordained Assistants currently seeking a charge, and sends monthly to all Probationers, Ministers in charges, and other eligible persons who desire it a list of current vacancies and appropriate appointments with, in each case, the name and address of a contact person.

(b) They may invite the Presbytery Advisory Committee to arrange that they be supplied with a list of Ministers (and Probationers) deemed suitable, and confine their selection among these.

(c) There is always the difficulty in remote areas that methods effective in other parts of the country may not for them be practicable. In such a case the Presbytery Advisory Committee may, if so requested, arrange for a number of "possibles" to preach in the vacant pulpit, not as a leet to be voted on by the congregation, but to enable the Vacancy Committee to bring forward a nomination to the congregation.

(d) In response to a plea from the then Overseas Council (who were seeking to further the desire of Churches overseas that they be enabled to play a more reciprocal part in mission by sending Ministers to serve in parishes) it was agreed to introduce legislation whereby a vacant congregation might resolve in respect of that vacancy to restrict their right of call by appointing, for a period of three years only, a Minister of a Church furth of Scotland which is a member of the World Alliance of Reformed Churches, or of the Church of South India, or of the Church of Pakistan. The procedure to be followed in such a case is fully set forth in Para 12 (1d) of the Act.

Should the Committee decide that rather than submit one name (sole nomination) they wish to submit two or more (a leet) they are at liberty to do so, but if so the Presbytery Advisory Committee has the power (which it need not exercise) to nominate up to the same number, also to be heard and voted on by the congregation.

Procedure — It is at this point that the whole conduct of the vacancy moves out beyond the restrictions and guidelines imposed by statute and the Vacancy Committee have to be guided by their own good sense and feeling for the fitness of things.

First of all a decision has to be reached on the question of whether to go for a sole nominee or to settle for a leet. In considering this it is well to recognise that as thiings are today it is doubtful how many (if any) would agree to preach on a leet. When the 1984 Act was in preparation the suggestion was advanced that sole nomination might be ordained as the only way to proceed. The majority response from Presbyteries was that while this was highly desirable the freedom to have a leet was part of the hard-won right of free election and congregations should not be deprived of it. The Vacancy Committee is wise not to bind itself irrevocably in this matter. A situation could arise where they were so evenly divided between two that to force the issue and appoint one of them sole nominee would be unfair, misleading and unrealistic, and it might therefore be worth considering putting both names forward — the alternative being for the Committee either to start afresh or to resign. Not a perfect solution but a possible one. It has further to be borne in mind that not every candidate today would be prepared to preach on a leet.

The next problem to be faced is how a list of candidates is to be prepared — where are the names to come from? Should they advertise? If so, care must be taken not to make statements about stipend which have not been approved by the Maintenance of the Ministry Committee. There is in some quarters a reluctance to advertise — indeed a horror at the very thought, applications being seen as in conflict with the free working of the Holy Spirit through whom alone a valid Call can come. I find it hard to see that applying is any less spiritually-inspired than whispering to somebody that he might mention to somebody .... . And it has the advantage that the discriminating reader can learn a great deal from an application — and not all of it from the text. On the other hand a Committee would be ill-advised were it to confine its attention to applicants. It may well be that the person ideally suited to their needs is happy where he is with no thought of moving, but might well be interested if the approach came from the other side. The Holy Spirit can work at both ends of bringing the desired people together.

The greatest discretion should be exercised by groups who go on tour — their presence can have an unsettling effect on both Minister and congregation visited. Once they have got down to a short-list opportunity will be taken to have a talk with the person concerned and in any such "interview" the Committee must remember the limits of propriety. Both sides can learn a lot from an interview!

Where the interest centres on someone too far distant to be conveniently visited he may be invited to preach in some pulpit more readily accessible. If so he must be fully reimbursed for all outlays incurred. Not in any circumstances should he be asked, "Have you had any expenses?" He's bound to have, and the insistence on settling should come from the side of the vacant congregation.

First Charge Restriction — The list of categories of persons eligible for election is fully set forth in Para 13 of the Act. One general condition has to be borne in mind. A Minister is not free to be translated from his first charge of a church and parish of the Church of Scotlad until at least five years have elapsed since his induction. Allowance is made for "exceptional circumstances", but these must be genuinely exceptional, and before any such Minister is nominated for a vacancy a certificate that there are such circumstances must be obtained by the Interim Moderator from the Clerk of his present Presbytery. Indeed the Interim Moderator is required to lodge this certificate with the Clerk of the calling Presbytery before the nomination is reported to the Kirk Session.

In this connection one or two points should be noted. First it is a first charge and has nothing to do with the Minister's age. Secondly it refers to his "first charge of a church and parish of the Church of Scotland" — that is to say, years spent as a Chaplain in the Navy or in a charge of another denomination do not count. Thirdly, the quinquennium is to be calculated from the date of induction to the date of nomination. And fourthly if recourse is to be had to "exceptional circumsances" the appropriate certificate must be procured prior to nomination — given the publicity attending an election the releasing Presbytery is put in an awkward position when asked to vouch for the exceptional circumstances.

Who May be Chosen — Subject to this restriction a congregation may call any Minister of the Church of Scotland provided he has not reached his sixty-fifth birthday, any licentiate of the Church of Scotland who has satisfactorily completed, or has been granted exempion from, his probationary period, any former Minister or licentiate of the Church of Scotland who can produce a Certificate of Eligibility, any Minister of a Presbyterian Church in the United Kingdom or of a member church of the World Alliance, or of the Church of South India or of Pakistan, again in each case provided he can produce a Certificte of Eligibility. The foregoing is a considerably condensed satement and reference should be made to the terms of Act v 1984 Para 13.

Nomination — Once the choice of a nominee or of a leet has been made and accepted in writing the work of the Vacancy Committee is at an end and the Kirk Session takes over responsibility for what of the course is still to run. This ending of the Committee's task is signalised by a Minute of Nomination passed by the Interim Moderator to the Kirk Session. Before this, however, the Moderator must secure and lodge with the Presbytery Clerk whatever certificates are relevant to the case of the nominee. The Presbytery Advisory Committee is also to be informed as soon as a sole nominee or a leet has been approved. Should there be any doubt at all about a candidate's eligibility this point must be fully cleared up before the nomination is reported.

ELECTION AND CALL

Preaching by Nominee — At this point the Interim Moderator is to make arrangements for the sole nominee to conduct public worship in the vacant church or churches on the first convenient Sunday. If there is a leet they should if at all possible preach on consecutive Sundays. The Moderator will also arrange for the meeting to elect, or for the holding of a ballot as the case may be, and cause intimation of this to be made on two Sundays. If there is a leet the greatest care must be taken to avoid any appearance of unfairness — as, for example, would be the case were one of the candidates to preach on a local holiday weekend.

Normally the Interim Modertor will preside at all meetings connected with the election, but if unable to do so he may appoint another ministerial member of Presbytery (not a member of the congregation) to act in his place. He may have the assistance of others in the event of a ballot. In the case of a deferred union the nominee has, of course, to be heard also in the charge which has a Minister. The fullest consultation with the said Minister must, of course, take place. The Act is silent on the subject, but for myself I see no reason against, and a great deal to be said in favour of, the nominee conducting worship in only one or other of the churches, the congregations uniting for the occasion.

Open Vote — When it has been decided to proceed by way of open vote this will be done at a congregational meeting presided over by the Interim Moderator who will put the simple question, "Elect Mr X or Not?" The votes are counted (whether contested or unanimous), the result recorded in the Session minutes, and a Declaration of Result completed and signed by the Interim Moderator. If there be a leet a week must be allowed to pass between the last preaching and the meeting to elect. At that meeting the names of the candidates are put and voted upon in the order in which they preached. Unless one candidate has a clear majority of the votes cast the lowest-ranking name is dropped and a second vote taken, and so on until one candidate emerges with a clear majority of the votes cast. That, however, is not yet the end of the story, for the Moderator has still to put the question, "Elect Mr X or not?" Should this motion be carried for "or not" in either of the circumstances described the Interim Moderator declares there has been "Failure to Elect".

By Ballot — When it has been resolved to elect by ballot a rather more complicated situation emerges. Voting papers have to be printed which conform to a type stipulated in Schedule K to the Act. The Interim Moderator or someone authorised by him sits with a copy of the Electoral Register and ticks off the name of everyone to whom a voting-paper is issued — but no identifying mark is put on the paper. Provision has to be made for "crossing" in privacy and a ballot-box provided. Voting may take place at more than one station, but at different times — you cannot tick-off one Electoral Register at two places simultaneously.

As soon as practicable (at most within twenty-four hours of the close of voting) the Kirk Session is constituted by the Interim Moderator who proceeds in presence of the Elders to count the votes. If voting has been held in different places the contents of the boxes are first mixed. If there be a sole nominee and the "Fors" exceed the "Againsts" he is declared elected. If the latter are in the majority a Failure to Elect is declared. If there be a leet a count is taken of the First Choice votes cast, and if one candidate has a clear majority of these he is declared elected. If not the papers of the lowest return are distributed according to Second Choice, and so on until a clear majority has been reached when a Declaration is issued. Should a majority of votes have been cast "Against any of the Above" the Interim Moderator declares there has been Failure to Elect.

The preferential-vote system of First, Second, and Third Choices is a novelty of the 1984 Act. Under the old method a second and if need be a third election had to be held, each of these being preceded by pulpit intimation, and being held not sooner than the Thursday nor later than the Tuesday next following. In a hotly contested case with a large field it must have helped the winter to pass!

When a ballot election has been held the final step is for the Interim Moderator to seal-off the voting papers and stubs along with the ticked-off copy of the Electoral Roll and transmit these along with the other relevant documents in the case to the Clerk of Presbytery, to be destroyed by him after the person elected has been inducted.

Frustrated Procedure

Should a nominee withdraw before the election notice has been read the fact has to be reported and the wording of the election notice adjusted accordingly. If he is a sole nominee the situation is now one of Failure to Nominate. Should the withdrawal be made after the election notice has been read then in the case of a ballot vote a notice is to be prominently displayed in the voting station, and, as each voting-paper is issued, the name is to be struck out from it. If such withdrawal has resulted in Failure to Elect, the Vacancy Committee are to be summoned and have to decide whether to make a fresh nomination or to resign.

It is expected of the Vacancy Committee that they will bring in a nomination within six months of their appointment. If not, any ten qualified electors may put into the hands of the Interim Moderator a paper requiring that steps be taken with a view to a nomination being made. Receipt of this is intimated in writing by the Interim Modertor to the Clerk of the Vacancy Committee and has the effect of allowing them a further two months, after which they are to be regarded as having Failed to Nominate. Intimation of this failure will be made to the congregation and steps will be taken towards the election of a new Vacancy Committee.

Where there has been Failure to Elect as described above, the Vacancy Committee may either themselves start afresh or they may resign. In the latter case, after due intimation, a congregational meeting will be held to appoint a new Vacancy Committee.

A person who has actually been elected may, because of the state of the poll or for some other reason, decide not to accept, and in that case he must give the Interim Moderator notice in writing to this effect. A meeting of the Vacancy Committee is then summoned and the facts reported. Here again the Vacancy Committee have the choice either to make a fresh nomination or to resign and allow for a new Vacancy Committee being appointed.

Where there has been Failure to Elect or the person elected has declined appointment there may be lodged with the Interim Moderator a requisition for a meeting of the congregation to be held to determine whether the Committee is to be continued or a new one appointed. Such a requisition must be over the signatures of at least one-tenth of those on the Electoral Register and it must be lodged within a week of the failure being intimated. Two Sundays' notice must be given of such a meeting which, if it resolves that a new Committee is the answer to its problem, should go on and elect one there and then.

Precautions — Contingencies like those outlined above are the sort of thing which every self-respecting Vacancy Committee wishes to avoid. There are a few precautions well worth taking.

For instance, every effort should be made to ensure that before a nomination is made there is the maximum of unanimity within the Committee. To put forward a name on a narrow majority or with luke-warm support is to ask for trouble. If, however, the Committee is determined to take such a step the nominee should be fully informed — anything less is grossly unfair to him, for it may well be that he himself will not wish to proceed in such circumstances. Sometimes a situation is reached where a division has arisen within the Committee as between two names and neither side is prepared to yield. In such a case it is ofen wise to drop both names and start afresh. If there is to be friction and frustration it should as far as possible be confined within the Committee. One other thing, a Vacancy Committee must never panic. Time may be seen to be running out with no progress to report. The Committee do well to remember that their task is to make the right nomination, not necessarily an instant one. Given patience and faith things have a way of working out.

From the other side a Minister invited to accept nomination should treat the matter with the utmost seriousness and should not allow his name to go forward unless he is genuinely interested to accept a Call when, as is to be expected, that follows. In that connection he should be at pains to find answers to all the questions he considers important before agreeing. He must be afforded every opportunity to see church, halls, manse (including garden) etc. If he has any predilection — should he insist on occupying his own house rather than the manse, for example — this would seem the time for the matter to be discussed, in the case of the Manse very seriously discussed (see p 148). The Act requires that if the temporal affairs are administered on a constitution peculiar to the congregation (the normal UP case) the nominee is to be at this stage provided with a copy of that constitution.

Ius Devolutum — Six months are allowed in which the right to call must be exercised, the time being calculated from the date when permission to call is given up to the date of appointment (not induction) of the new Minister. The congregation may apply to Presbytery for an extension, in which case a further three months is normally allowed without reason asked — though not by right. At the end of this period a further application may be made, but this time for specific cause shown. If by the expiry of that time still no appointment has been made the permission to call is regarded as having lapsed and the Presbytery is free, if it so chooses, to raise anew the question of readjustment. On the other hand the Presbytery may itself resolve to make an appointment *tanquam jure devoluto*. What happens in that case is that a Minister and an Elder are added by the Presbytery to its Advisory Committee and to that enlarged body is entrusted the task of bringing forward to a subsequent meeting of Presbytery the name of a Minister or Probationer deemed suitable for, and prepared to accept, the appointment. If satisfied, the Presbytery will then itself make the appointment and record accordingly. The Presbytery Clerk having received written acceptance from the appointee, arranges for him to preach in the vacant pulpit as soon as convenient. There is, of course, no election, but facilities are provided for signing a Call and normal procedure is then followed through to induction. It is remarkable how many very successful ministries have begun in terms of this legislation.

The *ius devolutum* is a carry-over from the days of patronage — the right of the principal heritor to present expired if a presentation had not been made within six months of the vacancy occurring, and the right fell to the Presbytery. In the eighteenth century it was not uncommon for patrons deliberately to allow this to happen so as to avoid what were increasingly coming to be the unpleasant consequences of exercising their right of presentation. The Act of 1874 which abolished patronage laid this restriction upon the congregation who were now being given the right to elect, and at first it seems to have been very strictly enforced. In 1945 an Act (vii) changed the *terminus a quo* from the date of the vacancy to the more realistic date of receiving permission to call, and in modern times the *terminus ad quem* is usually accepted as the date of "having an end in sight." Occasions arise, however, when a congregation is beset with internal dissension so that the happiest (maybe even the only possible) solution can be for the Presbytery to intervene and itself make an appointment.

A new feature of the 1984 Act is that failure to elect within the time-limit supplies the Presbytery with an option to re-open the question of readjustment. Two reasons are advanced in support of this — "First there is the fact that after a very considerable time the congregation has been unable to interest anyone in their vacancy and this represents a new and significant piece of evidence on the question whether the charge is a necessary one: and, secondly, before a Presbytery can be expected to approach a Minister and put to him that he has a duty to go and minister to the congregation of X it must itself feel assured that the congregation of X is a necessary element in the continuing work and witness of the Church." (Reports 1981, p 465)

SETTLEMENT

The Call — In every case where an election has been successfully completed this is to be followed by the preparation of a Call to the person elected. The form of this will be found in Schedule L to the Act — a more modern form of words having replaced the archaic language that so long prevailed. When the election has been by open vote it will be convenient to have the Call available for signing before people leave the meeting, but where there has been a ballot the signing must await the issue of the Declaration of the Result. In either case adequate opportunities must be provided for the Call to be subscribed and full intimation made of these. Members not able to be present may sign by mandate. Adherents who have registered as such may sign the Call itself — other regular worshippers in the congregation, provided they are over fourteen years of age, may sign a Paper of Concurrence. The Call must simply "lie for signature" — it is illegal to have it canvassed.

When it comes to deal with the election the Presbytery will have the Call before it and by then it should have "lain" for at least ten clear days. The number of signatures is to be taken into account by the Presbytery when deciding whether to sustain. The Call may at the request of the Kirk Session, or at the will of the Presbytery, be sent back for further subscription.

The Call is of very ancient origin and does not today enjoy the importance once attaching to it. In time of patronage it represented the only possible response of the members to the appointment of their Minister — concurrence in a choice which had not been of their making. In the years leading up to the Disruption it gained a negative kind of significance in that the only way open to the members to express their discontent with the system lay in refusing to sign the Call. Today there is a tendency to see the Call as a needless duplication. "We all turned out and voted for him — what more do we need to do to show that we want him?" The answer is that voting for him and signing a Call to him are not identical. I might well vote Against him as candidate because he was not my choice and at the same time be prepared to promise him as appointee my whole-hearted loyalty and support.

The Presbytery if it is convinced that a Call is not sufficiently well subscribed may, and indeed should, return it for further signatures before dealing with the sustaining of the appointment. This can create a difficulty at local level, though the element of shock can be most effective in awakening the dreamers. The Kirk Session is not allowed to canvass the Call, and in any case if there is so little life in the congregation that they cannot get a Call decently subscribed, the conclusion might fairly be drawn that the sooner they get a new Minister inducted the better!

Consideration by the Presbytery — After a successful election the Interim Moderator has to secure from the appointee a letter of acceptance which has also to include an assurance that no undue influence has been exercised by him to secure the appointment. This letter along with the minute of nomination and all subsequent intimations duly attested, the voting-papers and ticked-off copy of the Electoral Register in case of a ballot, and any appropriate certificates covering the appointee's eligibility for the post (including in case of a Gaelic-essential charge a certificate of competency to preach in Gaelic) are lodged with the Presbytery Clerk, who lays them on the table at the first meeting of Presbytery thereafter. He also arranges for the congregation to be informed by edict of this meeting and of their right to be present in their interest. Should the inductee be a licentiate he is entitled to be present in person for his interest. The Presbytery Clerk should carefully retain all papers lodged with him in connection with the vacancy until after the induction when he is expected to destroy them. The papers having been laid on the table the Presbytery hears anyone whom it considers to have an interest — normally the Interim Moderator or other representative of the congregation. It may also hear its own Advisory Committee. It then proceeds to sustain the Call. Where it is a licentiate that has been appointed a day, hour and place will be fixed for his ordination and induction. If the person elected be a Minister but not in a Church of Scotland parish the time and place of induction will likewise be appointed. Since both ordination and induction are Presbyterial acts the Presbytery will appoint a meeting *in hunc effectum* for this purpose.

Translation — If the Call be addressed to a Minister of a charge within the bounds of the Presbytery the Clerk will have arranged for his congregation to be edictally cited for their interest. If commissioners are present they will be heard after those from the calling congregation. If Election and Call are sustained a time and place for a meeting to induct will be duly appointed.

If the Call be to the Minister of a charge in another Presbytery then if Election and Call are sustained the Clerk will be instructed to forward the papers to that Presbytery and, if so desired, commissioners may be appointed to prosecute the Call there. These may be members of the congregation, but they go as commissioners from the Presbytery. Advantage of this provision is rarely, if ever, taken today. Presbytery then goes on to make provisional arrangements for the induction. On receiving intimation in this way a Presbytery Clerk has to communicate with the Minister concerned and with his Session Clerk and will cause intimation to be made to the congregation (one Sunday will suffice) citing them for their interest to the meeting at which the translation is to be considered. If the Presbytery resolves to place the Call in the Minister's hands this will be duly done by the Moderator and the Presbytery will resolve to translate, declaring that the Minister remains Minister of his present charge until he has been inducted elsewhere and instructing him to await the orders of the other Presbytery as to the time of his admission.

Should the releasing Presbytery resolve not to translate it is open to the Minister, having been a party at the bar, to appeal there and then, as may also the commissioners from the calling Presbytery if they are present, and also, although it would be an awkward situation, the congregation that was *not* going to lose its minister. Provision is made, however, that the calling Presbytery, even though it did not compear at the meeting, may appeal, so long as this is lodged along with its reasons with the Presbytery Clerk within ten days of judgment being given.

When Demission Appropriate — A Minister who wishes to accept a Call to a charge in another denomination or to take up a non-parochial appointment within the Church has to proceed by way of demission. It has particularly to be noted in this context that any appointment to which the Minister is not to be inducted or introduced is a non-parochial appointment — translation can take place only between one charge to which the Minister has been inducted and another to which he is to be inducted.

"The Usual Assurances" — In 1888 an Act (xvii) was passed to bring the legislation against Simoniacal practices into line with the new system that emerged consequent on the abolition of patronage four years earlier. The story from the Book of Acts (chapter 8) will be familiar, of how Simon the Sorcerer wished to purchase with money the gifts of the Holy Spirit. The legislation had been directed against what, under patronage, was quite a possibility — that a Minister would enter into a bargain with a patron that if presented he would not at any time seek augmentation of stipend, or ask for improvements to be carried out at the Manse, or enlargement of the Church, or what-have-you. It was ordained in the

1888 Act that the whole text (a page and a half of octavo) was to be read at every act of admission. Not surprisingly, perhaps, an Act of 1903 (vii) provided that in place of this reading it would suffice if the candidate gave written assurance that the Act was known to him and that he had done nothing at variance with it. Normal practice today is that in accepting appointment by letter the appointee also gives "the usual assurances" — which most certainly do not include an assurance that he has read the Act anent Simoniacal practices, or even that he knows of its existence! The standard form of words is "that he has used no undue influence either by himself or others to secure the Call."

Commissioners — Until about thirty years ago it was more or less standard practice to appoint commissioners who would prosecute the Call before the other Presbytery, and indeed failure to do so might be seen as a discourtesy. Today, however, such appointment is very much the exception — indeed today it is the sending of commissioners that might be seen as a discourtesy!

Confidentiality — A question sometimes asked has to do with the position of the Minister being called — when does he disclose the fact to his own congregation? There is no law on the subject, but my own impression is that as soon as he has accepted nomination in a vacancy a Minister should call the members of his Session together and tell them, passing on the information officially to the congregation the first Sunday thereafter. To make a disclosure earlier is strictly a breach of confidentiality; to delay longer is to risk the news being "leaked", which is always unfortunate. Telling his people that he has accepted nomination does not commit him irrevocably to going.

Objections — When an induction (whether or not preceded by ordination) has been appointed the Presbytery Clerk arranges for an edict to be served on two Sundays giving intimation of the Presbytery's intention to proceed unless objection to the life or doctrine of the inductee be made and immediately substantiated, and giving intimation of the time and place when the Presbytery will meet to deal with such objection (generally the Church half-an-hour before the time of the Service). The court being met and constituted the edict, duly attested, is laid on the table along with the minute of the other Presbytery agreeing to translate, when this is appropriate. The Presbytery Officer then gives further intimation in terms of the edict. To be valid at this stage an objection must be specifically directed at life or doctrine and must be reasonably fully substantiated. Should this in fact occur procedure would be sisted and the Presbytery would take suitable steps to deal with the situation. If there is no objection, or if the objection is not substantiated, or is seen as manifestly irrelevant, the Presbytery proceeds.

In olden days this edict was read "at the most patent door" of the church, and the fact that this is no longer done (it being read to the assembling congregation) has meant a loss symbolically, for what is about to happen should be of no less importance to the careless and the unconcerned out there than to the committed who are within. Should an objection be raised the Presbytery would delay proceeding only if it were satisfied (a) that the objector had an interest — that is, that he was a member or parishioner, (b) that the objection applied to life or doctrine, and (c) that a strong *prima facie* case had been put forward. One cannot be too careful when character is being called in question, for it is only too easy to stray into the field of defamation. The objector, certainly, would enjoy a considerable measure of privilege — he would plead that he was answering an edictal invitation and seeking to fulfil a public duty, though even that would not prevail if it could be shown that he was activated by malice or that there was no probable cause for his allegation. It is the members of Presbytery who have to be particularly careful, and if satisfied that a strong case has been presented the wise course is to remit the matter to a small committee to investigate and report, to suspend proceedings, to make an intimation in the most general terms to the assembled congregation, and to leave it at that for the time being.

Admission — The proceedings at a Service of Ordination and/or Induction begin with a short act of worship after which the Clerk reads a brief narrative of proceedigs. The Moderator reads the Preamble and puts the prescribed questions, the inductee signs the Formula, and the Moderator leads in prayer, all the ministerial brethren joining physically in the laying on of hands in the case of ordination. The person is then declared to be inducted and the right hand of fellowship is given by all members of Presbytery present. A question is then put to the congregation (p 3). Finally charges are given to the Minister and to the congregation by a Minister designated for this purpose. After service the Presbytery resumes its session when the new Minister's name is added to the Roll of Presbytery and the Interim Modertor is thanked and discharged. A certified intimation of induction is given by the Presbytery Clerk to the Session Clerk to be engrossed in the minutes of the next

Session meeting. The Presbytery Clerk also hands to the new Minister an extract from the minutes of the Assembly's Maintenace of the Ministry Committee setting forth the stipend arrangements for the incumbency.

When the induction is to a linked charge the Presbytery has to decide in which of the churches the service is to take place and if there is particular difficulty in members of the other church or churches attending this then a Service of Introduction may later be held in one of these other churches. There will, however, be only one Service of Induction, for this has the effect of admitting the inductee as Minister of both or all of the congregations in the linked charge.

Induction is the appropriate service even when the appointment is under terminable tenure, though this was not so in terms of earlier legislation.

Ad Vitam aut Culpam — In olden days induction was invariably *ad vitam aut culpam* (till death or serious fault) — a system that conferred great security, even if at the price of considerable rigidity. In the past thirty-odd years the degree of security has been steadily whittled down —

(a) Act xxi of 1960 anent Congregations in an Unsatisfactory State gives power to Presbyteries in certain circumstances to "dissolve the pastoral tie" without having to prove *culpa.*

(b) Act iii of 1972 provides that a Minister's attaining his seventieth birthday (while not culpable!) is to have the same effect "as if he had resigned his charge and such date had been appointed by the Presbytery of the bounds for his demission." This applies to all Ministers inducted since 1972 except that one inducted to a charge before that date and whose charge has become a new charge as a result of readjustment is deemed to have an interest *ad vitam aut culpam* in that new charge (Act xxi 1974).

(c) At the time of writing a proposed Act is with Presbyteries under Barrier Act procedure reproducing the text of the above 1972 Act but substituting "sixty-fifth" for "seventieth" birthday as the occasion for compulsory retiral — to apply in all cases of induction after the passing of the Act (if it is passed).

(d) In 1977 the Assembly agreed that for purposes of National Insurance ministers would be regarded as "employed persons not contracted out" in terms of the 1975 Social Security Act. This obviously puts the Minister in a relation to the Church in respect of his living vastly different from that of his eighteenth century predecessor.

(e) Act vi of 1984 anent Congregations in Changed Circumstances conferred upon Presbyteries in certain circumstances the right "to terminate a Minister's tenure of his charge" — though it protected all existing rights.

Any induction to a charge today, while still nominally *ad vitam aut culpam* is subject to these various qualifications. When induction is to terminable tenure there is the further qualification that the incumbency being created is temporary in character. It may in exceptional circumstances be for a specific guaranteed period — of three or five years perhaps. More likely it is terminable at the will of the Presbytery on giving six months' notice in writing and a minute of these conditions having been in the hands of the inductee and a written acceptance of them obtained from him at the time of his appointment.

The term "induction" is of modern origin. It came into usage only after 1843, the word generally employed before that being "admission", though entry, collation, institution and settlement are also to be found. Prior to the passing of the Patronage Act of 1874 admission was a matter of profound legal significance comparable with infeftment (the symbolic entry into possession of land) and as a consequence of it the Minister took "actual, real and corporal possession" of "parsonage and vicarage teinds, manse, glebe and kirklands". All that induction confers today is security of whatever tenure it has been agreed the inductee shall enjoy.

Introduction — When an Associate Minister has been appointed by a congregation the fact has to be reported to the Presbytery which has to satisfy itself that the appointment has been duly made and that the person is qualified for it. If so satisfied the Presbytery goes on to ratify the appointment and to make arrangements for a Service of Introduction. In virtue of his appointment the Associate is entitled to a seat in Presbytery. As distinguished from the Minister, however, he does not hold an office but is an employed person.

When an appointment has been made to an extra-parochial office wholly or mainly under control of the Church (Hospital, Prison, University, Industrial Chaplaincy, Community Ministry, etc) a Service of Introduction may be held in a Church conveniently situated or in some other suitable place, but only if ordination is involved is it necessary for edictal intimation to be made. Again the fact of appointment entitles to a seat in Presbytery. In the case of Deferred Union or Linking the Service will take place in the vacant Church of X, but the person will be inducted "to the Parish of X in deferred union (or linking) with the Parish of Y" and when the time comes for the union or linking to be effected a Service of Introduction should be held, probably in the Church of Y. When as a result of agreement to unite or link the Minister of one of the charges is to become Minister of both there is to be no Service of Induction to the second charge, but a Service of Declaration of Union and of Introduction of Mr AB should be held.

My attention has been drawn to the fact that when the non-parochial appointment is to a post in the Edinburgh Offices no service of Introduction is held to mark the event. This seems an omission to which the Presbytery of Edinburgh might care to give some thought.

DEMISSION

Once a Minister has been inducted to a charge there is no such thing as resignation of or retirement from it, the only way out (apart from translation) is by demission, and for this application has to be made to the Presbytery.

Application to Demit — The tie knotted by induction cannot be loosed at the will of either party or even by the parties jointly but only by the Presbytery which created it or by the Assembly. For a Minister to take the law into his own hand and depart constitutes desertion and leads to deposition. In the normal course a Minister may wish to demit on grounds of age or infirmity, or with a view to taking up some extra-parochial appointment. His first step is to lodge an application with the Presbytery Clerk indicating his desire to demit and the reason for it and stating when he wishes to go. At the first ordinary meeting of Presbytery after its receipt this document will be laid on the table and arrangements made to confer with the Minister if thought wise and to put on the agenda for next meeting the business of dealing with the application. To this meeting the congregation will be cited for its interest. It is most important that these rules be scrupulously observed. In a case in 1820 the Presbytery had failed to do so, had accepted the demission and had gone so far as to induct a successor. The General Assembly set aside the whole proceedings and declared the "demitted incumbent" to be still minister of the parish.

At this meeting a report may be given, if deemed appropriate, by those who met with the Minister, representatives of the congregation will be heard, and, usually, the applicant will be asked merely if he adheres to his desire to demit, though, of course, in case of challenge he may be heard at length. If the ground of application be age or infirmity the retired

Minister has the option of retaining his seat in Presbytery and being eligible for a commission to Assembly provided he is willing to attest in writing and to renew annually a statement of "his intent to continue to attend Presbytery and to participate in its committees" — though in any case this right is exhausted on his attaining his seventy-fifth birthday. On the other hand he may wish to relinquish his Presbytery membership while retaining his status in terms of Act viii of 1980. In other cases, unless there are grounds for withholding it, a Presbyterial Certificate will be issued. Where a Minister demits as a consequence of readjustment he will already have given written agreement to terms and no further legal action is necessary. Such a Minister retains his seat in Presbytery subject to the age-limitation indicated above.

In a case where a Minister leaves the service of the Church but retains his ministerial status he remains under supervision of the Presbytery which released him unless he moves to the bounds of another, in which case he must lodge his Presbyterial Certificate without delay. The fact that he does not enjoy a seat in Presbytery does not relieve him from being answerable to the Presbytery or from notifying any change of residence.

In the case of a Minister retiring on grounds of age or infirmity care must be taken to ensure that his application to the Retirement Scheme Committee for an annuity has been dealt with to his and to the Presbytery's complete satisfaction before his demission is formally accepted. Steps must also have been taken to discover whether his proposed going can be seen as being in the interest of readjustment (see p 65).

Conference with Minister — The purpose of conferring with the Minister as referred to above is to enable the Presbytery to satisfy itself regarding his reasons for wishing to go. A situation can arise when life is being made exceedingly difficult for a Minister, and a young man in particular may think the simplest solution is to get out. In such a case the Presbytery has a clear duty to protect its Minister against such pressure and not to allow demission to be resorted to as an easy option. There is also the case where there is a *fama* in the background and demission seems to offer an obvious way escape from "unpleasantness".

"Age or Infirmity" — Time was when this phrase had a perfectly clear meaning — age meant you were seventy, infirmity meant you had a doctor's certificate testifying that for reasons of health you were not fit to continue. Under today's pension regulations a man may earn entitlement to full pension rights before reaching the age of seventy and will probably want to take advantage of this. In such a case he should certainly be regarded as retiring on grounds of age. The present regulations also provide, however, that a man may retire at a reduced pension at, say, age sixty. Is this retirement on grounds of age? I know no official answer but would take the view that, provided he is not engaging in any full-time employment, it should be so regarded. The point is important insofar as it may determine whether he is to retain his seat in Presbytery.

Other Cases — If demission is with a view to entering a non-parochial post recognised by the Church in terms of Act iii 1992 as entitling to membership of Presbytery the applicant will be free to choose whether to sit in the Presbytery of which he is presently a member or in that within whose bounds he is to be working. If the post does not so entitle he will be under the discipline of the Presbytery of his residence or of his congregational affiliation and he should report without delay to the Clerk of the Presbytery concerned. If he is leaving to go to another denomination he will take a Presbyterial Certificate and his connection with the Church of Scotland will be at end, though he may, of course, apply for re-admission (see p 137).

Demission of Status — It occasionally happens that a Minister applies for permission to demit status. I remember discussing with the then Principal Clerk, the late James B Longmuir the fact that there seemed never to have been any legislation to deal with this situation. He advanced the view that to our fathers the status of Minister was a thing so precious that for anyone to wish to relinquish it was in itself an act of contempt of such gravity as to merit deprivation of status. I think he may well have been right; and in any case anyone applying to the Presbytery for permission to demit status should have the gravity of the situation made very clear to him, along with the fact that while he could always petition the Assembly for restoration of status the supreme court would not be likely to look too favourably on such an approach. If he persists in his resolve to go then obviously his plea will be granted.

SPECIAL CASES

Appointment to Church Extension Charge — The appointment of Minsters to Church Extension charges is governed by a series of Assembly Regulations — 1955, Reg 1; 1969, Reg 9; 1975, Reg 2.

The responsibility for making such appointments lies with the Extension Projects Committee of National Mission, the procedure being as follows.

Where there is no congregation the Committee make choice of a Minister or Licentiate and seek the concurrence of the Presbytery which now goes on to take steps, as far as possible along normal lines, towards a settlement. The Service of Induction will probably be held in a neighbouring church, the edict being served there also. If there is church property in process of building a copy of the edict may also be displayed in a prominent place on the site.

Where there is a congregation — a second ministry, for example — the initiative lies with the Presbytery which has to consult with the Extension Projects Committee about an appointment. The latter body will tender a suggestion and if acceptable to the Presbytery the Interim Moderator will arrange for the nominee to preach. He is then to "learn the mind" of the congregation and the result of his enquiries will then be conveyed to the Assembly Committee. If dissatisfaction is expressed a second nomination will be made, and a third; after which the Assembly Committee will proceed to an appointment with concurrence of Presbytery. The issue having been resolved it will be for the Presbytery to proceed as nearly as possible in the normal way, including encouragement for the congregation to sign a Call.

Any Minister appointed as above has full ministerial standing in the Presbytery, and, with his Provisional Kirk Session, is responsible in the usual way for the area allotted to the charge.

No indication is given in the regulations as to how the mind of the congregation is to be "learnt" by the Interim Moderator. One imagines it should be done by holding a meeting of the congregation after the nominee has preached and asking for reactions, the main thing being to avoid conveying the impression that this is an election — it is more nearly akin to an exercise of the power of veto.

Appointment to a Church for the Deaf — This is governed by the provisions of Act xxiii 1969 and Act iii 1973.

Ministers may now be ordained specifically and exclusively for work among the deaf. The local Welfare Society is to approach the Presbytery of the bounds where their church, or one of them, is situated asking for the ordination of a named candidate, producing evidence that he (a) is a member in full communion with the Church of Scotland, (b) holds a diploma of the Deaf Welfare Examination Board, (c) has attended classes in a Divinity Faculty making satisfactory progress in Divinity and Scottish Church History, and (d) has served with acceptance for at least five years in a Society for the Deaf. The Assembly Mission Committee is to confer with the Presbytery and the Assembly Education for the Ministry Committee as to whether further training is required. A petition may then be presented to the Assembly and if granted the Presbytery will take the candidate on trials for licence, after which he may be ordained, but exclusively for work among the deaf, a restriction which only the General Assembly have power to remove.

Alternatively any Minister or licentiate of the Church of Scotland, provided he holds the appropriate diploma for work among the deaf, may be invited to become Minister of a Church for the Deaf, and if he accepts he will be introduced by the Presbytery on the basis of a tenure which may be terminated by the Society for the Deaf, but only with concurrence of the Presbytery.

In either case the Minister so appointed and introduced has full ministerial status and is entitled to a seat in the Presbytery.

Chapter 4

PROPERTY AND FINANCE

MUCH OF WHAT APPEARS in this chapter quite inevitably has been or will be dealt with in parts here and there throughout the book. It seemed desirable, however, even at the expense of some repetition, to gather it together for ease of reference in a short chapter on these two themes that figure so largely on the agenda of today's church management committee.

PROPERTY

In 1985 the Presbytery of Glasgow submitted to the General Assembly an Overture expressing its grave concern about how large a proportion of the annual income of the Church was, of necessity, being spent upon repairs and other work on Church buildings. Some idea of the magnitude of the problem facing the Church, it was claimed, could be gleaned from the fact that within that Presbytery during the first six months of the previous year applications had been approved for permission to spend on fabric work of various kinds a total sum just short of a million pounds. When there was added to that the cost of work involving less than £6000 (for which permission was not required), and the not inconsiderable sums involved when the final bill exceeded the estimate (cases of the other kind were few) the total outlay involved was well over the million pound mark. A simple calculation showed that that represented rather more than £20 per annum for each nominal member, which was just about half of the total givings for all purposes put together contributed by the said nominal member. Quite simply, the Presbytery was spending more than half of its total income in maintaining its buildings, in keeping a roof over its head — and that, the Overture pleaded, was a highly critical state of affairs.

The Overture asked that steps be taken in four different directions to deal with the problem — (1) Education — that every effort be made to alert congregations to the financial implications of neglect of property and the consequent need to deal with necessary repairs in a speedy and realistic fashion; (2) Government Aid — at a time when substantial grants were being made available to house-owners to have their property put into good order an approach might be made to secure grants for Church buildings which in so many cases form an important feature of the townscape; and in particular to have such expenditure exempted from VAT; (3) Necessary Buildings — that Presbyteries be encouraged to conduct surveys with a view to determining what are "necessary buildings" and while ensuring that these are maintained making sure that large sums are not spent on those which on a long-term view are not essential for the work of the Kirk; and (4) Fund Raising — to examine the possibility of securing a large capital sum for investment the income from which would render possible the making of substantial grants in needful cases.

The Overture was received and the matters raised therein were remitted to the General Trustees which have since struggled hard and earnestly with the problems highlighted. In particular they have been successful in creating an enhanced interest and awareness among congregations, in instituting a meaningful system for the regular examination of all Church property and the submission of reports thereon, and in grappling with the complicated "necessary buildings" problem.

Earlier Legislation — In 1960 the General Administration Committee reported to the Assembly that the existing Act (ii of 1955) covering the care of Church property was proving "cumbrous and unworkable" and proposed in its stead what became Act xxi of 1961 anent the Care of Ecclesiastical Properties. The principal changes were that each Presbytery was instructed to inspect "on its own behalf or by whatever agency it deemed wise" all properties within its bounds at least once in each five-year period, that a second Schedule be introduced showing what work had actually been done, that the Property Register should be submitted not merely for attestation by the Presbytery but for critical examination by its Fabric Committee, and that it should record in whose name the titles are held and where exactly the deeds are retained. This Act was repealed by Act ix of 1979 which, however, repeated most of its provisions with the addition of a requirement that at least once in each five-year period the Presbytery Fabric Committee should instruct an inspection and report of all ecclesiastical property within its bounds to be carried out by a person, the Reporter, approved by the General Trustees (the cost to be met by the Presbytery), this first and each alternate report to be known as a "Principal Report". The inspections carried out between these Principal Reports to be known as "Interim Reports" and were to be conducted by a person approved by the Presbytery.

The Property Register — In terms of this legislation it had been required that the responsible body in each congregation was to appoint a Fabric Committee, including at least one person of experience in such matters (who might be co-opted), which would carry out an annual inspection of all ecclesiastical property and which would maintain a Property Register containing a list of all property, together with details of title and insurance, and an inventory of all furnishing and equipment. It was also to contain a record of the matters found to be requiring attention at the annual inspection and of the action taken thereanent. This Register was to be produced for examination on the occasion of the Presbytery's annual inspection of records. A number of duties were laid upon Presbytery, Synod, and Assembly's General Administration Committee — mainly to do with reporting. As was perhaps to be expected this Act, more insistent on reporting than repairing, did not go far enough to produce really significant results.

Professional Surveys — With a view to making the legislation more effective the General Trustees in 1987 brought forward an amending Act (iv) which made provision for Presbyteries to instruct and pay for professional surveys of all properties belonging to every charge within their bounds. The effect of this was to secure a list setting forth details of work requiring to be undertaken and its probable cost, and that under three heads — of work urgently needed, of work requiring to be put in hand without undue delay, and of work that clearly had to be done but for which there was no urgent rush. An inspection by the local Fabric Committee was to be carried out once a year as before, and the professional survey was to be repeated every fifth year. In 1989 a motion was successfully advanced from the floor of the Assembly that a second professional inspection should not be obligatory till ten years after the first, but two years later the Assembly agreed to return to the original pattern of quinquennial report on being told that a conference of Presbytery Property Conveners had overwhelmingly approved of this as a proper interval.

Necessary Buildings — At this stage a new feature of considerable importance entered upon the scene — was it realistic to be spending large sums on a property which, so far as could be guaged had no long-term part to play in the future life of the Kirk? Work of an urgent repair type must, of course, be instructed in the interest of public safety no less than to ensure that the building would be in a sound and marketable condition when the time came to dispose of it, but ambitious (and expensive) schemes of additions, improvements, redecoration, rebuilding of organs, and things of that nature are in a different category. An obvious instance of the latter kind arises when it is clear that two adjoining congregations will be united on the first opportunity and each is determined that if and when arbitration between buildings is resorted to theirs will be without fault. The difficulty here is compounded by the fact that before terms of union are agreed upon no-one can say with any certainty which of the two buildings will be chosen — we all know there is only one "necessary building" but no-one can say with certainty which that should be. So long as Ministers enjoy induction *ad vitam aut culpam* and so long as buildings enjoy dry rot infestation with all its capacity for playing tricks no confident forecast can be made on the subject of which will be the better building when an ultimate decision has to be reached.

The Financial Limit — Regulations were approved by the General Assembly of 1989 and amended three years later and these govern the position today. They begin by differentiating between "repairs" and "alterations", the former referring to making good deficiencies without altering the appearance or the character of the subjects, while the latter refer to works which result in change to a building and include demolition (even partial), erection, extension, reconstruction, restoration and redecoration insofar as any of these extends beyond the character of "repairs". A sum is fixed, the "Financial Limit", being the maximum that can be spent on work in either category without certain consents. At the time of writing the figure fixed by the Assembly on the recommendation of the General Trustees is £15,000 (inclusive of VAT, professional fees and all other outlays), though in some Presbyteries a lower figure applies. In the case of "repairs" if within the Limit then normally the work may be put in hand at the instigation of the congregational authority responsible. If it exceeds the Limit there is also to be sought (though not necessarily obtained) the consent of the Consultative Committee on Church Properties (see hereunder). In the case of an "alteration" there is required the consent of the Presbytery, of the General Trustees, of the Consultative Committee on Church Properties (if over the Limit), of the Advisory Committee on Artistic Matters (if the Church building is involved), and of the Energy Consultant (if any alteration to the heating system is envisaged).

Some Hints — As will have been gathered, the whole affair is highly complicated and the following suggestions are offered with a view to simplification of what consents are required if work is to be carried out on Church property. (1) The responsibility for obtaining Presbytery's and General Trustees' consent rests with the Financial Board of the congregation, and while the sequence would normally be to seek these in that order time may be saved by approaching both simultaneously so that each may approve subject to the approval of the other. (2) Where the actual Church building is affected consultation with the Advisory Committee on Artistic Matters should be sought at the earliest possible stage and certainly before proposals have become hard and fast. (3) Properties where the titles are held locally are subject to the Regulations in exactly the same way as those vested in the General Trustees. (4) Where work is urgently necessary in the interests of health or safety or for preservation then subject to immediate intimation being given work may proceed without consent. (5) Both the Artistic Questions Committee and the CCCP work under the aegis of the Board of National Mission, though as from 1995 the Artistic Matters Committee is to be an independent Committee reporting directly to the General Assembly. (6) In the case of Listed Buildings no longer in Church use the consent of the Local Authority Planning Committee must be obtained for any proposed alterations. The position in Scotland still is that ecclesiastical buildings in use as such are exempt from the need to get Listed Building consent. Alterations to the exterior will, however, very often require Planning Permission (which is, of course, quite different from Listed Building Consent.

Consultative Committee on Church Properties

This is a body which was created in 1992 at the instigation of the Assembly Council. It has twenty-six members — a Convener and a Vice-Convener, four from each of General Trustees, Parish Re-appraisal and Advisory Committee on Artistic Matters, and twelve from Presbyteries by rotation (Reps 1992, p 92). It has the rather odd remit — I quote in full (Reps 1992, p 90 2(d)) —

"When Presbytery is dealing with applications for approval of work at a building the cost of which exceeds the Financial Limit, the following procedure shall be followed:

(i) Presbytery shall consider whether the building involved is a necessary building in terms of the ongoing missionary strategy of the Church. If the building is not considered necessary in this context, the approval for the work shall be withheld unless Presbytery considers that the work is necessary in the interests of safety or to preserve the value of the building as a marketable asset. Any decision by Presbytery to withhold approval on the ground that the building is not necessary or the work is not necessary on the foregoing basis shall be minuted accordingly.

(ii) If the Presbytery having applied the criteria in the following sub-paragraph wishes to give approval, it shall, before doing so, refer the matter to the Consultative Committee on Church Properties, which shall either concur with the Presbytery's wish to give approval and, in writing, advise Presbytery and the General Trustees accordingly, in which case Presbytery approval will be deemed to have been given, or decline to concur and, in writing, advise both Presbytery and the General Trustees of the areas of concern it has with regard to the work.

(iii) When the Consultative Committee has declined to concur with the wish of Presbytery, Presbytery shall give due consideration to the response from that Committee and thereafter reach a decision on the merits of the case."

The Property Commission

This body, also created in 1992 (Reps 1992, p 92) consists of a Convener, a Vice-Covener and ten members of whom at least four have expertise in property matters, to be nominated by the Nomination Committee and appointed by the General Assembly, the quorum being seven. In terms of the procedure outlined above if "the Presbytery withholds on any ground, approval for work the Financial Board will have a right of appeal to the Property Commission of the Church of Scotland whose decision will be final. It shall be the duty of Presbytery in such circumstances to advise the Financial Board forthwith in writing both of its right of appeal and of the time limits that apply in this regard. The congregational representives have twenty-one days in which to lodge, in writing, an appeal to both Presbytery and Property Commission (why to both I cannot understand). Where dissent and complaint was taken when the Presbytery judgment was given the Presbytery Clerk is to intimate this to the Property Commission and to the congregation concerned. All parties are entitled to be present when the Property Commission meets to consider the case. This it shall do within six weeks of the papers having been lodged with it, unless all are agreed to a later date. A final judgment rests with the Property Commission which has in due course to report that final judgment to the General Assembly (Reps 1992, p 93).

It is not beyond the bounds of possibility that this whole area involving the above Committee and Commission may be the subject of review and revision at an early date.

FINANCE

It is just thirty years ago that I produced a little booklet which I called "The Changing Face of Church Finance", and by way of setting forth a brief statement of the historical situation in regard to finance within the pre-Union Churches I think I can do no better than reproduce herc the relevant part of that survey.

The Matter of Stewardship

During these past few years a complete transformation has been effected in the financial organisation of our congregational life and it makes a profitable study to consider this, and in particular to note some of the side effects which have resulted from the changes.

Following on the Union of 1929 it was more or less accurate to say that congregations — of whatever pre-Union tradition — paid their bills (including their assessment towards meeting the expenses incurred by Assembly, Synod and Presbytery), and that out of the balance remaining they met such things as supplement to stipend, contribution in aid to the Maintenance of the Ministry Fund, and givings to Schemes of the Church, which included Aged and Infirm Ministers' Fund contribution.

In the matter of upkeep of fabric there was some variety of practice, but by and large the position was that expenditure on ordinary repairs on the buildings came out of the ordinary revenue along with the price of the coal that heated the buildings and the salary of the beadle who cleaned them, but that if exceptional expenditure was involved — if the roof called for reslating, or there was an outbreak of dry-rot in the vestry or the kirk needed redecorating — this was the subject of a special appeal and was met out of "extra" income.

Within that general pattern there was of course a fairly wide diversity of practice. Take the matter of stipend. In the old *quoad omnia* parish there still lingered the idea that stipend was no concern of the congregation — hardly surprising, considering that for generations the congregation had been sternly discouraged from so much as wondering what the Minister was paid. In the old *quoad sacra* the bulk of what was left "in the kitty" on 31st December went to the minister, schemes having been taken care of by the casual "retiring collection". In the Free Church there were often schemes to which particular congregations were thirled — in especial the Central Fund and Foreign Missions — and in almost every case stipend was a matter which received much concern. In the former UP congregations stipend was in many cases fixed by the congregation as such and that usually in advance — that is to say the stipend for the current year was fixed at the Congregational Meeting in light of the financial reports for the previous year — as opposed to *quoad sacra* and Free where something more like a bonus was given for the year whose financial returns were under review.

Effect of W F O

The first thing to bring about a considerable change in this general pattern has been the adoption on an increasing scale of some form of Freewill Offering with the consequent restriction on undertaking special efforts either in the way of retiring collections, additional calls for particular objects, collections by visitors, etc. Inevitably, and quite properly, the Freewill Offering has had the effect of confining congregational giving to one channel. Another effect, however, has been to make it possible to foretell with reasonable accuracy what the congregational income for the year may be expected to be. In consequence it becomes important to plan congregational spending and possible within limits to know in advance what there will be to spend. Thus the machinery is available to escape the utterly haphazard financial set-up that was forced on congregations so long as they were completely dependent on the random generosity of those members actually in regular attendance at Church services.

It is, however, within recent years that there has come, quickly one on the back of the other, that series of changes on the expenditure side which have created among them the present revolutionary situation.

Effect of Vacancy Schedule

First of all there was the appearance of the Vacancy Schedule issued by the Maintenance of the Ministry Committee. While it is true that this does not constitute a contract its effect is much the same as if it did. No longer is it possible to leave stipend to be determined in light of the financial situation revealed when the balance-sheet has been struck. With the proviso that no absolute compulsion will be exerted it is now true to say that a congregation is committed to find £x for stipend and £y for Aid and that this obligation is as final as the need to find £a for the organist and £b for the beadle.

A further step is taken when you empower Presbyteries to determine what are Appropriate Figures for Stipend and Aid in all its congregations and to decline to pass Schedules which do not conform to these figures. And yet a further step when you add Listed Expenses and then Travelling Expenses and make them a "must." And still further are you travelling the same road when you fix Aged and Infirm Ministers' Fund contribution at a proportion of stipend and ordain that it is to be a charge comparable to Assembly and Presbytery dues.

Effect of the Co-ordinated Appeal

The most vitally significant step in this progression, however, was taken when the General Assembly of 1960 finally committed the Church to the principle of a Co-ordinated Appeal for the Support of the Schemes of the Church and authorised Presbyteries to determine sums which congregations would be expected through all their agencies, to contribute to the support of the whole work of the Church. No longer is it to be possible out of the fragments that remain to give to favourite schemes and to withhold from others — every congregation is now committed to a definite sum which it is its duty to find for the support of the whole work of the Church.

I am sure it was never envisaged as a step in this same direction when the Act anent the Care of Ecclesiastical Properties was put on the statute book (in its original form in 1955), and yet in practice it must be taken to represent just such a movement. It is now for the Presbytery to take oversight of all Church property and to see that it is adequately maintained and preserved; and it seems to me to require only a little time till the logical outcome follows and the Presbytery says to each congregation that it is to set aside a named sum of money each year for fabric maintenance, any of it which is not actually spent in that year to go towards building up a local Fabric Fund.

A most intensely interesting and significant situation now emerges, because for the first time it is to be possible for those responsible for the finances of any congregation to sit down in November 1963 and to have before them the following figures — (a) the probable income from Freewill Offering in 1964 (got from the promise-cards which should be completely in by that time) along with a guess of what will come in through the open plate; (b) an indication of what the Woman's Guild, the Sunday School, the Youth Fellowship and the various other congregational agencies are going to contribute towards the Co-ordinated Appeal in 1964; (c) the amount to be spent on stipend along with the amounts of Listed and Travelling Expenses; (d) the amount of the contribution in Aid to the Maintenance of the Ministry Fund; (e) the amount to be given to the Aged and Infirm Ministers' Fund; (f) the amount required for Assembly, Synod and Presbytery dues; (g) the assessment for Schemes under the Co-ordinated Appeal (fixed by the Presbytery and intimated in October); (h) commitments in connection with fabric; and (i) the amount likely to be required for ordinary "housekeeping" during the year — that is, heating and lighting, salaries, rates and taxes, insurance, printing, and so on (an easy budget to prepare in light of spending in previous years). It is equally clear that by adding the items on the income and expenditure sides and comparing the totals it should be easy, towards the close of 1963, to say definitely whether the accounts for 1964 should just balance, or whether there is likely to be a deficit and if so to what extent, or whether there can be expected a credit balance on the strength of which to contemplate capital expenditure such as the purchase of a new manse, the building of a hall or similar project.

Co-ordinated Appeal — A Weakness — On that confident and optimistic note ended my view of the prospects thirty years ago. But unfortunately it has not proved the complete answer. The Co-ordinated Appeal suffered from one rather obvious but quite inescapable weakness in that it substituted a tax on cogregations for a freewill offering from individuals, and while people (generally) pay their taxes they do not derive from the exercise the kind of pleasure and satisfaction that comes from sending, out of sheer good-will, a subscription to what they believe to be a deserving cause. I have yet to hear of the person meeting a demand from H M Collector of Taxes who adds an additional hundred pounds because, he says, he understands the Exchequer is in a bad way and needing all the money it can get! But I have heard often in days past of a visit paid to a congregation by a missionary on furlough who spoke with knowledge and feeling about the work in, perhaps, some leper colony under our care with a resulting "Retiring Collection" that broke all records and involved a deal of sacrificial giving. For all its manifest disadvantages a system which had the various Schemes engaged in cut-throat competition for larger slices of the very limited cake ensured that they obtained publicity for and maintained enthusiasm in the work they were doing. I doubt just how well-informed today is the ordinary Church member about what exactly is being done with what he puts in his weekly envelope — or how concerned he is.

Co-ordinated Appeal — Its Inadequacy — A more serious flaw in the organisation of the Co-ordinated Appeal lay in the fact that it did not include all the aspects of expenditure involved in "Schemes". It had been hoped when the plan was first considered that it would be possible to make it all-embracing, but the Department of Ministry presented a very strong case for going its own way, so that givings for Stipend and Aid as well as for pension provision (at that time the Aged and Infirm Ministers' Fund) continued to make their own demands, and indeed advanced a preferential claim, as the powers attaching to the Vacancy Schedule enabled, whether or not it entitled, them to do.

Mission and Service Fund

At this stage, then, a congregation had four separate calls upon its total income —

a) the cost of "running" the congregation — heating and lighting, insurance, salaries, and so on;
b) the cost of Ministry, embracing stipend and expenses, Aid to the Fund (where appropriate), and pension responsibility;
c) its share of responsibility for administration etc at the Church Offices, for the cost of the Assembly meetings (enormously increased since 1962 with the payment of commissioners' expenses), for the outlays of "committees without funds", and so on; and also its share of the costof running the Presbytery — Presbytery Dues; and
d) its assessment under the Co-ordinated Appeal (which in 1970 adopted the name of "Mission and Service Fund").

The two last were largely under the direction and control respectively of the then General Finance and Stewardship and Budget Committees which together formed the Department of Finance.

When at the close of the financial year the Financial Board of a congregation was wrestling with the problem of the required outgoings being greater than the available incomings it needs little imagination to know under which of the four heads savings would be effected. Our donations don't begin till all our bills have been paid.

Personnel Committee — In 1978 there appeared a new body, the Personnel Committee for Staff in the Church Offices, a committee of fourteen with the function of determining the salaries, length and conditions of service of Assembly-appointed Secretaries, the General Treasurer, the Solicitor of the Church, ministerial Committee-appointed Secretaries and all other Office Staff. The Committee is required to take steps to consult fully about pay and conditions with those who work in the Church Offices. See also p 401.

Stewardship and Finance

One has to go back to 1976 and the "Committee of Forty" to come upon the roots of the next major change on the financial side of the Church's administration. The Assembly Council, created in 1978, brought to the following Assembly a report in which they advocated "setting up a system of Operating Boards and Servicing Boards", and in 1981 the Assembly agreed to the restructuring of the Committee system on the basis of seven Boards of which one was to be Stewardship and Finance. This Board was in fact established by the Assembly of 1983 and consisted of a Convener, a Vice-Convener and twenty-four members, of whom eight were to be Ministers and sixteen lay members of the Church — an unfortune term since it is meant to include Elders. Its principal functions are as follows —

1) to promote Christian stewardship;
2) to prepare a Co-ordinated Budget which will include the whole costs of ministry both active and retired, the Mission and Service Fund, and the General Purposes Fund, and to secure for this the approval of the Assembly;
3) to allocate among congregations the Co-ordinated Budget this being a joint exercise involving also Maintenance of the Ministry and Presbytery; and to administer the financial services of the Church.

The Board also exercises control of the work of the General Treasurer's Department, viz:

a) Preparing and issuing a Schedule for congregational financial returns;
b) Preparing and presenting to the Assembly the Accounts of the Church;
c) Considering reports from the Auditor;
d) Operating a central banking system among the various Boards and Committees;
e) Exercising custody of Funds;

f) Attending to all relevant issues of Taxation; and
g) Distributing all unallocated legacies.

The Board was responsible for the care and maintenance of the Church Offices, including the provision of services thereat and the allocation of accommodation therein among the Boards and Committees. This responsibility has now passed to the Assembly Council wich engages an Office Manager. The Board maintains a close liaison with the Personnel Committee and with the Church of Scotland Trust.

Co-ordination of Budgeting and of Allocation — It was agreed at that stage (1983) that there should be co-ordination at the level of budgeting whereby "an overall view of the Church and its requirements could be obtained, priorities could be wisely decided, and the financial support required could be fairly assessed and allocated." The Report (1983, p 73) goes on to say, "The Assembly Council proposes that the Maintenance of the Ministry Committee should continue to allocate contributions required for the Maintenance of the Ministry Fund by a method which relates allocations to each congregation's stipend, while the Board of Stewardship and Finance should continue to allocate contributions for the Mission and Servce Fund, and in future the General Purposes Fund also, by a method which relates allocations to each congregation's Total Normal Income less the net costs of ministry. This makes it likely that disparities in the various allocations, which are a frequent cause of complaint, will continue to arise. The Committee is therefore glad to note the Assembly Council's commitment to continuing negotations with these two Boards in an effort to bring the Total Normal Income of congregations, stipends and other ministry costs, and allocations for the Mission and Service Fund into a more reasonable relationship, both within Presbyteries and among Presbyteries."

One is entitled to wonder how the most recent arrangements about stipend (see pp 203 ff) are going to dovetail into a just basis of allocation as between congregations.

Board of Mission and Aid — In view of linking the needs of Ministry and Schemes the Fund generally was in 1987 awarded the new title of "Mission and Aid" and embraces the requirements for Mission and Service, for Aid to Maintenance of the Ministry and for the General Purposes Fund, the responsibility for allocation the budget being placed on the Board.

Chapter 5

ENTERING THE MINISTRY

THE CHURCH OF SCOTLAND, as the National Church, has, ever since the Reformation, acknowledged its distinctive call and duty to provide the ordinances of religion to the people in every parish of Scotland through a territorial ministry. It is in line with this insistence on the work of the parish that the General Assembly recognise no ecclesiastical rank higher than that of Parish Minister. All Ministers are equal and any apparent exception to this rule is quite illusory. During his year in office the Moderator of the General Assembly is designated "Right Reverend" and thereafter as "Very Reverend" and on civic occasions and the like has a distinctive place accorded him, but at no point is he invested with any authority in thc Kirk beyond that necessary for the control of Assembly business. The Deans of the Thistle and of the Chapel Royal and the Principal of St Mary's College St Andrews (if a Minister) claim the designation "Very Reverend" but the General Assembly has issued no deliverance on their status or on the use of the designation referred to. The parish ministry is, then, a most important office and entering it is a most significant step in anyone's career.

The Path of the Entrant — The early stages of the career of the normal aspirant for the ministry are governed by Act v of 1985 as amended by Act v of 1989, Acts xvi and xviii of 1992 and Act xi of 1994. These in turn supplanted Act xx of 1973 as that had been amended by Act x of 1980. The main matters connected with training for the ministry are related hereunder, but there is a wealth of detail for which reference should be made to the text of the Acts as enumerated above.

Committee on Education for the Ministry — The whole business of selecting men and women for the full-time ministry is put under the care of the Assembly's Committee on Education for the Ministry, which for administrative purposes is within the Department of Education and consists of a Convener, four Vice-Conveners, and twenty-four members all Assembly appointed, along with one member appointed by each of what used to be the Scottish Divinity Faculties. (There is some uncertainty today as to the correct designation of these bodies so I am sticking strictly to the terms of the Act both here and throughout the rest of the chapter). These are the voting members. In addition there are members without voting powers — the four Deans of the Faculties of Divinity, four student members (who, however, do not sit with the Committee when it deals with questions of selection or with the circumstances of individual students), and one member from the Department of Ministry. There are Sectional Committees — on Recruitment and Selection, on Supervision of Students, on Admission of Ministers, and on the Auxiliary Ministry. For convenience' sake the Education for the Ministry Committee will be referred to throughout this chapter as "the Committee". There are also four Liaison Committees, one attached to each of the four Faculties, which take a pastoral interest in the students "advising the Committee on all College matters relating to the candidates and their progress towards the successful completion of their prescribed Course."

Three Routes — Traditionally there have been two ways in which one might become a Minister of the Church of Scotland. First there is the way of Candidature — the aspirant starts from scratch as an applicant, becomes a candidate, then a student, a licentiate, a probationer, and then a licentiate again, after which he is free to accept a Call. Secondly there is the way of Admission — the aspirant is already a Minister, perhaps of another denomination, if so then in cases where there is mutual eligibility acceptance will be a formality, but in other cases will involve a Petition to the General Assembly; or perhaps he is a former Minister of the Church of Scotland who for some reason no longer enjoys that status, in which case again a Petition is called for. And thirdly today alongside the full-time ministry there has (since 1980) been an Auxiliary Ministry, part-time, non-stipendiary and exercised always under supervision, and that is governed by its own regulations. It is proposed, therefore, that the subject of entering the ministry be dealt with under these three heads — (1) The Way of Candidature; (2) The Way of Admission; and (3) The Way to the Auxiliary Ministry.

THE WAY OF CANDIDATURE

Women and the Ministry — Until 1968 the ministry was an exclusive male preserve, but an Act of Assembly of that year declared women to be eligible for ordination to the ministry on precisely the same terms as men, and thereafter to exercise their ministry on exactly the same terms as men. As explained in the preface I have used male pronouns throughout.

Acceptance for Training

Application — The first step on the road towards the ministry is the submission of an application schedule, and this has to be in the hands of the Committee on Education for the Ministry (hereinafter referred to as "the Committee") not later than 31st January of the year in which the applicant hopes to begin his course, by which time he must have attained his seventeenth birthday. It actually involves completing two copies of a Schedule which may be had from the Secretary of the Committee, to whom one is to be returned and the other to the Clerk of the Presbytery of the applicant's place of residence or of his congregational allegiance. It is provided that these two Schedules do not need to be completed "in exactly the same way, using the same words throughout" — in other words it is two Schedules, not one Schedule in duplicate. At this stage the applicant must, in terms of regulations approved in 1994 (Reps 1994, p 171) "have been, over a recent period of three years, a communicant member of, or appropriately involved in, the Church of Scotland." Exception is permitted "where the Committee deem it appropriate", but in such a case the Presbytery of residence must be informed. "No Prospective Candidate may be nominated by Presbytery as a candidate for the Ministry in advance of being a communicant member of the Church of Scotland." An applicant cannot attend Selection School in advance of his eighteenth birthday, and at the other extreme an application will not be accepted from anyone who by 30th September in the year of beginning his course will have attained his forty-fifth birthday, or if in normal circumstances he could not have completed the appropriate course by 30th October in the year of his fiftieth birthday. Normally the applicant who has been accepted must have begun his course within three years or the acceptance will lapse.

Candidature — It is the duty of the Presbytery which has received such an Application Schedule to transmit to the Committee comments in writing on the character, beliefs, vocation, motivation and general suitability of the applicant. A Presbytery must not in any case recommend an applicant for training unless satisfied as to his physical fitness (Regulations 1941, 3). A difficulty arises at this stage in the case of an applicant presently in secular employment in that his position and prospects therein may be severely prejudiced if it becomes known that he has it in mind to leave this occupation and enter the ministry. It is important, therefore, that the fullest confidentiality be observed. It is suggested that the Presbytery should take this item of business in private, or better still should remit to a Committee to conduct the interview and prepare the report, giving powers for this to be transmitted without submission to a meeting of the full court. While this latter method has much to commend it judgment must be exercised. It should be kept clearly in mind that at this stage the Presytery is not nominating, it is merely sending comments on suitability — the distinction is a nice one!

It is now for the Committee having received the written report from the Presbytery and being itself satisfied that the Prospective Candidate does not suffer from any obvious disqualification to arrange for him to attend a Selection School.

Selection School

The possibility that the medium of the Selection School might be employed in the selection of candidates for the ministry was first advanced in the Report of the Committee in 1966 (Reps 1966, p 597), it being argued that there was need for "a more effective method of detecting the less suitable candidates." An experiment was conducted at St Andrews over a period of rather more than a full day, ten applicants in two groups being assessed by a total of six assessors in an extended interview situation involving discussion as well as written and *viva voce* tests. As a result it was recommended to and agreed by the 1967 Assembly that the idea of the Selection School be adopted. The following year it was reported that five further schools had been held, the length of the session having been extended to two full days and the procedure followed being an adaptation of that employed by the Civil Service Selection Board and including such down-to-earth exercises as writing a tactful reply to a "difficult" letter of the kind that might be encountered in a typical parish situation. While the subjects embraced were wide and varied an assurance was given that assessment was based on the overall performance.

In 1984 the matter of the selection of candidates and of the role the Presbytery should play in their promotion and in the care of them at all stages was remitted for fresh consideration to the Committee, which in turn appointed a Special Review Committee to carry out this task. A very full report was submitted to the Assembly in 1985 (Repts 1985, p 441). In general terms the Review Committee came to the conclusion that a centralised selection system was much to be favoured and that the Selection School worked well. As a consequence of their investigations, however, certain changes in detail were effected.

Assessors — Presbyteries were in 1985 invited to submit names of personnel, ministerial and lay, male and female, deemed suitable to act as assessors, and they may be asked again as need arises. The actual appointing, however, is done by the Committee, and for this it is answerable only to the Assembly. Assessors serve for a period of not more than six years after which they withdraw for at least two years before becoming eligible for re-appointment — but then for only one term. The same time-limits apply in the case of Directors of Selection Schools. To these rules there are certain exceptions which are set forth at length in the Report (Repts 1985, p 450).

Object of Assessment — The purpose of the Selection School is stated as being to attempt an assessment of the candidate's suitability, taking into account — always in the context of full-time ministry — such factors as a sense of vocation, an understanding of the faith, maturity, personality, commitment, power of communication, ability to relate to other people, ability to study, leadership, age, and health. And presumably anything else considered relevant — maybe even a sense of humour!

Recruitment and Selection

The Sectional Committee on Recruitment and Selection consisting of thirteen persons chosen by the Committee from within its own Assembly-appointed membership along with the four representatives from the Faculties or their alternates, and one representative from the Department of Ministry is the body which carries the responsibility for reaching a decision in respect of every applicant, and in discharging this duty it has before it the full report and recommendation of the assessors from the Selection School, and available to it all other papers that had been available to the assessors. It may decide to accept the applicant, in which case it will prescribe an appropriate course of training for him and will instruct him to seek forthwith nomination by his Presbytery. On the other hand the Sectional Committee may decide not to accept the applicant, in which case it will inform him he may return to a second Selection School and, as necessary or desired, to a third. Indeed an applicant may have a fourth "try", but that only on appliction to the Committee itself. Normally there must be a twelve-month gap between appearances at Selection School, and at each fresh appearance the applicant will be in the hands of assessors who have not seen him before and who have no access to the report(s) of his earlier appearance(s). In cases where the Selection School report does not recommed acceptance it is expected wherever possible to include a paragraph making specific comment on the applicant's future Christian involvement as that appears to the assessors.

It has to be clearly understood that in cases where an applicant has to avail himself of a second or subsequent appearance he may find he has been overtaken by age-restriction — that is to say, the age-limit applies to the date of acceptance and not the date of his first appearance at a Selection School.

Counselling — In the letter to the applicant conveying a negative decision there will be included a note saying that he may expect to hear fairly soon from a counsellor appointed to offer him counsel and support in his disappointment. The first approach from the counsellor will take the form of a letter which will make clear to the applicant that he is under no obligation to accept the service offered. The counsellor may if he so requests have access to the report of the assessors, but this is not recommended and must not in any circumstances be disclosed to the applicant. It is most important that the counsellor be not regarded as a coach with the responsibility of training the applicant for his next appearance, nor as an advocate to present his case. The function of the counsellor is simply to be a friend to the applicant, to lend a listening ear, and, so far as possible, to assist him in coming to terms with the decision reached and in shaping his future in the light of it. It is suggested that real advantage would accrue from the applicant's own Minister being brought in at this stage and that in some circumstances a meeting of all three could prove most helpful.

A Difficulty — A weakness of the system lies in the fact that while the Church can delay recognition of a student as being in training for its ministry it cannot prevent him — given that he has the necessary preliminary qualifications — from studying within a Faculty of Divinity. Let it be that he is accepted on his next appearance at Selection School he has avoided the loss of a complete year on his way to the ministry, and who would blame him for wanting to do this. If, however, he is still not accepted, what then? He may go on hopefully to take another year's classes; and so on until he has completed the entire academic course (possibly with considerable distinction) and has graduated BD but has still not been accepted as a candidate in training for the ministry of the Kirk. A desperately unhappy human situation can emerge. The career-choices open to graduates in theology are, to put it mildly, limited if the door to service within one or other of the denominations is closed to them. When this kind of scenario is seen to be building up counsellor and parish minister have a particularly heavy responsibility.

Review — The applicant not accepted at his first appearance is not bound there and then to avail himself of the second chance — he may, and often does, come back for a second "try" after a lapse of years. Apart, however, from the choice of reappearing at Selection School the unsuccessful applicant may apply to, and appear in person before, the Sectional Committee stating why he is convinced he has had less than a fair hearing at Selection School. For this he must have lodged a written submission within three months of receipt of the Selection Committee's decision showing why he feels he has had less than justice, pointing to procedural irregularities which he alleges occurred there, or other like complaint. When he appears before the Committee he may be accompanied by an Observer of his own choosing, such Observer having no right to take any part in the proceedings and no access to any confidential documents. Having heard the applicant the Sectional Committee has a choice of three courses — (a) it can adhere to its original decision; (b) it can resolve to recall its original decision and accept the applicant; or (c) it can uphold the appeal to the extent of making it possible for the applicant to return to the earliest possible Selection School and arranging that he will be seen by a different group of assessors; and if this is done then for the purpose of calculating the total number of appearances the School whose decision has been successfully appealed against is not to be included.

If the review procedure outlined above leaves the applicant still with a negative answer and still dissasfied he may, not later than three months after receiving notice of the Committee's decision, have recourse to the main committee on Education for the Ministry and thereafter, if still not satisfied, to the General Assembly's Panel of Arbiters whose decision marks for him the end of the road. (see hereunder). The whole procedure for review is highly complicated and the relevant sections of the Act should be studied with great care by those concerned.

Nomination

The applicant who after passing through Selection School has been accepted by the Sectional Committee is, in terms of the Act, known as a "Prospective Candidate" and is now in a position where he may be nominated by his Presbytery, which will normally be that within which is situated the congregation of which he is a member, and he should make written application through its Clerk. A prospective candidate who has been refused nomination by one Presbytery is expressly forbidden from making application for nomination by another unless with the prior written approval of the Committee which has to satisfy itself that such application is "in the best interests of the Church". For my own part I find it difficult to envisage how this test is to be applied.

An Act of 1992 amended Act V of 1985 by the introduction of a new Section (10) in these terms, "A Prospective Candidate who has been refused nomination [by his Presbytery] may submit a re-application for nomination on two further occasions, provided that at least one year elapses between each application. Alternatively a Prospectve Candidate who wishes to appeal against the decision of the Presbytery may have recourse to the General Assemly's Panel of Arbiters, whose decision shall be final (see hereunder).

Panel of Arbiters — The Assembly of 1992 approved a Deliverance of the Board of Education (26c), (Repts 1992, p 451) which made provision whereby the Assembly should, on the recommendation of their Nomination Committee, appoint a Panel of Arbiters consisting of seven persons at least one but not more than two of whom should be former Directors of Selection Schools, with the Principal Clerk as Secretary, to dispose of appeals against decisions of Selection Schools and of Presbyteries as indicated above. The following year the Board of Practice and Procedure framed Rules of Procedure for such Panels (see Repts 1993, p 17). Since the Board had been instructed to "determine" these it was held they required no further approval from the Assembly. It seems unfortunate that a quorum is not fixed for meetings of the Panel. One of the rules is "that in each case the prospective candidate and the

Presbytery agree to accept the decision of the Panel as final." This is to deal with the point made in the Report (Repts 1992, p 521) that "an applicant who wishes to have his or her case discussed in the very public arena of the General Assembly cannot be prevented from exercising the right to petition the General Assembly." Since what is being challenged is a Presbytery judgment in a case to which he was a party I should have thought the constitutional right was to appeal, not to petition, but under whatever form he has a right to take his case to the Assembly.

There are, then, two separate points at which the intervention of the Panel of Arbiters may be sought. First (in time) there is the point at which the Sectional Committee on Recruitment and Selection having on the strength of three appearances at a Selection School decided not to accept as a Prospective Candidate the person concerned he may elect to have his appeal dealt with by the Panel of Arbiters whose decision he must accept as final. The second case is where the applicant has been accepted as a Prospective Candidate but where his Presbytery is not prepared to nominate him as such, and at this stage, as I see it, he is entitled to appeal against that Presbytery judgment in the usual way, though the Regulations (Repts 1992, p 529) seem to suggest he has first to re-apply on two further occasions at not less than yearly intervals. The alternative, however, is provided that the person may elect to peril his case on a judgment of the Panel of Arbiters. This will be effective, however, only if both he and the Presbytery commit themselves in advance to the acceptance of the Panel's judgment as final — otherwise it is to the supreme court itself that the case must go.

An interesting problem arises as to what form the Assembly's judgment should take were it to uphold the appeal against the Presbytery refusal to nominate. Normally they might be expected to instruct the Presbytery to nominate, but that would be to require the lower court to perform a complete *volte face* on a matter on which after the most serious consideration it had come to a firm conclusion. Clearly the Assembly can over-rule the judgment of a Presbytery, but can they instruct it to change its mind? What was possibly a precedent arose in 1991 when the Synod of Forth referred to the Assembly an Appeal against a judgment of the Presbytery of Stirling which had, after three separate applications, resolved not to nominate an applicant as a candidate for the ministry. The mind of the Presbytery was that this was not a suitable applicant. On a division the Assembly upheld the appeal and approved a motion that they instruct the Presbytery of Stirling to nominate. I much doubt the regularity of this. As I see it the Assembly could have overruled the

Presbytery decision by themselves nominating the petitioner, which I am sure they were entitled to do, but I do not see how they could instruct the Presbytery to declare that they considered a suitable candidate one who on three separate occasions they had found unsuitable.

Types of Candidate — Once nominated by the Presbytery the "Prospective Candidate" becomes a "Candidate" and will belong to one or other of four classes —

a) *Ordinary Candidates* — being persons under the age of twenty-three on 30th September in the year when they begin, or are deemed to have begun, their prescribed course. To be accepted these candidates must possess passes in Higher and Ordinary Grade examinations or their equivalent sufficient to qualify them for admission to University, and if these qualifictions are such as to enable them to enter a Faculty other than Divinity they will be encouraged to take the Regular Course. They are eligible for either the Regular or the Alternative Course of full-time study lasting not less than six years. If *completed in five years* a year's *further study will be prescribed.*

b) *Intermediate Candidates* — being persons over twenty-three but under thirty on 30th September as above. To be accepted for the appropriate course these must fulfil the requirements for admission to a Faculty of Divinity, but in cases where their qualifications entitle them to enter upon a Degree course in a Faculty other than Divinity they too are to be encouraged to take the Regular course. They are eligible for either the Regular or the Alternative Course lasting not less than five years, or for the course for Intermediate Candidates consisting of three years leading to the LTh qualification with two years further study on a Certificate Course, the course for Diploma in Ministry or Pastoral Studies (being open normally only to graduates).

c) *Mature Candidates* — being persons between the ages of thirty and forty on 30th September in the year when they begin their course. Otherwise as in (b) above. They are eligible for the Regular or the Alternative Course of not less than four years, or for the course for Mature Candidates, consisting of three years leading to the LTH followed by one year's further study on a Certificate course.

d) *Older Candidates* — being persons over forty but under forty-five on 30th September as above. To be accepted they must have good educational qualifictions or recognised professional or vocational experience as deemed satisfactory by the Committee. The Committee shall prescribe what it considers a suitable course in each of these cases. Further (Regulation 32), "the Committee shall have power, but only in the most exceptional cases, to prescribe Special Courses for Candidates under the age of forty years, as well as for Older Candidates."

General Requirements — Each candidate before his course can be recognised has to pass examinations, three in all, in Bible Knowledge. Also each candidate in course of his theological study has to engage in three periods of practical work prescribed by the Committee, taking the form normally of an "attachment" to a congregation. Presbyteries are expected each May to supply the Committee with the names of congregations within their bounds which could provide suitable training, experience and supervision for such attachments.

Course of Study

There are four normal courses of study, each of which includes the following subjects — (1) the interpretation and use of Holy Scripture of both Old and New Testaments; (2) the development and growth of the Church including special reference to the Church of Scotland; (3) the principal doctrines of the Christian faith, their interpretation, defence and application; (4) the principles of Christian ethics; (5) the practice of the ministry, attention being given to public worship, the Sacraments and preaching, the pastoral ministry, Christian education, pastoral discipline, Church law and procedure, and speech training.

The Regular Course — This consists of —

(a) a First Degree in Arts, Social Science, Medicine, Science, Music or Law or such other degree as may be accepted as qualifying the applicant to study for the BD as a second degree in one of the four older Scottish Universities, followed by a course of not less than three years' study leading to that Degree. A candidate who contrives to complete both degree courses within five years will be required to take a further year's study unless he has attained the age of twenty-three before beginning the later of the two courses.

(b) a Course of not less than three years' study leading to the attainment of a BD degree at one of the said Universities. (How the applicant contrives to be allowed to enter upon this course without the preliminary requirements set forth in (a) above is not explained.)

The Alternative Course — The Alternative Course consists of four years of study leading to the attainment of the BD as a First Degree and has to be followed by two years' further study at University level as shall be determined by the Committee not later than the end of the third year of the course. In the case of a Candidate commencing the first BD course after the age of thirty no further University study is required after the attainment of the said degree.

The Intermediate Candidates' Course consists of a three years' course leading to the attainment of the LTh qualification followed by two yers' full-time study for Certificate in Ministry or Pastoral Studies; or other course approved by the Committee.

The Mature Candidates' Course consists of a three years' course wholly within the Faculty of Divinity leading to the attainment of the LTh qualification, and has to be followed by one year's study for a Certificate in Ministry or Pastoral Studies; or of such other course as may be approved by the Committee.

Special Courses may be arranged by the Committee in light of the whole circumstances of the case where the applicant holds a First Degree other than a BD in a Faculty of Divinity, or who has pursued his theological studies at other than a Scottish University. As already stated, in exceptional circumstances the Committee may prescribe a Special Course for a candidate under the age of forty.

Supervision

Liaison Committee — There are four of these — each connected with one of the Universities — and they consist of representatives of the Sectional Committee on the Supervision vision of Students, with appropriate members of staff, and representatives appointed by neighbouring Presbyteries (for full details of membership see Repts 1994, p 528). They advise on all matters relative to candidates and their progress towards the completion of their prescribed courses. When a Liaison Committee becomes aware of significant difficulties affecting a Candidate it informs the Committee which in turn communicates with the Presbytery.

Sectional Committee on the Supervision of Students — This consists of twelve members and a Convener drawn from the main Committee, the four Faculty representatives (or their nominees) and the four Student Members from the main Committee (or their alternates), and, as its name implies, it is responsible for the oversight of candidates, and that from their being accepted until their being licensed.

Presbytery Responsibility — Throughout the whole of his course the candidate remains under the pastoral supervision of the Presbytery which nominated him, unless during the period he has moved his place of residence, in which case he must, within two months of moving, give to the Clerk of the Presbytery which nominated him notice that he wishes to be transferred, whereupon the latter will furnish him with a certificate which he must without delay lodge with the Clerk of the Presbytery to which he has moved.

Presbyteries are required to confer at least once a year with candidates under their care and, to assist them in this, they are to be supplied by the Committee not later than 25th July with a report relating to progress during the previous academic year. The Presbytery has thereafter to satisfy itself as to the candidate's fitness to continue and must intimate its decision to the Committee not later than 25th September. The Presbytery has power, after conference with the Committee, to suspend or terminate a person's candidature, and in such cases the Presbytery's decision will be final, but subject to the candidate's right to petition the General Assembly for a review of his case. As I see it, this provision relieves the Presbytery of the need to cite the candidate to its bar when the case is being considered.

I can find no authority for this, but I am firmly of opinion that if a Candidate has been guilty of some grave moral lapse it is for the Committee in consultation with the Presbytery to consider his position relative to his candidature. The actual exercise of discipline, however, I should take to be the affair of the Kirk Session of the congregation to which he belongs, and the responsibility for pastoral caring lies with the Minister of that congregation.

Licence

Candidates entering their final year are, not later than 31st October, to inform the Committee to which Presbytery they intend to apply for licence, and they are, not later than 30th November, to make such application to their supervising Presbytery. The Committee is to prepare a full list of all such proposed applications and to circulate a copy thereof not later than 15th December to all the Presbyteries of the Church stating that the Presbyteries concerned may take these candidates on trial and, subject to their course being sustained, may license them, but without prejudice to the right of any other Presbytery to object to any one of them.

Objection — This covering letter indicates also that the Presbytery is at liberty to object to any candidate whose name appears on the list being taken on trials, and that if this is to be done the supervising Presbytery must be informed not later than 15th March. Commissioners may be appointed to prosecute the objection before that Presbytery. Since it will normally be the conduct, character, or ability of the candidate that will be in question it would seem to me that he should be cited and be at the bar for his interest, and that this item of business should be taken in private. The Presbytery having heard the objection may dismiss it and proceed with the trials; or it may decide to sustain it and not to proceed; or it may refer the matter to the General Assembly. Since the Act does not specifically confer upon the Presbytery finality of judgment the normal right of appeal will lie with the applicant or with the objecting Presbytery, while any member of the supervising Presbytery may dissent and complain.

Late Application — Where timeous application has not been made a Presbytery may, if satisfied with the reason for the delay, proceed to take the candidate on trials, but it must first circulate all the Presbyteries of the Church setting forth the name and particulars of the candidate and calling for objections within three calendar months, the expense of the exercise to be borne by the candidate. In a case where the lateness of the application has been attributable to the Committee's having shortened the candidate's course the procedure will be as above but the expense will be met by the Committee.

Trials for Licence — The candidate may be taken on trials for licence any time after 1st January following receipt of his application. The object of the trials is to enable the Presbytery to discover whether the applicant "is acquainted with the present legal and sacramental practice and traditions of the Church of Scotland, and that he is a fit person to proceed to its ministry." They consist of — (a) an examination, which may be oral or written or both, on the principles and practice of the Church, and (b) the conduct of public worship at a principal service in presence of two Ministers and two Elders from the Presbytery. A meeting is then held of those who have supervised the course, the examiners in (a) above, and those who were present at the service in (b) above, and a decision is reached as to whether or not to recommend that the trials be sustained. This may be done although the Presbytery is not yet in a position to license.

The Exit Certificate — This is a document which the Committee is to issue to the Candidate's Presbytery testifying that in his case the general and the academic requirements have been completed to the satisfaction of the authorities, that is, the necessary standards have been achieved in the relevant classes, that the Bible examinations have been duly passed, and that the periods of practical work have been satisfactorily performed or that other acceptable arrangements have been made and approved. It is also provided that "in exceptional circumstances, however, permission to proceed to licence may be given after full consideration by the Committee with the relevant Faculty of Divinity, the supervising Presbytery, and the candidate concerned when it is considered to be in the best interests of the Church." My comment in an earlier place about how this condition is to be assessed is equally apposite here.

Service of Licensing — The actual Service of Licensing of a Student may not take place until the Presbytery has received an Exit Certificate in his favour, has sustained his trials, and has made known to him in detail the vows he will be expected to take.

Because of the dates of the Faculty examinations the necessary information to enable the issue of the Exit Certificate is not available before the closing days of June, and because of holiday and other summer commitments it is desirable that the licensing should take place not later than the opening days of July it is usual for Presbyteries in fixing an *in hunc effectum* meeting for the Service of Licensing to do so "subject to the necessary certification in the case of Mr A B being received by that date." If, for any reason whatever, the Certificate is not in the hands of the Presbytery Clerk the licensing must not proceed. For this reason some Presbyteries are delaying the Service of Licensing till August or September.

It is possible to begin a Probationary Period without an Exit Certificate (and therefore unlicensed) given the prior written permission of the Committee (Act v 1985 as amended, Para 58).

The Licensing Service used generally to be held on a week night in a suitable Church within the bounds, but increasingly a service on a Sunday evening is standard. If there is only one Candidate the service may appropriately be held in the Church with which he is closely associated. In course of the service, Presbyery being constituted, the Moderator will read the Preamble and put to the Candidate(s) the Appointed Questions, after which he (they) will be required to sign the Formula. After service each Licentiate is furnished with an extract minute of his licence, and it is customary that in course of the service he is presented with a copy of the Scriptures which he has just been authorised to "open" to the people.

Purpose of Licensing — The extract minute referred to will, after narrating the circumstances, declare that "the said Mr AB was licensed to preach the Gospel of the Lord Jesus Christ and to exercise his gifts as a Probationer for the Holy Ministry." Two questions have of late been raised in regard to this, and indeed in relation to licensing in general — first a question raised by the Panel on Doctrine as to whether it is sound theologically to license for the preaching of the Gospel while withholding the dispensing of the Sacraments of the Gospel; and secondly, and more cogently I think, whether it is not something of a nonsense to license as preachers of the Gospel people who for years past have, without let or hindrance, been occupying pulpits in full knowledge of the Church. It was not always so. Writing a century ago Mair in his Digest of Church Laws says that "ministers are expressly prohibited from giving countenance or permission to students to engage in the public ministry of the Word before being regularly licensed to preach the Gospel. Hitherto the Church has considered that on the one hand the conducting of public worship was a service not to be grasped at, or even undertaken, immaturely, and that on the other hand the time and power of students were required for, and ought to be devoted to, their own studies. It is remarkable that in these days .... there should appear an inclination to permit students to leave their work and hasten to the pulpit."

Whatever one may think of Mair's strictures the fact has got to be accepted that the candidate has been permitted, and indeed is required, to preach and therefore to that extent the authority given at licensing is meaningless. The business of "exercising his gifts as a Probationer" is, however, still very relevant. And in any case it is surely a good thing to mark in a significant and memorable fashion the passing of so important a milestone on the road towards so important an office.

Probationers and Licentiates

As a consequence of the Licensing Service the "Candidate" has now become a "Licentiate" and the way lies open for him to become a

"Probationer". For long these latter terms were interchangeable, other synonyms being "Preacher of the Word" and "Expectant". All alike referred to one who had completed his training for the Ministry. (If he occupied the status overlong without acquiring a charge he was disparagingly referred to as a "stickit minister.") The terminology was given statutory definition in terms of Act vii of 1985 and this has been confirmed in the new Act xi of 1994. As a Licentiate he is under supervision of the Presbytery which licensed him, but if he were guilty of some grave moral fault it would now be to the Presbytery and not to his Kirk Session that he would be answerable. Incidentally, if found guilty and deprived of his status the traditional term for the sentence would be that he was "silenced" — a peculiarly apt term for a Preacher!

From the moment of licence onwards the position of the Licentiate is governed to a considerable extent by the Act anent Students, Probationers, Licentiates and Transference of Ministers referred to above (but now simply the Committee on Probationers) as well as by the Act anent Training for the Ministry.

Definitions — The new Act (xi 1994) opens with a series of definitions. A Probationer is defined as a Candidate who has completed his course and obtained his Exit Certificate, has been licensed by his Presbytery and is performing his Probationary Period (see hereunder). A Licentiate is defined as either (a) a Probationer whose period of compulsory service has been satisfactorily completed or one who has been exempted from such service; or (b) a Student who has been licensed and who, having no ambition — at this stage at least — to enter the parish ministry has been content to leave it at that and has not gone on to serve a probationary period. It seems unfortunate, and almost certain to lead to confusion, that these two completely different classes should share a common title. It seems hard too that a Licentiate satisfactorily completes a compulsory period of eighteen months as a Probationer merely to become a Licentiate once more!

At this point the aspirant for the ministry is passing from the control of the Committee on Education for the Ministry to that of the Probationers Committee within the Department of Ministry. Those Licentiates who elect not to serve a Probationary Period continue in the care of the Education for the Ministry Committee to the extent that they cannot be inducted to a charge until that body has either prescribed, or has granted exemption from, a Probationry Period. It is provided that those who have satisfactorily completed their course of study are to be granted an Exit

Certificate (see above) and in due course a Certificate of Entitlement which has to be submitted to the Presbytery within which the Probationary Period is to be served.

Roll of Probationers and Licentiates — Presbytery Clerks are, without delay, to forward to the Committee on Probationers particulars of all students who have been licensed, and the Secretary of the Committee is to send to each a form for completion in which *inter alia* he will enter certain personal particulars as well as indicating the kind of ministry he wants to pursue and also a brief "personal profile" (Act xiv 1994). Only after this form has been returned will his name be entered on the Roll which the Committee is obliged to keep.

Probationary Period — In days long past some probationers sought Assistantships where they might remain for one, two, or three years, while others immediately looked for a parish of their own. It was accepted that those in the former group were there earning their modest salary by services rendered in the parish, it being believed that in the performance of these duties they were "gaining experience". Later there was introduced the principle of a compulsory period of probation. In the early years exemption was fairly freely granted on the rather naive assumption that those with "extensive experience in the big wide world" were not in need of such training. The fallacy of this was soon exposed and today exemption is very much the exception and is likely to become even more exceptional since the age-limit for entrants has come down. Before becoming eligible for election to a home charge today a Licentiate must have served a Probationary Period under the Probationers' Committee in an assignment to which he has been directed by the Committee on Eduction for the Ministry. Originally the length of the period while nominally "a year" was actually from eight to twelve months — beginning usually in September and lasting till 30th April of the following year. Two one-day non-residential conferences were held. The period had to be served in full-time employment (usually as a parish assistant) and Presbyteries were by 30th May in each year to submit to the Committee on Education for the Ministry a list of charges in which suitable training could be acquired.

In 1990 the Assembly Council after discussion with all interested parties brought in a Report which was accepted and which introduced what was essentially a new form of probation. Its provisions included — (1) that while the Committee on Education for the Ministry should continue to determine placements, supervision of the candidate should then pass to the Board of Ministry, (2) that the length of the Period was to be extended to eighteen months, (3) that the system would be introduced gradually and only those accepted after coming to Selection School later than 1st February 1992 would be required to serve eighteen months though others might elect to do so, and (4) that for the first year of the period Probationers would be paid at the rate of 80% of the Minimum Stipend and for the remaining six months at the full Minimum. A series of conferences is held during the period. As mentioned above a new Act was passed in 1994 and Act vii of 1985 was repealed.

The situation created by the 1990 Act is under threat these days and that on grounds of finance — can we afford it? This is most unfortunate, for it has many advantages. One obvious weakness of the earlier arrangement was that an appointee did not usually begin his "year" before September/October and by the end of the calendar year his thoughts were far away in search of suitable vacancies. For so short a period it was not worth while moving house, changing children to another school, and so on. So the Period came to be not so much a welcome preparation as a resented interruption. The other great advantage has been that the affair being centrally funded the Probationers can be placed where they will receive the training they require and not just sent to a congregation which can afford from its own resources the considerble cost of their employment.

Certificate of Entitlement — At the same time that the Exit Certificate is issued the Candidate receives from the Committee on Education for the Ministry a Certificate of Entitlement in the absence of which he cannot undertake a Probationary Period, and this he is to lodge with the Clerk of the Presbytery within whose bounds he is to be working, and that Presbytery thereupon assumes responsibility for his oversight. This Certificate has a validity of five years. A Licentiate who wishes to begin serving a Probationary Period after his Certificate has lapsed has to apply to the Sectional Committee on Admission of Ministers which notifies the responsible Presbytery which, after enquiry and interview sends its opinion to the Committee — and in due course a fresh Certificate may be issued. In the event of refusal the applicant has a right of appeal to the Panel of Arbiters (see Revised Regulations, Repts 1994, p 611).

Change of Placement — If in the opinion of the Probationers Committee the placement has proved unsatisfactory it is in order for the Education for the Ministry Committee, after consultation with the Probationers Committee, with the Probationer, with the Minister and Kirk Session of the charge where he is working, and with the Presbytery, to resolve to remove a Probationer or to make alternative arrangement for his placement during the remainder of his period. It is the Committee on Probationers that has power to prescribe supplementary training. A Probationer must obtain permission from the Committee on Probationers to proceed to ordination and induction. While serving his period the Probationer is free to accept pulpit supply in vacant charges.

Sustaining the Period — There is some confusion here. It is required that reports are to be presented by both the Probationer and the Minister with whom he is serving to the Probationers Committee which "shall make a recommendation at the end of fifteen months on whether the probationary period shall be sustained or not." The foregoing is quoted from Act xviii 1992 (being a new Sect 61 for the 1985 Act), and it will be noted that it does not say to whom the "recommendation" is to be made. On the oher hand in an Appendix to their report to the 1994 Assembly the Probationers Committee declares *inter alia* "although the Committee is responsible for sustaining the Probationary periods ....." It would seem, then, that the Probationers Committee actually do the sustaining.

If the decision is favourable the Probationer becomes eligible for election and appointment to a home charge or to some extra-parochial ministerial appointment and may take steps in this direction He may not, however, be inducted to such a charge or begin the work of such an appointment until he has completed the full Probationary Period. Should the decision on sustaining be unfavourable a further Probationary Period may be prescribed — almost certainly in a different appointment — and this will be made by the Education for the Ministry Committee.

There is a possibility of confusion arising from the fact that we still have two systems working side by side — that for those on the short Probationary Period and that for those under the eighteen months rule and that the provisions of Act vii 1985 (repealed in 1994) still apply in the former cases. For those on the eighteen month period the Education for the Ministry Committee does not have any say in the matter unless where a second placement has to be arranged (see above).

Preaching in Vacancies — From January onwards the Committee is to provide Probationers and Licentiates with opportunities of preaching in vacant parishes. The Probationer may himself apply for a vacancy, but in every case the Vacancy Committee must obtain permission from the Probationers Committee before the congregation may hear him as a nominee.

The Probationers Committee is to compile and maintain a list of all Probationers seeking a charge, together with such documentation, including personal profile, as may be submitted to the Committee by each Probationer or Licentiate. The Committee shall send monthly to any eligible Licentiate and to Probationers whom the Committee has agreed might make application to vacant charges the list of current vacancies and appropriate appointments issued monthly to all ministers in charges and to any other minister who may request it, with in each case the name and address of a contact person. The Committee is also to make available in a vacancy the complete list of available Probationers. On the request of an Interim Moderator a selected list based on knowledge of the expressed wishes of each Probationer or Licentiate is to be provided. Where a selected list is supplied the names shall be accompanied by the appropriate personal profiles which may have been submitted to the Committee; and of these vacancies they are to keep a detailed record. All of this in terms of Act xi of 1994 anent Candidates, Licentiates and Probationers for the Full-time Ministry.

Subsequent Procedure — Every Licentiate who has not been ordained by the second anniversary of his licensing is required to complete a fresh form from the Probationers Committee indicating his up-to-date position. If on the third anniversy of his licensing he has failed to provide this information his name is to be taken from the Roll; and this will happen too to any Probationer of at least three years' standing whose whereabouts are unknown to the Committee. Once a name has been so removed it may be restored only by application to the Sectional Committee on Admission of Ministers for a Certificate of Eligibility, or by petition to the General Assembly.

Admission by General Assembly — It has occasionally happened — though rarely of late — that a Minister of another denomination has been accepted, but with the status of a Licentiate. This would happen where the Assembly were prepared to accept the validity of the petitioner's ordination but were not happy about the adequacy of his training — he would be accepted as a Minister subject to fulfilling certain conditions about classes to be taken and/or an assistantship to be served and put under the care of a Presbytery. It is, I think, universally accepted that there is no authority for requiring such a person to undergo trials for licence (I received this opinion from no less an authority than Dr Cox himself) — he has been granted the status of a Licentiate in the old-fashioned meaning of that term and, so soon as whatever conditions were imposed by the Assembly have been purged, he is free to accept a Call.

To me it has always seemed odd that in the case of people from a totally different tradition and background we are thus prepared to assume their knowledge of the legal and sacramental practice and traditions of the Church of Scotland when we are at such pains to examine those brought up within that tradition. The General Assembly of 1946 laid it upon the Presbytery in such a case "to satisfy itself as to the knowledge of those admitted regarding the practice and procedure of the Church as contained in the first ten chapters of "Cox". I imagine, therefore, that, short of calling them "trials", a Presbytery is entitled to take whatever steps it considers reasonable in discharging this responsibility.

Ministerium vagum — The Church has always been reluctant to create such a ministry, that is, the ordaining of a person who is not intending to proceed to a definite charge. There is now authority on the subject (Regulations 1969, 1). With regard to extra-parochial offices it is only when the Church has some control over, or some right to approve of, the appointment and some ongoing oversight of how it is to be operated that ordination is to be granted to a licentiate wishing to take up such an appointment. It has also to be shown that there will be need for the appointee to baptise and/or dispense Communion ere ordination will be granted. These services where appropriate should be rendered by the parish minister.

The End of the Candidature Road

On being ordained either for a charge or for service in some other capacity a Probationer or Licentiate may be said to have completed the journey along the Way of Candidature, and so to have become a Minister of the Church of Scotland, a status he will continue to enjoy for life or until he has been deprived of it by judicial process, or has voluntarily relinquished it and had his resignation of it accepted by the Presbytery, or until he has entered the service and come under the jurisdiction of some other denomination of the Church. This last applies in the case of the Church of Scotland minister serving overseas who enters the ministry of the indigenous Church.

BY WAY OF ADMISSION

As a method of entry into the ministry of the Kirk the Way of Admission is divided into two branches, it may be by Petition or it may be by Certificate of Eligibility. In either case the procedure was in the hands of the Committee on Probationers and Transference and Admission of Ministers whose procedure was governed by the terms of Act vii of 1985 anent Admission and Re-admission of Ministers and Eligibility for Nomination, Election and Call, or for Appointment. This seems likely to be superseded in 1995 by an Act anent Admission and Re-admission of Ministers and Eligibility for Nomination, Election and Call, and Appointment. The supervising body for Probationers is now called the Committee on Probationers, and all matters concerning admission to the ministry of the Church of Scotland fall within the province of a new Committee on Admission and Re-admission of Ministers, being a Sectional Committee of the Committee on Education for the Ministry.

Petition for Admission

A Minister of any denomination other than one with which our Church has a mutual eligibility agreement, or one within the Anglican communion, if he desires admission as a Minister of the Church of Scotland must approach the General Assembly by Petition. For this purpose a form has to be completed setting forth certain particulars, including the applicant's age, present Church connection, educational curriculum and ministerial career, and containing also a statement of his reasons for wanting to enter the ministry of the Church of Scotland, and also of the kind of service he hopes to undertake there. He must also lodge documentary evidence in support of the information supplied. It is usual also to submit the names of referees. The closing date for receiving a Petition is 1st January immediately preceding the Assembly to which it is addressed. At the time of lodging the petition the applicant also has to pay a fee the amount of which is determined from time to time by the Committee — at the time of writing it is £50 whether for a Minister, or for a Licentiate; and that whether or not the applicant is a former Minister or Licentiate of the Church of Scotland.

Interview by the Committee — Synopses of Petitions received are circulated to members of the Admission Committee which meets some time before the end of January and, unless for very special reason he is excused, the Applicant appears then for interview. Thereafter the Committee reaches a provisional decision as to the recommendation it will make to the General Assembly and this is conveyed to the Applicant who is required to reply in writing stating whether he wishes to proceed or to withdraw, and in the former case whether he would like in any way to alter the terms of his Petition. Should he decide to withdraw he is entitled to have a proportion of anything up to one-half of his fee returned. In exceptional circumstances, and for reasons to be stated in its report to the Assembly, the Committee may refer a case *simpliciter* to the Assembly.

Reference to Presbytery — The opinion of the Presbytery has now to be obtained — that is, the Presbytery of the applicant's place of residence, or if he has not resided within one Presbytery during the past three months, the Presbytery of Edinburgh. If, with permission of the Committee, the petitioner is already being employed within the Church (see hereunder) and has been so for at least a month prior to 1st January the Presbytery within whose bounds he is so employed is also to be consulted. Copies of the Petition in full, of the synopsis, and of the recommendation shall be forwarded to the appropriate Presbytery or Presbyteries, which are asked to consider the case and to forward their opinions not later than 15th April.

Something of a difficulty presents itelf at this stage since the object of the reference to the Presbytery is clearly designed to uncover any local knowledge relevant to the Petitioner and with this in mind the Presbytery would wish the matter to be afforded the widest publicity. Since at this stage the Petition may still be withdrawn it would be unfortunate for it to be widely known that the Applicant was so much as contemplating leaving his denomination. The Presbytery has, therefore at this point to treat the matter as confidential, dealing with it behind closed doors. Not the ideal way to uncover the slightest whiff of scandal.

Review by Committee — The Committee then meets again and considers the recommendation it proposes to advance — for granting, for partially granting, for deferring, or for refusing to grant. The decision is intimated to the Petitioner who may alter his crave or withdraw his Petition, and in the latter case all documents lodged will immediately be returned to him.

Older Applicant — In the case of an applicant over sixty years on 1st January in the year of his application and who has not held a charge or charges in a Presbyterian Church for at least ten years the Committee is not to make a recommendation, but it may resolve to transmit the Petition *simpliciter*. This provision, designed to make the path of the older applicant more difficult has, in my opinion, had the opposite effect. The Petitioner arranges for an eloquent friend to make an impassioned *ex parte* statement on his behalf. At this point a balanced assessment of the situation from a member of the Committee which had gathered and collated the facts might seem more helpful. The Regulations prevent it being offered.

At the Assembly — When the Petitioner is called to the bar comissioners have in their hands copies of the Petition itself and of the reports of the Committee and Presbytery. The Petitioner may answer questions put from the floor, or may speak to any inaccuracy which he claims appears in the synopsis (with a copy of which he has been supplied at least seven days before the hearing) but he may not speak in support of his Petition, except that he may do so briefly when the petition has been transmitted *simpliciter* or subject to an adverse recommendation.

If the Assembly agree to admit they remit to the Presbytery concerned, or to some other, to take the necessary steps for admission, but they do not define these. This, as I see it, means that on receipt of the relevant minute of Assembly the Presbytery adds the name of the Petitioner to the List of Ministers without Charge resident within its bounds, though I think that before doing so it is entitled to require him to sign the Formula — merely coming from another Presbytery he would have to do this. Courtesy demands that he be welcomed at a Presbytery meeting, but he is not entitled to a seat in that court. If no action has been taken on the strength of the Assembly minute within six months of its date of issue it loses its validity. From which it would seem to follow that the status of Minister of the Church of Scotland is acquired not when the Assembly grants the crave but only when the Presbytery enrols.

Partial Admission — The Assembly may resolve upon partial (or interim) admission — that is to say, they may impose a condition that certain classes are to be taken or that an assistantship is to be served. In the former case the classes have to be taken at the Petitioner's expense, but in the latter case the Church will fund this from central sources and the Petitioner will receive a salary. During such period of partial admission the Petitioner may not preach in a vacancy (except a continued vacancy) or administer the Sacraments, but he may exercise all the other functions of the ministry. He is put under the supervision of a Presbytery and within the context of discipline will be treated as a Probationer. The following Assembly will receive a report from the Committee as to whether he has fully and satisfactorily complied with the conditions, and if they now resolve to admit then procedure will be as above.

For any reason which it deems adequate the Assembly may decide to defer consideration of a Petition for Admission.

Ordained Status

If the Petitioner has been ordained to the full status of the ministry by a Presbyterian Church within the United Kingdom, by a Church overseas which is a member of the World Alliance of Reformed Churches, by any Church in the Anglican Communion, by any regularly consituted branch of the Methodist Church or of the Congregational Union, of the Scottish Congregational Church or of the Congregational Federation in Scotland (provided in the latter case the ordination was in accordance with by-laws 1959 or 1976 of the Congregational Union of Scotland), or by the United Reformed Church in the United Kingdom, then his admission will be with the status of a Minister. In other cases the question of the acceptability of the Petitioner's orders will be the subject of a report by the Committee and of consideration by the Assembly. If not prepared to recognise the Petitioner's ordination the Assembly will admit him as a Licentiate and remit to a Presbytery to take the necessary steps. I do not think this would mean steps to ordain him there and then (see *Ministerium Vagum*, p 132) — he would have, as a Licentiate, to await a Call to a parish or a ministerial appointment, when ordination would follow in the normal way.

Interim Employment — A Petitioner may apply to the Committee for permission to accept employment within the Church pending the outcome of his Petition, and if agreeable the Committee will grant such permission subject to the condition that he may not dispense the Sacraments, that he may not preach in vacant charges (except in a continued vacancy) and that he report to the Clerk of the Presbytery where he is employed — though he remains under the care and supervision of the Presbytery of his residence. The "employing" Presbytery may be required to provide within three weeks a report as to the manner in which he is performing his duties, and the permission may at any time be rescinded.

Lapsing of Admission — This part of the Act concludes with what appears to me an odd provision — "in the event of a Petitioner not having received a Call to a Church, or a ministerial appointment, by the fifth anniversary of his admission by the General Assembly, his admission will be deemed to have lapsed, and, if the Petitioner still seeks admission it shall be necessary for him to present a new Petition to the General Assembly." I find it strange that the Act should apply the term "Petitioner" to one who for the past five years has appeared on a Presbytery Roll as a Minister Without Charge. I find it difficult to understand how a person upon whom the status of Minister of the Church of Scotland has been conferred by the Assembly can be deprived of that status except as the result of a judicial process. And I wonder what status exactly such a person will have. He cannot automatically recover the status he enjoyed in the Church which he left five years before. It looks as though he had ceased to be a Minister at all. I can only hope it is a situation unlikely to arise!

Licentiates and Students — A Licentiate of another Church may petition the General Assembly craving to be received as a Probationer of the Church of Scotland, and, with the necessary adjustments, the foregoing regulations and conditions will apply. If accepted, the Petitioner will be put under the care of a Presbytery which has to take "the necessary steps".

A Student who has been, or is being, trained under another denomination does not come within the scope of this legislation. is for him to apply to the Committee on Education for the Ministry which will deal with his case on its merits and the Student will then enter by way of Candidature which includes attendance at Selection School, this latter being a must.

Petition for Re-admission — A former Minister of the Church of Scotland who has been deprived of, or has voluntarily relinquished, his status may desire re-admission, and in such a case he must submit a Petition to the General Assembly. Such a Petition will *mutatis mutandis* follow the same lines as apply in the case of a Petition for Admission.

Certificate of Eligibility

In certain cases, the number of which has been steadily increasing in recent years, it is not necessary for a Minister of another denomination to petition the General Assembly to be received as a Minister of the Church of Scotland — his course is to obtain from the Admission Committee a

Certificate of Eligibility which when lodged with the Presbytery Clerk through the Interim Moderator of a vacant congregation will entitle him to be nominated in the vacancy, and thus, after election and induction (or introduction), he will become a Minister of the Church of Scotland. Should he for any reason be refused a Certificate the applicant is at liberty to approach the General Assembly by Petition craving to be received as a Minister (see above).

Requirements — The requirements for obtaining a Certificate of Eligibility vary according to the Church from which the applicant comes —

Presbyterian Church in Ireland — To obtain a Certificate of Eligibility a Minister of that Church has to produce a certificate from the Clerk of its General Assembly to the effect that he was ordained in that Church and has held charges or appointments within it for a period of at least five years.

Reformed Churches — A Minister of any regularly constituted Presbyterian Church in the United Kingdom, of the United Reformed Church in the United Kingdom (exclusive of Ministers of the Churches of Christ now within the U R C), or of any Church outwith the United Kingdom which is a member of the World Alliance of Reformed Churches, or of a Church within the Anglican Communion, may obtain a Certificate of Eligibility on condition that he satisfies the Admission Committee that he is a Minister in full standing in his own denomination, having held charges or appointments within it for at least five years, that his educational qualifications are comparable with those within the Church of Scotland and that his character and conduct are becoming his profession. The fee is 8.

Partnership Plan — A completely new conception was introduced in the 1985 Act anent the Settlement of Ministers whereby a congregation may decide to have as their Minister for three years a Minister of a Church furth of Scotland which is a member of the World Alliance of Reformed Churches or of the Church of South India, or of the Church of Pakistan. A Minister chosen in this way by a Vacancy Committee must, before nomination, secure from the Committee a Certificate of Eligibility, and this will be supplied provided he can satisfy the Committee that he has fulfilled the eductional requirements of, and has been ordained by, his own Church, that he is a Minister in full standing, that he has served for at least three years in charges or appointments therein, and that his character and conduct are becoming his profession.

Such a person will be introduced as Minister of the vacant charge on conditions of terminable tenure for a period not exceeding three years. With concurrence of the Presbytery and of the Board of World Mission his incumbency may at the request of the congregation be extended for one further period of three years. Throughout the time of his ministry he will enjoy to the full the status of a Minister of the Church of Scotland. At the end he will revert to being a Minister of the Church from which he came, though I imagine he could apply for a Certificate of Eligibility that would entitle him to accept nomination in a vacancy in Scotland were he so minded.

Former Minister of the Church of Scotland — A former Minister or Licentiate of the Church of Scotland who has neither relinquished nor been deprived of his status but who falls into one of the following categories may acquire a Certificate of Eligibility on the conditions set out hereunder. The fee in each case is £25.

a) One who with approval of the Board of World Mission has entered the courts of an indigenous Church as a full member — on ceasing to be such a member.
b) One who has become an accredited Minister of the United Reformed Church, or of the Presbyterian Church in Ireland — on production of a certificate from his Assembly Clerk as to status, record and character.
c) One who has served furth of Scotland in a Church which is a member of the World Alliance of Reformed Churches — provided he satisfies the Admission Committee or its Executive as to status, record and character.
d) One who has accepted employment outwith the jurisdiction of the Church — with the provision as in (c) above, and on condition that he gives a written assurance of his intention to terminate such employment.
e) One who because of maternity commitments has not for a period been in a charge — with the provision as in (c) above.

It should be noted that in the case of Ministers within the catergories (d) and (e) the Certificate of Eligibility is necessary for re-entry into the parish ministry, but the person concerned has in fact never lost the status of a Minister of the Church of Scotland.

Conditions — All certificates issued by the Committee as above are subject to the following conditions — (a) they will not be issued in a vacuum but only in connection with a particular vacancy; (b) unless under very special conditions they will not be granted to persons over sixty years of age, and (c) their validity extends to only one year after the date of issue.

A New Act

As has been said earlier, a new Act is presently being considered by Presbyteries in terms of the Barrier Act, and, I am told, is likely to be approved and enter the statute book in 1995. It varies only slightly from the position set forth above, the main changes involved being (a) to restrict petition to those intending to serve in a charge or appointment under the jurisdiction of the Church of Scotland or in an appointment qualifying for membership of a Presbytery; (b) to reduce the age limits to a comparable reduction in age limits for prospective candidates for the ministry, and to allow of no exceptions; (c) to require documents to be lodged one month earlier; (d) to request more information of petitioners including their medical history and any employment outwith the church; (e) to require petitioners without exception to be interviewed by the Committee; (f) to send *full* documentation of a petition to the appropriate Presbystery; (g) to allow for withdrawal of, but not as at present alteration to, a petition after the Committee has finally decided on its recommendation to the General Assembly; and (h) to dispense with interim admission as a possible recommendation.

The End of the Admission Road

It will be clear from the foregoing that in the case of Admission by Petition the status of Minister of the Church of Scotland is conferred when the Presbytery to whose care the Petitioner has been committed takes the necessary steps; whereas in the case of Admission by Certificate of Eligibility the status of Minister of the Church of Scotland is acquired only in virtue of being inducted or introduced to a charge or installed in an appointment. Once acquired — in whichever way — the status continues to be enjoyed until relinquished or deprived, or until the person has entered the service of another Church — except in the special case of the Partnership Plan referred to above when, in my view, the person ceases to be a Minister of the Church of Scotland on the termination of his service therein and that irrespective of whether he intends to return to the service of the Church from which he came. Incidentally I have not heard of any case where advantage has so far been taken of this Plan.

THE WAY TO THE AUXILIARY MINISTRY

The suggestion, first mooted in 1975, that the traditional full-time ministry of the Church might be supplemented by a part-time ministry, took shape in the report submitted by the "Committee of Forty" to the Assembly of 1977. Two reasons, principally, were advanced in support of the proposal — first, that as things seemed to be developing there was never again likely to be an adequate supply of ordained personnel to man, nor an adequate flow of finance to maintain, throughout Scotland a full territorial ministry of the kind known to an earlier generation; and, secondly, that "the Church has a huge potential resource in terms of her lay men and women which is not being fully used." It was resolved that, in consultation with other interested Committees, a Draft Act should be prepared for submission to the following Assembly. In 1978 a report was presented further elaborating what was envisaged, and it was remitted to the General Administration Committee, in consultation with the Department of Education and the Home Board, to "draft an Overture to enable the ordination of auxiliary part-time Ministers of Word and Sacrament." This Overture, finally approved under Barrier Act procedure (27 Presbyteries voting in favour and 20 against), became Act iv of 1980. It contained also regulations for the selection and training of such a ministry. It was later amended in terms of Act iii 1987.

An Auxiliary Minister is defined as "a person who has been ordained for life to a ministry of Word and Sacrament exercisable under supervision on a part-time and non-stipendiary basis."

Recruitment — The recruitment of candidates is in the first instance a duty of Presbyteries and in this they are to satisfy themselves that there is a reasonable expectation of spheres of service being available within their bounds where such auxiliary Ministers could appropriately and usefully serve. An applicant for the Auxiliary Ministry must normally have been over the past three years in full communion with the Church of Scotland and must carry the recommendation both of his Minister and of his Kirk Session as well as of the Presbytery. He must have a good educational background, and "proficiency in spoken and written English will be regarded as of material importance." He has to submit a formal application to the Committee on Education for the Ministry (referred to throughout this section as "the Committee") which arranges for him to appear at a Selection School where the standard expected in the matter of suitability is as it is for the regular ministry. The Committee if satisfied with the assessors' report, accepts the Candidate as a Prospective Candidate for the Auxiliary Ministry, subject to his being nominated by his Presbytery. Since the service to be rendered is part-time and without financial reward it appears to me most important that before encouraging anyone to commit himself to the considerable work of preparation the Presbytery should be quite clear it is going to be able to avail itself of his services in a meaningful way. So far as legislation is concerned, however, the Presbytery may now nominate a candidate although it does not itself have, or expect to have, a sphere demanding the services of an Auxiliary Minister. I imagine this is all right so long as it is made perfectly clear to the aspirant that there is no obvious outlet, now or later within the Presbytery of his residence for the services he hopes to be able to render. The maximum age for entering on the course was in 1989 raised from fifty-eight to sixty-one.

It was reported to the Assembly of 1994 that in the previous year the number of applicants for the Auxiliary Ministry who came to Selection School was ten, eight of whom were selected for training. There was one candidate in second year and eight serving the required periods of probation. At the same time it has to be said that the total number of Auxiliary Ministers is as low as twenty-three after something like fifteen years.

Course of Training — The course extends over a twenty-four month period, is part-time and consists of —

a) central residential training involving attendance at extended weekend training sessions held in the summer in each of the three years of the course and covering both academic disciplines and the experience of worship;
b) extension study under central tutors carried on through supervised reading and seminar work, the written essays being submitted to the tutors; and
c) practical training taking the form of a six-month period each year served in a parish (not normally the Candidate's own) and relating to preaching and the conduct of public worship, to pastoral work, and to Christian education.

In each year of the course the Candidate must satisfy the Presbytery and the Committee of his continuing progress and suitability, and, if not satisfied, the Committee has power to extend or to discontinue the course.

Although the Regulations for Selection and Training went down as part of the Overture under the Barrier Act it is specifically provided that these may be amended on the recommendation of the Committee without being subject to Barrier Act procedure.

Licence — The Committee, if the course has been completed to its satisfaction, transmits an Exit Certificate to the Presbytery which has then to take the Candidate on trials for licence. These are exactly as with Candidates for the full-time ministry, the only distinction being that in this case the Candidate is licensed not "as a Preacher of the Gospel" but "to the auxiliary ministry of the Church of Scotland."

Probationary Period — "The first year after licence shall normally be a probationary period" though in exceptional circumstances exemption may be granted. The Committee will assess the adequacy of the Probationary Period in light of a report from a Minister or Ministers appointed by the Presbytery, and, if the Committee sustains, the Candidate then becomes eligible for ordination at the hands of the Presbytery — or of any other.

Ordination — The new Act says nothing about when ordination may take place but one is entitled to assume that the Candidate will first have undergone trials for licence and will have an appointment lined up. On completion of, or on having been exempted from, the period of probation the Licentiate for the Auxiliary Ministry may be ordained by his Presbytery. Since the service he is to render is part-time and unpaid it is reasonable to assume that his assignment will lie within the bounds of his Presbytery of residence. It may take one of a variety of forms and may even, I imagine, consist in a kind of roving commission within the Presbytery, or within some part of it. He cannot be inducted to a parish, but is given an assignment which may consist in ministering to a parish (under supervision) and in such a case he may be expected to begin his duties with some sort of Service of Introduction. It would seem right that in the case of his first assignment this should be coupled with the Service of Ordination. The Act makes no reference to the matter, but I take the view that an edict in common form should be served either in his own Church or in that connected with his assignment, as would be done in the case of either Minister or Elder. The Service would follow a pattern identical to that for the ordination of a Probationer for the work of an ordained assistantship.

When ordained the Auxiliary Minister comes under the care of the Board of Ministry and a form of "contract of employment" has been drawn up by them. Once assigned to an appointment the Auxiliary has a seat in the Presbytery within whose bounds he is working and is on all fours with other ministers in his relation to that body.

An Auxiliary Minister may function "ministerially" outwith the Presbytery within which his assignment is located only if prior permission has been given by the Presbytery into which he proposes to intrude. This has particular relevance to the conduct of services, the administering of the Sacraments, and the performing of marriages. It is not enough that consent has been given by the Minister in whose parish the Auxiliary Minister is proposing to function.

Non-Stipendiary — The Auxiliary Minister receives no salary, honorarium or other payment in respect of services rendered, though necessary and approved outlays incurred will be refunded. If he preach in a parish other than that to which he is assigned he is entitled to receive the customary Pulpit Supply fee, but not in respect of services conducted in the Church of his assignment. In terms of a provision approved in 1992 (Repts 1992, p 507) he is entitled to receive an allowance of up to £150 per annum towards the cost of purchase of books and this is to come from central funds.

The End of the Auxiliary Road

Having been duly ordained the aspirant to the Auxiliary Ministry has now gained the status of a Minister of the Church of Scotland. So far as his "standing" ecclestically is concerned he is in the fullest and most complete sense a Minister of Word and Sacrament. The Act says (Para 2), "Except in so far as modified by the terms of the Act, an auxiliary minister is hereby declared to be a minister of the Church of Scotland for all necessary purposes in connection with his or her assignment as hereunder provided." So far as the exercise of his ministry is concerned he is strictly limited in that he cannot be inducted to a parish, in that his employment is necessarily part-time and unpaid, and in that he can serve only under the direction and control of some other Minister. For the duration of the assignment he is awarded a seat in Presbytery. His status — with its consequent answerability to the Presbytery — continues for life unless he is deprived of it or relinquishes it of his own will with consent of the Presbytery. In a number of cases Auxiliary Ministers have returned to complete the normal course of entering the full-time ministry by way of candidature. I do not know how this "part-time status" would affect, for instance, his position were he to decide to contest a Parliamentary election. I imagine we'll have to await an answer till someone does so aspire!

Chapter 6

THE DUTIES OF THE MINISTER

THE DUTIES WHICH FALL TO THE LOT of a Minister will vary considerably according to the position which he holds. I propose to deal in the first place with the standard situation, that of a Minister inducted to a parish; I will then go on and look at the peculiarities affecting the position of chaplains of one sort and another; and I will conclude with a brief note about those who hold the status of a Minister but are either retired or engaged in secular employment. While the principal object of the chapter is to define duties, opportunity will be taken to comment also on rights and privileges belonging to the Minister — for, after all, the two go very much together.

THE MINISTER OF A PARISH

The Parish

Induction — When a Minister (or a Probationer) has been elected and appointed to a Parish the Presbytery convenes *in hunc effectum* to conduct a service in which the appointee is inducted (or ordained and inducted) as Minister of the parish, and when this is done "certified itimation of the ordination and/or induction shall be sent to the Session Clerk to be engrossed in the minutes of the first meeting of Session thereafter." (Act iv, 1932). Likewise at the first meeting of Session after the occurrence of the vacancy it should have been recorded that "the parish became vacant on .... by reason of the translation/death/demission of..... ."

In virtue of his induction the Minister is Moderator of his Kirk Session (or Kirk Sessions in case of a linking), he has a seat in the Presbytery, he is eligible to receive a commission to the General Assembly, and, where the Model Constitution is in operation, he is entitled, if he so wish, to be Chairman of the Congregational Board. Immediately after induction he will receive from the Presbytery Clerk an extract minute of the Assembly

Maintenance of the Ministry Committee setting forth the stipend arrangements that are to obtain. This is an odd document in that while it represents a solemn undertaking on the part of the congregation it has no contractual force. All that a Minister is guaranteed in the matter of stipend in virtue of his induction is the current Minimum Stipend (with, now certain Seniority Supplements (see pp 203 ff)) and nothing more. He also acquires certain rights in the the use of Church property (see hereunder).

Residence — In the years immediately following the Reformation the law was most strict in the matter of the absentee minister — understandably so. For a Minister to be absent from his flock for forty days without reason approved by the General Assembly was adequate cause for deprivation. Today many manses are outwith the parish (see hereunder), but the Presbytery is entitled to insist that the Minister reside within reasonable distance of his parish, and for any protracted absence he must seek permission in advance. Six weeks is the period; if the absence is to be for longer the Presbytery must be consulted, leave of absence will be granted and an Interim Moderator appointed. Should a Minister absent himself from his parish without leave for longer than this he may be treated as being in desertion and be deposed. This in fact is the way to resolve the difficulty where a Minister in a fit of pique "resigns" and walks out without seeking demission at the hands of the Presbytery, or where, perhaps, he just vanishes. After due citation and non-appearance he is deposed on the ground of desertion — deposed not only from the parish but "from the office of the Holy Ministry".

Leave of Absence — This is invariably granted for a specific period, and during the whole of that time the Interim Moderator is in full charge. Should a Minister on leave for health reasons feel he is sufficiently recovered to resume duty before the expiry of the full period he must apply to the Presbytery to discharge the Interim Moderator — he cannot at his own will return during the period of the leave.

Manse — From the days of the Reformation the Manse has been a prominent feature of every Scottish village, and that both architecturally and socially. In this regard things are changing, and that very rapidly. For a full discussion of the place of the Manse today (see pp 205 ff). So far as our present interest is concerned let it suffice to say that where a Manse is provided the Minister is expected to occupy it. The Presbytery may give him permission to live elsewhere, and in such a case the congregation were accustomed until recently to make him an allowance but were not bound to do so. Today such payments are frowned upon if not actually forbidden, though existing agreements will continue to be honoured. When, however, a Manse is not provided there must be paid a sum in lieu at the rate for Manse Allowance determined from time to time by the Maintenance of the Ministry Committee. On the death of a Minister in service a reasonable time will be allowed for his family to vacate the house.

Because he is held bound to occupy it the value of the occupancy of the Manse is not chargeable for Income Tax. In every case the Council Tax is payable by the Congregation and provision for this has been made in determining stipends.

Where permission had been given to a Minister to live elsewhere than in the Manse an acute problem may arise as to what to do with the vacant house. It may be sold and the income invested and allowed to accumulate in the hope that the fund so created will be adequate to furnish a new Manse when the occasion arises — though it rarely is. In no circumstances should the whole income from it be used to pay the Manse Allowance. If it is decided that the house should be let care must be taken that the tenant does not acquire rights to an indefinite tenancy. A condition can be written into the lease ensuring that the tenant can be put out if and when the house is needed as a Manse (not to allow of its being sold) but with this restriction it may not be easy to find a tenant. In the present state of the law requiring that a Manse be availbale, a congregation should at all times ensure either that it has a suitable house or that it has the capital required to buy or to erect such a house. The General Trustees operate a rule that unless in the most exceptional circumstances they will not authorise the erection or purchase of a house as a Manse which is of less than six apartments — boxrooms not being accepted as apartments. Where for special reason a smaller house is accepted it is strictly on an interim basis till proper provision can be arranged.

Non-Intrusion — A Minister's sphere of duty lies within the bounds of his own parish and he may overstep these to perform ministerial functions only with the previous consent of the Minister of the Parish concerned, or on the order of the Presbytery or of the Assembly, or to minister to members or adherents of his own congregation, or to conduct a marriage or funeral by private invitation. Special rules apply in the case of Auxiliary Ministers (see p 144).

Access to Church Buildings — "The place of worship and other ecclesiastical buildings connected with every charge are at the disposal of the Minister for the purpose of his office." Further, "he may use these, or grant permission to others to use them, for all purposes connected with the congregation or its organisations, and also for all purposes of an ecclesiastical, religious or charitable nature even if they be not connected with the congregation." He may not use them, or grant the use of them, for any other purpose without consent of the body responsible for the temporal affairs of the congregation" (Act xvii 1932).

The Minister has sole power over the ringing of the Church bell, and, according to Mair's "Digest of Church Laws", he is "keeper of the Communion vessels and furniture, and is answerable to the parish if they are lost or put to any profane use."

Public Worship

According to the Westminster Confession public worship consists of prayer with thanksgiving, reading the Scriptures, preaching and hearing the Word, singing of Psalms, and the due administration and worthy receiving of the Sacrament; and God is not to be worshipped in any way "not prescribed in Holy Scripture." (Westminster Confession xxi). The only rule-book in this field is the Directory of Public Worship of God (1645) which in its preface is at pains to point out that it is not to be treated as a litany, but as a base that allows the individual Minister "to furnish his heart and tongue with other materials of prayer and exhortation, as shall be needful upon all occasions."

In a day when the Word is rarely being heard at home and only very occasionally at school or elsewhere it is doubly important that it should be read at public worship. There are those who insist on three passages at each service — Old Testament, Gospel and Epistle. For myself I feel that relevance to the subject of the sermon is of more importance than source, but that is a personal opinion. While for many years the Authorised Version alone was in use, and while the Assembly have given their blessing to the New English Bible, there is no prescribed translation, and the choice here, as in so many aspects of the service, lies with the Minister. It has always seemed to me odd that in many Churches with a "high Church" tradition, where the pulpit is reserved exclusively for the preaching of the Word, the "opening of the Scriptures", there is no copy of the said Scriptures there to be "opened". The only item of "ceremonial" which our fathers tholed in worship was the solemn carrying in of the Book by the beadle — and it was to the pulpit that he carried it.

Book of Common Order — From time to time a "Book of Common Order" has been published bearing the imprint of the Church of Scotland. The most recent, published in 1994, replaced those of 1978 and 1940 which had taken over from the former United Free Church of Scotland Book of 1928 with its Parish Church counterpart of 1923. The interesting point about all of these is that while they were prepared at the behest of the General Assembly and their publication carries the blessing of that court their content was never formally approved by the Assembly. The deliverance accepting the Book in 1978 acknowledged the considerable work of the Committee in its preparation and commended it to the whole Church. In the Introduction to the volume, however, the Convener of the Committee explains that a certain course is followed because "it is an order which the Committee believes best reflects the logic of the Gospel." The Assembly has never at any time declared its acceptance of this view of the logic of the Gospel, and there can be little doubt that many would challenge it. The book generally departed so seriously from accepted practices in many particulars that in 1977 it produced a counterblast in the appearance of "The Reformed Book of Common Order" published by the National Church Association — which was unfortunate but almost inevitable. The new Book (1994) takes a more realistic line when it claims to offer a rich provision for worship which is faithful to the Bible and to Christian experience. 'Comprehensive in its content, fresh and contemporary in its language, attractive in its layout the book may be used verbatim, or for providing models to be followed, or as a resource facility."

The Book of Common Order, therefore, is a guide to Ministers in the conduct of public worship, in the administration of the Sacraments, and in other services of the sanctuary. It is not binding upon anyone. As was said in the 1928 Book, a Service Book is necessary "to express the mind of the Church with regard to its offices of worship, in orders and forms which, while not fettering individual judgment in particulars, will set the norm for the orderly and reverend conduct of the various services in which Ministers have to lead their people."

Innovations in the Order of Public Worship — How often one hears it claimed that the Minister and he alone is in charge of the worship of his congregation. This is true to the exent that no-one else in the congregation has any standing in regulating the conduct of public worship, but it is not true if it is meant to imply that the Minister is absolute master in this field. It is the Presbytery which carries the responsibility for the conduct of worship in all the congregations within its bounds, and the Presbytery appoints each Parish Minister its executive within his own domain. This means on the one hand that the Presbytery may at any time call one of its Ministers to account in this regard and on the other hand that anyone who is dissatisfied with the way in which worship is being conducted in his congregation has, to hand, a remedy in the form of a petition to the Presbytery.

The Act of Parliament of 1592 (the Magna Carta of the Kirk) deals with the matter of innovations, and the General Assembly of 1866 construed the relevant section thus — "It belongs to the Presbytery to regulate matters concerning the conduct of public worship and the administration of ordinances in accordance with the laws and settled usages of the Church; and they are to take cognisance of the alleged existence or proposed introduction of any innovation or novel practice coming regularly to their notice, and after enquiry, if this appears necessary, are to give such deliverance as seems to be warranted by the circumstances of the case and the laws and usages of the Church; and it is their duty to enjoin the discontinuance or prohibit the introduction of any novel practice inconsistent with the laws and settled usages of the Church, or a cause of division in the congregation, or unfit for any cause to be used in the worship of God either in general or in the particular kirk."

One or two points here are worthy of note. First, that the Presbytery is not merely empowered but is put under obligation to deal with the matter of unwelcome innovations; secondly, that it is to do so when "such matters come regularly to its notice", and this would certainly be the case were any member or group of members to present a petition; and thirdly, that the fact merely that the innovation is causing division within the congregation is declared sufficient to condemn it — it does not have to be proved that it is inconsistent with the laws and settled usages of the Kirk.

Who May Conduct — As has been said, the conduct of public worship has been delegated to the Minister and the law is very strict as to whom he may allow to function in his stead. The authorised persons are Ministers (including Auxiliary Ministers), Probationers, regular Students of Divinity, Deaconesses licensed to preach and approved candidates for such licence, and Readers. The employment of anyone outside these categories is prohibited, though exception is made in certain circumstances for lay missionaries and agents of the Mission Department. Anyone engaging a person other than as above is required to give written intimation to the Presbytery Clerk within fourteen days along with an explanation of why that person was employed, and the Clerk is to report at next ordinary meeting of Presbytery (Act ix, 1934).

This Act has not to my knowledge been repealed, but it is treated with contempt these days. It is quite common today for a special service of some sort to be conducted by a group of Elders, or by members of the Woman's Guild, or by a Youth Group. However desirable this may be its legality seems to me highly questionable and in my view the Minister should at least be present throughout and should nominally be in charge of affairs — if anything is done amiss it is he and not the perpetrator who will be held responsible. It is he, certainly, who should pronounce the benediction — see hereunder.

Blessing the People — The Westminster Confession lays down that one of the principal functions of the ministry is to bless the people. This may be seen as fulfilled in the pronouncing of the benediction at the close of every service of public worship. It seems to me important, therefore, that this should be a blessing and not a prayer — "be with you", not "with us." I regard as quite wrong in this context a practice which is coming into fairly common use called "The Grace" whereby all present repeat together the words of the Pauline benediction, "The grace of the Lord Jesus Christ ...." Whatever attraction this may have liturgically I cannot believe it meets the requirement that the Minister should bless the people. And I have a personal conviction that his blessing should be confined to those who are there to receive it.

The Sacraments

One of the things listed above as belonging to the Minister subject to the direction and control of the Presbytery is the dispensing of the Sacraments. What that means is that no-one in the congregation has any say in how the Minister may dispense the Sacraments or whom he may appoint to do so in his place. The Assembly, however, has imposed certain restrictions in regard to the latter point.

Who May Dispense — The subject of who may dispense the Sacraments within a charge of the Church of Scotland is covered by the terms of Act iv of 1975. This distinguishes between the authority required for regular dispensation over a period (locum, exchange, etc) and permission to do so only on some once-only special occasion (baptism by the child's grandfather, and the like).

Those entitled to dispense on the former basis are —

a) Ministers holding the status of Ministers of the Church of Scotland;
b) Ministers of the United Reformed Church or of a Presbyterian Church whose doctrine is in keeping with our own and who has been duly authorised by the Presbytery of the bounds — such authority to be given only in special circumstances of which the Presbytery it sole judge;
c) A duly ordained Minister of one of the Lutheran or Reformed Churches in Europe, of the Waldensian Church, or of the Church of the Czech Brethren — all with authority of the Presbytery as in (b) above; and
d) An ordained Minister of a non-Presbyterian Church who holds an appropriate certificate from the Committee on Probationers and Transference of Ministers — again with authority of Presbytery as in (b) above.

A Parish Minister may on occasion invite a Minister of another denomination whose orders are in accordance with our standards to administer one of the Sacraments. This he may do completely on his own authority, but, if the invitation is accepted, the matter is to be reported in writing to the Presbytery Clerk within fourteen days after the event. I do not think this is ever done.

Baptism

In 1953, in response to an Overture from the Presbytery of Glasgow asking for a fresh examination of the Doctrine of Baptism with a view to securing "theological agreement and universal practice" with regard to this sacrament, the Assembly appointed a Commission which laboured for the next nine years over the production of a Statement on the Doctrine of Baptism. Interim reports had been remitted from time to time to Presbyteries for study and comment, until finally in 1962 the Statement went down as an Overture under Barrier Act procedure, being passed by the following Assembly into a standing law of the Church. Along with it went down another Overture designed to translate the theology into terms of practice. Both Overtures were approved and merged into one Act (xvii of 1963) anent the Administration of Baptism to Infants. This is a complete misnomer, for the theological part of the Act covers the whole subject of Baptism. This is the legislation which now governs the administration of Baptism to children, though how far it has achieved "theological agreement and universal practice" is an interesting question.

Infant Baptism — Baptism is to be administered to a child only in the case where one or both parents have been baptised and are (a) members, (b) *bona fide* adherents, or (c) desire to seek admission to full membership of the Church; or in the case where, the parents being unknown or having been separated from the child, the Kirk Session is satisfied that the child is under Christian care and guardianship. The parents or guardians who have to udertake the Christian upbringing of the child are to receive such instruction in the meaning of Baptism as the Minister may deem appropriate. In 1964 (Repts, p 64) the Assembly in connection with (b) agreed that absence from public worship due to "causes which render such attendance a practical impossibility" was not to be a barrier. In the case of (c) above an Elder is to be appointed to shepherd the parents into full communion and to exercise pastoral care over the child.

A Minister is not to baptise a child from another parish (unless the parents belong to his congregation) without consent of the Minister of that parish, and where a Minister has declined to administer baptism no other Minister may do so without consent of the Presbytery. It would seem, therefore, that when a Minister is approached by people not known to him with a request for the baptism of their infant he should first ask them whether an approach has already been made to some other Minister.

Baptism is normally to be administered in Church, but this is not essential; the facts of the baptism are to be entered in the Baptismal Register of the congregation; and a Certificate of Baptism is to be issued. Baptism is to be in the name of the Father, the Son, and the Holy Ghost, with water, and by sprinkling, pouring or immersion. Other elements may not be used. The Act makes no reference to this, but there is much to be said in favour of making an entry on the child's birth certificate recording the date and place and affirming that baptism was administered in water in name of the Trinity.

Change of Name — The name to be used in the service of Baptism should, naturally, be the name or names entered on the Birth Certificate. If, however, the Baptism takes place within twelve months of the date of birth a change of name may be effected at the request of the parents, and baptism should be administered using this name, otherwise the change will not be allowed. It is for the parents if they have not already done so to obtain the appropriate form from the Registrar and for the Minister to complete it. On its being returned (which must be within two years of the date of birth) the Registrar will enter the new name in the Register of Corrections.

Tinkers — In 1967 (Repts, p 12) the Assembly adopted certain guidelines for the baptism of the children of tinkers. A request for such baptism should be seen as an opportunity for evangelism, and it should be kept in mind that a refusal could easily be interpreted as meaning that the Church was not interested in tinkers. "Against this there is a considerable danger of an element of superstition being associated with the Sacrament unless the teaching and practice of Ministers deliberately guards against this. Every case would have to be regarded on its own merits. We would favour the administration of baptism whenever some kind of assurance of Christian upbringing could reasonably be given, and we would bear in mind that such assurance in the case of tinkers might not be quite what we would look for in the case of settled parishioners." Baptism should be administered in Church at a service in the usual way, and even where this is not possible "it should at least take place in the Church, and, of course, by the Parish Minister."

Adult Baptism — Baptism may also be administered to adults, the only qualification being that the person must be prepared to make profession of sin and promise of new obedience. It is common for baptism to be so administered at the time when the person is seeking to enter into full communion with the Church. It is important to note that admission to Communion does not supersede or include baptism and that care should be taken to ensure that only those already baptised are accepted for admission. The two may fittingly be encompassed in the one ceremony.

Service of Blessing — I digress for a moment from the Act to say that while the Church of Scotland has accepted infant baptism as its norm it has not insisted upon it as its rule. There are in the Church those who, while utterly committed to providing their children with Christian training and upbringing, are completely convinced that "believers' baptism" is the proper course, and so do not seek baptism for their children. Such parents may approach their Minister with a request for a service at which they may give thanks for the gift of their children, may seek a blessing upon them, and may commit themselves to their Christian nurture. In such circumstances I imagine the Minister would want to explain to them the tradition and significance of infant baptism, but if they remained unconvinced I am not aware of anything in the law or usage of the Church to prevent him acceding to their request, and I can see much to be said in favour of his so doing.

"Second Baptism" — In 1976 there came to the General Assembly an appeal which raised a question regarding the propriety and validity of "second baptism". The circumstances briefly were these. An elder who had been baptised as a child sought and received second baptism and appealed to the Assembly against a judgment of the Presbytery of Hamilton to the effect that he had erred in so doing. After a most interesting debate the Assembly rejected the appeal, reaffirming the confessional belief, shared with the Universal Church, and particularly with all branches of the Reformed Faith, that re-baptism is in violation of the doctrine of one baptism whether of infants or of believers, and of the article that baptism is administered but once to any person.

Then in 1982 a case came to the Assembly from the Presbytery of Caithness, involving this time a Minister and an Elder. The Assembly found that the two men, by their acceptance of second baptism (in the sea), had been guilty of repudiating the validity of their baptism as infants. A Special Commission was appointed to meet with the Presbytery and with the men concerned, who were to be admonished and rebuked, and in the case of the Minister an undertaking was to be obtained that he would uphold the doctrine and practice of the Church of Scotland in regard to the baptism of infants.

The Lord's Supper

Along with his general duty in relation to the administration of the Sacraments the Minister has, in terms of Act i of 1929 and Act xvii of 1931, the responsibility of the preparation of first communicants.

Confirmation — It has long been accepted in the Church of Scotland that the objective of the preparation which the Minister is here seeking to provide is for the confirmation by the candidate of the vows taken on his behalf at the time of his baptism, leading to his reception into the full communion of the Church. The Directory of 1592 has nothing to say about a service of admission. At that time, and for long afterwards, Kirk Sessions examined all members of congregations before each celebration of the Lord's Supper and decided whether or not they might be "admitted to the Table". It was in the latter half of the last century that there was introduced an Order of Admission in which first communicants made public confession of their faith. The Order Book of 1923 included a Form and Order for the Confirmation of Baptismal Vows and Admission to the Lord's Supper. What was in mind there, as it clearly states, was the confirmation of baptismal vows — the preamble reads that having in infancy received baptism "you have now of your own choice come forward to acknowledge before God and His Church the covenant made on your behalf......"

The use of the term "confirmation" can lead very easily to confusion with the confirmation which is conferred by a priest. This is illustrated by the fact that by the time of the Book of Order of 1940 the reference is to an "Order for the Confirmation of Baptized Persons and for their Admission to the Lord's Supper." It is the person who is to be confirmed, not the vows. This is a subtle but significant change. By the 1979 Book the Service has become simply "Confirmation and Admission to the Lord's Supper" and, interestingly, the candidate is asked to subscribe to a confession of faith but not to confirm baptismal vows. References in the 1994 Book to "the newly-confirmed" seem to indicate that the confirmation is something that happens to the candidates and not something that they do. It is clear that we now have a difference between people confirming vows and a priest confirming people. The latter position is clarified when a 1973 publication of the Committee on Public Worship and Aids to Devotion refers to confirmation as being "what God does to those who truly put their faith in Him and have committed their lives to him" and as meaning "making strong."

This latter, and very different, meaning of the word confirmation does not appear at any time to have been received at the hands of the General Assembly, and it is therefore to be accepted that the confirmation for which Ministers have to prepare candidates is something which is to be done by, not something which is to be received by, the candidate who has to confirm on his own account vows which had of necessity to be taken on his behalf. It is vows that are to be confirmed, not people.

Preparation of Communicants — It is the duty of the Minister to take under special instruction in the truths of the faith all who would enter the full communion of the Church — having first satisfied himself that they are all baptized persons. It is then for the Kirk Session to agree that they be admitted and have their names added to the Communion Roll of the congregation. The Minister will then, in face of the congregation, put to the candidates questions along the lines appointed, and on receiving satisfactory answers will in prayer receive them and commend them to the prayerful acceptance and care of the congregation. So far as I can discover, the Assembly have not approved any group of questions since those contained in Act xiii of 1935, and I conceive it is for the Minister concerned to devise his own list. Those on p 117 of the new "Common Order" seem admirable from every point of view.

Communion Service — The Communion is dispensed by the Minister, not by the Kirk Session, and it is not necessary that the court should be constituted for the celebration, though the fact should be recorded in the Session minutes. It is a custom of long standing that the Elders assist the Minister in the distribution of the elements, but there is no law requiring this to be so. At, say, a Dediction Service for the Woman's Guild it would be fitting and perfectly in order that Guild members should render this service. The Minister is in full charge of the Service, but it is the Kirk Session which determines the frequency and the times and seasons.

Private Communion — In 1690 the Assembly by Act x "hereby discharge the administration of the Lord's Supper to sick persons in their houses, and all other use of the same except in the public assemblies of the Church." No doubt this arose from the horror of idolatry (which could easily be detected in the use of reserved elements) that was so chacteristic of the Church of that day. I am not aware that the Act has been repealed, but the practice of taking Communion to the sick can today be said to have become legally established by use and wont. I think it most important, though, that such celebrations be seen as complete occasions and not as some kind of extension of a service already held, using "reserved elements". I think it very desirable, too, if the local Elder can attend so as, in a symbolic way, to bind the occasion into the corporate life of the congregation.

Marriage

Marriage was one of the Sacraments of the Roman Catholic Church which was discarded by the Reformers and the connection between Marriage and the Kirk has been of an odd character.

Prior to 1940 — The historical situation regarding marriage in Scotland was that there was a choice of two ways in which a couple could be wed

— the regular and the irregular. The former of these was a marriage conducted by a Minister of religion, the latter might take any one of three forms — *declaration de praesenti*, promise *subsequente copula*, or cohabitation with habit and repute. The first of these, *declaration de praesenti*, was in very popular use before it was abolished in terms of the Marriage (Scotland) Act of 1939. It consisted essentially in the parties taking one another as man and wife, usually, but not necessarily, in presence of witnesses. The introduction in 1855 of compulsory registration of births, marriages and deaths produced a complication — in order for such a marriage to be registered the fact of the consent had to be proved and this was most conveniently done by having a Sheriff examine the witnesses, after which he gave authority for registration. The simplest way to achieve all of this was to have the whole affair encompassed in the one exercise. Hence the tendency for those who so wed to claim (quite wrongly) that they had been "married by the Sheriff". *Promise subsequente copula* (also abolished by the 1939 Act) was of fairly rare occurrence because the promise had to be established, and it could be so proved only by writ or oath and neither of these was likely to be forthcoming if the claim was being contested. *Habit and repute* continues to this day. It refers to the case of a couple who are both free to marry and who have been living together as man and wife, being known to the world as such, but who have never gone through any ceremony. The issue arises usually over a question of succession after one of the parties has died and the surviving spouse approaches the court with a view to having the *de facto* situation regularised. The cohabitation may have begun when one of the parties was not free to marry, but if it is continued after the barrier has been removed it will still be valid (Campbell v Campbell 1867).

Civil Marriage — The Marriage (Scotland) Act 1939 considerably altered the position, in that it provided a new form of regular marriage. It could be said to have introduced a new division into marriage — as between religious marriage and civil marriage, This latter was marriage contracted in the office of an Authorised Registrar of Births, Marriages and Deaths. It demanded the same preliminaries as religious marriage (see hereunder) except that the Registrar would not accept a Certificate of Proclamation.

Preliminaries — Before a religious or a civil marriage could be celebrated certain preliminaries had to be gone through and a Schedule obtained from the Registrar of the District within which the marriage was to take place. There were three possibilities. The first of these was *Proclamation of Banns*, a practice of very ancient origin. In the Church(es) of the parish(es) of residence of the parties at the principal service on one, two, or three Sundays intimation was made of the intention to marry and opportunity was provided for anyone to object. Proclamation had to be in a Church of the Church of Scotland. (It was customary for a proclamation of intention to marry to be made in a Roman Catholic place of worship, but this had no legal validity.) To have the proclaiming confined to one Sunday was an irregularity for which an additional payment had to be made — this was a kind of fine and went to the Poor Fund. The second method was *Publication of Notice of Marriage* which was introduced by the Marriage Notice (Scotland) Act of 1878 and which consisted in having a notice of the proposed union exhibited for eight days on a board outside the Office of the Registrar of the District or Districts of residence of the parties. The third possible preliminary was a creation of the 1939 Act — *Licence*. Where "because of illness of one of the parties or other emergency" neither of the above methods had been pursued a joint application might be made to the Sheriff who could, if satisfied, grant a licence whose validity lasted for only ten days. It is not clear of what the Sheriff had to be satisfied, and it is difficult to imagine how "illness or other emergency" could prevent the doing of things that ought to have been done before the emergency arose. This provision was resorted to quite frequently during the war years, for obvious reasons. It should be noted that this form of licence was quite different from the licence and special licence which may be procured south of the border.

Proclamation No More — In 1975 the General Administration Committee reported to the Assembly (Repts 1975, p 11) that in connection with Lord Kilbrandon's examination of the operation of Scots Marriage Law it had been represented on behalf of the Church of Scotland that in modern days neither proclamation nor publication enjoyed effective publicity-value and that a system of annotation of birth-entries coupled with a much more rigorous examination of the credentials of those applying for a Marriage Schedule could prove more effectual in preventing bigamous and other illegal unions. The Assembly ratified the action that had been taken. The new Marriage Act was passed in 1977 and as from the beginning of the following year the calling of banns and the publication of notices officially ceased. The proposal for the annotation of birth entries has, however, never been implemented; though in fairness it has to be conceded that no noticeable increase in bigamous unions has occurred!

Marriage (Scotland) Act 1977 — In conformity with the demands of a multi-racial society the scope of religious marriage has, under the 1977 legislation, been extended to embrace those of other faiths so long as monogamy is accepted and adequate vows undertaken. In place of the former preliminaries the couple have now to present themselves at the office of the Registrar of the District within which the marriage is to be celebrated, and this a fortnight to three months before the crucial date, taking with them their Birth Certificates. The Registrar will issue a Marriage Schedule, and this must be presented to the Minister before the wedding begins. In terms of the Act the Minister is guilty of a criminal offence if he conducts a marriage service in the absence of such a Schedule. No matter what the pressure from a swooning bride, an hysterical mother, or a threatening father, the Minister must set his face as a flint against any kind of ceremony until the Schedule is in his hands.

Although proclamation is no longer a necessary preliminary to marriage in Scotland, and although Act iii of 1978 repealed all earlier legislation concerning it, rescinding Schedules and Regulations relevant thereto, the same Act conserved the right for any person usually resident in Scotland to have banns proclaimed in a church in his parish of residence if this is going to facilitate marriage furth of Scotland where evidence of proclamation is required. This will apply to marriages to be conducted south of the border in the Church of England where not only is evidence of proclamation demanded, it must have been made on three separate Sundays. It has been agreed, however, that if the parties are known to him the Minister may proclaim on one Suday only, otherwise on two.

Marriage of Foreigners — The marriage in Scotland of a pair of foreigners, or of a foreigner with a British subject is, if it satisfies the requirements of Scots law, valid throughout H M Dominions, but it will not necessarily be accepted in the country to which the foreigner (the bridegroom, say) belongs, and to which it may be his intention in the long run to return. It will be so only if the legal requirements of that country are complied with. In the interest of his partner (the bride) and of her possible children the Minister will do well to ensure that steps are timeously taken to secure from the Consul or other diplomatic representative of the country concerned a satisfactory assurance that the marriage will be accepted as valid in the country concerned. If not he should warn the bride very seriously of the possible consequences, though, of course, the decision must be hers, and so long as he has a Schedule in his hand the Minister has no legal justification for not proceeding.

Form of Service — Under the Act of Parliament it is left to Ministers of the Church of Scotland to follow their own form of service, but the Assembly of 1977 passed a Declaratory Act setting forth the basic minima which the Church currently requires as essential to constitute a valid marriage service — first that the marriage must be celebrated by an ordained Minister in a religious ceremony wherein before God and in presence of the Minister and at least two competent witnesses, (over fourteen and *compus mentis)* the parties take each other as man and wife for life and are declared by the Minister to be so united; and secondly that the Minister assures himself that the legal requirements have been met and that the parties know of no legal impediment; and that he ensures the due completion of the Marriage Schedule (Repts 1977, p 10).

Legal Requirements — The legal requirements referred to above are that the parties are of age and are not related within the forbidden degrees. There is in Scotland no need for parental consent. The minimum age for marriage is sixteen and some years ago the then Procurator gave the opinion that a Minister should not celebratc a marriage until at earliest the day after the sixteenth birthday of the younger party. To be a "competent witness" the person must be at least fourteen years of age and *compus mentis.* In a case where one of the parties is illiterate he should make a cross where the Minister writes "John Bloggs X His Mark" and this should be subscribed by two witnesses — preferably not the same as those signing as witnesses to the marriage.

When Are They Married? — While it is most important that the Minister should ensure the due completion of the Schedule I am clear that this is not an essential constituent of the actual marriage but only a piece of machinery connected with its registration. Suppose, for example, that the bridegroom suffered a fatal heart attack on the way from the sanctuary to the vestry there could be no signature and therefore no completion of the Schedule. I am quite clear, however, that in such circumstances there had been a marriage and that the bride had thus become a widow with all the legal implications in regard to property, pension, etc which that condition carried. I am fairly sure the Minister and the witnesses would need to appear before a Sheriff to testify to the fact that mutual consent had been given and the couple had been declared wed. On the strength of this the Sheriff would, as I see it, authorise the registration of the marriage in the absence of the completed Schedule.

Who May Celebrate? — Although the tenet that marriage is a Sacrament was departed from by the Reformers the Assembly have consistently resisted any attempt to allow other than an ordained Minister to celebrate marriage. In a very few cases authority has been given to a Lay Missionary on an island where there was no resident Minister. The suggestion in 1985 advanced by the Education for the Ministry Committee (Repts 1985, p 6) that a Probationer in course of his Probationary Period might be permitted as part of "his supervised training and experience" to conduct a marriage service was rejected by the Assembly. When a Minister is to be involved in an extended exchange it can be an advantage, and is perfectly in order, for the Presbytery to "authorise Mr AB, Minister of the Presbyterian Church of ..... at ..... to solemnise marriage according to the forms of the Church of Scotland." Both Registrar General and local Registrar should be informed and furnished with an extract minute.

Place of Marriage — Civil Marriage may be contracted only in the Office of an Authorised Registrar. There is no restriction upon where Religious Marriage may be celebrated and from time to time one reads of the most outrageous choice of venue. Because of its association with Runaway Marriage and the blacksmith's anvil (see hereunder) Gretna is still a popular choice. For a very long time most Scots marriages took place either in the Manse, in the hotel or hall where the reception was later to be held, or, occasionally, in the home of the bride. Today this is very rare, most weddings being celebrated in Church. Although the service is to be in Church it need not be in public and the doors may be kept closed.

The Marriage Schedule specifies where the marriage is to take place. A problem can arise if through some emergency the locus has to be changed at the last moment. Suppose, for example, that a wedding has been fixed for a Saturday afternoon in Church but is complicated by the bridegroom being in hospital as the result of an accident. Provided the hospital is in the same Registration District as the church the marriage may proceed, the Minister making the necessary alteration in the Schedule and signing the change as well as enclosing a note explaining the circumstances. Otherwise I think every effort should be made to contact the Registrar of the District (of the Hospital), though I still think the marriage could proceed.

"Ecclesiastical Marriage" — I have throughout this section used the term "religious marriage" which I believe to be much preferable to the term "ecclesiastical marriage" which made its appearance for the first time in the 1977 Act. It seems an unfortunate choice since the object of the Act is to confer authority to conduct marriages upon a variety of religious groups some of which would emphatically deny that they are Churches.

Gretna Green — In a distant day when south of the Border a bride had to be of a certain age before she could marry without parental consent the road which crossed the Sark to enter Scotland at Gretna became a road of romance, and many an exciting tale was told of the post-chaise heading north at incredible speed to outdistance the pursuing carriage of the bride's enraged father. Post-boys from hotels in and around Carlisle specialised in the art of evasion. In many cases the whole affair was more sordid than anything else, but the element of romance was accentuated by the custom of the local blacksmith (there were two of them competing for the business) of conducting a service of sorts over his anvil. A change in English law in 1754 brought the business to a close. In the 1950's, however, the practice re-emerged, this time for couples under twenty-one from the continent. Now, however, Scots law demanded a fifteen-day residential qualification on the part of one of the parties before application for either proclamation or publication could be accepted with a further eight days for objections to be lodged and young people were living in and around Gretna (on the Scottish side) in many cases in conditions of great squalor for the requisite three weeks. This, which had become little short of a scandal was brought to an end, but the aura of romance lingers and the Authorised Registrar at Gretna boasts by far the highest marriage rate in all of Scotland.

Re-Marriage of Divorced Persons — In terms of Act xxvi of 1959 a Minister is at liberty to marry a divorced person whose ex-spouse is alive, but is expected to adhere to the following requirements —

a) He should not accede as a matter of course but should carefully inform himself concerning the life and character of the parties, the grounds and circumstances of the divorce, the future facing any children concerned, whether any other Minister has refused to celebrate, and regarding the ecclesiastical affiliation of the parties.
b) He must carefully consider the possibility of scandal should he accede, and of doing spiritual hurt should he refuse.
c) He must assure himself there has been repentance where guilt was involved.
d) He is not required to solemnise such a marriage against his conscience. Each Presbytery is to appoint certain individuals with one of whom a Minister in doubt or difficulty may consult.

The Act also required that the number of such marriages should be reported in the annual statistical returns, but this condition was repealed by the Assembly of 1985.

Funerals

The only law one can find on the subject of funerals comes from the Directory of 1645 which says, "When any person departeth this life, let the dead body upon the day of burial, be decently accompanied from the house to the place appointed for public burial, and there immediately interred without any public ceremony." It is added, "Howbeit it is convenient that the company apply themselves to suitable conference; and that the minister, if he be present, seek to edify, as at other times."

The long-established custom of the Church is that, unless in very exceptional circumstances, when this is asked-for a Parish Minister will conduct a funeral service in respect of any of his parishioners deceased. Where such a service is desired it is important that the Minister should be consulted before times are finally fixed. It is all too common today for undertaker and crematorium authority to fix the affair and then expect the Minister somehow to "fit it in". In the case where the Minister may feel that the life of the deceased was such as to make something of a mockery of Christian burial it is well for him to remember that there are relatives and friends who are in sore need of comfort (a need all the greater, doubtless, because of the character of their loved one) and that towards them he has a special pastoral responsibility. Indeed the occasion of a death can provide an admirable entry to a home where otherwise there might have been scant welcome and to hearts not always so very receptive to the Christian message.

Before the days of cremation the custom was for there to be a fairly full service in Church or in the house of the deceased where either the person had died or the body had been "brought home", and then a brief committal service at the graveside, the degree of brevity being dictated by the weather conditions. With the shelter provided by the crematoria and the tendency for folk to attend there in considerable numbers it seems unfair to have only a brief committal service there, with the result that there has inclined to be a duplication of the whole service. I think those arranging the funeral should be advised to choose which is to be the place for the public gathering and to reserve the other as a private affair for family and intimate friends. The minister can then adapt accordingly.

The crematoria are, understandably, becoming fussy about timing —

some threatening to charge an extra fee for time over-run beyond the half-hour allowed. Ministers should note that the thirty-minute limit has to include getting folk into their places and emptying the hall afterwards and accordingly the maximum time available for the actual service is twenty minutes at the very most. The whole day's schedule can be upset and other people greatly incommoded when this time-limit is not observed — and there is no excuse for the failure.

The Instruction of the Young

The instruction of the young also belongs to the Minister under direction and control of the Presbytery. It is a duty which he shares with the Kirk Session who "have to make provision for systematic Christian education through the establishment and maintenace of such supervised learning opportunities as seem appropriate to all ages and stages of development of the young people." The Session also acts along with the Minister in the appointing of the Leader of the Sunday School, and it has to approve the appointment of Sunday School teachers (Repts 1985, p 431).

The Minister is "head" of the Sunday School (even when, as is almost invariably the case, someone else acts as Superintendent). There is here in this divided responsibility the possibility of trouble where, for example, the Minister as "head" sees things differently from the Superintendent as "leader" and both disagree with the Kirk Session as "supervisor". As I see it, the Minister would have the final word at congregational level, but the Kirk Session, if it took the disagreement very seriously and was convinced that the Minister was wrong, would be entitled to reach its own decision on how things ought to be done, and if the Minister indicated he was not prepared to comply the Session could petition the Presbytery under whose direction and control, it will be remembered, the Minister is acting.

Notarial Execution of Wills

The Church of Scotland (Property and Endowments) Amendment Act of 1925 provides (Sec 13) that "a minister of the Church of Scotland who has been appointed to a charge without limit of time or for a period of years to officiate as minister shall, in any parish in which such charge or part thererof is situated, have the like power as regards the notarial execution of wills or other testamentary writings as is conferred by Section 18 (1) of the Conveyancing (Scotland) Act 1924 on a parish minister acting in his own parish." The Act further provides that a certificate by the Principal Clerk of Assembly stating the parish in which the charge of any such minister is situated will be accepted as conclusive evidence thereof.

What Is It? — The power of notarial execution in this limited context is the authority to write out a will for a person who is blind, or illiterate, or too ill to be able to write. For such a will to be valid the utmost care must be taken to ensure that cerain conditions are complied with. First, obviously, the testator must be blind, illiterate or too ill to be able to write. Secondly, the Minister must be acting within the civil parish in which his own ecclesiastical area or part of it is situated — that is to say, he is strictly confined, but not confined within the bounds of his own ecclesiastical parish, for his power extends over the whole of the civil parish in which the other lies, and may indeed include a second civil parish as well. Thirdly, the Minister has to have the will written out or typed out, and he has to read it over to the grantor in presence of two witnesses who must also hear or see authority given to the Minister to sign. Fourthly, the Minister is to add the docquet as shown hereunder. It is essential that this docquet be in the Minister's handwriting. Fifthly, he has then in presence of the grantor and of the two witnesses to add his own signature to each page as well as to the docquet, being particularly careful on the last page to add the date of signing. This last can be of great importance as otherwise it may not be possible to establish that the will supersedes one of an earlier date. Sixthly, the two witnesses have now to sign in the spaces indicated, adding the word "Witness" after their names. And lastly, the Minister may not be an executor, a beneficiary, a trustee, or have any other interest under the will.

Custody of Will — When a Minister has been asked to act in this way he will be wise to have the will scrutinised by a solicitor to verify that it is all in order. Should the grantor express a desire that the Minister retain the will "for safe keeping" he should treat the request sympathetically — for it may well suit next-of-kin (who usually have ready access to the house and effects following on the death) that the will should not be found. If he agrees to hold the document the Minister should arrange that there be put among the grantor's papers a note to the effect that there is a will in his keeping.

Form of Docquet — The following is the form of docquet prescribed by the Conveyancing (Scotland) Act 1924 in the case where the grantor of the deed is blind or cannot write.

Read over to, and signed by me for, and by authority of, the above-named AB (without designation) who declares that he is blind (*or* is unable to write), all in his presence and in the presence of the witnesses hereto subscribing.

Signed by me at ...... this ...... day of ...... Nineteen hundred and .... Minister's Signature Minister of the Parish of ....

Signature .... Witness
Address .... Designation ....

Signature .... Witness
Address .... Designation ....

Limitation — It is important to note that notarial power vests in the Minister only for this limited purpose and that he has no authority to attest any document which requires to be sworn in presence of a Justice of the Peace or of a Notary Public.

Extra-Parochial Activities

Civil Judicatories — Until fairly recently Ministers were, under pain of deposition, forbidden to be members of any civil or criminal judicatory or of Parliament. Act xxvii of 1959 removed this disability and there is now no Church impediment to a Minister being, for example, a Justice of the Peace, or sitting in Parliament (but see hereunder), and the ban did not extend to being a member of the House of Lords.

Acting as a Juror — In terms of the Jurors (Scotland) Act 1825 all Ministers were exempted from sitting on juries and therefore were never called for such service. This has been altered in terms of a Law Reform Act of 1980 which provides that Ministers may be called as jurors but that if they do not wish to accept service they are automatically excused.

Clergy Disqualification — It has been stated above that there is no Church impediment to prevent a Minister sitting as a Member of Parliament. There is, however, a civil disqualification banning Ministers of any of the Established Churches and of the Roman Catholic Church, and that not merely from sitting as Members but from even entering as candidates in a Parliamentary election. Before he can be nominated as a candidate a Minister of the Church of Scotland must resign not only his charge but also his status. This is serious if he is elected, but even more so if he is not! There seems no reason why the national Churches should be singled out for this disability and I understand the matter is under discussion with the Library of the House. It would appear that the Church of England has a procedure whereby in such circumstances a clergyman may submit his resignation to his Bishop in such a way that if elected to Parliament his resignation is seen as having taken effect, otherwise it is regarded as having been withdrawn. The Church of Scotland was asked whether it could devise similar machinery but replied that since the trouble arose from the existence of a law for which there was no justification it would seem appropriate that the change should be made at that end. The Assembly have now indicated a specific desire to have the civil law amended with a view to the removal of this anomaly.

Employment Outwith the Church — There came to the Assembly in 1942 (Session 9) a case in the form of an appeal against the judgment of a Presbytery deciding that a Minister who had accepted the position of Town Clerk (in a very small burgh) which he proposed to exercise in conjunction with his charge must relinquish the Town Clerkship. The Assembly upheld the judgment of the Presbytery.

In 1950, in response to an Overture from the Presbytery of Kirkcaldy, the General Assembly passed an Act (xxii) to the effect that no Minister in a regular charge may undertake any contract of remunerative employment within or outwith the jurisdiction of the Church without previously having obtained the approval of the Presbytery of the bounds or of a higher court of the Church. The Assembly went on to enjoin Presbyteries to exercise the utmost care in dealing with applications from Ministers for permission to undertake such employment, to obtain the opinion of the Kirk Session concerned, to satisfy itself as to the number of hours involved and the suitability of the proposed employment, and to secure that the Minister would be free at any hour when pastoral duties were required, and that he would have adequate time for the proper discharge of all his ministerial responsibilities, including visitation, study and preparation for the pulpit, oversight of congregational organisations, and attendance at Church courts.

In-Service Training

Courses on various aspects of the work of the ministry are organised on a residential basis by the Board of Ministry, but the "less than stisfactory recruitment" to these courses has been consistently commented upon. In 1984 (Repts, p 465) reporting on the proven worth of the courses the comment is offered that they are of value "not least for the Minister who claims to be 'too busy to take time off' but for whom an opportunity to evaluate his or her ministry, its priorities, its motivation, and its theological base might well be precisely what makes it worthwhile, necessary even, to take time off to be at a course."

Ministerial Workload

The Maintenance of the Ministry Committee in its Report to the 1991 Assembly referred to the fact that its Medical Panel was disturbed at "the haphazard arrangements for ministerial time-off" and urged that steps be taken to provide a system whereby ministers could have two days off each week. The Assembly gave a qualified approval but recognised there were problems.

In 1993 it was reported that "the Committee wishes to reiterate the reasons which appear to make this necessary. First, recreation is an important factor in the health of any human being — ministers are no different in this respect from the rest of the congregation. Secondly, it can only be to the benefit of ministers, their families and their congregations to be working at peak efficiency — a situation which cannot obtain when the minister is exhausted. Thirdly, while ministers are the first to advise others on the need to have time for themselves, for their families and their friends, they do not at present set a very good example. Fourthly, because of the life-style commitment of the role, many ministers find it difficult to take any time off without feeling guilty — there is a need therefore to confirm a minister's right to time off from parish and congregational duties" (Repts 1990, p 87).

"Basic Tasks of the Ordained Ministry" — In this connection the Assembly Council in 1990 brought in a report to the Assembly and this was printed with a limited circulation in view, primarily to encourage discussion. Much interest has been manifested in the booklet — and that not by any means exclusively within the Church of Scotland.

Balance of Ministerial Duties — An Appendix is added which is perhaps worth reprinting at length, setting forth those aspects of ministry that have to be kept in mind in any study of this subject.

1 A minister is ordained to the Ministry of Word and Sacrament.

2 The minister is responsible for the conduct of public worship and the Sacraments.

3 A minister will have duties to undertake at the specific request of

Presbytery, the General Assembly or its Committees, in addition to the duties of congregation and parish.

4 The minister is inducted to a specific pastoral charge as pastor to congregation and parish. The care of the sick, the bereaved, and others in a wide range of pastoral need, is a prime task of Christian ministry to be undertaken both personally and with others.

5 The minister is responsible for the conduct of both marriages and funerals within the charge and parish, and also for the counselling related to this work.

6 The minister has the responsibility for the supervision of youth work and of educational work for both young and old including the instruction of new communicants.

7 Ministers may be asked to undertake chaplaincy work in schools, colleges and universities, hospitals, prisons and industry, and other work within the local community.

8 Ministers are required in the course of their work, to undertake administrative functions in relation to congregations and their courts, the Presbytery, the General Assembly and its Committees.

9 A minister is the Moderator of the Kirk Session. In most congregations he/she may also act as chairperson of the financial court of the congregation. In either capacity, a minister is required to uphold the decisions of superior courts as they pertain to the inferior court.

An admirable statement in its way, but it does not go very far towards helping the over-zealous and over-worked minister to find the equivalent of two days per week when he can be completely free of parish responsibilities. There can be no doubt that many Ministers would benefit both in their personal and family lives and in the discharge of their duties if their affairs were more orderly organised but it is difficult to see how a job many of whose most demanding calls inevitably arise in the most haphazard and unpredictable way can be made to fit into a neat and tidy work-programme. One can only hope the day will not come when a minister receiving a sudden and unexpected call of need will respond, "I'll see what I can do tomorow — this is my day off." Like so many other aspects of the calling ministerial time-off does not readily lend iself to legislation.

THE MINISTER AS CHAPLAIN

The introduction of — and in recent times the vast increase in the number of — chaplaincies of one sort and another raises problems in connection with the rule that no Minister may perform ministerial functions within the parish of another. Such chaplaincies today are connected with the Armed Forces, with Hospitals, with Prisons, with Universities, with Schools, and with Industry. Obviously the field of work of such Chaplains will often lie within someone else's ecclesiastical parish, for only in a very few cases of part-time chaplaincies will all the duties of the office be confined within the Chaplain's own parish. The matter was the subject of a report to the General Assembly of 1954.

For a variety of reasons — all of them administrative — most such appointments are made by the National Mission Committee which is also responsible for collecting and transmitting the salary. It is, though, most important that every such appointment should have the authority and approval of the Presbytery concerned. For in terms of Act viii of 1933 it is the Presbytery of the bounds which alone may permit one Minister to enter the parish of another for the discharge of limited ministerial functions, including the administration of the Sacraments, as the Presbytery may specifically authorise. Appointment by the Presbytery to the chaplaincy may therefore be taken as implying that this degree of authority has been conferred. *Industrial Chaplains* — These are chosen by an Inter-Church Committee, the Presbytery being notified by the Assembly Committee and asked merely to note that the appointment has been made. It seems to me that if the appointee is a Church of Scotland Minister then unless the factory lies in his parish the least that can be required is that the Presbytery authorise his intrusion into the parish concerned and to that extent approve of his appointment, for I do not think a minister can officiate within the parish of another on the mere say-so of an Assembly Committee, still less of an Inter-Church Committee.

Hospital Chaplains — It is not uncommon that a long-term patient in hospital (to take an example) expresses a desire to enter into the full membership of the Church. In such a case the Chaplain should get in touch with the patient's own Minister, or if he has no Church connection with the Minister of his parish of residence, should arrange for the patient to receive a short course of instruction, should with the approval of the Kirk Session concerned admit and receive him, and ensure that his name has been entered in the appropriate Communion Roll.

Baptism — When there are urgent reasons or special circumstances rendering necessary, or at least advisable, the administration of baptism to a child within the context of the Hospital Chaplain's work he should so administer, and as soon as possible thereafter should send particulars of the baptism to the Minister of the congregation with which connection is claimed, or to the Minister of the parish within which the parents reside, or to the Clerk of the Presbytery involved so that he may pass these to whoever is responsible and in this way they may be entered in an appropriate Baptismal Register. I understand that in some Maternity Hospitals a Baptismal Register is kept. I incline to the view that a baptism in the parish should also be recorded in the Parish Register.

School Chaplaincies — These are in a class by themselves in that a Minister is not appointed to a school chaplaincy by a Presbytery or any other Church authority — he is invited to accept the position by the Head Teacher and continues in office during the latter's pleasure. The Parish Minister, though he will usually be welcome as a visitor to the school, has no rights in the matter, and in particular has no claim *ex officio* to act as Chaplain.

Forces Registers — The General Assembly of 1970 approved Regulations whereby the Committee on Chaplains to H M Forces is required to maintain a register of all persons admitted to full communion during the period of their service in the Forces. The Committee is further required to issue to each such person on request on his returning to civilian life a certificate testifying that he has been so admitted. The Committee also maintains a register of all who have received baptism during their period of service. These registers are meticulously prepared and maintained and Certificates will be issued on appliction to the Secretary of the Committee. His only complaint is that he so rarely receives such requests.

RETIRED MINISTERS

Age Limit — Up till now it has been accepted that a Minister retiring in the normal way from a charge or an appointment on account of age or to facilitate readjustment will retain his seat in Presbytery and will be entitled to exercise all the functions of the ministry — always, of course, subject to the supervision of the Presbytery. This is no longer the situation, the position since 1995 being that demission of a charge involves loss of the seat in Presbytery unless in the case of the Minister who, following notice of his desire to demit, lodges in writing a declaration of his intention to attend Presbytery and to participate in the work of its Committees. This of course applies only to those retiring after the date of the Act (1985). The declaration has to be renewed annually and will cease to be effective after age seventy-five. While the right to a seat in Presbytery has thus been restricted there is no age limit imposed on the right of retired ministers to undertake ministerial duties except as noted hereunder.

Ministerial Certificate — The Ministerial Certificate (sometimes called the Practising Certificate) first emerged in terms of Act i of 1976 which has now been superseded by Act ii of 1987. The new Act substantially repeats the provisions of the earlier one and I propose to deal only with the latter. The functions of the ministry are defined as — (a) the conduct of public worship, (b) the administration of the Sacraments, and (c) the solemnisation of marriage, and the possessor of a valid Ministerial Certificate is authorised to exercise these "generally and particularly" — to wit — (a) on an occasional basis, (b) in employment as *locum tenens*, and (c) in connection with an assistantship or office under the jurisdiction of the Presbytery or an appointment which has been approved by the Presbytery. The Certificate is issued on an annual basis its validity expiring on 30th June in each year.

Issuing and Renewing — Within two months of demission or resignation involving loss of seat in Presbytery application for a Certificate should be made in writing to the Presbytery Clerk. However, whether or not an application is submitted the Presbytery is to take the case into its consideration and is to resolve to grant or to withhold or to take other action, a decision to withhold requiring that cause be shown and recorded in the minute. The unsuccessful applicant is to be cited to the meeting when the matter is reported and to be given an opportunity to speak in defence. I imagine also he has a right of appeal to the General Assembly. Application for renewal of the Certificate is to be made in writing to the Clerk of Presbytery not later than 30th April in each year, otherwise the Certificate will lapse and cannot be renewed before the following year. The application is to set forth "details of present employment and of ministerial functions discharged since the issue of the current Certificate. On moving to the bounds of another Presbytery the Minister is to exhibit the Certificate to the Clerk within two months of arrival. In the absence of a Ministerial Certificate a Minister may not be associated in the work of a Kirk Session.

Review by Presbytery — Section 15 of the Act reads — "In the event of a Ministerial Certificate being withheld when first applied for, or on failure to make application, or on appliction for renewal, the Minister concerned may, after the expiry of at least two years from the date when it was withheld, make application for the issue or restoration of such Certificate to the Presbytery which withheld it; and that Presbytery may, after such enquiry as seems necessary by its Superintendence Committee, or other Committee as above, and after giving opportunity for the Minister to be heard, issue a Certificate, either immediately or after such period of supervision as may be determined, whether within its own bounds or as may be arranged with another Presbytery." I have difficulty with the second of the three situations referred to, failure to apply for renewal. First, I find it difficult to see how something can be "withheld" if it has not been applied for. And secondly, and more seriously I cannot believe it is intended that someone who overlooked the need to apply for renewal should be denied the right to function for at least two solid years.

List of Ministers with Certificate — I quote Section 19 — "Each Presbytery shall keep a list of Ministers who have been granted a Ministerial Certificate or have exhibited such Certificate to it. A copy of this List shall be sent to the Principal Clerk of the General Assembly on 30th June each year, or as soon as possible thereafter, and any changes in the course of the year shall be intimated as they occur."

"Practising Certificate" — For myself I much prefer this title. Its possession is not primarily proof of status but of authorisation to exercise the functions of that status — two quite different things. There are those who have the status of Ministers of the Church of Scotland but who from their own choice do not want, as well as those who because of a Presbytery judgment do not hold, a Ministerial Certificate. For my own part I think it most important that a Presbytery should maintain a list of those resident within its bounds who are Ministers of the Kirk, and they might mark in a suitable way those of them who hold valid Ministerial Certificates.

The Act is unsatisfactory in many ways. To take a simple instance, as the Act stands a Minister on his retiral has no intention of carrying out any ministerial functions in the days ahead, he just wants to be retired and enjoy the relaxation he has missed, so he does not apply for a Certificate. Six months later his grand-daughter is about to be wed and insists Gran'pa must officiate. But he can't. He has no Certificate and he cannot get one till June two years away. That surely is a nonsense. Or again, conduct of worship is defined as a ministerial function. It is being performed, none the less, by all kind of folk, but it daren't be performed by a retired Minister who has forgotten to apply timeously for renewal of his Certificate. Another nonsense, surely. In cases like those quoted the general reaction, I know, is that the situation is so ludicrous you just have to shut your eyes to what the Act says and go ahead in a responsible way — everybody knows the law is an ass. This is an attitude to regulations that one does not want to see encouraged. The Act, I suggest, is needing to be looked at very carefully and to be completely revised.

Relation with Former Parish — This may be a suitable point at which to introduce a word about the relation between the retired Minister and the parish from which he has gone. I have no knowledge of any law covering this subject, and indeed find it difficult to conceive what kind of legislation would prove of value in a situation which depends so completely on good sense. What only too often happens is that a want of thought and consideration on the part of the retired Minister and a super-sensitivity and readiness to find cause of offence on the part of his successor creates much needless unhappiness. One cannot expect a Minister whose whole working life has been spent in the one community to cut himself off completely from all his friends; on the other hand the new Minister hurrying to offer his services in a case of bereavement of which he has just heard cannot but resent meeting his predecessor leaving the premises. In a case, where, for example, the Minister has been granted occupancy of the manse he might consider (or be urgently advised to consider) transferring his membership to another congregation. One of our men never went to a Session meeting but found four men with clerical collars, one of them his immediate predecessor, occupying the front seat. His nervous breakdown took none of us by surprise.

As I have said, this is a realm where consideration, imagination and good sense — on both sides — must take the place of legal enactment. A word of advice offered by a trusted neighbour could often prove of considerable value.

Chapter 7

MAINTENANCE OF THE MINISTRY

THE NAME USUALLY APPLIED to the upkeep of the ministry is "maintenance of the ministry", and the name all but universally applied to the income of the Minister of a parish is "stipend". The same term is often used for the income of ministers generally even though holding appointments other than parochial charges, though this is not strictly correct. Properly speaking "stipend" is to be distinguished from salary in two important respects. For one thing it was not paid by anyone comparable to an employer but belonged to the benefice or living and vested in the Minister in virtue of his having been inducted as Minister of the parish. In early days it was paid in two half-yearly moieties at Whitsunday and Michaelmas and vested in the Minister who was incumbent on those days. Why it should have been Michaelmas rather than Martinmas is not clear — the latter would have represented a fairer division of the year, and by November the season's crop would have been gathered. The other distinctive feature of stipend was that the first charge upon it was to meet all expenses incurred in the performance of the office, only the balance which remained thereafter being available for the support of the Minister and his dependants.

Neither of these considerations applies today. The ministry is still a *munus publicum* and there is no master-servant relationship, but stipend is now invariably paid *de die in diem* through the Committee on the Maintenance of the Ministry; and in recent years the introduction of Listed Expenses has ensured that first one and then another of the outlays necesssarily incurred by the Minister in the performance of his duties are met from congregational funds, so that the whole of the stipend is available for his private enjoyment. For all practical purposes the Minister of today is in receipt of a salary, though since tradition dies hard (nowhere harder than in the Kirk) it is still quite invariably referred to as a stipend.

PRIOR TO 1929

The Union of 1929 brought together three separate strands of Churchmanship and each of these had its own method of paying its ministers, hammered out over a long period in each case. Let us trace these briefly.

The Old Parish

The old Parish Churches (there were some nine hundred of them) was supported by a charge on the fruits of the land, stipend being paid by the heritors (the local landowners) out of teind. The history of teind is of considerable significance and of no little interest and merits a brief historical survey.

Teind — The pre-Refomation Church in Scotland had been an extremely wealthy institution. From the fourteenth century the principle had been accepted that the Church enjoyed a right to a share in the produce of the land, and the practice had developed of awarding a tenth or teind. Within fifty years, thanks to the spontaneos generosity of some and to pressure applied by a powerful Church in the case of others, the system of teinds for the support of the clergy had come to be established throughout the country. These came to be known as the "spiritualities", and until the mid-nineteenth century they constituted the principal — indeed almost the only — source of ministerial income. There were also, however, the "temporalities" — things like glebes and also vast grants of land made by the Crown and others and said, before the Reformation, to cover one-third of the area of Scotland and to represent one-half of the country's wealth. At the Reformation the leaders of the new Church were generous to a fault in allowing the former Romish priests to retain two-thirds of the teinds they had been enjoying, the remainder being for the Ministers who were doing the work of the parishes. This, needless to say, was intended as a temporary measure to see out the life-time of the priests, but it got itself established, so that in the end of the day the Reformed Church found itself with roughly one-third of the spiritualities and even less of the temporalities. For some reason which no-one seems able to explain the Reformers did not advance any claim to these rich lands so that they reverted, some to the Crown, others to adjoining proprietors. John Knox's dream of every parish in Scotland equipped with a school, a schoolhouse and a dominie, as well as with a kirk, a manse and a minister was destined to remain a dream.

In 1617 an Act of Parliament reformed the law of teinds to the effect that they were no longer paid into a common pool but were kept to their parishes of origin for the support of the Ministers of these parishes. This gave rise to the tag *decimae debentur parocho* — the teinds are owed to the parish — a principle that has been largely honoured ever since (but see "Area of Preference" p 184).

Burgh Churches — In the mid-eighteenth century the whole face of Scotland was changed as the Industrial Revolution moved the base of the nation's economy from agriculture to manufacture. One result was a massive migration of population and the creation of new communities often far from a parish church, which in any case was probably inadequate to cater for the new numbers. Additional buildings and an enormously increased ministry were desperately needed, but there were no heritors who could be required to put up the buildings and there was no spare teind from which the stipends could come. The first attempt to cope with this acute problem took the form of legislation to establish Burgh Churches in the cities and principal towns where the problem was most urgent — Edinburgh had fourteen, Glasgow eight, Aberdeen six, Dundee four, Paisley and Perth three each, Greenock and Stirling two each and one in each of Queensferry, Dumfries and Kilmarnock. In these cases it was the municipal authorities who were required to erect the buildings and also to provide the stipends — all out of funds within their control. These, forty-five in all, were the Burgh Churches.

Parishes quoad sacra — So far, however, merely the fringe of the problem of Church Extension had been touched, and all over the country Chapels of Ease were coming into being on local initiative, and in 1844 it became possible to have these converted into Parishes *quoad sacra*. Before a Chapel could be so upgraded there had to be endowments, in the form of feu-duties and ground annuals, sufficient to provide an annual stipend of £120, or of £100 where a manse was also being provided. The idea of a congregation paying directly towards stipend out of regular income was being very reluctantly accepted in the Old Kirk, even if by this time it was established practice in the congregations of the Secessions. A hint of things to come was to be found in most *quoad sacra* constitutions which provided that surplus income was to go to stipend. A recommendation of the Assembly of 1884 was to the effect that surplus revenue should go to stipend after a certain limited percentage had been set apart as a sinking fund for fabric repairs.

Stipend Augmentation — In the eighteenth century stipends generally stood at a miserably low level. Just after the rebellion of 1745 it was reported that out of 834 parishes in Scotland 800 had a stipend of £100 or less, 147 being lower than £40, and the highest being £140. Throughout the troubles of the '45 the Kirk had remained loyal to the Hanovarian cause, and the time was thought propitious to press for legislation that would secure for its Ministers a larger share of the available teinds. Such an attempt was made in 1750 but failed miserably — as might have been foreseen considering that the landlords were the people of influence in Parliamentary circles and any increase in stipends meant a corresponding drop in their incomes! To the argument that a hundred Scottish ministers had less than one hundred pounds a year the answer was given that in England and Wales there were seventeen hundred with less than twenty An interesting comparison, an appalling situation, but surely not a compelling argument for the retention of the *status quo!*

Victual Stipend — The amount of the teinds that had to be paid as stipend was fixed not in terms of currency but of "victual" — that is to say so many chalders of meal, and so on. In 1808 an Act was passed requiring stipend to be paid in cash of the realm and setting up the machinery for making the necessary calculation. For all the criticisms that can be levelled at it the original system had advantages — on the short term the fortunes of the Minister fluctuated with those of his flock, and on the long term the stipend of a parish retained for all time a constant relationship with the cost of living. Had the principle been adhered to it is believed that most *qoad omnia* stipends today would be in the £20,000/£30,000 range without any contribution from the congregation.

Exchequer Grants — It was not until 1810 that a further approach was made to Parliament for augmentation of stipends, this time consequent on the considerable drop in the value of money that followed on the Napoleonic wars, and this was successful to the exent that there was set aside from public funds an annual sum of £10,000 for the purpose of ensuring that no stipend would fall below the level of £150. The Clerks of the various Presbyteries were to make up lists of all parishes within their bounds where the stipend was below that figure, and the Lords of Session were empowered to make appropriate allocations. On the first time round this was done with great mathematical precision, so that for the first time in the Kirk's history there was a true Minimum Stipend — of £150 per annum with an additional £30 if there was no manse or no glebe and of

£50 where there was neither. There was a further provision that the situation would be reviewed every five years, but this was not implemented, with the result that the original awards came to be regarded as additional endowments, the property of the congregations concerned. In 1927 the administration of this fund was put into the hands of the Church, and it is now used for its original purpose (see hereunder).

Parliamentary Parishes — Into the nineteenth century a serious problem still persisted in parts of the Highlands where distances were great and many people lived in areas remote from their parish Church and Ministers cold not cope with the enormous areas under their caare. New parishes had to be created. To assist in this situation the Government in 1824 set aside a sum of £50,000 to enable churches and manses to be built and stipends to be provided in such cases. In fact no fewer than forty-three new parishes were created in the Highlands as a result of this legislation, and these are still called Parliamentary Parishes, and the 120 which had constituted the original stipend is known as an "Exchequer Living".

Under an Order and Scheme of the Scottish Ecclesiastical Commissioners of 21st June 1926 redemption money was paid over in respect of the £1200 of Exchequer Livings and £5040 of stipends remaining out of the Parliamentary Parishes grant. In 1932 this came under the control of the Committee on the Maintenance of the Ministry who have framed regulations to ensure that Exchequer Grants, as they are now called, are allocated to charges on, or very near, the Minimum Stipend.

Standardisation — For the next century nothing very significant happened in the field of stipend until in 1925 there passed through Parliament the Church of Scotland (Property and Endowments) Act, which had the effect of transforming the whole stipend structure of the Kirk. This Act, designed to facilitate the Union of the Churches, had the object of putting completely within control of the Church all her assets in property and funds so that she would not even seem to be "State-subsidised". The main provisions of the Act so far as stipend was concerned were two — first to standardise all teind stipend by converting it from a fluctuating sum into a standard charge upon the land affected, and secondly to make this payable to the General Trustees, a new body created by Act of Parliament some four years earlier. The money was still intended for its parish of origin (though see hereunder) but it was no longer to vest in the Minister of that parish. Standardisation would take place automatically on the first occurrence of a vacancy, but any Minister in enjoyment of teind stipend could elect to standardise, and since these were years of depression the standardised terms represented a distinct advantage over current rates, so standardisation progressed fairly rapidly as the result of election. A few Ministers preferred to continue on the old basis but today all stipends have been standardised, the latest being effected in 1974. The basis of computation was the average fiars' price for fifty years since 1873 plus five per cent. All charges not exceeding a shilling were extinguished, those between a shilling and a pound had to be redeemed by payment of a capital sum, while those over a pound could be redeemed by choice of the heritor.

Area of Preference — Monies ingathered in this way for a particular parish are, in terms of the Act, to be "appropriated by them in the first place to meeting the proper requirements of that parish or its neighbourhood (as such requirements may be determined by the General Assembly or by any body to which the General Assembly may delegate the necessary power), and any remainder after these requirements have been fully met shall form part of a general fund at the disposal of the General Assembly" (Section 36). In terms of Act xli 1971 the Assembly delegated to the Committee on the Maintenance of the Ministry the power referred to. As the outcome of this the Assembly of 1953 passed an Act (xxvii) renewing the delegation but providing machinery whereby a dissatisfied party might bring the issue to the floor of the Assembly.

The decision on what are "proper requirments" is an issue considered on the merits of each case by the delegated committee after conference with interested parties. Though the Act does not say so it has always been accepted that only stipend requirements are relevant (though that presumption is being earnestly looked at today), and indeed an application to use some part of the fund for an Assistant Minister working in the parish has been refused.

There is a movement afoot at the time of writing to have these monies made available for other than stipend purposes, particularly fabric. Indeed steps are being taken to promote Parliamentary legislation revoking the restriction to "the parish or its neighbourhood", but the present position is as set forth above. Counsel's opinion was taken on the question of defining "the parish or its neighbourhood" and this was given to the effect that it was "the civil parish, or the parish *quoad omnia*, or an area approximating to these units." Though what the Act creates is an area of preference it has been the practice of the Church to see the formerly benefitting charge as having a preferential claim and only the balance remaining after its reasonable needs have been met has any part been made available for distribution among other congregations within the area of preference. The amount of endowments nowadays represents so small a figure in relation to stipend that questions in this field have ceased to be of much practical significance. While the Act envisages the possibility of endowments going to a general fund the all-but-universal practice has been to allocate them to a particular congregation. And it is quite invariable practice that allocations whether to the formerly benefitting congregation or to any other are only for the duration of the existing or the anticipated incumbency. The reason why available balances were not simply added to the Minimum Stipend Fund was that in 1929 certain former congregations of what had been the the "voluntary" persuasion entered the Union only on a guarantee that they would not be asked to accept any money that had come from such sources.

Law of Ann — Three further features of teind stipend fall to be noted. First of all there is Ann or Annat governed by Acts of Parliament of 1547, 1571, and 1672. Ann consists of the half-year's stipend vesting first after the death of a Minister who died in office. Of this, one-half was payable to the widow, the other half being divided among surviving children, though all went to the children in the absence of a widow. Ann was not part of the Minister's estate and did not require confirmation, nor was there any way in which the Minister could direct what was to happen to it. It was not exigible on the income from a glebe. The Act of 1925 brought these payments to an end, but a Widow's or Next-of-Kin Grant has been instituted to take its place.

Vacant Stipend — This is stipend which vests during a vacancy and is not Ann, and it applies to the endowments of *quoad sacra* parishes as well as to teind. In terms of an Act of 1814 it was payable to the Widows' Fund, but in 1930 legislation was passed whereby the Trustees of the Widows' Fund surrendered their right to Vacant Stipend to the Maintenance of the Ministry Committee, receiving in compensation the sum of £140,000 payable in half-yearly sums of £17,500 over a period of forty years. So Vacant Stipend is now the property of the Committee on the Maintenance of the Ministry, and is used in part to assist in payment of pulpit supply during vacancies.

Assistant and Successor — It was a peculiarity of the Old Parish system that a Minister did not retire on grounds of age or infirmity. Instead he applied to the Presbytery to have an Assistant and Successor appointed. If a probationer was chosen he was ordained, but there was never any induction, for the senior colleague continued as Minister of the parish and it was in him that the stipend continued to vest. He had the right — but not the duty — to preside over the Kirk Session, to sit as a member of Presbytery and to attend the General Assembly — that is to say, it was only if the Senior Minister elected not to do these things that the Assistant could act as Moderator of Kirk Session or occupy a seat in Presbytery. At the time when he applied to have such an appointment made the Senior Minister set forth in the form of a contract the payment to be made to the Assistant and by way of security he assigned his right to that portion of the stipend to the Moderator and Clerk of the Presbytery. It was for the Presbytery to satisfy itself that the proposed provison was reasonable and adequate before agreeing to an appointment. On the death of the Senior Minister the Assistant was, without further election of any kind, inducted as Minister of the parish. The normal arrangement reserved three tenths of the stipend to the Senior Minister.

The Churches of the Secession operated a similar system of Assistant and Successor — though sometimes they called him Colleague and Successor — but in their case it was the congregation that determined how much was to be paid to each of the men concerned — after all, it was they who were paying it.

The United Presbyterians

The idea that the support of its Minister should be the direct responsibility of a congregation must in 1733 (the year of the First Secession) have been a completely revolutionary one. The people of Scotland had been accustomed to an ecclesiastical economy wherein church, manse and glebe were provided and maintained and the stipend paid by the heritors as a statutory obligation, so that all the givings of the people could go to the support of the poor. It must have been a harsh new experience for the congregation to accept responsibility for the payment of stipend, over and above having to equip themselves with heritable properties, and all by direct voluntary giving. In fact the first Seceders were allowed a breathing-space in which to prepare for taking on the new burdens in that Ebenezer Erskine and the other three Ministers who left the allegiance of the Kirk in 1733 to form the Associate Synod were for seven years allowed to continue in the enjoyment of church, manse, glebe and stipend before finally being deposed in 1740. By that time "praying societies" in many parts of the country were petitioning the Associate Synod for "supply of sermon" and were indicating a readiness to provide a stipend comparable to the average figure within the Establishment. The Relief congregations, from the time of their very beginning in 1761, accepted this obligation with apparent enthusiasm.

In his "Stipend Within the Church of Scotland" A H Gibson says, "The First Secession had an important bearing on the Maintenance of the Ministry because the Seceders proved that when a Minister was liked and respected by his people, and left church, manse and stipend for conscience' sake, particularly when it was a reason that was understood by the common man, he would not be left to starve but would be supported by the people themselves." In both Secession and Relief Churches the standard practice was that before a body of people were "received as a forming congregation" they had to satisfy the Presbytery of their willingness and ability to provide a reasonable stipend for their Minister — or Ministers when application was made for a colleague and successor.

In 1847 when what had by then become the United Secession Church (with 400 congregations) came together with the Relief Church (with 118 congregations) to form the United Presbyterian Church their Basis of Union proclaimed (Article 9) — "that as the Lord hath ordained that they who preach the Gospel should live of the Gospel .... this Church asserts the obligation and privilege of its members, influenced by regard to the authority of Christ, to support and extend, by voluntary contribution, the ordinances of the Gospel." And lest there should be any misunderstanding of the word "voluntary" a statement was issued in these terms, "Chistian Churches are required to regard provision for the support of their Ministers as part of their Christian duty, and are prohibited from transferring this service to the State. When this is called voluntary giving, it is not meant that the contribution is optional, so that the Christian disciple is at liberty to give or not to give as he chooses, but that the obligation does not arise from civil statute, but solely from the law of Christ." The price might be high, but it was being paid gladly because it was the price of independence.

The Augmentation Fund — Within the United Secession Church there had been acceptance of the principle that the weak should be helped by the strong, and, at stipend level, this had manifested itself in the making of grants ranging from £5 to £50 from Home Mission funds to needy congregations to assist with the payment of their Ministers. In 1868 the

U P Synod resolved to set up an Augmentation Fund under a new standing committee of the Home Board. This fund (unlike the corresponding Sustentation Fund of the Free Church) dealt only with the contributions in aid made by the stronger congregations and with their distribution in an equitable manner to assist with the stipends of the lower-paid Ministers. It was not in any methodical sense a minimum stipend fund.

Until comparatively recently the stipend of a Minister of a former U P charge was in most case determined by the congregation at their annual meeting and was paid by the Treasurer of the Managers. A special feature was that it was paid in advance, usually monthly but occasionally quarterly. The system had considerable advantages, though it was unfortunate that it encouraged the view that the Minister was the servant of a particular congregation rather than of the Church as such.

The Free Cuurch

As 1843 approached and it became increasingly apparent that a vast secession from the Church was inevitable the leaders of the "popular party" (as it was then called) realised that they were going to be faced with a problem of terrifying magnitude and urgency in organising some system whereby the day-to-day maintenance of those Ministers who "came out" would be met. In the event some 450 Ministers left manse and livelihood behind them, casting themselves upon the goodness of their people. But goodness has to be organised, and that at the very least takes time, whereas hungry wives and children need to be fed, and that does not allow any time.

The Sustentation Fund — The answer which was found was the establishment of the Sustentation Fund, and this was owed to the genius — and faith — of Thomas Chalmers. A convocation of Ministers and Elders interested in cutting adrift from the Establishment was held in November 1842 when Dr Chalmers advanced the idea that since it would be quite wrong, not to say utterly unfair and impracticable, to leave every Minister to be looked after by those of his former flock who had come out with him, there should be set up an annual fund which would take the place of the endowments of the *quoad sacra* charges. At their stipend figureof £120 this would mean an annual sum of, say £54,000. Set against the kind of collections that were being gathered at parish churches at that time the whole conception seemed preposterous — nor were there wanting those who said so! But Chalmers persisted in his idea, and before the

Disruption had taken place at all "associations" were being set up in many parts of the country to whip up support and organise machinery to get the system running. Besides which the new Church revived the Scriptural office of Deacon primarily with a view to taking charge of the Fund. Every member of the new Free Church congregations was visited monthly in the interest of the Sustentation Fund, and such was the enthusiasm generated that in the first year of its history instead of the £54,000 that had seemed an idle dream there was ingathered £68,704 which steadily grew over the next ten years till it passed the £100,000 mark.

The Equal Dividend — Out of this annual fund an "equal dividend" was paid to every Minister of a charge — £105 in the first year and rising each year until in 1861 it had reached £160 at which it was held constant. Congregations were, of course, encouraged to make payments direct to their Minister in supplement of the equal dividend. Once this figure had been achieved a further elaboration was introduced whereby the available balance in the Fund was divided each year among the most poorly-paid Ministers of the Church. Just before 1900 something very close to a minimum stipend had been attained within the Free Church of £183,10s. And the principle had been firmly established that each Minister, irrespective of the character of his charge, was the servant not of a congregation but of the Church as a whole.

The United Free Church

The Wee Frees — In 1900 the Free Church and the United Presbyterian Church came together to form the United Free Church, but quite a substantial minority on the Free Church side opted out, retaining, of course, the title Free Church of Scotland, though more popularly known as "the Wee Frees". After the union the Ministers of this minority were solemnly deposed and actions instituted for recovery of the property they were still occupying. Not surprisingly this was resisted, the actions were defended and counter-actions were raised. For the Free Church it was argued that in two essential matters the new body created by the union had departed from fundamental principles to which the Free Church was bound to adhere if it was to retain its identity and therefore the title to its property. The property, it was argued, was held for principles not for persons. The matter went to the House of Lords which in 1904 gave judgment in favour of the continuing Free Church, awarding them the whole property and funds of what had been the Free Church. This created a quite impossible situation in that the remanent Free Church could not so much as administer, much less occupy or use, the vast property that had thus become theirs. A Parliamentary Commission was appointed the following year to allocate the property on a fair and equitable basis. For our present purpose it is important to note that the United Free Church lost in this way £100,000 of the capital of its Sustentation Fund.

It was largely due to all this financial uncertainty that not until 1908 were any steps taken to come up with a co-ordinated scheme for the maintenance of the ministry within the new body. During this interim period — and for long afterwards — the two sides continued to function as they had been accustomed to do, the only change being that in many former Free Church congregations the amount of the equal dividend was paid direct to the Minister, and when this was done it was regarded as their contribution to the Sustentation Fund.

The Central Fund — In 1908 the Central Fund was established, though this seems to have been primarily a change in nomenclature, both branches of the united Church continuing esssentially as before. After the equal dividend had been received by all Ministers there was a Surplus Fund and this was divided among all Ministers whose stipend from all soures was less than £200, and that in such a way that those who had least received most, but still not on the basis of a strict minimum stipend. New regulations were approved by the U F Assembly of 1925 whereby a true Minimum Stipend was achieved, no Minister who was in receipt of Aid having a stipend higher than that of any other.

The City Minimum — One interesting exception to the above rule was that an additional £50 was paid to some city Ministers. Prior to 1900 there had existed within the Free Church a custom whereby Ministers of certain Churches within the four cities were singled out as deserving of special treatment from a Home Mission point of view and received an additional £50 per annum, paid in part from the Central Fund and in part from Home Mission sources. To select the deserving charges had always proved an invidious task, so that the 1925 regulations provided that every charge within the four cities would enjoy a stipend of not less than £50 above the normal minimum. This was known as the City Minimum, was adopted in the united Church in 1929 and continued until 1961 when it was resolved to depart from the practice, no Minister inducted to a city charge after 1st July in that year qualifying for any addition beyond the normal Minimum Stipend.

Supplement to Stipend — Within the U F Church it was further required that the Deacons' Court or Board of Management after providing for payment of feu-duties, insurance, salaries, Presbytery, Synod and Assembly Dues, and the expenses of heating, lighting, etc should "provide a suitable supplement to the Minister's stipend out of congregational funds before these funds are held applicable to any other purpose whatsoever."

SINCE 1929

Territorial Ministry

The third of the Articles Declaratory of the Church of Scotland concludes, "As a national Church representative of the Christian faith of the Scottish people the Church of Scotland acknowledges its distinctive call and duty to bring the ordinances of religion to the people in every parish of Scotland through a territorial ministry." It was in fulfilment of this obligation that the Church, as re-united in 1929, committed itself to the creation of a "Fund for the Maintenance of Gospel Ordinances for the People in every Parish in Scotland through a Territorial Ministry." A title of this kind is more of an *apologia* than of a name and inevitably it had to be abbreviated, so that today the official title is simply "the Fund for the Maintenance of the Ministry", the unofficial and still simpler form being "M of M". It is important, though, to keep in mind that the justification for the fund is the maintenanace of ordinances throughout Scotland, the maintenance of a ministry, not the maintenance of ministers. One wonders whether we whiles tend to forget this when deciding on priorities.

Committee on the Maintenance of the Ministry

To administer this fund the Basis and Plan of Union of 1929 provided for the appointment of a Committee which would ingather from the General Trustees and others all sums ear-marked for stipend, which would collaborate with Presbyteries in securing adequate congregational support for the Fund, and which would administer all monies available with a view to securing "a Standard Minimum Stipend to be fixed each year, for all ministers inducted to a charge whose ministerial income for the year from all other sources shall be less than the minimum possible to "provide a minimum stipend beyond the sum of £300 and a manse which both uniting Churches have regarded as inadequate support for the work of the ministry." It was, in fact, stated that "the Committee shall aim at providing such an annual amount as shall secure for all regular charges of the Church a minimum stipend of not less than £400 and a manse, insofar as this has not been provided otherwise." Nearly forty years were to elapse before this figure was attained, by which time the increase had been far outstripped by the upward march of inflation.

For many years the Committee operated under a common secretariat with the Committee on Readjustments, on Aged and Infirm Ministers' Fund and on Probationers and Transference and Admission of Ministers as the Church and Ministry Department. As a consequence of large-scale reorganisation effected in 1984 the Committee became part of a much larger Department of Ministry and Mission, and is today part of the Department of Ministry.

Ingathering of Funds — It is the responsibility of the Committee to collect from the General Trustees the income from standard charges, glebe rents and other similar payments destined for stipend, and from other trustees the income from funds held in trust for stipend purposes. The Committee also ingathers the income from feu-duties and ground-annuals held principally for behoof of *quoad sacra* congregations. The Committee has also to encourage as well as to ingather the response of congregations. Over the years a number of different methods have been devised to encourage and maintain this support.

The Vacancy Schedule — Immediately it is agreed that a vacant congregation is to be allowed to call a Minister a Vacancy Schedule is sent by the Commitee to the local Treasurer for completion in conference with representatives of the Presbytery's Maintenance of the Ministry Committee. This schedule sets out the amount of stipend to be paid in the new incumbency, detailing the various sources from which the money will come (Standardised Stipend, Statutory Endowments, Local Trust Fund, Exchequer Grant etc, as well as Congregation Direct.) It shows also whether a Manse is provided and if not what Manse Allowance is to be paid, and what arrangements are proposed about meeting Listed Expenses. Lastly it shows the amount of Aid to be given to, or to be derived from Mission and Aid.

In the case of a linked charge a separate Vacancy Schedule is sent to each of the component congregations, each being expected to provide a portion of the stipend and to accept a part responsibility for the upkeep of the manse and the payment of Council Tax, all in terms set forth in the Basis of Linking (p 52). Should one of the congregations subsequently default in its share the responsibility for making good any resulting deficiency does not automatically fall upon the other partner or partners.

Once the Vacancy Schedule has been completed at congregational level it is forwarded to the Presbytery which has the duty of transmitting it to the Assembly Committee. If the Presbytery is satisfied that the proposals are reasonable in light of all the circumstances known to it it transmits with approval; if it is not so satisfied it can either transmit without approval or it can itself take the schedule back to the congregational authorities for further consideration. The Assembly Committee will then examine the Schedule and may either approve or disapprove. If the Schedule is approved the Presbytery is free to take the final steps towards the settlement of a Minister, and when this occurs the Presbytery Clerk is bound to put into the hands of the inductee an extract minute of the Assembly Committee's deliverace setting forth the detailed stipend arrangements agreed. In the event of disapproval the schedule will be returned to the Presbytery which may either take the matter up afresh with the office-bearers concerned or adhere to its decision that the proposals are resasonable, in which case the Assembly's Committee may seek conference with the Presbytery on the matter.

In the early years the consideration of Vacancy Schedules at both Presbytery and Committee level were very much an *ad hoc* affair, each schedule being assessed wholly on its apparent merits and in the absence of any kind of standard — particular or general — against which it could be compared. Naturally enough, comparison would incline to be made among schedules presented at the same sederunt and a schedule which one day would be rejected out of hand might in the very different company of another day be accepted as reasonable or even generous. The only absolute available was the current Minimum and setting sights on that had the effect of keeping stipends down rather than of encouraging them to move upwards.

Appropriate Stipends — The year 1952 saw a completely new concept introduced — that of "Figures for Appropriate Stipend and Aid". In the first place, in fact, they were called "Desirable Stipends", but the name was changed soon after the scheme became operative, and it will be convenient to use the term "appropriate" from the outset. The late Karl Greenlaw, at that time Assistant Secretary of the Committee, was author of the idea and for purposes of plotting the scheme he took as model his own Presbytery of Dundee. Starting with the congregation of St Mary's he asked himself, "What in all the circumstances of this congregation would be appropriate figures for them to pay by way of Stipend and by way of Aid to the Fund?" Having arrived at what he considered a fair answer he went on to assess all the other charges on a comparable basis in all the varied circumstances of each case. When this principle had been applied throughout the Church as a whole there were determined in respect of each congregation figures for Stipend and Aid which, while they might not be immediately attainable, were considered reasonable and "appropriate". Every Presbytery of the Church was instructed to prepare and submit a list of "appropriates" for its various charges, and these had to be approved by the Committee which in fact had already prepared a list covering the whole Church. It should be noted that while congregations might be consulted at the time when the lists were being prepared their consent or approval of the figures finally determined was not required — the Presbytery with the concurrence of the Assembly Committee decided what were the Appropriate Figures. For the first time there existed a yard-stick with which to measure the adequacy of Vacancy Schedule proposals. Ere long a schedule was unlikely to be approved unless the Appropriate Figures were promised — and certainly it could not be disapproved if the Appropriate Figures were proposed. The vacant congregation was now looking up to its appropriate figure instead of looking down at the Minimum and this led to a marked improvement in stipend levels.

Formula for Determining Aid — In 1982 the Assembly approved a scheme whereby figures for Aid — which in the past had been determined largely on the tradition for generosity established by each congregation — were to be fixed on a graduated scale related to stipend, rising from a token 1% in the case of the barely self-supporting congregation to 90% in that of the congregation paying £10,000 and over. Obviously to introduce a change, which in many cases must have been quite dramatic, in a single year would be unrealistic and would lead only to ill-will and acrimony. It was therefore agreed to phase-in the new system over a four-year period. It was conceded that Presbyteries would "retain their right to adjust individual Aid figures in the light of local knowledge." In almost every case, therefore, the fixing of Appropriate Stipends has the effect of automatically fixing the figures for Appropriate Aid.

The Revision Schedule — The figure entered on the Vacancy Schedule, it has always been emphasised, does not constitute a contract — it represents merely an undertaking on the part of the Committee that they will not interfere with the endowments, and on that of the congregation that no effort will be spared to meet their share, and they apply (with appropriate adjustments for inflation) throughout the incumbency. In the case where the circumstances of a congregation alter appreciably — whether for better or, more commonly, for worse — a Revision Schedule may be obtained on application to the Presbytery which will transmit it to the Assembly Committee with a recommendation and it is then dealt with exactly as the original Vacancy Schedule had been. In the event of a congregation which is not vacant becoming involved in union or linking a Revision Schedule will automatically be issued.

Shortfall — In its 1993 Report the Committee expressed concern at the increasing tendency "to shortfall on stipend payments as a result of paying for major fabric costs." They state that the Committee now resists writing off these amounts and directs the attention of the General Assembly "to the long-term crisis which could develop in maintaining the level of the Minimum Stipend if the Committee is expected to provide Minimum Stipend Fund reserves to help pay for fabric repairs." The following year a more ominous note was struck when a deliverance was approved (No 6) in which the Assembly "acknowledged the serious consequences of the increased use of General Funds for fabric repairs and approved the policy of accumulating shortfalls which will be considered at the time of a vacancy." The Report for 1994 merely repeated this statement without condescending upon what specific steps were contemplated.

Payment of "Bonus" — If stipend is to be increased this should, as indicated above, be done through the meduium of a Revision Schedule, but if a congregation one year find themselves in a position of unusual financial strength and wish their Minister to share in their good fortune, they may make a "bonus" payment for that year only, but only on condition that an identical sum be paid, half in Aid to the Fund and half to Mission and Aid.

Supplement to Retired Minister — At one time it was not uncommon when a Minister retired after a long ministry for the congregation as a mark of appreciation to undertake to pay him an annual grant in supplement of his pension. Such an open-ended commitment could have hurtful effects on the future financial position of the congregation, and in particular could be prejudicial to the stipend prospects of his successor. In 1976 the Assembly approved a Report of the Aged and Infirm Ministers' Fund Committee in these terms, "The Committee believes that a congregation which wishes to pay its retired Minister an annual sum by way of augmenting the annuity paid to him from the Fund is free, and should be encouraged, to do so, but only if it has met the appropriate stipend, its appropriate contributions as Aid to the Fund and to the Mission and Service Fund, and is able by the provision of a capital sum to purchase an annuity from a reputable insurance company at the time of the Minister's retirement." A proposal to augment a Minister's retiring allowanec in this way must secure the approval of the Presbytery, which will insist that the payment be covered by a settlement along the lines indicated.

Minimum Stipend

For many years after 1929 the Minimum Stipend was determined and "declared" at the regular meeting of the Committee in February of the year after that to which it applied, and all who were entitled to benefit received a back payment as soon as possible thereafter. This was the only way in which it could be done. For at that time the principle was simply that the whole amount contributed during the year was distributed in respect of the stipend for that year. But the General Treasurer does not close his books until a few days into January, and many congregations did not send up the bulk of their contributions until the close of the calendar year, so that it was well into January before it was known how much was "in the kitty". On the other side was the fact that information had to be got from Ministers as to precisely how much they had received from all sources in respect of their year's ministry, and this could not be supplied till after the year had ended. Only when both of these exercises were completed was it possible to determine how much would be needed to maintain the existing level of the Minimum and how much, if any, would be available to make an increase — which in those early days was generally in the region of £5, or even £10 — and gratefully welcomed at that!

Declaring the Minimum — It was as recently as 1963 that an innovation was made, the Committee declaring what was to be the level of the Minimum at the Assembly in May and payment of the respective balances being made to the recipients before the end of the year for which they were due. This involved a measure of informed guess-work, but now there were balances which could act as buffers in case of over-optimism. In that year, incidentally. the increase had been one of £70 (bringing the Minimum up to £870 — the biggest annual increase in the history of the Fund. The position today is that the Committee determine the minimum figure in the calendar year before it is due and later report this to the Assembly to be "noted" by them. It was, of course, in the days when the declaration could not be made before February and when, in any case, no policy was at stake and only a simple matter of arithmetic was involved, that power to declare had to be assumed by the Committee. They still, however, continue to exercise that power and "declare" to each Assembly what the Minimum Stipend is to be for the ensuing year.

All Other Sources — Aid from the Minimum Stipend Fund becomes payable only when the ministerial income "from all sources" does not amount to the figure determined as the Minimum. The question of what items of income are to be seen as income from other sources is one that has created difficulties, and these have come from two different directions.

First of all the question arose in respect of payments received by Ministers who had been appointed part-time Hospital or Prison Chaplains or who gave part-time service as Chaplains to the Forces. It was tempting to see these payments as ministerial income — they could not have been earned had the man not been a Minister. On the other hand such a payment did not represent income received by the Minister in virtue of his incumbency in that particular charge, and, even more serious, if his were a heavily aid-receiving charge he was not a penny better off for undertaking this extra burden. And while the exclusion of these might create an anomaly, it was no less of an anomaly to include them while taking no account of, say, the payment for a regular weekly article contributed to the local newspaper. All such payments are accordingly omitted from the calculation.

From the other side a question was raised very sharply by the Trustees of the Pringle Bequest Fund. There had been established in Elgin a trust one of whose provisions was that all Ministers of charges in Presbyteries in the Moray Firth neighbourhood were to receive from the Trust an annual spplement of £x. The Pringle Trustees insisted that this sum would be paid only if it were to constitute an addition to the sum to which the Minister was entitled had there been no such fund. The Committee for their part were equally insistent that the Trust represented one of the "other sources" and that the £x from the Pringle Bequest ranked on all fours with the £y from a local endowment and the £z from Standardised

Stipend. The net result, it had to be admitted, was that the better-paid Ministers in the neighbourhood enjoyed the full benefit of the bequest whereas those in aid-receiving charges received no benefit at all. It was strenuously argued that this had not been the testator's intention. With no less force it was argued that the testator was perfectly familiar with the working of the Minimum Stipend Fund and must have known this would be the result.

The issue aroused intense public interest. The Assembly appointed an *ad hoc* committee under Mr L Hill Watson KC, and in 1944 that committee reported, upholding the line taken by the Committee (Repts 1944, p 535). This was accepted by the Assembly, but the Pringle Trustees, being the Provost, Magistrates and Councillors of Elgin, were still dissatisfied and withheld payment. An action against them was raised by one of the deprived ministers and decree in his favour was granted by the Lord Ordinary in 1946. The Trustees appealed but subsequently withdrew in favour of a Petition to the court to alter the terms of the Trust. This went to the Second Division where it was unanimously rejected. The leading judgment of Lord Cooper is to be found in Assembly Reports 1947 at page 101. So ended the rather pathetic Pringle story.

Supplementary Payments — When nowadays there is a declaration of the Minimum Stipend there always appears the phrase "with the appropriate additions in special areas and cases." The "special areas" is a reference to a system of Supplementary Payments introduced in 1977 and applying to Island Parishes. This has been replaced by a system of Island Allowances set at two levels, the Outer Island Allowance (set at £1000) applying to Tiree and Coll, the Western Isles, Orkney, Shetland, Jersey and Guernsey; and the Inner Island Allowance (set at £400). These Allowances have increased from year to year at the rate of inflation and are paid in addition to the Appropriate (not the Minimum) Stipend. The special cases were two in number — first the case of a Minister already incumbent in a charge who undertook a linking — and to him went an additional £100, but this no longer obtains; and secondly the Minister of a Minimum Stipend charge declared by the Assembly to be in an area of special responsibility or of strategic importance — and in that case the supplement is £200. (Reference has already been made to the City Minimum discontinued as from 1st July 1961.)

Seniority Payments — In 1965 in answer to pressure from the floor of the Assembly a system of Seniority Supplements was approved and operated for some five years after which it was discontinued. These payments increased in amount according to whether the Minister had given ten, fifteen, twenty or twenty-five years' service. The total to be received from supplementary payments in any one year was not to exceed £200, and in this connection payments received in respect of Hospital, Prison or other chaplaincies were to be regarded as supplementary payments. The situation created a number of anomalies and its operation involved a geat deal of extra work at office level. There were those who thought the whole conception unwise in that a family's needs are generally far greater in the middle years when children have to be educated than towards the end of the road. The outcome was that the Assembly accepted the view urged by the Committee (which had never been enthusiastic) that the best and fairest way to help the largest number of Ministers was to press on with increasing the level of the Minimum Stipend. So in 1970 when the Minimum was increased by a sum sufficient to encompass the various supplements without anyone suffering a reduction opportunity was taken to terminate Seniority Payments. They are now (1995) being reintroduced on a completely different basis (see "New Stipend Structure" hereunder)

Basic Stipend — In 1964 with a view to securing a steady flow of income to Ministers in Minimum and marginal cases there was introduced a system whereby each year a figure is struck, rather lower than what had been paid during the previous year, and this, the Basic Stipend, is paid monthly in advance to Ministers where this is desired, it being understood that the congregation will remit quarterly payments in settlement, and that they will do so not later than the end of the year by which time they will have refunded *in toto* the amount of the Basic Stiped for the year.

Centralised Stipend System — In 1975 there was put into operation a system whereby all stipends are now paid directly into the bank account of the Minister concerned in monthly remittances from the Church Offices. Congregational Treasurers remit to the said Offices all sums for Stipend and for Aid, and they are expected to do so regularly and timeously. The scheme gained the approval of the Commission of Assembly in February 1975, powers having been given by the previous Assembly. The payment of stipend is today a highly complicated affair involving deductions for Pension Fund and Endowments Assurances contributions, Car Loan or Young Ministers' Furnishing Loan repayments where appropriate, and the application of two code-numbers, one for deducion of PAYE income-tax and the other for National Health Insurance contributions. While, therefore, the loss of the feeling of direct personal involvement must be regretted, the new system is proving highly efficient and works in the long run to the advantage of all concerned.

At the end of each year and at the beginning of the next Statements are issued to Minister and to Congegational Treasurer showing the situation as it has been in the year just ended and as it is going to be in the year just begun.

An Equal Stipend — From time to time the suggestion is advanced that there should be an identical stipend enjoyed by all Ministers irrespective of their congregation's ability to pay. Suggestions have also been made in favour of Children's Allowances, and also of Responsibility Supplements. After due consideration by the Committee all of these proposals have been rejected by the Assembly. The system to which we are committed is a Minimum Stipend system; after many years of adjustment in the light of experience it has been developed to a point where it works as well as any scheme can be expected to do. Beyond the level of the Minimum, it is true, the amount of the stipend depends on the financial ability of the congregation and takes no account of the experience, or qualifications, or special needs of the Minister, or of the amount of work or degree of responsibility involved. It is hard indeed to conceive a system which would take account of all these factors (not to mention all the hidden differences) and achieve anything near a true equality. In any case the remit of the Committee is to ensure a reasonable standard of living for the most poorly-paid section of the Church's ministry.

Endowments

Statutory Endowments — The New Parishes Act of 1844 supplied machinery for the creation of parishes *quoad sacra*. This was done on application to the Teind Court which had to satisfy itself that a stipend of at least £120 per annum (or, at first, £100 with a manse) would be available in perpetuity, and this would be assured by setting aside a sum which would provide an annual income of the sum required, and this in the form either of consols or of feu-duties. The latter being less expensive it was almost without exception in this form that endowments were provided. Normally one-half of the total required had to be supplied by the congregation (though the Baird Trustees were generous in giving help) and the other half was given by the Endowment Committee (merged in

1920 with the Committee on the Maintenance of the Ministry). Because they were provided in conformity with the statute of 1844 these came to be known as "Statutory Endowments". Since 1925 all such endowments have been collected by the General Trustees and paid over to the Committeee on the Maintenance of the Minisdtry for behoof of the Ministers of the charges concerned.

Initial Endowment — One of the effects of the 1925 Act was that it was no longer necessary to go to the Court of Teinds for the erection of a new charge and simplified procedure had been introduced. In particular the new congregation has been relieved of the burden of finding capital for endowment, the practice being that when it is granted full status a Church Extension charge qualifies for an Initial Endowment of £150 — £100 from the Committee and £50 from the Baird Trust. In certain cases where a charge having no, or very limited, endowments has been transported to a Church Extension area while retaining full status it may be granted an Initial Endowment as above.

Further Endowment — All through its history the former Parish Church has upheld the principle of having stipend covered by endowment, and in furtherance of this policy today help is extended to existing congregations to increase the amount of their endowment cover. There is fixed a maximum average stipend over the previous three years and a maximum figure for existing endowment. The limits set for 1993 were the average of the congregation's contribution to stipend over the previous three years, together with the current year's endowment, must be not more than £13,800 and the endowments must be raised to not more than £3,800. It is recommended that, where appropriate, legacies and similar windfalls may profitably be invested in this way.

Compulsory Redemption of Feu-Duties — Extensively during the 'sixties older properties within the cities were coming to be occupied by squatters and to be abandoned by their owners. In such cases the local authority usually took possession (with a view to demolition) and instituted proceedings to have the subjects cleared of ground burdens so that they could themselves take over and demolish the property subject to a lien thereon. Since by that time the feu-duties were bringing in no income derisory prices (commonly one year's purchase) were being fixed by the District Valuer. Many such feu-duties were held against the statutory endowments of *qoad sacra* parishes and as a result hardship was being suffered by Ministers in cases where the congregation was not in a position to make good the drop in income. In 1972 the Committee reported that "in an endeavour to mitigate in some measure this situation the Committee has been setting up by transfer a new Capital Fund, presently amounting to £99,998. The purpose of this Fund will be to give a partial replacement of endowment income lost in this way to certain aid-receiving *quoad sacra* parishes."

Basal Endowment — Where in any year funds available for endowments grants have not been fully taken up the Committee has, with Assembly approval, established a custom of choosing a charge having a stipend of not more than £100 above the minimuim, which is held to be a necessary charge, and providing it with a Basal Endowment at the rate of £120 per annum.

Dealing with Endowments — The Act of 1925 lays the responsibility for determining the use of endowments on the General Assembly "or any body on which the General Assembly may delegate the necessary power." Such delegation was made to the Committee on the Maintenance of the Ministry in 1951, confirmed in 1953. The procedure which the Committee adopts is as follows. Immediately the Committee is informed in terms of Act iv 1984 of the occurrence or anticipated occurrence of a vacancy in a charge where there are endowments for stipend it will consider whether or not it wishes to raise the question of the future use of these endowments — though if the question of readjustment is being raised the issue is delayed until that is settled. Should the Committee resolve not to raise the question this is without prejudice to the right of any other interested party to do so. The Presbytery, or any Minister or Kirk Session within the area of preference would certainly have interest — it is doubtful whether any other party or person would. When the Committee has decided upon the amount to be allocated to the formerly benefitting charge it informs the Presbytery seeking its opinion, though it is not bound thereby.

It is only after agreement has been reached on the amount that is to remain with the formerly benefitting charge that a question arises as to the use of the balance, and no moneys will be available until the vacancy has been filled, for all endowments which had been payable as stipend during the vacancy qualify as vacant stipend throughout the entire vacancy. In determining the use of the balance the following points are important — (a) every necessary congregation within the area of preference has a valid claim; (b) a necessary aid-receiving charge within the area of preference has a first claim; and (c) a congregation outwith the area of preference can receive an allocation only to the extent that that congregation is aid-receiving, which is to say in effect, that when you go beyond the area of preference the money must be applied solely to relieve the Minimum Stipend Fund.

Such cases must now be very rare, for no single congregation is still endowed to any extraordinary extent.

NEW STIPEND STRUCTURE

For quite some time the Committee has proclaimed as its objective the establishment of a Minimum Stipend at the level of the Scottish National Earnings for Male Non-Manual Workers (which I propose hereunder to abbreviate to "Non-Manual Average"), but in 1993 it was agreed that this would involve an immediate increase of around 5000, and that this seemed quite out of reach given the current standard of liberality. It was remitted to a Joint Committee of Assembly Council, Board of Stewardship and Finance and Committee on the Maintenance of the Ministry Committee to bring forward plans for implementing the proposed Minimum Stipend equivalent to the Non-Manual Average as soon as possible. One might have expected that this would be seen as demanding a new level of liberality. The report of this Joint body to the Assembly of 1994, however, indicated that it saw no hope of achieving this objective with the existing machinery and recommended the adoption of an entirely new Stipend Structure.

The New Features — The object of this new structure is declared to be a substantial increase in the level of the Minimum Stipend. "The major new element in the new Stipend Structure proposed is the introduction of a Service Supplement to be paid to all parish ministers who are under sixty-five and have at least five years' eligible qualifying service." The details of what constitutes such "eligible qualifying service" are set forth in Repts 1994, p 186.

This Service Supplement (a) is to be paid in addition to the stipend for the charge; (b) is to be paid after five years' qualifying service and until age 65; (c) will be phased in from the beginning of 1995; (d) will begin at £1000 per annum (at 1995 Constant Prices) in each of the next five years up to 1999, amounting to a total Supplement of £5000. That is to say, the Minister of an Aid-receiving charge will for the first five years of his ministry or if he continues beyond 65 receive the present inadequate

Minimum while the Minister of five years' service in any charge will receive up to an additional £5000, and that without any additional burden directly laid on the congregation. The congregation, however, is, along with all others, to bear a levy ranging from five to twenty-five per cent of gross stipend (exclusive of supplement), and that whether or not its Minister is at the time in receipt of any supplement. "In every case the Service Supplement will be paid to qualifying Ministers not by their cogregations but from central funds."

As things are at present self-supporting congregations make payments to Ministry Funds for (a) Stipend; (b) National Insurance; (c) Main Pension Fund (20% of gross stipend); (d) Housing and Loan Fund (2% of gross stipend); (e) Insured Pension Fund (voluntary); and (e) Travelling Expenses. To this list will now fall to be added, (f) Service Supplement, and this will continue to be paid throughout a vacancy.

It is envisaged that the Minimum Stipend will be increased annually by the percentage increase in the Retail Price Index until the new Stipend Structure is fully implemented. No explanation is offered of why it should stop then. At the other end it is agreed that a self-supporting congregation which meets in full all its contributions to central funds (including Mission and Aid) may pay a stipend above the recommended scale provided the Presbytery approves and the congregation undertakes to contribute to the Service Supplement Fund a certain amount for every £1 they propose to pay beyond the scale. Initially (for 1995) the contribution will be at the scale of £2 for every £1 by which the stipend exceeds the agreed Stipend Scale.

The General Assembly of 1994 accepted the report and ordered its implementation forthwith.

Manse

Historic Note — From earliest days of the Reformed Kirk the heritors were under obligation to provide and to maintain a Manse, which term was judicially defined as including all necessary and usual offices, garden and garden walls. In itself it is to be such a house as is considered suitable at the time for others in the same class as ministers. Its accommodation should be sufficient for an ordinary family and due hospitality, and it should be "decently and comfortably furnished without and within." Mair adds an interesting list of offices court decisions have ordered from time to time — poultry house, pighouse, butler's pantry, cook's pantry — all adjuncts to a substantial house of at least ten apartments with garden of generous proportions — such was the typical manse of that day. It is hard to believe that it was less than a hundred years ago that Mair records that "a bathroom with hot water is now provided without demur", adding that "the provision of hot water would include a kitchen range."

Unlike the position of the Church building, of which the heritors were proprietors holding in trust for the Church, the Manse was seen as the property of the incumbent for the time being *ex officio* and he acted on behalf of himself and his successors in office. Only very rarely was there any written title. In the event, however, that, for example, the house had to be rebuilt the Minister was entitled to a payment in compensation to enable him to provide himself and his family with accommodation. This was known as Manse mail.

It was the invariable custom of the Churches of the Secessions and of the United Free Church to provide a manse for the occupancy of their ministers. In the case of *quoad sacra* congregations the provision of a "Manse with appurtenances" was one of the things necessary before a cause could be created. I can find no record of such Ministers declining to occupy.

The whole situation was changed, of course, by the 1925 Property and Endowments Act.

The Position Today — The contemporary situation is that the Manse is available to the Minister for use in fulfilment of his ministerial functions and for the accommodation of himself and his family — but not for letting. It is not so very common today but there are still many parishes in rural areas where parts of the Manse are used exclusively by Church organisations, there being no suitable hall available. Sunday School meets there, Kirk Session and Woman's Guild hold their regular gatherings there, and so on. The Minister is held bound to occupy the Manse and for that reason the value of its occupancy is not chargeable for Income Tax. There used to be a statutory remission on local rates, but that was brought to an end with the introduction of Council Tax. This tax on Manses has to be paid by congregations. The Assembly of 1993 "acknowledged the new financial burden which is being placed on congregations in meeting the Council Tax in respect of Manses and note that the Committee will take this into accout when determining the 1994 Minimum Stipend."

Until very recently when for any reason a Minister did not want to occupy the Manse — he had a house of his own conveniently placed to the parish, or it was far too big for his needs, or it had a great acreage of ground and his doctor had warned him to keep away from a spade — in these or similar circumstances he could seek consent of Presbytery to live in a house of his own providing and receive a Manse Allowance in lieu. Due, I imagine, to difficulties with Inland Revenue this is no longer an option. The Minister may be excused from occupying the Manse, but there can be no payment in lieu. Where there is no Manse a Manse Allowance has to be paid at a figure ordained by the previous Assembly — the present rate is £1300.

The Position Tomorrow ? — I quote from Reports 1994, p 309 — "The General Assembly asked the Committee to look at the economics of selling off manses and using the money towards ministers' stipends with a view to helping ministers purchase their own houses, and report to next Assembly.

"Initial investigations show that there are many complex issues which demand close and detailed study. The Committee recognises there are economic, legal, pastoral, fiscal, and mobility considerations as well as regional variations. In order to explore these further the Committee wishes to continue its research and to report to a future General Assembly.

"In the meantime the Committee feels that the best way forward is to continue to provide manses which are of good quality, well maintained and of a suitable style to be effective bases from which Parish Ministers will undertake the duties of the office to which they have been called."

Twenty-five years ago in the then "Manse Mail" I contributed an article on what I then saw as the Manse problem, concluding by saying, "The Manse in the form in which we have known it is on its way out. We should therefore give some hard thought to the detail of a proper system of house allowance for ministers. It would be necessary to establish a fund from which long-term loans of large sums could be made to those at the start of their parish ministry. The initial money for such a fund could be found from the sale of existing properties and, as a loan fund it would be self-perpeptuating. Stipends would have to be considerably adjusted to provide the equivalent of the manse. Some part at least of this supplement would go direct to Edinburgh to pay off the minister's loan. The titles to such houses could be taken in name of the Church with a back-letter conveying to the minister when the loan had been fully paid off — treating the Church exactly as a building society in fact. Special provision would have to be made in those cases where a manse had still to be provided because suitable accommodation was not available. It will take much hard thinking to work out a satisfactory scheme, so the sooner we start thinking the better."

It would seem that authority has now caught up with my conclusion of all these years ago. My suggestion of a possible pattern might well provide a starting-point for the further research we have been promised is to go into the subject. It is quite essential that we find a worthwhile solution, and find it soon.

There is, of course, another consideration complicating the situation — the desirability that the Minister should be living among his people, mixing with them in the ordinary contacts of daily life. Linkings have already made an inroad into the application of this principle, but it would be sad, as I see it, were the day to come when the whole of rural Perthshire, for example, would be served by ministers occupying their own houses in either Perth or Crieff.

And yet another problem is that of what to do in the really remote areas where, take away the Manse, there is just no suitable housing.

Those entrusted with the examination of the manse problem have indeed a considerable task on their hands.

To return from this considerable digression the situation today in regard to Manses is, briefly, that where a Manse is provided the Minister is expected, though not bound, to occupy it. If, with permission of Presbytery, he occupies his own house no compensating payment is to be made.

The Glebe

The Minister of a landward *quoad omnia* parish was, under the old regime, entitled to a glebe. This was an area of arable land extending to at least five acres imperial measure, or a larger extent of grazing land, chosen by the Presbytery, in proximity to Church and Manse. A certain area of grazing, varying in its position from one year to another was a possible substitute and was known as "minister's grass". The glebe was designed essentially as pasture for the minister's pony, the equivalent of a petrol allowance today.

Today the ownership of such land is vested in the General Trustees who arrange for its letting or as occasion arises for its feuing. As a general rule they are reluctant to sell. In 1974 the Trustees reported a total income from glebe rents of just under £250,000. At the same time their policy is to encourage Kirk Sessions and Congregational Boards themselves "to work glebes for the benefit of the Church." When a glebe is sold the total price is to be invested and only the income may be expended (Act xxxiii 1966). Strictly they have become an endowment the income from which is to be used for stipend.

MISCELLANEOUS

Widow's or Next-of-Kin Grant — Reference has been made to the Law of Ann (p 185) which provided that the half-year's stipend vesting after the death of a Minister in service was paid one half to the widow and one half among the surviving children, but this was brought to an end by the 1925 Property and Endowments Act. In the U F Church a practice had been followed that immediately on the death of a Minister there was sent to his widow, or if no widow to his next-of-kin who had kept house for him, from the Central Fund a grant which in 1920 amounted to £60. For purposes of this payment no distinction was drawn between active and retired ministers. The practice was continued in the united Church, and as cases began to occur of widows not entitled to Ann these, the widows of former Church of Scotland Ministers, were accepted as qualifying for the same grant. In recent years a differentiation has been made in the amount of the grant according to whether the Minister died in office or as an annuitant of the Main Pension Fund. Difficulties have recently been raised to the latter payments from the side of Inland Revenue so that the grant in such a case is now a nominal one and further provision is made for the widow by means of an increased Widow's Pension. The sum paid to the widow or next-of-kin of a minister who dies in pensionable service is now set at three times the level of the Minimum Stipend and is paid by the Retirement Scheme Committee from the Main Pension Fund (formerly the Aged and Infirm Ministers' Fund). It is no longer made on an *ex gratia* basis being fully provided for in the Regulations of the Church of Scotland Retirement and Death Benefits Scheme for Ministers and Missionaries.

Vacancy Expenses — The Committee helps with the payment of pulpit supply during a vacancy, the cost being borne jointly by the Committee and the congregation in proportion of their respective responsibility for stipend during the last full year of the incumbency. In cases where stipend is paid wholly or mainly from the Fund a supply of weekly vouchers may be obtained providing an undertaking is given to remit the required contributions throughout the period of the vacancy.

Travelling Expenses — It was as comparatively recently as 1963 that the General Assembly resolved that the travelling expenses incurred by a Minister in performance of his duty should be one of the obligatory Listed Expenses to be paid by the congregation. In 1967 the regulations governing Listed Expenses were amended so that where there is no Driving Grant payable from central funds and the Presbytery and the Committee agree that the parish is car-essential the congregation is bound to pay "on the same basis as the Committee's grants, the cost of such travelling either by car or by public transport, as may be approved by the Committee" (Repts 1967). In cases of union and linking and in certain other car-essential parishes in remote areas a Driving Grant may be provided by the Committee, usually on the basis of an agreed contribution to expenses incurred, on the understanding that the congregation will meet any balance outstanding on the permitted expenses — and in cases where they fail to do this the grant may be withdrawn.

From 1994 the level of the Car Travelling Allowance was increased to — For the first 4500 miles, 48p per mile; For the next 3000 miles 29p per mile; For all additional miles 19p per mile. For motor cycles the rate is one-half of that for cars. The pedal cyclist can claim 5.5p per mile — no matter how many thousand miles!

Car Loans — Loans may be advanced to assist with the purchase of cars, these being governed by Regulations passed in 1992. These are available (interest free to Ministers on the Minimum and to others at modest rates according to stpend) to assist with the purchase of new or nearly new cars up to a maximum of £5040 and of second-hand cars with a mileage up to 36,000 up to a maximum of £3600. The Regulations are set forth in full in Assembly Reports 1992, p 215. Application should be made to the Department.

Listed Expenses — The General Assembly of 1957 gave their approval to the introduction of Listed Expenses, that is to say, expenses necessarily incurred by a Minister in the discharge of his duty — these should be met by the congregation and not paid by the Minister out of stipend. There have been modifications in the actual List over the years, the present position being as approved by the General Assembly in 1991 (Repts 1991, p 276).

1 (a) The Communion Expenses incurred.

(b) Any fee or expenses due to a visiting minister at Communion Seasons if such payments be authorised by the Kirk Session.

2 Holiday Supply on six Sundays in any calendar year, and Supply during the minister's attendance at the General Assembly as a Commissioner.

3 Telephone Rental and calls incurred in performance of ministerial duties.

4 Stationery and postge stamps for official use

5 Travelling expenses incurred in the fulfilment of ministerial duties, at the rates agreed from time to time by the Committee on the Maintenance of the Ministry.

It should be particularly noted that the Council Tax is the responsiblity of the congregation and not of the individual Minister, appropriate allowance having been made for this in the fixing of Appropriate Stipends.

Removal Expenses — It used to be that when a congregation within its bounds called a Minister the Presbytery was to draw attention to the heavy costs of removal, and that wherever possible they (the congregation) should meet at least part of these outlays. In 1992 it was ordained by the Assembly that payment of Removal Expenses in full should be obligatory in all cases. Where it is an Aid-receiving charge the Committee on the Maintenance of the Ministry will meet the account in full; in a Self-supporting charge the congregation is to be responsible though the Committee are prepared to pay the bill and recover the outlay over the next three years. A Manse Disturbance Allowance of up to £1200 is also available. For full details regarding these allowances reference should be made to Assembly Reports 1992, p 217.

Presbytery of Shetland — Special Regulations covering the staffing of charges in Shetland were approved in 1991. These are set forth at length in Repts 1991, p 277, and should be studied carefully by anyone interested in serving there. Briefly they include the following. A Supervisory Committee is to be appointed to supervise all aspects of the working of the Regulations. Appointments to charges are to be made on the nomination of the Committee, the congregation having a right of veto. A Minister appointed to Shetland under the Regulations has to undertake to stay for at least five years and will not be allowed to take up another charge during that time unless with special permission; he is to be paid not less than the Minimum Stipend with appropriate allowances, to be provided with a car and running costs, to be allowed six weeks' holidays to be taken in two instalments for one of which full travelling expenses will be met to a point on the mainland. At the end of the period he will have the choice of continuing in Shetland for a further agreed period. If not he is to be paid the full cost of returning to the mainland, to be paid the Minimum Stipend and provided with a house or allowance in lieu for up to a full year until finding a suitable appointment.

A report on the working of the Regulations is to be given to the 1995 Assembly and it is understood this will be to the effect "that while it has been necessary to adjust some of the terms and conditions in the light of changing circumstances the arrangements are still a very significant package of support for those ministers who are willing to uderake the special challenge of ministry in the Shetland Islands." It is hoped there will not be a need to review further these regulations until the year 2000.

Young Ministers' Furnishing Loan Fund — This Fund, whose origin lay in the former U F Church, made loans to Ministers in first and Minimum Stipend charges to assist with the furnishing of the Manse. The Fund was administered by the Committee on the Maintenance of the Ministry. As from 31st December 1988 it has been amalgamated with the *Young Ministers' Loan Fund* which had been administered independently of the Offices and had made loans for the same purpose to Ministers who, however, might be on stipends above the Minimum. The Fund is now known as *The Young Ministers' Loan Fund* and is available to provide loans for furnishing purposes to recently ordained Ministers on entering their first charge or appointment. The "young" does not apply to the age of the applicant.

Decennalis et Triennalis Possessor Non Tenetur Docere de Titulo — This is a rule to which we have rarely to refer — mercifully! It means that one who has enjoyed peaceful possession for thirteen years is not bound to instrtuct his title, applies exclusively to Churchmen, and has to do with fishing rights. I mention it here because the General Trustees are presently engaged with a case where it applies. I quote from R A Paterson, our own Solicitor, writing in the Stair Memorial Encyclopaedia — "In the well-known Lochbroom case the propietor of an estate on the north side of a sea loch and river held on titles capable of embracing the whole fishings on both sides of the loch and river *ex adverso* his land. On the opposite side of the water, however, lay the parish glebe in respect of which there had never been any formal designation. Further, there was no feudal title to the salmon fishings on the south side of the river. These had been possessed by the incumbents of the parish from time immemorial and not by successive estate proprietors. It was held that the minister, as a Churchman, was entitled to the benefit of the rule, and having possessed for the requisite period must thereforee be presumed to have a valid title to fish for salmon in the loch and river from the south side *ex adverso* the glebe; interdict against him for so doing was refused."

Chapter 8

SUPPORT FOR THE MINISTER

SUPPORT FOR THE MINISTER comes in a variety of shapes — as pulpit supply, by way of assistance (which in turn takes many forms), and through the Field Staff of the Board of National Mission, many of whom will be Deacons and Deaconesses, members of the Diaconate.

Pulpit Supply and Locum

A Minister is entitled in course of a year to six (which may be extended to eight) Sundays' holiday supply and also to have his pulpit supplied on the occasion of his attending the General Assembly as a Commissioner. In order to qualify he must have been absent from his pulpit on these Sundays — that is to say he cannot deny himself the holiday and claim payment of the sums in lieu. He is also entitled to have his pulpit filled in a time of illness. When the period of absence is to be of any length — Maternity Leave, extended Sick Leave, Study Leave — a locum will normally be engaged and an Interim Moderator appointed.

Whose Responsibility?

The responsibility for organising the availability of Pulpit Supply lies with the Committee on the Maintenance of the Ministry; but, of course, Ministers, Interim Moderators, and Session Clerks are the people who do the actual arranging. If as a result of sickness, holidays or other cause or during a vacancy pulpit supply is required there must be strict adherence to the rules governing who may be engaged (see hereunder).

Supply Agents

Application may be made to one of the Supply Agents appointed by the Assembly, and of these there is one in each of the four cities. These

Agents are under obligation to keep lists of those they employ, indicating how they conform to the restrictions. They are further instructed that in allocating engagements preference is to be given to (i) Probationers and Licentiates, (ii) Ministers without charge, and (iii) Accepted Candidates for the Ministry who have completed two full sessions of their theological course; and that no unauthorised person is to be employed.

Who May Be Engaged — This is governed by the Act anent the Conduct of Public Worship (Act ii 1986) which ordains that public worship may be conducted only (1) by the Minister; (2) by the Minister together with another person(s); (3) by another person(s) under suprevision of the Minister, he being present; or (4) by another person in full charge, but in that case the other person must belong to one of the following classes — Ministers and Auxiliary Ministers of the Church of Scotland; Ministers of other Churches as defined with great particularity in the Act; probationers, licentiates, and students in training for the ministry; members of the Diaconate who have been licensed to preach; Lay Agents; Readers. A person who does not qualify as above may be employed on occasion, but the whole facts of the case are to be reported to the Presbytery Clerk within fourteen days. Should a preacher fail to appear the Session Clerk whom failing the senior elder present is to "lead the congregation in an act of devotion, or invite someone else to do so" and again "the circumstances are to be reported to the Presbytery Clerk as soon as possible thereafter." What the Presbytery Clerk is to do in either of these cases is not set forth in the Act.

Which Committee? — Oversight of the organisation of Pulpit Supply has for long been the business of the Committee on Probationers and Transference of Ministers. In 1994 that Committee had its responsibilities altered, becoming the Committee on Probationers and among other things Pulpit Supply was moved under the umbrella of Maintenance of the Ministry. That body has now carried through a revision of Fees and is asking the Assembly of 1995 to approve of these. They represent quite massive changes and I am in difficulty as to which to quote — so I am quoting both.

Pulpit Supply Fee — The Scale of Fees and Regulations for Supply passed by the Assembly of 1991 (Reps 1991 p 282) to have effect from 1st July of that year are still in force at the time of writing, and the Assembly being what it is (and the proposals what they are!) the scale may well continue thereafter.

Pulpit Supply Fees as Proposed from 1st July 1995

1 Pulpit Supply Fee shall be a Standard Fee of £35 (or as from time to time agreed) for the Principal Service conducted in any charge of the Church of Scotland.

2 In charges where there are additional diets of worship on a Sunday, the person fulfilling the Supply will be paid £10 for each additional Service.

3 Where the person is unwilling to conduct more than one diet of worship on a given Sunday he or she will receive a *pro rata* payment based on the total available fee shared on the basis of the number of Services conducted.

4 The fee thus calculated shall be payable in the case of of all persons qualified to conduct services under Act ii 1986.

5 In all cases necessary Travelling Expenses shall be paid. Where there is no convenient public conveyance the use of a private car shall be paid for at the lowest rate for Travelling Expenses. In exceptional circumstances, to be approved in advance, the cost of hiring may be met.

6 Where week-end board and lodging are agreed as necessary these may be claimed for the week-end at a maximum rate of that allowed when attending the General Assembly, but it is expected that where possible weekend board and lodging will be provided voluntarily or at a reduced cost by members or adherents. The fee and expenses should be paid to the person providing the supply before he or she leaves on the Sunday. Alternatively he or she may be handed a voucher to forward for payment to the Secretary of the Department of Ministry.

Pulpit Supply Fees as Presently Payable

1 The Pulpit Supply Fee shall be at the rate of 3p for every £10 of stipend (0.3% of Stipend). In the case of Minimum Stipend Charges some of which have Supplements of one kind or another (Unions, Linkings, Islands, Shetland, etc) the fee shall be calculated on the basis of the Basic Minimum Stipend, *i e* no account is to be taken of the Supplement.

2 The fee thus calculated shall be payable in the case of Ministers (including Auxiliary Ministers, but in such cases only with permission of the supervising Presbsytery, and only in the case of occasional pulpit

supply, and not in respect of the conducting of services in connection with duties to which they have been assigned by the Presbytery), Licentiates, Probationers, Candidates for the Ministry (including the Auxiliary Ministry) who have been duly accepted as such, Readers, Deacons and Deaconessses licensed to preach, of the Church of Scotland. In the case of Ministers of other denominations, the same fee thus calculated shall be payable, and, in the case of all others conducting Pulpit Supply with the consent of the Presbytery of the bounds, a reduced fee of 0.15% of the Minimum Stipend shall be payable.

3 A Minister in a charge who supplies an empty pulpit without requiring to provide Pulpit Supply in his own charge shall not receive a fee, but may receive an honorarium not exceeding 0.15% of the Minimum Stipend each Sunday.

4 The same fee shall be payable irrespective of the number of Services conducted, but, if the preacher is not prepared to conduct all the services which the Parish Minister would normally undertake, so that it is necessary to engage one or more other preachers, the Fee shall be shared between them or among them.

5 and 6 Exactly as in the new Proposed Scheme above.

Cost of Supply During Vacancy — Assistance is available from the Maintenance of the Ministry Committee towards meeting the cost of pulpit supply during a vacancy, the cost being borne jointly by the Fund and by the congregation in the proportion that applied to stipend during the last year of the incumbency. When the stipend is paid, wholly or nearly wholly, from the Fund and local resources are limited a supply of weekly vouchers may be obtained on giving an undertaking to remit the required contributions throughout the vacancy. One such voucher is given to the preacher and remitted by him to the Department. I understand that it is proposed to discontinue the issue of Vouchers.

Supply by Readers

A Reader is defined in Act xvii 1992 as "a person who has been set apart by a Presbytery to an office which qualifies him or her to carry out duties within the Church of Scotland which are principally concerned with the ministry of the Word and the conduct of public worship." Each Presbytery is required to maintain a List of Readers within its bounds.

The Office of Reader — This in the Church of Scotland is of very ancient origin. The Reformed Church in its early stages was inevitably desperately short of qualified Ministers, and that largely because from the outset it was insistent on the importance of its ministry being fully equipped academically, so that those many priests who came over had to undergo considerable educational training before being allowed to take charge of a parish — they were in fact given the chance to return to their former sphere. The temporary dearth of Ministers was met by the employment in many parishes of Readers, a number of whom functioned under the direction of a Superintendent — a system not unlike that of the Methodist Circuit. In time the qualified Ministers were forthcoming, and the office of Reader lapsed. It was significantly revived after the First World War, again in a time of acute ministerial shortage, and again it lapsed when a flow of students was re-established. The office was again revived in 1958 and is presently governed by the provisions of Act xxviii of 1974 as amended by Act xxiv of 1978 and again (extensively) by Act xvii of 1992.

Selection — Any member of the Church of Scotland may apply to his Presbytery to be taken in training as a Reader, enclosing evidence of commendation in the form of a letter from his Minister and an extract minute from his Kirk Session. The Presbytery having considered the application and met the applicant and being satisfied as to his suitability refers the whole affair to the Board of Parish Education where it is duly dealt with and the applicant becomes a Candidate for the Readership.

Training — The course of training is one of guided study extending over three years, and it includes experience of conducting public worship, attendance at one week-end conference, and two six-months' attachments to congregations (not the candidate's own). Full details are set forth in Schedule A to the Act (Repts 1992, p 532). Further, a Regent (not his own Minister) is appointed by the Presbytery and is responsible for pastoral oversight throughout the course. The course having been completed the Presbytery will arrange a final hearing after which it may decide that the Reader in Training be now set apart, or that he undergo further training, or that he be not set apart. In certain circumstances a candidate may be exempted from some part of the course (Act xvii 1992, Para IIc).

Admission — It is now for the Presbytery to arrange for the admission of the Reader. This will normally, though not necessarily, take place at an ordinary meeting of the court. After the reading of the Preamble the prescribed questions are put (with the phrase "to discharge the duties of Reader" taking the place of "to discharge your ministry") and the candidate signs the Formula. He is then set apart by prayer (no laying-on of hands) and welcomed as a Reader of the Church with authority to conduct public worship anywhere within the Church. His name is entered on the Roll of Readers which every Presbytery is enjoined to keep, as well as on the Roll maintained by the Board of Ministry.

What He May Do — It shall be competent for a Reader (a) to provide occasional pulpit supply and to receive the standard fee therefor; and (b) to be attached to a charge within the bounds and in that conection to take services, to act as Chaplain in residential accommodation, to conduct Funeral Services, to conduct School Assemblies, to perform any other duty to which the Minister assigns him and which may include pastoral work. For activities of this kind he shall receive such fees as are agreed by the Presbytery in consultation with the Kirk Session and the Department of Ministry.

Supervision — Readers function under authority of the Presbytery with which they are enrolled, and on leaving the bounds of a Presbytery the Reader should apply for a certificate which he will lodge with the Clerk of the Presbytery within which he has gone to reside — the certificate testifying to status and character. Readers are required at least once every two years to attend an in-service conference approved by the Board of Parish Education. At his own request a Reader may have his name taken from the Active List without affecting his status as a Reader.

So far as life and doctrine are concerned it is my opinion that the Reader, like any other layman, is answerable to his own Kirk Session. Were it to be averred that he was preaching heretical doctrine it would be for the Presbytery to conduct an enquiry into the facts, to instruct him if he were in error, but, if he proved obdurate, to order the removal of his name from the Roll; but so far as any official censure was concerned the matter would, it seems to me, need to be referred to the Kirk Session to take whatever action it deemed proper.

Availability — The obvious weakness of the system at the present time is that the supply of Readers is most plentiful in the populous districts where the demand is at its lowest, while in the remote areas where their services would be invaluable the Readers incline to be thin on the ground. It is difficult to see how this situation can be remedied. In my own experience Glasgow Presbytery was at one time beset with complaints from Readers that they had been at considerable pains and no little inconvenience equipping themselves for a function which they were rarely if ever given the opportunity of exercising. The suggestion was made that their services might be profitably employed on a part-time basis not in the pulpits but in the pastoral work of the Presbytery's parishes. For this little enthusiasm was manifested — their ambition was to be Readers not pastoral assistants, and in fairness it has to be admitted these are two entirely different things. On the other hand it has to be said that an experiment of appointing a team of three Readers to supply, under the direction of the Interim Moderator, the non-ordained needs of a congregation suffering a protracted vacancy, proved reasonably successful. At the present time there is a growing interest in the possibility of a part-time ministry (p 141), the first part-time charge — at Abercorn and Dalmeny — having already been approved, and the changes introduced into the Act of 1992 are moves in the same direction. It remains to be seen how this commends itself. In any case, of course, this takes care of only one part of the problem — the over-abundance of supply in one part of the land — and does nothing for the dearth of supply in the other.

Supply by Locum

Where the need for supply is likely to be protracted — during a vacancy, to cover a long period of sickness, during maternity leave or study leave — it is customary to appoint a *locum tenens* who will not only supply the pulpit but will cover the work of the parish generally. In every case of this kind the Presbytery will have appointed an Interim Moderator who is ultimately responsible for the ongoing work, and it will be for him in consultation with the Kirk Session to determine just how much cover will be expected to be given by the locum and also how much he is to be paid for his labours. Locums are generally recruited from the ranks of retired ministers and with the drastically reduced age for retirement advocated today there is always quite a pool of available labour. Where, however, someone is appointed who had been granted early retirement on health grounds the financial arrangements must be cleared with the Pension Fund Commitee.

It is of crucial importance that the locum should constantly remember the limitations of his role. As he becomes known and respected among the people it is natural — inevitable indeed — that members and office-bearers should approach him with problems — not just factual questions but policy decisions — and while he is perfectly at liberty to answer those of the former description he must guard like the plague against having anything to do with the latter. For all such matters he must studiously direct the enquirer to the Interim Moderator.

Sick Leave — There was a time in the history of the Kirk when a Minister having been granted sick leave it fell to his neighbours to take turn of "giving sermon" and the hours of worship would be adjusted to make this a possibility. As a system it was most unsatisfactory, and so most Presbyteries substituted a scheme whereby all congregations made an agreed contribution towards a Sick Supply Fund and out of this the fees for pulpit supply, engaged in the usual way, were met. Things today are rather different. Quite simply, a Parish Minister is entitled to receive stipend as long as he remains Minister of the charge regardless of his state of health. He has, of course, to ensure that Pulpit Supply is provided and appropriate funding to allow such supply to be underaken is available from the Committee on the Maintenance of the Ministry, primarily from Statutory Sick Pay recovered from the Department of Social Security in the past and also from recovering monies from congregations in respect of National Insurance at a rate slightly in excess of the charge levied by the Department of Social Security. In the case of a probationer or a Minister serving other than as a Parish Minister the arrangements for pay will depend upon that particular Minister's contract of service.

Sabbatical Leave — As long ago as 1979 the General Assembly having considered an Overture from the Presbytery of Inverness about Sabbatical Leave remitted to the Maintenance of the Ministry Committee to prepare a scheme. In its Report the following year the Committee declared, "Whether it be a Scheme of Sabbatical Leave, or Study Leave, or Continuing Education Leave, the primary aim must be to afford to every Minister in a pastoral charge the opportunity of sharing in a period of renewal and recreation from time to time. The evidence of other Churches indicates that a Minister on leave continues to receive stipend at the full rate and that the congregation has to bear the cost of supply fees and expenses either directly or by means of a levy to a Central Leave Fund. It was obvious from the replies received that a Scheme of Sabbatical Leave could not be made compulsory."

Little more was heard on the subject until 1988 when an Interim Report claimed that detailed arrangements would have to be made regarding funding and administration, regarding provision of pulpit supply or locum, regarding the effect on congregation and manse families, and conference held with Presbyteries to enlist co-operation and support. The following year the Committee reported that "conscious of the financial implications of a national system for Sabbatical Leave [the Committee] have no firm proposals to make to the Assembly at this time." They went on to encourage Presbyteries themselves to take initiative, and promised that they would "come forward with a national scheme at some point in the future." Then in 1991 the Assembly Council's report recommended that the Department of Ministry should outline proposals for a nation-wide scheme (Repts 1991, p 88), with the result, however, that in 1994 the Council reported with regret that in the present financial climate the Chuurch should not proceed with such a national scheme but that the matter should be kept alive with a view to a further report in 1998.

In quite a number of cases Presbyteries have in fact taken steps in this field and operate a scheme of Study Leave. This in most cases involves a period of three months' absence from normal duty (with, of course, a ban on earning during that period), it may confine itself to simple "study" in the everyday sense of that word (by, for example, the writing of a thesis or the taking of a diploma), or it may involve travel, or it may mean occupation in some denomination or some other sphere or even some other country — in fact it is very much open-ended so long as it has the advance approval of the Presbytery which may even provide a capital sum to make the exercise possible. The evidence coming from Presbyteries which operate a scheme is that it is highly successful, and it is generally felt that a national scheme would be of considerable advantage.

Maternity Leave — A Minister is entitled to Maternity Leave and Maternity Pay in terms of regulations agreed with the DHSS. The Minister is to cease work during the period of the leave, which will normally be of eighteen weeks' duration — eleven weeks prior to the expected date of confinement and until the sixth week after the actual confinement. Advance notice is to be given in writing fifteen weeks before the expected date, and this has to include an assurance that her absence will be partly or wholly due to the pregnancy and that she intends to return to her work at the expiry of the period and to continue therein for at least three months. Payment of full stipend will be maintained for a period of eighteen weeks. It is stressed that when on Maternity Leave a Minister may not be involved at all in ministerial duties within her parish or in the Church at large. In case of special hardship, terms may be arranged in consultation with the Maintenance of the Ministry Committee who should be timeously approached .

These terms are, I understand, presently the subject of review.

ASSISTANTS

Ministerial assistance can take quite a variety of different forms — there is the assigned student, the student assistant, the ordained assistant, the associate minister, the auxiliary minister, and increasingly a system is developing where an arrangement is made with a Retired Minister to render part-time service. Besides which there is the Community Minister.

Student Attachment

It is a prescribed and important part of the preparation for the ministry that a candidate has to engage in a certain amount of practical work concommitantly with his academic studies, and this is achieved by his being assigned to a series of parishes by the Committee on Education for the Ministry during his years in the Divinity Faculty. The regulations governing such Assignments (Reps 1970 p 586) provide that they are to operate only in winter and spring terms with no obligations over the Christmas vacation period, that the student is to conduct at least one, and not more than three, full services of worship, that he is to participate in one (not always the same) Sunday activity, that he is to spend not more than one afternoon or evening per week in the work of the attachment, and that while there is no salary a refund of expenses incurred will be made. Each student is to underake three such attachments during his course — in a different parish each year.

Clearly the object of this particular exercise is to provide the student with, at first hand and at close quarters, an insight into the work of the parish ministry, and any measure of assistance coming to the Minister concerned is minimal and purely coincidental, and is in any case likely to be more than offset by the burden of guiding and supervising imposed. The extent of the service is determined by the Committee which also evaluates its success.

Student Assistant

Student Assistantships were at one time a regular and — from the impoverished students' point of view at least — a highly popular feature of the years of training for the ministry. At any time during his University course, and particularly during its closing stages, a student might expect to be engaged as Assistant in some busy congregation, and in a day before the payment of Student Grants the (generally modest) sum paid by way of salary was a most welcome addition to the student exchequer. The object in view was not primarily the training of the student but the provision of help for an over-worked Minister in a busy city parish. In 1969 it was proposed in a deliverance to the General Assembly that this system should be brought to an end, it being deemed that the "attachment" system provided a better form of training.

The deliverance was approved, but the following year a Petition was presented to the Assembly by the Divinity Students' Council of Trinity College, Glasgow, asking that Student Assistantships be re-introduced as an optional alternative to Student Attachments. The Assembly provisionally granted the crave and remitted to its Committee to examine the whole field afresh. The researches of the Committee revealed that in the other three centres there was a preference for Attachments, but that it was generally agreed that an option should be available. The position today is that the Attachment principle has prevailed.

Probationer Assistant

Almost without exception students, after licence, are required to serve a Probationary Period under surveillance of the Committee on Probationers in a charge to which they have been directed by the Committee on Education for the Ministry. In the first place this was called the "probationary year" and was intended to be for a twelve-month period, the students concerned starting immediately after licence and being permitted to apply for vacancies any time after the passing of the New Year. In fact congregations (who were paying the salaries) were rarely interested to engage till the summer was past, so the "year" started in October and by January the assistant's eyes were on the ends of the country in search of a vacancy. Effectively the "year" had been reduced to six months. A Report in 1983 suggested the possibility of a two-year period of Probation being introduced, but while the desirability was accepted the idea was not pursued because of the expense involved.

However the Assembly of 1990 approved proposals advanced by the Assembly Council, that for all accepted by the Committee as Candidates for the full-time ministry the Probationary Period be extended to eighteen months and that such probationers (1) shall receive for the first twelve months of the period a salary at the level of 80% of the current Minimum, upped to 100% of that Minimum at the end of the first year's service; (2) shall be given rent-free housing or a housing allowance, and the refund of travelling expenses; and (3) shall be eligible at the close of the first twelve months' service for admission to the Minister's Pension Fund. (Reports 1990, p 73). Since it was of the essence of the scheme that every type of parish should be involved the choice must not be restricted to those congregations which could afford to pay, and so the Committee accepts the bill in every case. Very serious questions are being raised as to whether the Church can afford this level of cost on the Probationary Period in this time of financial stringency.

Auxiliary Probationers — Those in training for the Auxiliary Ministry also, on being licensed, have, unless in very rare circumstances, to serve a Probationary Period, and this they will do in exactly the same way as students for the regular ministry except that they will be available for only a limited number of hours (ten perhaps) per week, and that they will not be in receipt of any salary though they will recover out-of-pocket expenses.

Commitment — The Probationary Period may commence any time after licence, but it will usually begin with the opening of the season's activities sometime in September. The Probationer is required to give his full time and energy to the work of the assistantship and is specifically prohibited for doing any concurrent study towards, for example, a higher degree. He acts under the direction and control of the Minister, and if the appointment has involved moving into the bounds of perhaps a new Presbytery he has to lodge a certificate with the Clerk and comes under supervision of that Presbytery. In any matter of life or doctrine it is to the Presbytery that he is answerable. He serves his Period under supervision of the Board of Ministry (not of Education as formerly).

Period of Service — Each Probationer and each supervising Minister is to submit a report after three months and again after fifteen months from the start of the Period to the Committee on Probationers which is to make a recommendation as to whether the Period should be provisionally sustained. At this point the Probationer is eligible for election in a vacancy but may not be inducted until the full Period has been completed and sustained. Should the Period not be sustained a further period of Probation may be prescribed, to be served in an attachment — almost certainly a new one — chosen by the Committee on Education for the Ministry, All of this in terms of an Act of 1991 amending Act v of 1985 (see Reports 1991 p 563). It is not unknown for a Probationer to elect to continue in his Assistantship for a further year, though in such circumstances there will more than likely be an application for him to be ordained. It has to be borne in mind that in the eventuality of the assistantship being continued the entire cost will have to be met by the congregation and, in the event of his being ordained, this will include the contribution to the Pension Fund.

Ordained Assistant

His Probationary Period having been completed to the satisfaction of all concerned the Probationer may elect instead of proceeding immediately to a charge to serve for a further spell as an Assistant, either in the congregation wherein he has been for the past eighteen months, or in some other, and in such a case it is usual that he should be ordained, both to allow of his rendering a fuller service and to give him a deeper and more comprehensive range of experience. As has been indicated in the previous paragraph there will at this stge be no financial assistance available from central funds.

Request for Ordination — The request for the ordination of an Assistant should be directed to the Presbytery by the Minister and Kirk Session of the congregation where the Probationer is serving or proposing to serve, and should indicate that he has satisfactorily completed his period of Probationary Service and has given an underaking to continue in the position for at least a year after ordination. In considering the request the Presbytery is enjoined to bear in mind that ordination should be granted to licentiates only for very good reasons (either because of the size of the congregation in which they propose to serve or because of the amount of pastoral and parochial work involved) — though I imagine only some very cogent reason would lead to refusal.

Ordination — The Service of Ordination is exacly as it would be for a Probationer going to his first charge and an edict in common form has to be served in the usual way. There is, of course, no question to the congregation. Since 1972 (Act ii) ordination as an Assistant has carried with it the right to a seat in Presbytery.

Conditions — The same conditions apply in regard to salary and expenses as outlined above in case of Probationers except that the salary is to be at the rate of 80% of the Minimum prevailing during the year when ordination takes place. In this case, however, these figures represent minima and better terms can be given so long as the congregation is meeting all its commitments. It seems reasonable that better terms should be given since the ordinand had been in receipt of the full minimum during his previous year's service (see p 224). Generally the appointment may be terminated (after the promised year) by one month's notice on either side.

ASSOCIATE MINISTER

This is a creation of fairly modern times and so far there is little law applying to it. Since its introduction by the Board of National Mission through its Committee on Parish Reappraisal as an option under New Forms of Parish Ministry no fewer than thirty Associate Ministries have been established.

Creation — It is for the Presbytery to determine when an Associate Ministry should be created in a charge. When so deciding the Presbytery is expected also to define with some precision what are to be the duties of such a ministry, and this it will do in conference with the Minister and Kirk Session of the charge concerned. Normally an Associate Ministry will be created for one of two reasons — either (a) because perhaps as a result of readjustment a charge has become of such a size as to demand the services of a second Minister; or (b) because there is in the parish an area of special character sufficient to require a Minister freed from other parish responsibilities to look after it. In the former case care must be taken by the Presbytery in framing the job-specification to ensure that the Associate while ultimately under control of the Minister is given scope for the fulfilment of his own personal ministry and is not seen simply as an Assistant with a fancy title. In the latter case the danger is that of over-departmentalising the work of two men who should be seen as sharing one common ministry. And in both cases it should be borne in mind that the whole idea of Associateship is still very much at the formative stage and that a good measure of freedom should be allowed to discover how the arrangement can be employed to the best advantage.

Tenure — The length of tenure has to be stipulated in the agreement reached when the appointment is made and a copy of the whole terms should be supplied to the appointee before his final acceptance. It should be kept in mind that the achieving of some kind of continuity is one of the principal reasons for having an Associate (rather than a string of Assistants). There is nothing to prevent the contract being for, say, five years in the first instance with the option of being renewed for a further five, and this is, on the whole, to be preferred to the idea of "ten years with the possibility of review at the end of five." When a period is stipulated I imagine the congregation is bound, though a situation could arise which no-one would wish to see continued longer than necessary. During the period of his service the Associate will be a member of the Kirk Session but will not act as its Moderator. A point which dare not be overlooked is that while the Parish Minister is the holder of an office and not an employed person this does not apply to the Associate who is an employed person working to a contract. In his own interest the Associate should satisfy himself regarding the terms of this before becoming involved.

Introduction — The Associate who will have been chosen by the Kirk Session with concurrence of the Minister (ratified by the congregation itself if the Kirk Session so resolve), will have his appointment confirmed by the Presbytery (which has satisfied itself as to his status and credentials) and is introduced to the congregation at an appropriate service. Only where ordination is involved is edictal intimation required. He enjoys the right to a seat in Presbytery. Obviously since he will be working in such close fellowship with the Minister the latter's concurrence in the choice is of paramount importance.

Payment — The stipend of an Associate Minister will be by arrangement of Kirk Session and Presbytery. He will be provided with a Manse or paid a Manse allowance in lieu, as well as recovering the usual Listed Expenses. In certain circumstances the Assembly's Reappraisal Committee may be prepared to recognise the Associate Ministry as a "new form of parish ministry" and to take over, in part or in whole, the responsibility for stipend, but such agreement must have been reached in advance of any appointment being ageed to.

AUXILIARY MINISTER

Full particulars regarding the selection, training, and employment of Auxiliary Ministers will be found at page 141 ff.

Assignment — "Auxiliary Ministers may be allotted to such assignments as the Presbytery of the bounds may from time to time determine." Such assignments may be expected to vary considerably in character as between one Presbytery and another. In some cases relief to the overworked Minister in an area of deprivation may be in view, or help to a Minister in a multi-charge linking, or provision to cover a continued, or at least continuing, vacancy. Whatever the circumstances the Auxiliary, in discharging the duties of his assignment, is subject to the supervision of a Minister or Ministers appointed by the Presbytery of the bounds.

Conditions of Service — These are to be determined by the Presbytery in consultation with the Minister of the parish within which the assignment is to operate and are to include a definition of the minimum number of hours per week and the number of weeks per year to be devoted by the Auxiliary, arrangements for the reimbursement of expenses (which will include travelling up to a maximum of 4500 miles a year), a "book allowance" up to £150 a year, and the payment of pulpit supply fees, though fees are not to be exigible in respect of the pulpit of the parish to which he has been assigned. A list of "Proposed Conditions for the Assignment of an Auxiliary Minister" was approved by the Assembly of 1985 (Reps 1985, p 206), but these were revised and updated two years later (Repts 1987, p 430). A very exhaustive review of the experience of the office of Auxiliary Minister was undertaken by the Committee on Education for the Ministry in 1986 and is extensively reported in Repts 1987 pp 413 ff. They admit that their enquiries evoked "few undiluted hymns of praise" for the new office, "but equally there was an almost total lack of any call that this new Ministry should as soon as possible be discontinued.

Relation to Courts — During the period of the assignment the Auxiliary is a member of Presbytery and as such eligible for appointment as a Commissioner to General Assembly. During that period also he is associated with, though not a member of, Kirk Session and may be invited by the Minister to act as Moderator *pro tem* of Session, but only on the strict terms applying to such Moderatorship (p xxx). During any period when he is not assigned, it would seem, the Auxiliary cannot be a member of Presbytery, for so long as he retains the status of Minister he cannot sit in Presbytery as an Elder.

RETIRED MINISTERS

A practice which is spreading fairly widely, at least in the cities, is that a Minister who has retired from his parish on grounds of age accepts appointment as a part-time Assistant in some busy charge, with a view principally of lightening the Minister's load of pastoral work. This is a local and domestic affair where agreement is reached with the Minister and Kirk Session and the Retired Minister in regard to duties, remuneration, etc. The Retired Minister retains his seat in Presbytery (so long as he undertakes to attend same and until the age of 75), but he does so as Retired Minister of X and not as Ordained Assistant at Y. He may be associated with the Kirk Session but is not a member of it and can function as Moderator only on the *pro tempore* basis (p 288).

Locum Tenens — A Retired Minister may act as locum during a vacancy. Again this is a domestic arrangement not requiring outside approval except in one of two events. First, there are Presbyteries which do not approve of the Interim Moderator (being a retired Minister) accepting office as locum — a difficulty easily overcome by appointing a different person as Interim. (When delicate readjustment negotiations are in progress this dual role can lead to complications better avoided.) So Presbytery approval should be obained. Secondly, when some part of the vacancy expenses are being met out of Maintenance of the Ministry funds the approval of that Committee is a *sine qua non* of any financial agreement with the locum.

There is no rule governing the salary of a locum — it is a matter for local agreement and will depend to a considerable extent on the amount of service to be given. This may vary from the supply of the pulpit, the conduct of funerals and marriages and urgent sick visiting to what amounts to the full work of a ministry, and the emoluments fall to be determined accordingly.

In a number of cases a Licentiate with no pastoral charge is employed as a locum during a vacancy. Clearly such locums cannot underake Baptisms or Communion services, but this can usually be got round by an occasional exchange with the Interim Moderator.

COMMUNITY MINISTER

This office has had a very odd history. In 1971, arising out of the Report of the Special Commission on Priorities of Mission, the Advisory Board was instructed "to take up the question of what area might most suitably be named as an area for organisational experiment of the kind suggested in the Report, to consider the possibility of the appointment of an "Enabler", and to bring forward specific proposals to next General

Assembly (Repts 1971, p 700). The following year it was reported by the Advisory Board that the area of Drumchapel had, with the approval of the Presbytery of Dumbarton, been chosen as the area, but that the question of the appointment of an "Enabler" was still under consideration, the functions of such a person not having been very clearly defined in the original report. The Board promised that this would receive the most careful consideration. The following year the Board was happy to report that the appointment had been made of a "Community Minister" but said nothing at all in fulfilment of its promise to define duties or responsibilities. The matter now moved into the field of the Home Board which was financing the venture.

In 1974 the Home Board reported to the Assembly on what was being done at Drumchapel where, it was said, the work of the Community Minister "covered many aspects of the life of the community, such as participating in the activities of the community, helping to set up a newspaper, promoting amenities, supporting self-help groups, arranging parties for deprived children and co-ordinating distribution of gifts at Christmas, seeking to formulate answers to the real needs of the people of the area. A close relationship is kept up with all the congregational agencies in the locality." It is added that his duties have also included the promotion of ecumenical understanding and Christian action, the establishment of house-churches, and keeping in touch with churches in the area.

Responsibility for the experiment now passed from the Home Board to the Maintenance of the Ministry Committee and from them to the Unions and Readjustments Committee under the umbrella of "New Forms of Parish Ministry". So far as I am aware no statement has yet been before the Assembly setting forth the precise (or even general) duties of a Community Minister. Despite this it was possible in 1994 to report that there were eight Community Ministers employed within the Church.

Assignment — It will be only indirectly that any one parish Minister will benefit from the setting up of a Community Ministry in his area, and so the initiative in this field must lie with the Presbytery which has to make approach to the Reappraisal Committee. If it is agreed in principle that such a project should proceed consultation will take place regarding the area to be served and the nature of the work to be undertaken. The appointment is for five years with review at the end of the fourth, and salary is at the level of the Minimum and either housing is made available or a housing allowance is paid. The appointment will be made by the

Committee in consultation with the Presbytery. For the discharge of his duties the Community Minister is answerable to the Committee; for life and doctrine he comes under the jurisdiction of the Presbytery. I incline to think that a Parish Minister could take exception to the creation of a Community Ministry that included all or part of his parish area, though in the absence of any clear definition of the duties of such a ministry he might find it difficult to prove that any kind of intrusion was involved.

THE DIACONATE

The Diaconate of today represents what resembled very closely the merging in 1988 of two separate and quite independent streams of Christian service each of them with a long history — the Lay Missionary (exclusively male) and the Deaconess or Church Sister or Parish Sister (exclusively female), though in fact what happened was that in 1988 (the centenary year of the first appointment of a Deaconess — at Bowden) the Diaconate Committee agreed to recommend acceptance as Deacons of seventeen (out of the nineteen) active Lay Missionaries, the event being marked with a Special Meeting of the Diaconate Council in Glasgow on St Columba's Day, 1988.

The Lay Missionary

The Lay Missionary was an agent of the Parish Assistance Committee of the Home Board, appointed by that Committee to assist in certain parish situations, empowered to preach and that regularly, but not ordained. They were to be found working in two quite different types of situation. In many sparsely-populated areas particularly in the Highlands and Islands a lay missionary would be found supplying the need for a Minister — supplying in fact the want of a parish minister — but, of course, enjoying none of the powers that go with ordination. In all such matters he was dependent on the Minister of the parish in which his station was situated and under whose direction and control all his work was done. Usually he operated from a Mission Church or Mission Hall or Mission Station and was provided with the equivalent of a manse. From time to time over the years the suggestion has been advanced that because of the isolation of his station it would be good that he be given some kind of ordination however limited in character that would enable him to baptize and to give communion and celebrate marriages, but this has been consistently and successfully resisted. In the case, however, of a few island communities agreement has been reached with the Department of the Registrar General that he be recognised as authorised to conduct marriage according to the forms of the Church of Scotland.

The other locations in which Lay Missionaries were commonly found were in densely populated areas of the cities — what today we should call areas of deprivation — where again they operated very often from a Mission Hall with the financial and personal backing of what amounted to an independant group within a city congregation. The number of Lay Missionaries in both types of situation has been steadily dwindling over the years. I have been able to identify no fewer than ninety-two of them in 1934; in 1985 it is recorded that there were twenty-seven, eleven of them in Highland and Island parishes; in 1988 the total had, as indicated earlier, dropped to nineteen.

Conditions of Service — The aspiring Lay Missionary had a course of study set for him by the Parish Assistance Committee, he served for a probationary year in a post to which that Committee directed him and all being well he was then commissioned "by the General Assembly or by such subordinate court as may be named by the General Assembly" — generally the Presbytery. The Parish Assistance Committee appointed him to his sphere of service and might at any time transfer him to another location. He retired at age seventy, though in exceptional circumstances his service might be extended for a further period. If an Elder he might be enrolled in the local Kirk Session and if so could be appointed Representative Elder to the Presbytery — and in any case had a right to sit in Presbytery as a Corresponding Member. Lay Missionaries were on the pay-roll of the Parish Assistance Committee which also arranged for them to receive a pension if they had given twenty years' service.

The Deaconess

In one form or another Deaconesses had been functioning within the Church for a hundred years, sometimes under the name of Church Sisters, but it was not until 1962 that they received formal recognition through the medium of a "Scheme" which regularised their position, functions, relation with courts, etc. This Scheme was slightly amended twenty years later. In 1985 it was agreed that the Diaconate Board should become the Diaconate Committee operating within the Department of Ministry, and, as has been said, in 1988 Lay Missionaries were invited to join in the scheme, an invitation accepted by all but two of the then nineteen holders of the office.

Definition — A Deacon or Deaconess is described as "one who has, under a call from God, pledged himself or herself to the service of Jesus Christ and His Church and has been trained and commissioned thereto in conformity with the doctrine and discipline of the Church of Scotland. It is a distinctive office, agreeable to the Word of God."

It is emphasised that the office is open to men on the same terms as women, and the revised Scheme is at pains to use "he or she" and so on throughout. As explained in the Preface I have consistently used the masculine form alone to avoid dreary repetition of alternatives and crafty constructions to avoid the choice. In this case, however, the *de facto* position is that the office is mainly held by women and some of the regulations apply exclusively to them, so it has seemed reasonable to use the feminine form throughout — it being understood that men are included.

Function — The function of a Deaconess is to exercise a ministry of an evangelistic, pastoral, eductional or social nature in the work of a parish or chaplaincy or in some other service approved by the Diaconate Committee.

Candidature — A candidate has to apply to the Deaconess Committee and will be interviewed by that body. If satisfied regarding sense of vocation, fitness and basic background the Committee may accept the candidate, and if so will notify her Presbytery for its interest. In case of rejection the candidate has a right to petition the General Assembly.

Training — Every candidate must satisfy the Committee that she has a knowledge of the Bible, of Christian doctrine, of Church History (particularly Scottish), and an understanding of the Church, and is able to relate these to individual and corporate life today, and that she has practical experience and understanding of Christian education and the communication of the Gospel to different ages and groups. Training is normally taken at St Colm's Education Centre and College. Over and above this the Deaconess may be expected to take more specialised training prescribed by the Department or Committee for which she is to be working. The Committee prescribes a probationary period (which may be extended) and informs the Presbytery within which it is to be served.

Commissioning — A candidate having satisfied the requirements in regard to training and probation and being a communicant member of the Church of Scotland and over twenty-one years of age may be commissioned, an exercise performed by the Presbytery at a special service arranged for the purpose. This will normally be held in the Church where her work is to be centred, and the Presbytery will associate with it in the service those Deaconesses who are in attendance. Having been so commissioned the Deaconess is entitled to append after her name the letters "D C S" (Deaconess of the Church of Scotland) and to wear the badge and uniform of a Deaconess.

Answerability — For the due performance of her service the Deaconesss is answerable to the Department or Commitee or secular body which is employing her, but of course if she is working in a parish she will take orders from its Minister. In the matter of life and doctrine she is under the jurisdiction of the Presbytery within whose bounds she is serving, or failing such a Presbytery, of that which commissioned her. She may voluntarily resign her commission, but may be deprived of it only by Presbytery, with the usual right of appeal to the General Assembly.

Relation to the Courts — There is nothing to prevent a Deaconess being ordained an Elder and as such admitted to the Kirk Session of the parish where she is serving. The Assembly of 1958 ruled that Deaconesses should be invited to attend Session meetings when matters affecting their work was under discussion and that they should be appointed to membership of Presbytery Committees. In 1980 it was ordained that Deaconesses serving within the bounds should *ex officio* be Corresponding Members of Presbytery; and then by Act ii of 1990 they were granted full membership of Presbytery during their period of service, to continue on retirement on grounds of age or infirmity. When granted a seat in Presbytery the person was no longer entitled to be a member of a Kirk Session.

Salary — Terms and conditions of service are as determined by the Department, Committee, or other employing authority concerned.

Licence to Preach

In 1956 it was agreed by the General Assembly that certain candidates for the Diaconate having the required qualifications should receive a course of theological training which would "fit them to act as Assistants in parishes, Chaplains in Universities and Training Colleges, Teachers of Religious Instruction in Schools and Colleges, and similar spheres of service"; and

(a) that such candidates if found suitable by the Deaconess Committee are to be recommended to the Presbytery not only for commissioning but also for licensing as Preachers of the Word, without reference to probation for the Holy Ministry;

(b) that regular preaching and regular participation in the conduct of public worship is to be only by Deaconesses so qualified and licensed; and

(c) that any Deaconess may apply to the Committee on Education for the Ministry to have such additional training prescribed so that she may qualify for such licence.

The decision in 1968 that women should be eligible for ordination as Ministers on the same terms as men was bound to render rather superfluous the legislation for Deaconesses to train for licence to preach since in effect this was now equivalent to becoming a Probationer for the Holy Ministry.

It will be noted that the restriction of preaching and conducting public worship to Deaconesses licensed to preach refers to the "regular" exercise of these functions, which might seem to indicate that all duly commissioned deaconesses are available for occasional pulpit supply, although in the Act of 1986 they are not included among those eligible.

FIELD STAFF

This is the general name given to lay staff who work mainly in parishes and who are the responsibility of the Board of National Mission under its Committee on Field Staff. In accordance with the overall policy of the Board and where appropriate in the light of financial guidance offered within the terms the Strategic Plan by the Assembly Council in consultation with the Board of Stewardship and Finance this Committee is responsible (a) for matters concerned with the selection, training, deployment and pastoral support of full-time Lay Agents, and (b) for liaisoning with the Diaconate Committee. Most Field Staff work in parishes, three in Gaelic-speaking crofting communities, one in the Shetlands, and others in large city housing areas — fifteen in Glasgow alone — where Ministers are few in relation to population in many parts.

The majority of Field Staff are commissioned Deacons or Deaconesses or Missionaries who have undergone a period of training usually extending over a period of two years followed by a probationary period of one year in a parish, after which they are commissioned to their task by the Presbytery under whose jurisdiction they are serving — in case of the Missionaries by instruction of the General Assembly, in that of the Diaconal candidates by recommendation of the Diaconate Committee. In 1994 they were paid at the rate of £11,826 with certain seniority payments as well as expenses for travel, telephone and stationery. Housing is provided or a payment in lieu, removal expenses are met and there is a contributory pension scheme. The total average cost to the Committee of employing a Field Worker was reported in 1993 as being £15,681.

Chapter 9

DISCIPLINE

IN THE CONTEXT of the life of the Kirk the word "discipline" has come to acquire a chilling sound, we are instantly reminded of a day when what appear to us as none too scandalous doings brought down the terrifying wrath of a self-righteous Kirk Session, we picture the cutty-stool, we are perchance reminded of Holy Willie and of the hypocrisy with which the bitter sarcasm of Burns adorns his prayer. The word, however, is a perfectly respectable one, filling an honourable place in the vocabulary of the Kirk, as I shall try to indicate.

We find the term in use in three separate contexts, first as referring to the government of the Kirk as a whole, secondly in respect of that aspect of the work of the Kirk Session that had to do with the care of the wrongdoer in the flock, and thirdly in connection with the duty of the Presbytery to deal with *fama* or scandal affecting one of the Ministers or Probationers under its oversight.

THE DISCIPLINE OF THE KIRK

A passage from the Articles Declaratory which enthusiasts of the ecumenical movement love to quote is found in Article VII which declares that "the Church of Scotland ..... recognises the obligation to seek and promote union with other Churches in which it finds the Word to be purely preached, the Sacraments administered according to Christ's ordinance, and discipline rightly exercised, and it has the right to unite with any such Church without loss of its identity on terms which this Church finds to be consistent with these Articles." Discipline has to be rightly exercised ("richtly entertaynit" had been the original form of words). There are those who see this as a reference to the way Kirk Sessions dealt with antenuptial fornication and such-like misdemeanours. This is quite wrong. It is a reference to how the Church itself is governed, in our case to the Presbyterian form of Church government. We have not to look far for corroboration of this meaning of thc term. The post-

Reformation Scottish Kirk was governed in the first place in terms of Knox's First Book of Discipline of 1560 and then on the more elaborate work of Andrew Melville, the Second Book of Discipline of 1592.

It would seem to me, therefore, that one crucial question posed in Article VII in the ecumenical context is whether a Church based upon a Presbyterian polity can agree that, say, an Episcopal form of Church government is a right way of ordering its affairs, whether discipline is being rightly exercised therein. We can, if we so care, abandon the one discipline and adopt the other, but we cannot superimpose the one upon the other, nor can we identify the one with the other. We have squarely to face up to the question whether within the Church with which we are conversing discipline is being "richtly entertaynit." There can, certainly be no doubt as to how our fathers would have answered that question.

Question of Identity — It is interesting to note how insistent were the framers of the Articles to declare that such a union would not involve any loss of identity. It would seem a fair assumption that they had at the back of their mind the outcome of the famous Free Church litigation of 1900–04 where in the House of Lords it was held that the question of the ownership of property following a Church union was to be determined on the basis of whether either of the parties had lost its essential identity. Not satisfied with declaring that such a union could be effected without loss of identity the Article goes further and asserts that on this question the Church is to be judge in her own cause. While the civil courts would almost certainly concede this claim on a purely ecclesiastical issue I cannot but wonder whether they would do so on a question of ownership of property.

It is not my intention to pursue this issue further (however tempting the prospect) but merely to draw attention to the fact that any consideration of discipline within the Kirk must direct itself towards Church government as the integral and crucial part of that subject.

DISCIPLINE EXERCISED BY THE KIRK SESSION

One of the traditional duties of the Kirk Session — and one which exercised them greatly in an earlier day — was that of seeking to maintain a proper standard of Christian behaviour within the flock. They seem to have had a firm belief that people could be obliged to be good. Alleged deviations from the path of rectitude were regularly reported to the Kirk Session which generally instituted at least an enquiry to be followed by a trial and which if the offence was proved could lead to rebuke, delivered in public, to the lesser excommunication, being suspension from privileges for a stated period, or to the greater excommunication which involved being completely cut off from Church membership. This represented discipline being richtly entertaynit.

So far as I have been able to look into this aspect of congregational life in those earlier days two things have struck me very forcibly — first the enormous power which the Kirk Session was in a position to wield in the lives of the people of the close-knit communities of those days, and secondly the extremely responsible way in which they tackled their task in such cases.

The Power of the Session — Not only was the Kirk Session in a position where it could summon the suspect delinquent to its bar, it had also the power to cite and compel witnesses, and it could make its censures effective. I quote an instance from around 1830. In my own parish of Houston the Kirk Session resolved after due deliberation that the Thanksgiving Service on the Monday after the Communion Week should be discontinued. A group within the congregation submitted a petition (in the most respectful terms) praying that they be not deprived of this so valuable opportunity of spiritual enrichment. The Kirk Session apparently saw this as an attempted encroachment into their territory and summoned the delinquents to answer for their impertinence. Most of them claimed they had not properly understood what they were about and expressed contrition for any offence given. They were admonished and told to be more circumspect in future. Half-a-dozen hardy citizens stood by their guns. They were suspended from sealing ordinances *sine die*. Over the succeeding years the records testify how one after another had to come crawling back and make his peace — one wanted a child baptised, another dearly wished to take communion, a third one — and I found this especially interesting — was a joiner who had moved to Irvine and could not find work in that town because he could not produce a certificate of good behaviour from his Kirk Session.

The emergence of the Secession bodies broke what had been in effect the monopoly enjoyed by the Auld Kirk in matters religious and the iron grip of the Session had to be loosed.

Form of Trial — The other very interesting feature of the exercise of discipline by Kirk Sessions of yester-year is how seriously they took their responsibility, the pains to which they went to secure a fair trial. They would devote three or four whole evenings to a simple case — say of drunkenness — hearing witnesses and indeed writing down their testimony in long hand and having it read over and signed. Witnesses did not undertake to tell the truth, the whole truth, and nothing but the truth, they were instead "purged of malice, partial counsel and good deed done or to be done," The interrogation was led by the Moderator, but the accused had the right to cross-examine and to lead evidence in rebuttal of the charge. It all took time, but time as I say, seemed to be no object. With the best will in the world one cannot but wonder whether some of the time could not have been better spent in devising a more positive approach to improving the moral condition of the parish.

The Contemporary Situation — We have a vastly changed position today. On the occasion of a quinquenniual visitation when the question of discipline is reached there is generally a hush during which the Minister explains that he looks to these things privately and confidentially and that unless in some exceptional case no report is made to the Session and nothing appears in the minutes. It is good that this should be so, so long as some gross scandal is not simply ignored. The sinner can be made ashamed of his conduct without needing to declare his penitence in face of the congregation, and there is more hope for his regeneration if he remains within the fellowship of the congregation than if he is thrown on to the rubbish-heap of the excommunicated.

DISCIPLINE EXERCISED BY THE PRESBYTERY

Discipline is still a most important, if mercifully not very common, function that has to be exercised by Presbyteries. In what follows I propose to quote fairly extensively from what I wrote in my little "Guide to the Presbytery". It should be kept in mind that every Minister so long as he retains that status is subject to the discipline of some Presbytery, that of which he is a member or was a member until he lost his seat on account of age, or of that within whose bounds he resides. Every Probationer is likewise subject to the discipline of the Presbytery within which he holds a post or resides or of that which licensed him.

A Caution to Clerks — If any breath of scandal affecting one of its members comes to the knowledge of a Presbytery — and for practical purposes this means reaches the ear of the Clerk — he will normally take steps to discover what exactly is amiss and whether there is anything he can do "off the record" to put things straight. This is both understandable and commendable, but in an area where the utmost caution has to be exercised the Clerk must here proceed with great discretion, keeping in mind that if his efforts are unavailing the issue may well develop into a full-scale libel case in which he will be expected to act as prosecutor and when everything will be "on the record". It would be most unfortunate if the unhappy Minister concerned had been encouaraged to weep on the Clerk's shoulder to the extent of making an incriminating confession to him in his role of "friend of the accused." The Clerk could find himself in a most embarrassing position — to put it at its mildest — were he required to give evidence of such an interchange, in a civil no less than in an ecclesiastical court.

In a situation of this kind the Clerk is well advised to visualise from the outset the issue becoming a "case" and see himself responsible for the conduct of a trial. What can be an honest attempt to help can so easily be represented as unauthorised interference. The Clerk most certainly should see to it that someone well known to the accused and trusted by him is put in touch to help and advise. The Clerk cannot himself move too warily in the affair.

Instituting Proceedings — The Act (vii of 1935) underlines the need for the utmost caution in instituting proceedings against a Minister or Licentiate, requiring that before this is done a complaint shall have been lodged either in a writing subscribed by the complainer or in a statement made by the complainer in presence of the Presbytery, in either case along with some account of its probability. It may be, of course, that there is a *fama clamosa* (a public scandal) of such intensity that the Presbytery for its own vindication feels bound to take the initiative and institute an action even in the absence of a complainer. The wise course at this stage is to remit the business to a small select committee including if possible someone with legal experience. The first duty of such a Committee is to conduct a preliminary enquiry.

Preliminary Enquiry — The accused person is to be informed of the arrangements for the preliminary enquiry throughout the whole of which he has the right to be present and to defend himself thereat with the help if desired of a solicitor or other agent. It has to be kept clearly in mind that this is not a trial but an enquiry to establish (a) that there are grounds for believing that there may be guilt, and (b) that the guilt is capable of being proved. In such an enquiry much will depend upon whether the fault alleged is moral or heretical in character. It is universally accepted that drunkenness, embezzlement, gross indecency are moral faults scandalous in a Minister and the business is simply that of showing that the accused has been guilty of such conduct. If, however, the charge is one of heresy the actual terms of what the Minister said or wrote will most likely be freely — perhaps proudly — confessed and the question before the Committee will be whether this represents a heretical opinion of such a character as to demand that the matter be taken farther.

Plea by Accused — The Committee may report that in their view no further action need be taken, and if the Presbytery agree then that is the end of the matter. If, however, the Committee are of opinion that there are adequate grounds on which to proceed they should, without elaborating on the matter in any way, simply state this and ask the Presbytery to authorise them to prepare a Statement setting forth the heretical opinions or the improper conduct alleged and submit this to the accused. He in turn has three options. He may plead Guilty as charged. Or again he may in writing state objections to the Statement in part or in whole, and in that connection it is wise that the Presbytery should have given authority to its Special Committee to act for it in the adjusting of the Satement if that is deemed appropriate in light of the objections received. Or it may be that the accused will simply tender a plea of Not Guilty.

Confession — The Act of 1935 says that "if the person concerned shall admit all or any of the allegations contained in the said Statement the Presbytery shall take such steps as shall seem to it to be necessary and proper according to the nature and extent of the allegations admitted by such person."

In the body of the text of the 6th Edition at page 321 Cox states, "If the accused confess and the matter confessed be of a scandalous nature censurable in others, such as the sin of uncleanness, or some other gross scandal (whatever be the nature of his penitence, though all be convinced of it) the Presbytery is *instanter* to depose him *ab officio*." This is a reprint of the precise terms of the old Act of 1707. It makes it clear that the Presbytery has no discretion in such a situation, it is bound to depose from office. While I should agree that the kind of offence referred to merits the greatest severity I am not myself satisfied that today's Presbytery is bound in this strait-jacket. The Act of 1935 quoted above repeals all prior Acts of Assembly "insofar as any of their provisions are inconsistent with this Act." To me it seems clear that there is complete inconsistency here and, that being so, the later Act must prevail. Besides which it would seem unjust that deposition should of necessity follow upon confession of guilt whereas proof of guilt after trial leaves it to the Presbytery to depose or to take "such other steps as it shall deem to be necessary and proper."

Deposition — The matter is of considerable importance because of the utter finality of a sentence of deposition compared with, for example, suspension from office *sine die*. The latter has all the force and effect of the former, but if at some future time the Presbytery is satisfied that the hurt is healed and that the transgressor might be restored to office it has it within its own power to lift the suspension, which it can do without too much reminiscing. If, on the other hand, the man has been deposed then only the Assembly can restore his status, and this means, of necessity, a petition which will rehearse the whole facts and circumstances of the original offence — a high price to pay with no guarantee of success.

I rather clearly remember a case when a Minister who had been deposed at least twenty years earlier petitioned for reinstatement. Interestingly the reason for his having been deprived of status was an irregularity that would not be looked upon half so seriously today as it had been at the time. The principal effect of bringing the whole affair to light was one of widespread dismay that so serious a consequence should have followed on so slight an offence and the crave of the petition was granted without demur. That is the only case that has occurred within my recollection, and I am prepared to believe that others, though they might well deserve to be reinstated, would rather leave things as they are than have the by-most-folk-forgotten episode dragged into the glare of the television lights on the Assembly floor.

Preparation of Libel — The document setting forth the charge is known in ecclesiastical parlance as a "libel" and the whole process is referred to as "trial by libel". Assuming that the accused has wholly, or at least substantially, denied the conduct attributed to him in the Statement a libel is to be prepared and subscribed by the Moderator and Clerk of the Presbytery. Before it is served it is to be reviewed by the Procurator of the Church. The accused person when served with the libel should also be furnished with a list of the witnesses the Presbytery proposes to call.

Committee to Conduct Trial — A Presbytery is a most unwieldy body to conduct a trial, particularly if it is going to involve examining many witnesses and is likely to occupy a fair amount of time. Provision therefore exists whereby the Presbytery may appoint a Committee of not fewer than three and not more than five of its number to act for it. It used to be that a Presbytery could ask for the appointment of two from the Board of Assessors, but that provision was withdrawn in 1980. The Presbytery has also to appoint one of its number (two if it so determine) to act as prosecutor and he in turn may instruct counsel or engage a solicitor to act in the affair. The Presbytery may feel constrained to engage — and even pay for — someone to represent the accused.

Temporary Suspension — A Presbytery may at this point, depending upon the whole circumstances, resolve that the accused should be suspended from the exercise of his ministerial functions until the case has been disposed of, and if so it is to make an order accordingly and appoint an Interim Moderator to act with the Kirk Session. The Minister's right to his stipend and occupancy of the manse shall, however, be in no way affected by such suspension.

Special Defence — Within twenty-one days of receipt of the libel the accused may lodge Notice of a Special Defence — that he was in quite another place when the event occurred (alibi) or that he was mentally deranged at the time. Since resort to a special defence transfers the *onus probandi* to the shoulders of the defender he ought when lodging his Special Defence to enclose a note of the witnesses he proposes to call in support of it.

Opening Sederunt of Trial — Once this has all been done a date is to be fixed for the trial proper to begin, and not less than seven days' notice thereof shall be given to the accused. At this first sitting the accused shall have the opportunity of stating any objection to the competency of the proceedings, to the constitution of the court, to the relevancy of the libel, or indeed to make any preliminary objection he may have to the regularity of the proceedings. As was hinted earlier, if the charge is one of heresy the whole burden of the case may turn on a challenge to relevance — that the facts alleged (and admitted) do not disclose any deviation from strict orthodoxy. Once that question has been disposed of one way or the other the trial is as good as ended.

Diet of Proof — Assuming that these various matters have been disposed of and the facts are still open to challenge the Committee shall appoint a date when the cause is to go to proof. At that said diet all evidence is to be given on oath — first witnesses for the prosecution, then those for the defence, with cross-examination and re-examination. A shorthand-writer is to be employed and put on oath and a record taken of all the evidence. Speeches shall be made for the prosecution and then for the defence. If it is the Presbytery itself which has heard the evidence it is then to go on and issue its verdict. If the hearing has been remitted to a Committee that body is to prepare a report of its findings in fact. If it is a unanimous report the Presbytery is bound to accept its conclusions and find accordingly. If the report is that of a majority the Presbytery may resolve either to accept the verdict or to have the evidence printed and of new to hear the parties (not the witnesses). It has then to reach its verdict.

Incidentally, the verdict has to be be one either of Proven or of Not Proven (not of Guilty or Not Guilty). This is sometimes made the subject of criticism on the ground that a Not Proven verdict leaves a stain on a man's character. Coming from the criminal courts (where it represents a third choice) it can be seen as meaning, "We're sure he did it, but they couldn't pin it on him!" I have always held the view that the Kirk is right in its choice of verdicts and that it is the criminal courts of the land that are wrong here. The accused pleads Guilty or Not Guilty of the charge and that is as it should be. If the latter the matter goes to trial when the Crown proves or fails to prove its case, the offence charged being thus Proven or Not Proven. The question of innocence is strictly an irrelevance. A boy is brought in in connection with the theft of a large sum of money. Under police pressure he takes them to a field and shows them exactly where the money is buried. He is found Guilty and sentenced. On appeal the sentence is recalled because he had not been told he could have his father present at the "grilling". Does this mean he was Not Guilty? But, if I may mix my metaphors, do not let me get side-tracked on to a hobby-horse! Suffice it that the Church's verdict is Proven or Not Proven.

Sentence — By whichever method the verdict has been reached if it be one of Proven the Presbytery shall hear the offender or his representative in mitigation. It shall then go on to consider what is the appropriate censure and "direct what steps shall be taken for carrying the censure into effect." The censures of the Church are admonition, rebuke, suspension from office (either for a stated period or *sine die*), deposition, or in a case of extreme aggravation and contumacy, excommunication. If a minister is suspended or deposed he is debarred from performing any of the functions of the ministry, including the conduct of public worship. Admonition and rebuke are administered by the Moderator in presence of the court. Suspension from office debars from the privileges as well as from the duties of the ministry. Where it is for a limited period and involves a Minister in occupancy of a Manse special arrangements will have to be made in this regard.

Record Apart — It is provided that the whole record of the proceedings in a libel case are to be kept in a Record Apart. If the proceedings end with a finding of guilt and a pronouncing of censure then there shall be entered in the ordinary minute-book of the Presbytery the first minute of the Record Apart, the terms of the libel, and the verdict and sentence. Should the case end in complete acquittal the Record Apart and all papers shall be sealed and held *in retentis* for five years, after which they shall be destroyed.

Proceedings in Other Courts — The proceedings of other courts, civil or criminal, cannot be accepted as a substitute for independent action in the courts of the Church. For example, citation as co-defender in an undefended divorce action does not prove adultery, nor does conviction of driving with an excess of alcohol prove drunkenness — though a plea of Guilty tendered by the Minister before the Sheriff in such a case would be a significant item of evidence.

A difficulty can arise when a criminal charge is being preferred at the instance of the police in that they have first claim on all productions, and in any case are likely to have been first on the scene and have impounded all the evidence they could find. Let it be that a Minister is being charged with embezzlement, the police will certainly have taken possession of all books, ledgers, vouchers etc and until there has been a criminal trial or the fiscal has decided not to proceed to trial, these papers will not be available for the Presbytery's prosecutor. In their absence there is clearly nothing he can do to establish a case. Police and fiscal are likely to prove co-operative (even sympathetic) but the situation is a difficult one to which neither side seems able to suggest a solution.

Appeal to Tribunal — It is a common occurrence these days to read of someone who has been dismissed from some post appealing to an Employment Tribunal which after a hearing has issued a judgment of wrongful dismissal, reinstating the appellant or awarding him damages or both. I have been asked whether a Minister deposed by Presbytery or

General Assembly after due process can take his case on either the procedure or the merits to such a Tribunal. My view would emphatically be in the negative. We have good authority in Ballantyne v Presbytery of Wigtown (Session Cases 1936 p 654) that where judgment has been given by a Church court in any matter affecting doctrine, worship, government or discipline in the national Church then "the matter is at an end and neither statute nor the common law, nor previous decision, whether upon statute or the common law, can avail to bring the matter within the jurisdiction of the civil authority." I cannot imagine that any Tribunal could stand up in face of that. I know there have been occasions when the Tribunal has ruled in the case of Ministers — but not of the Church of Scotland.

Chapter 10

THE COURTS IN GENERAL

UNTIL 1992 ONE WOULD HAVE inclined to open this Chapter by quoting Article II of the Declaratory Articles of the Kirk and have written that the Church's government is Presbyterian "and is exercised through Kirk Sessions, Presbyteries, Provincial Synods and General Assemblies, but that year saw the end of the road for the Provincial Synod, so that the situation today is that the strata of courts are three in number. While each of these functions independently in its own domain they share a great deal in common so far as the conduct of their business is concerned, and they are interconnected in a very intimate fashion. It will be the business of this chapter to look at these common factors and to examine these lines of communication.

CONDUCT OF BUSINESS

Meetings

This is an area where there are differences between one court and another. With the exception of the Kirk Session all the courts of the Church either are actually in session or are standing adjourned to meet at a time and place of which public intimation has been made before they rose at the previous meeting. For a Presbytery to close its sederunt without having taken this step of appointing its next meeting means that the court has lapsed and it will be necessary for it to be "revived" — at no little inconvenience. The Presbytery can, of course, meet for a specific item of business or in an emergency before the day appointed. In the case of the Assembly, adjournment is only from one session to the next. When the Assembly of 1994 concluded their business they "appointed the next General Assembly to be holden at Edinburgh on.... and the Assembly of 1994 became a part of history. A Kirk Session is quite different in that it meets when called or on a regular basis as has been arranged.

How Called — Since the Presbytery is standing adjourned and the next Assembly has already been appointed there is no need for either of these courts to be "called". Sometimes when the agenda for a Presbytery meeting is circulated it is referred to as "the notice calling the meeting", sometimes even there is a note over the name of the Moderator purporting to "call the meeting". This is quite incorrect. The meeting was appointed by order of the court, and any subsequent notice should take the form of a reminder that this has been done. Special meetings can be called by the Moderator and by him alone. If the Clerk sends out the notice he should do so stating that the calling is by order of the Moderator. A Kirk Session meeting may be called by pulpit intimation or by notice sent to all members.

Quorum — The quorum of the Assembly is thirty-one of whom at least sixteeen must be Ministers. In the other courts the quorum is three — in Kirk Session the Moderator and two Elders, while in the Presbytery at least two of the three must be Ministers (and the Elder must already have been enrolled, for otherwise the meeting could not be constituted and so his commission could not be received).

Constitution — The meeting (assuming there is a quorum) is constituted with prayer (normally but not necessarily led by the Moderator), after which the sederunt is taken, commissions are dealt with, a Moderator is appointed if this is necessary, and the minutes of the previous meeting or meetings are submitted for approval and signature. When the business has been completed the benediction is pronounced by the Moderator and this is accepted as satisfying the requirement that the meeting be "closed with prayer."

Public or Private — The Kirk Session meets in private unless for any special item of business it should resolve to meet as an open court — which it is never required to do. All other courts meet in public though they are at liberty to meet behind closed doors, and will do so in certain cases where the law so prescribes or where they themselves deem it expedient. In most cases the public is represented by the press which has the right to report on the proceedings. In a case in the General Assembly in 1984 it was agreed that reporters might be present but television cameras were banned. When in a case parties have been removed it lies within the discretion of the court to determine whether they must leave or may stay to hear the deliberations in their case, though normally this will be conceded. A court of the Church enjoys the protection under the Revolution Settlement Act of 1693 that the civil courts are bound "to render all due assistance for making the sentences and censures of the Church and judicatories thereof to be observed." And so a newspaper editor could find himself and his paper in trouble were he to report a case which the court concerned had resolved to take in private. The Presbytery being an open court facilities should be available for accommodating the public should they wish to sit in on the proceedings.

When Meetings Coincide — The general rule is that no court can sit when any court superior to it is in session unless the permission of the latter has been obtained — in craving which reason must be given. The principle is, obviously, that members should be free to attend both, and this will imply allowing sufficient time to elapse to cover travelling. On the same principle a Kirk Session, provided none of its members is a commissioner, may meet during any of the sittings of the Assembly. In 1890 it was ordained that it was not to do this "without urgent cause", but this is now completely relaxed.

OFFICIALS

Without exception the same officials are found in all three of the courts.

Moderator

In every court one of the members acts as Moderator. The Moderator of the Kirk Session must always be a Minister. In the Presbytery it is required that the Moderator be a Minister. Recent legislation (Act ii 1980), however, has made it possible that an Elder should be elected Moderator of the General Assembly — though that has not so far occurred. In every case, apart from the Kirk Session, he must be chosen by free election, he holds office for a year and is eligible for re-election. He remains in office until he has constituted the meeting at which his successor takes over. Until 1944 it had been customary for the Moderator of Presbytery to be picked from a rota and to hold office for only six months.

Arising from the ecumenical debate proposals have recently been discussed for the introduction of a system of permanent Moderators of Presbytery, or for Moderators who would hold office for an extended period of, say, seven years. These proposals, however, spring from a conception of the powers, status and function of the office of Moderator quite foreign to those that have all along obtained in the Church of Scotland. The proposals for change are not primarily concerned with the length of tenure of the office, but rather with its satus — ultimately with overturning the principle of the equality of the ministry.

Powers — The powers of the Moderator are very limited, being strictly confined to the conduct of the meetings of his court. He is responsible for calling, or declining to call, a meeting when such seems to be required or when requsitioned. He causes good order to be kept, ruling on points of order and refusing to put motions which he deems irrelevant, offensive or otherwise incompetent. Once the Moderator has ruled on a point of order his ruling becomes a judgment of the court and may be appealed like any other. The Moderator signs minutes, petitions, and other papers (but not extracts) in name and by authority of his court. It is now well established that the Moderator of the General Assembly visits many parts of the Church after the Assembly have risen bearing their greetings and expressing their concern. That, however, is the extent of his power, and if, for example, he addresses a Presbytery in course of his tour he does so quite simply as a visitor. It is perhaps worth saying that he is Moderator of the General Assembly of the Church of Scotland — not Moderator of the Church of Scotland as the media love to designate him.

Voting — A Moderator has a casting vote only, and if he declines to exercise this the matter remains unresolved and may be raised afresh at some later time. He cannot move or second a motion, and should not be seen to take sides when in the chair. There is a widely accepted convention that a casting vote should always be given for the *status quo*. This stems from the principle that change should not be introduced unless it carries a clear majority, and that is a very sound guiding principle for any chairman to follow even though it is not a binding rule.

Clerk

A court cannot function without a Clerk who, on appointment, takes the oath *de fideli*. In the temporary absence of the regular Clerk a Clerk *pro tempore* must be appointed, and he also has to take the oath, and this fact too has to be recorded in the minute. The form of administering the oath (whose full title, incidentally, is *de fideli administratione officii*) is that the person raises his right hand and says, "I promise that I will carry out with faithfulness the duties of Clerk.' In the case of a few of the larger Presbyteries a full-time Clerk is appointed; in other cases a parish Minister functions on a part-time basis. For some years past the office of Principal Clerk of Assembly has been linked with the full-time Secretaryship of the Board of Practice and Procedure, the Depute Clerkship being a part-time appointment. Any court may appoint a Clerk who is not one of its number — though I am not aware of any case where this is done. I imagine it could happen in future were a Presbytery to want to continue the services of a Clerk who had passed his seventy-fifth birthday.

Custodier of Records — The Clerk is custodier of the records of the court and he alone can give valid extracts from these, but he can do so only with consent of the court. On appoinment he should receive — and give a receipt for — the records as set forth in an inventory.

Signature — If on any document the Clerk append his official designation after his signature this is understood to mean that the writing carries the authority of the court.

Leaving the Desk — The same rule applies to the Clerk as does to the Moderator, that he must relinquish his place if an inferior court of which he is a member is called to the bar and a Clerk *pro tempore* is appointed and takes the oath. Unlike the Moderator, however, he may without leaving his place at the desk speak on any subject that is before the court and he may move or second any motion thereanent. Indeed when at the Assembly a Committee report is presented by the Convener he not being a commissioner it is one of the Clerks who moves in terms of the Deliverance.

Treasurer

Every court appoints a Treasurer regarding whose responsibilities reference should be made to the following chapters on the various courts. The financial affairs of the General Assembly fall within the province of the General Treasurer of the Church.

Officer

Every court of the Church appoints an Officer to wait on its meetings and to carry out its orders. He will not normally be a member of the court. In the case of the Kirk Session this is one of the duties of the Church Officer — largely nominal in modern days.

RECORDS

Minutes

The entire deliberations of every meeting of every court are recorded in a minute — usually referred to as "the minutes". These should represent an account of all the decisions reached by the court and should record in detail all the motions, amendments, etc that were before the court and the state of the voting in reaching these decisions, though unseconded motions are not generally recorded, though should the mover of such a motion be appealing then obviously the record must be complete. To enable this to be done those proposing motions should hand these in writing to the Clerk when they are proposed, or at latest before the vote is taken. The minutes are not intended to be — and are much better not to be — a detailed account of all the arguments that were advanced or of the speeches that were made. Ideally each item of business should be minuted and the minute approved at the time, but this is at once very difficult for the Clerk and extremely time-consuming for the court, so the standard practice in all courts is that the minutes of one meeting are taken in scroll by the Clerk and having been extended by him at his leisure are submitted for approval at next meeting. If, however, there be a particularly contentious matter before the court it is well that the minute covering it should be prepared, read over, adjusted if need be, approved there and then and signed by Moderator and Clerk. This may well occupy a little time, but it will be time well spent. In terms of Act iv of 1984 anent Readjustment when a final judgment has been reached by the Presbytery affecting the future of a congregation procedure is to be sisted, the minute is to be adjusted and approved, and an extract is to be forwarded to the Assembly Committee.

Content of Minute — A court has the right to say (subject to over-ruling by a superior court) what shall appear in its minute. It is in order to propose that some item or occurrence should not be recorded, but if there is opposition to this it is well to concede the point. There are certain matters which are not to be recorded in the ordinary minute book — see Record Apart (p 246).

Form of Minute — The minute of any meeting must begin with a definition of the place and time of the meeting "held consequent upon adjournment" or "called by the Moderator" or whatever the case may be, followed by a list of all those present, and it must record that the meeting was opened and closed with prayer. In the case of the larger Presbyteries it is usual instead of recording the names of those present to have a separate Sederunt Book in which people sign (or score off) their names. This book is part of the permanent record and should be carefully preserved and produced at the annual inspection of records. Even when there is such a record it is usual to print enough names in the body of the minute to constitute a quorum. No record is kept of attendance at sessions of the General Assembly.

It is ordained that the minute should contain a marginal index of subjects (a rubric) for ease of reference. I think that increasingly the rubric is giving place to a cross-heading in heavier type appearing at the top of each subject, and so long as the objective of easy reference is achieved I cannot see it matters very much how this is done. Blank spaces and blank pages must never be left as these would allow for unauthorised insertions — a line should at least be drawn through the empty space. Pasting pages on to the book is highly irregular.

Loose-leaf Minutes — For many centuries the first requirement of any record was that it be kept in a bound volume, and there was much to commend this idea. So long as there were people capable of writing magnificent copper-plate and happy to spend time doing so the system worked admirably. The emergence of the typewriter changed all that. It became both quick and easy to produce a highly legible minute — but you cannot get a bound volume into a typewriter! And of course the word-processor made it possible in a single operation to type a minute enough copies of which could be run off to supply one to each member. Insofar as it is thus possible to supply members of the court with a printout of the minute the change is very much to the good. A Regulation of 1964 accepts loose-leaf records subject to four conditions:

1) the pages must be consecutively numbered as they come into use;
2) the last word on each page has to appear as the first word on the next;
3) each page has to be initialled by the Moderator (over and above his signature at the end); and
4) at convenient intervals a suitable number of sheets are to be bound into a permanent volume.

The last of these regulations is perhaps the most important since it is so easy for failure to observe it to go undetected at the annual inspection and for this to result in sheets going missing. Loose leaves can disappear in a way that does not affect a bound volume. In regard to Regulation 3 I should think that if each sheet (rather than page) is initialled this should be sufficient protection against the introduction of spurious material.

Circulation — It is, I think, universal practice in Presbyteries, that copies of the minutes are printed and circulated along with the agenda and the notice reminding members of the date of the next meeting, the same practice being followed these days in many Kirk Sessions. In such a case when it comes to submitting the minutes for approval they may be "taken as read". When the only copy is in the hands of the Clerk he will read over the entire minute, unless it be agreed to take any part of it "as read". When the minutes of a Kirk Session are circulated in this way particular care has to be taken to ensure that their confidentiality is honoured as far as possible. When a meeting is held in private so also is the minute of that meeting. The same, of course, applies to those parts of the minutes of other courts which record business transacted behind closed doors.

Approving the Minute — As soon as the meeting has been constituted, commissions disposed of and a Moderator installed the next business is to have the minutes approved. The only question here is whether the minute is an accurate and adequate record of what happened. The fact that someone does not approve of what happened or has had second thoughts about the competence of what was done is utterly irrelevant. Confusion can easily arise when, as happens in some cases, the minute of a Committee is submitted to the whole court as the recommendation of that Committee, for here a clear distinction has to be drawn between approving the accuracy of the record and approving the recommendation.

If attention is drawn to a mistake of a fairly trivial nature this can be corrected by the scoring out of the wrong word and the superscription of the correct one, the alteration being initialled by Moderator and Clerk. Not in any circumstances should a word be rubbed out or painted over and another word written (or typed) in its place. The fact that a change has been made must be patent on the face of the record.

If any material alteration, addition or deletion is to be made then in my view this fact should be recorded in the new minute — that is to say, the minute should read, "The minutes of meeting of ..... were submitted, taken as read, and were approved subject to the addition in the third line of page 123 after the word "agreed" of the words "that ....." This should be done in addition to making the change in the permanent record along with a marginal note verifying how many words had been added, and duly initialled, To me it seems a nonsense to say, as I have seen done, "The Minutes were approved subject to adjustment" without condescending on the nature and extent of that adjustment. After all, any member of the court who retains his minutes is entitled to believe he has a complete and reliable record, and this can be the case only if alterations are fully recorded in the circulated material.

A resolution reached at a meeting of a court becomes operative immediately and does not need to await the approval of the minute at a subsequent meeting.

Signing the Minutes — The minutes having been approved (with or without adjusment) they have to be signed by Moderator and Clerk. This signing is done by authority of the court. It is therefore those who occupied these offices when the minute was approved who sign even though they may not have been present at the meeting whose business is recorded. In the event that a minute has not been signed at the time and, let's say, the Moderator has died it is always in order for the court, having heard the circumstances, to authorise someone else to sign, which he should do there and then, adding after his signature 'by authority of the ..... given at ..... on the .....'

Deletion of Minute — It has always been held incompetent for a court to delete or expunge any part of its record unless under order of, or at least with authority of, a superior court. This must not be taken to mean that part of a draft minute (the kind that is circulated beforehand) may not be deleted — so long as this is agreed and carried out before it has been approved and signed.

"Taking Instruments" — When someone has taken an appeal or dissented and complained the full minute used to read, "...against which judgment Mr AB protested for leave to appeal, took instruments in the Clerk's hands and craved extracts." The interesting piece of ceremonial enshrined in the phrase "taking instruments in the Clerk's hands" consisted in laying a shilling on the Clerk's desk, and is a survival from a day when litigation was much more common than it is now and when the sole income of the Clerk of a court came from charging so much a page for providing extracts from the minutes. Litigants were entitled to extracts, but Clerks were entitled to their fees. The shilling was an earnest of the appellant's good faith in the matter of paying, falling into the same class as the arles paid to a prospective farm-servant or the shilling paid to the soldier, or the half-crown which I myself remember handing over to the factor on renting a house. A shilling is no longer legal tender and the Assembly of 1994 agreed that the whole affair was now an irrelevance and should be discontinued. I'm sure that although instruments have not been taken all will go well with the appeal, but meetings may be a little duller without this modest piece of make-believe.

Record Apart

To keep the ordinary records of the courts, which have to be consulted and inspected for various purposes, free from the presence of undesirable matter, and to obviate their mutilation by the deletion of the proceedings, the principle of a Record Apart shall be adopted in all cases where moral delinquency is alleged. So far as the cases which ordinarily come before Kirk Sessions are concerned, involving communicants or baptized persons who are adherents, the desired end may be achieved by the use of a Minute Book of Discipline. In all other cases, such as pocesses against office-bearers the court of first instance shall resolve from the first to keep the proceedings of the case in a Record Apart, and said resolution shall be minuted in the Record Apart and not in the ordinary record. "When the judgment which finally disposes of the case, by whatever court of the Church pronounced, involves any degree of censure of the accused, then the court of first instance shall engross in its ordinary minute-book the first minute of the Record Apart, the libel or a summary of each of the charges thereof if a libel was served, and the final judgment. When a case has ended in entire acquittal, if there be a Record Apart in any court inferior to the General Assembly, it shall, with all papers in the case, so far as these do not affect the interests of third parties, be sealed up in presence of that court, docqueted with the name of the congregation and the date of final judgment, and kept *in retentis* for five years. When a process ends in entire acquittal, the person whose innocence has been approved ought to have a certified copy of the judgment of the court delivered to him.

'If a record be kept by the Kirk Session of all cases of discipline it shall be in a book reserved for this purpose alone. The names, and all that might lead to the identification of the parties, shall be rendered illegible after five years. In such cases the Kirk Session shall not, unless requested by the person accused, be required to keep a Record Apart but in the event of an appeal or a dissent and complaint to any superior court other than the General Assembly, a Rcord Apart shall be kept by that superior court

"In every case the inferior court must keep an Inventory of Process, in which the Clerk must enter and number all the documents."

It goes without saying that the Record Apart must not be duplicated and circulated to members with the other papers of the court.

Other Records

Apart from minutes there are records of various kinds belonging to courts, especially to Kirk Sessions, and reference should be made to the appropriate chapter in each case.

Long-term Custody

For many years Church records no longer in current use were stored in a strong-room in the old Tolbooth Church until, towards the end of the 'fifties, an approach was made by the late Sir James Fergusson, then Keeper of the Records of Scotland, offering to assume responsibility for the repair, care and keeping of all the Church's old records. The talks that followed resulted in an agreement approved by both sides in 1960 whereby all Church records of any age would be given on permanent loan to H M General Register House, Edinburgh. The records would be available for inspection and study, but only in the public search-rooms and under supervision of Records Office staff. Access would be free and photostat copies would be available on payment of the usual fees. Should a Kirk Session wish to have its records "re-loaned" for the purpose of, say, an historic exhibition, this would be done by applying to the Presbytery which, if satisfied, would transmit the application to the Principal Clerk, he being the person appointed to deal with the Keeper in such matters. Once the particular purpose had been served such volumes were to be immediately returned.

In 1970 the Presbytery of Shetland approached the General Assembly with a request that they be permitted to have their records kept by the archivist of the local authority on the plea that it was most inconvenient to have to travel to Edinburgh in pursuit of this branch of local history and that the books would be equally secure as well as more accessible in Lerwick. The General Assembly agreed. Since then permission has been granted to various Presbyteries to have their records put in custody of the

Regional Archivist. The terms and conditions of loan are in each case as in the original agreement except that approach is made direct to the Archivist by the Presbytery Clerk.

Transmission of Documents — In 1969 it was enjoined that all Church records of date prior to 1900 were to be transmitted to Edinburgh (or, where some other arrangement had been approved, to the appropriate authority) for custody, In 1985 this was updated (Repts p 6) in the case of congregational records which, if not in current use, are to be transmitted when more than fifty years old.

Inalienable — Church courts being courts of the land are in the position of holding their records inalienably for the benefit of the public. Such records are therefore *extra commercium* and cannot by sale or gift be passed out of the ownership of the court. Should any such records appear in some private collection or in some museum, library or sale-room steps should be taken for their recovery.

Subpoena — It could happen that a court of the realm passed an order requiring the production of some Church record and in such an event it is proper for the document to be made available.

SUBORDINATION OF COURTS

Each court (with the obvious exception of the Kirk Session) has authority over those below it and may recall their judgments when their proceedings are regularly brought before it. Only a very few items are excluded from this power of review and these only by specific enactment. In a case before the Assembly in 1933 it was argued that when an Act conferred powers of decision upon a Presbytery without saying its judgment was subject to appeal the Presbytery's determination was to be accepted as final. The Assembly rejected the argument. The presumption is in favour of the right of appeal and can be rebutted only by the specific terms of an Act. A Kirk Session, for example, has finality in all matters connected with the preparation of the Electoral Register in a vacancy, the Presbytery is the final court in the exercise of *ius devolutum* and in determining when permission is to be given to a Minister of another denomination to dispense the Sacraments in a Church within its bounds. For a long time the Synod was the final court of appeal in all matters except doctrine, worship, or censure of a Minister or office-bearer; but in

1947 the licensing of students was, in terms of Act viii added to the exceptions, and in 1962 Act xv deprived the Synod of finality in readjustment cases, but see what follows.

The Synod That Was

This may be the appropriate point at which to say a word about the disappearance in 1992 of the Synod from the second highest rung in the ladder of the courts of the Kirk. For a very long time before this (fifty years perhaps) there had been murmurings about the value of the Synod as a court, and in particular about its exalted position near the top. Evidence of this is to be found in the previous paragraph telling how in one field after another it was being deprived of finality of judgment.

The simple fact of the matter was that the Synod had outlived its usefulness. For many generations the Synod had filled a quite significant role as a half-way house between Presbytery and General Assembly. At a time when litigation was an everyday affair it was good to be able to reserve the General Assembly for the settling of really serious issues and at the same time to have an appeal court detached from the "local" influences that could so easily affect a Presbytery judgment. So the legislation provided that in a great many matters the Synod represented the end of the appeal road.

What significantly changed the whole pattern of Presbyterian polity was the emergence of the Committee structure. So long as the concerns of the Church were confined within her own parishes the four-tier pattern of government was both efficient and sufficient. But when (to take one obvious example) the Church became interested in missionary work overseas — and it is difficult for us today to realise the intensity of that interest — the four-court machine was not equipped to cope. Obviously the sending of missionaries abroad was not something to be undertaken by Kirk Sessions, Presbyteries or Synods — it was an affair for the Kirk as such and had to be taken under Assembly direction and control, as well as finance. So an Assembly Committee had to be appointed independent of the lower courts but, on the financial side, very much dependent upon them. And as the Assembly Committee structure expanded and developed Presbyteries found that these supplied the intermediate stage between them and the Assembly. No longer had we a neat little parcel of a case which Presbytery passed to Synod, and of which Synod in turn made a fresh parcel for transmission to Assembly. Under the new regime Assembly was involved almost from the outset.

When finality of judgment was taken away from it the Synod became merely a step — a wholly unnecessary and time-wasting one in most people's view — on the way to the Assembly. Less and less business came the way of the Synod and less and less interest came to be taken in its affairs. Attendances dropped to pitiful levels. The total strength of the Synod of Clydesdale, for example, was over the twelve-hundred-mark, yet to get an attendance of fifty was something of an achievement. In these circumstances when a case was being heard that put say thirty of these at the bar it was only too easy to "pack" the court with the right kind of voters! If one complained about the poverty of the attendance one was told, "Give the Synod some really worthwhile work to do and folk will attend." To which, of course, the answer was, "How can important work be entrusted to a court in which the members manifest so little interest that they won't even attend?"

In the hope of creating a deeper sense of responsibility in the work of the Synod an Act (vi) was passed in 1981 whereby a Synod might determine, given the concurrence of all its constituent Presbyteries, that it would confine its membership to an agreed proportion of its total strength. Members so appointed were to serve for four years one quarter being replaced every year. I cannot say how widely the option was taken up, but certainly in the case of Clydesdale the change was made but without any significant improvement being effected.

Other attempts were made from time to time to generate interest by devices like having someone to speak on a subject of contemporary interest followed by discussion. I remember an occasion on which I was such an invited speaker. A unique feature of the Synod was that it included in its membership a Correspondent from each of its neighbouring Synods. On the particular forenoon of my involvement after the opening exercises the Visiting Correspondents (three of them) were welcomed; a report in some detail was received from each of their own Correspondents on the visits they had paid during the previous year; they appointed Correspondents for the following year. This was followed by a collection of statistics thrown at us by a Committee Convener. I was then invited to speak, there was little or no discussion and we adjourned to meet in six months' time for, presumably, a repeat performance. We then proceeded to a local hostelry where a pleasant lunch was enjoyed. Could you wonder if people hesitated to undertake a perhaps hundred-and-fifty mile round trip for that?

I cannot imagine that the demise of the Synod was the occasion for widespread mourning throughout the Church, though it is certainly worth saying that in some of the more remote areas the biennial meetings will be missed, for they did provide an opportunity for people in fairly isolated situations to meet and exchange views — even if not all of them on ecclesiastical matters.

Inspection of Records

Apart from the possibility of having its judgments recalled the lower court is answerable to its superior for the responsible handling of its affairs, not least in the matter of its records. Every record which a court is bound to keep has to be submitted anually for inspection. Thus all congregational records which are the responsibility of the Kirk Session are examined by the Presbytery (p 336), the Presbytery's records used to be submitted to the Synod and those of the latter in turn to the Assembly, but now (Act vi 1992) "Each Presbytery shall appoint an Examination Committee to make an inspection of the Presbytery's Minute Book and Benefice Register, and report to the Presbytery at its first ordinary meeting of each year. An extract minute of the Presbytery's deliverance thereon shall be transmitted to the General Assembly not later than the 31st day of March in each year through the Board of Practice and Procedure." An Act of 1700 lays it down that the job of inspecting is to be entrusted to "a competent number of the most fit and experienced ministers for that work." During the sittings of the Assembly each year a Committee is appointed to examine all minute-books of Assembly Committees and report thereon to a later diet.

Objects of Inspection — The first object of the inspection is to ensure that the records actually exist and that they are being properly cared for and kept up to date. Attention is also to be given to ensuring —
1) that the doings of the court have been in conformity with the law and practice of the Church;
2) that minutes are properly kept, with rubrics, with alterations, additions and deletions properly attested, and in the case of loose-leaf records that these are kept conform to the regulations and are being duly bound;
3) that the minutes are signed, and alterations attested, by both Moderator and Clerk;
4) that attention has been paid to advice given on former inspections;
5) that the court has been diligent in executing all Acts of Assembly; and
6) that, in the case of Kirk Sessions, the inventory of Church property

has been revised annually and that the regulations concerning the care of ecclesiastical property are being fully implemented.

Attestation — After examination, in one of the records (preferably in the minute-book of the court) there should be written, 'These records, along with ..... have been examined from the date of last attestation and found satisfactory"; or "satisfactory with the following exception/s ....." and may go on to give instruction, "and ..... was instructed to ....."

Should any error disclosed in the examination be of so serious a character as to be censurable this fact may be recorded, but before this is done representatives of the court alleged to be at fault should be heard, and the fact that they have been so heard should be recorded in the attestation.

Who Produces — It is the Clerk of the court who, as custodier of all its records, is responsible for all the books being produced when called for. He should see that space is left after the last signed minute for the attestation to be entered in the minute-book. If the books are not forthcoming the court concerned may be ordered to produce them through a communication sent to its Moderator.

AVENUES OF APPROACH

The ways in which a lower court can bring its business, or have its business brought, before a superior court are four in number — (a) Appeal or Dissent and Complaint; (b) Petition; (c) Overture; and (d) Reference. The first of these, Appeal, or Dissent and Complaint, represents the way in which the judgment of a lower court can be brought before the superior court for review by a party at the bar or by a member of the court respectively. The second, Pwetition, is normally the machinery for asking that something be done which is of particular interest to the Petitioner, though in certain circumstances it can be used in connection with the review of a decision reached elsewhere. The third, Overture, enables the inferior court to raise in the superior some matter of general concern to the Church. The fourth, Reference, properly reflects a situation where the lower court is reluctant to reach a judgment on some issue where, for some reason, it feels that the more authoritative opinion of its superior should be taken. Each avenue has its own peculiarities.

Simple Dissent — Before dealing with the ways in which judgments may be brought up for review a word should be said about the fact that it is always in order for a member of a court to ask that he go on record as having dissented from its judgment on some issue. In days gone by this could be done only when the judgment reached was alleged to be "contrary to the Word of God, the Acts of Assembly, or to the received order of this Kirk," but today dissident will be recorded simply because the dissenter took a different view from the majority — and felt strongly about it. There is no need for a reason to be given. It is only when the matter has been finally disposed of that dissent may be taken, even in a case when the ground of dissent has to do with some earlier point of procedure. Other members of the court may "adhere" to the dissent, in which case their names will appear in the record — but they must have been present at the time and made their request then.

Appeal : Dissent and Complaint

The Difference — The distinction beween these two is one simply of nomenclature, and yet it is seen as of such importance that there are cases on record where an action has been found incompetent because it used the wrong words. The distinction is simple enough — the person at the bar says, "I appeal" and becomes the appellant whereas the person who is a member of the court says, "I dissent and complain" and becomes the complainer. A possibility of confusion used to arise when, for example, the complainer at the Presbytery had been repelled at the Synod and wished to go on to the Assembly, for he would go there as an appellant and that, of course, because at the Synod he was no longer on the bench but at the bar. But that is all now a bit of history for there is no longer a Synod. In what follows I propose always to refer to appeal, but all that is said is applicable equally to dissent and complaint.

Protest for Leave — An appeal is a subscribed document, but the process begins when the dissatisfied litigant, who has been recalled to the bar and informed of the judgment of the court, says, "I protest for leave to appeal." This is an important step and has to be taken immediately judgment is passed. It must be understood that the protest is not for permission to appeal (which cannot in any circumstances be refused) but for ten days' grace in which to lodge the document, which has to include reasons. It would be unrealistic to expect the party to be prepared to lodge such a writing there and then (though he may do so if he cares) and so he is allowed ten days. These start to count on the day following the judgment and end at midnight on the tenth day, by which time the appeal must be lodged with the Clerk or Moderadtor of the court who will endorse it, "Received by me at .... on .... AB, Presbytery Clerk." It is beyond the power of the court to extend the ten-day period.

It can be difficult for a party confronted suddenly with the judgment of the court, especially amid the general commotion and stir that usually follow the ending of a case, to collect his thoughts clearly and decide whether or not he wants to take the case further. His best course is to appeal there and then and so keep his options open — he can depart from the appeal at any time. With this situation in view the Presbytery of Glasgow some years ago introduced a Standing Order providing that when any case has been decided at a meeting it is in order at any time before the close of the sederunt for the party to ask to be recalled to the bar so that he may appeal, or for a member of the court to register dissent and complaint. I feel sure it is in order for a court to grant this consideration, and I think it reasonable it should do so.

As has been said, the appeal may be deserted at any time, and courtesy would demand that if this is to happen intimation be given to this effect without delay. In the event that the appeal is not lodged within the prescribed period it is treated as being departed from, and the Clerk will report accordingly. The minute of the meeting will record this fact and the sist upon execution of sentence imposed by the protest for leave to appeal will be lifted and the court's judgment will immediately become operative.

No Personal Bar — It might be expected that a member of a court who felt sufficiently strongly on an issue as to make him want to dissent and complain would at least have proposed a counter-motion, and it might seem that his failure to do so constituted a personal bar to proceeding to the superior court. The Church, however, puts no such obstacle in the way of the right to proceed by dissent and complaint.

Sisting Procedure — The taking of an appeal has the effect of sisting procedure in the execution of the sentence appealed against. It may be, however, that the lower court is so completely satisfied that the appellant has no case that, while it cannot deny him the right to appeal (since only the superior court can effectively determine that he has no case) it is prepared to take the risk of proceeding in face of the appeal. It would certainly be entitiled to do so were it convinced it could show that the appeal was frivolous, or was designed to frustrate by delay the objective of the decision appealed against. Going forward in this way, however, can lay the court open to the most serious censure.

Contumacy — Every court has the right to protect itself against evident insolence and contumacy, and it has a duty to protect outside parties from needless injury, so it may refuse to accept any document which appears to it to infringe in these regards.

Forms of Appeal — The appeal should be couched in some such terms as the following — "I, the undersigned, appeal to against a deliverance of .... given on .... regarding ...... and that for the following reasons — ...." If the appeal be in name of a group it is well to use the general term at the outset ("We, members of the congregation of .....") and to give the individual designations at the signature level.

Reasons — Appellants are charged to state their reasons with the utmost brevity and to state only such as they deem of real importance. It is not unusual to add "and for other reasons to be stated at the bar" though this is not necessary since his right to advance additional material at this stage is assured. The appeal must not contain any crave — the remedy, if any, lies wholly within the discretion of the court — and the presence of a crave lays it open to the penalty of being regarded as a Petition and dismissed as incompetent (Cox 6th Ed, p 93).

Answers — Provisions now exists (Assembly Standing Orders No 59) whereby "it shall be competent for all parties claiming an interest in the subject-matter of an Appeal, Dissent and Complaint, or Petition, to lodge Answers thereto ... . Answers may be lodged any time after the Appeal, Dissent and Complaint, or Petition is received by the Clerks, but not later than seven days before the opening meeting of Assembly. Answers shall be in the form of articulate numbered Answers to the narrative contained in the Appeal, Dissent and Complaint, or Petition, indicating in particular matters of fact that are admitted and denied and shall set forth a concise statement of the Respondent's case together with a crave specififying the action the Assembly are to take thereanent."

This raises for me four questions — at least. The first has to do with how the Respondent has had access to the papers lodged by the Complainer which normally become available only when the Assembly papers are issued to Commissioners — not usually much more than the seven days specified. Secondly, so long as the Complainer has the right to add reasons in his speech at the bar the Answers may well miss the principal point in the case they are attacking — it is difficult to answer a case of which you have heard only a part. Thirdly, one wonders why the Respondent should be entitled to lodge a Crave when the Complainer is so sternly forbidden to do so. And fourthly one wonders who is to pay for this printing.

Which Court — All appeals go to the next superior court, and that not later than the meeting which is at least ten free days after the delivery of the judgment made the subject of appeal.

Documents — No document is to be countenanced by the appeal court unless it had been before the court of first instance or had been offered to that court and been rejected, and no-one is to be allowed at the bar unless he was at the bar in the lower court or had applied to be so and had been refused. In a case of discipline the court of first instance may resolve either *ex proprio motu* or on application of a party, to transmit the record apart to the Clerk of the superior court, in which case parties will be informed accordingly. Whether or not this is done the Inventory of Process and all the productions are to be transmitted.

Intermediate Appeals — Should a party take grave exception to some step taken by a court in course of dealing with his case — were it, for instance, to allow production of a document which he maintained should not be allowed — then he will inimate his appeal at that point — but the case will proceed. When at the end judgment is delivered (and assuming it is given against him) he will formally protest for leave to appeal and he will be entitled, naturally, to found upon the alleged irregularity as one of the reasons — or it may well be the only reason — for contesting the ultimate judgment. If judgment is given in his favour it is likely he will be content to leave it at that and will not want to pursue the now academic question of the propriety of admitting the production. If appeal is not taken against the final judgment then all earlier appeals fall.

Sentence — A court will go on in face of all intermediate appeals and will conclude the case, where appropriate passing sentence, but an appeal against the final judgment will have the effect of sisting execution of sentence. In a libel, for instance, the minute would read, "It was moved, seconded and agreed that in respect of the charges found proven against him Mr AB be deposed from the office of the Holy Ministry. Parties were recalled and judgment was intimated." If at this point Mr AB appeals no further step is taken, but if no appeal is intimated the court will go on to depose. If reasons for appeal are not lodged timeously that fact will be reported at next regular meeting — which will then proceed to depose. In no circumstances should the matter be left unresolved because appeal had been intimated.

Taking Protestation — Let it be that appeal was taken to the General Assembly against a judgmentof a Presbytery, but when the case called the appellant failed to appear. The case would be regarded as departed from, and the Presbytery would be free to proceed with giving effect to sentence. In its own interest it shoud take protestation. It would be for the Clerk to take action in the matter and that in such terms as the following — "I, PC, for the Presbytery of X, take protestation that ... judgment has become final, and I crave extracts."

Sustaining the Appeal — An appeal may be sustained on the ground of irregularity in the procedure or of the incompetence of the censure. The case may then be remitted to the original court with instruction on how to proceed, or it may be disposed of by the superior court itself. Today the bulk of the material reaching the Assembly by this route has to do with readjustment issues and it is usual for the Assembly whether or not they uphold the appeal to go on and issue the case.

PETITION

Before dealing with the normal use of Petition I take the opportunity to comment upon two unusual but quite legitimate uses of this form.

In Lieu of Appeal — It is not the proper use of Petition to bring the proceedings of an inferior court under review, but recourse may be had to Petition when it has been put beyond the power of the aggrieved party to come by the proper avenue of appeal. A Kirk Session took up consideration of the conduct of one of its Elders in his absence and without his having been warned or cited to attend (it being the contention of the Session that being an Elder he had a duty to be present at all Session meetings) and then resolved to suspend him from office. In so doing they clearly put it out of his power to appeal since he had never appeared at its bar — he first learned there was to be a case against him when he received intimation by post of the sentence passed upon him. He petitioned the Presbytery, condescending upon the facts outlined above as his reason for taking this course. The Presbytery received the petition and after hearing parties recalled the judgment. Were a court to be misguided enough to refuse to accept an appeal the offended party would be entitled to approach the superior court by petition.

Minority Report — Another situation that can lead to the use of Petition is where a minority within the ranks of one of its own Committees wishes to bring its opinion to the attention of the court. The Assembly has ordained (Repts 1939, pp 3 and 7) that a minority report is incompetent The simple way to deal with the resultant situation is, of course, for a representative of the minority to move a counter-motion to the deliverance of the Committee and to speak to that; but resort to Petition has the advantage that it ensures that the case of the minority will be presented in print before the case begins. It has the disadvantage that the minority has to foot the bill for printing!

Ordinary Use — The normal use of Petition is to initiate business — generally the particular business of the Petitioner — in the court of first instance. A Kirk Session may be presented with a Petition from members of the congregation, or from parishioners, asking for something to be done in a region where the Kirk Session carries a responsibility — for example that there be a change in the hour of public worship. In like manner a Petition may be presented to the Presbytery from a congregation, or from a local voluntary assocation, or from an individual, asking the court to take some specific action. Probably the General Assembly is the main recipient of Petitions, and these fall into two classes — first there is the kind of petition submitted by a Minister of another denomination seeking admission to the Church of Scotland, or from a deposed Minister seeking reinstatement, or from a Presbytery asking for a change of boundaries; and secondly there is the kind of Petition which comes from an outside body asking for action in some area of public concern.

Crave — Since a Petition is always asking for something to be done it should contain a prayer or "crave", and there is much to be said for this being fairly specific in character. If what is being sought involves the passing of Kirk legislation then a Draft Act should be appended to the Petition.

Form of Petition — There is a standard form to which a Petition should conform no matter to which court it is addressed or what the nature of its business — though the form of Petition for the admission of a Minister does not adhere to this pattern. It should begin, "Unto the Reverend the Kirk Session/Presbytery of — [Unto the Venerable the General Assembly]", and it should go on — "the Petition of ..... *humbly sheweth*" — and here should follow in numbered paragraphs and succinctly set forth the various points upon which the Petitioner wishes to found. Thereafter comes the crave — "May it therefore please your Reverend/ Venerable court to do so and so — followed by some such phrase as "or to do further or otherwise as in the premises may to your Reverend/ Venerable court seem good." The document then closes with the respectful words, "And your Petitioner will ever pray" followed by the signature of the Petitioner.

How Dealt With — There are three separate steps which a court has to take in dealing with a Petition — first the document has to be read, or taken as read; secondly it has to be resolved whether or not it should be received; and further it has to be decided whether and to what extent its crave is to be granted. Unless in regard to either its subject-matter or its presentation it is so manifestly incompetent or so appallingly disrespectful as not to merit further consideration it will be read or taken as read. The decision whether or not to receive will turn largely on the question of competence. Suppose, to take an extreme example, that a Kirk Session were presented with a Petition from a group of members asking them to alter the order of public worship then obviously since they were being asked to do something outwith their jurisdiction the Petition should not be received. The issue, of course, will not usually be so clear-cut as this. When there is the slightest doubt the wise course is to receive the Petition and then go on and invite the Petitioner in the first place to address himself exclusively to the question of competence. If he cannot sustain this then the petition may be dismissed without more ado, but it could not have been dismissed had it not first been received.

Who May Present — If a member of a court have addressed a Petition to it, either alone or with others, he is or they are at the bar until it is disposed of. He may present it, but will do so from the bar. A membber who is not a signatory cannot present it either from the floor or at the bar.

OVERTURE

Overture is the vehicle for bringing to a court from an inferior court or from a group of its own members formal proposals for legislation or executive action of a general nature not limited to the business or interest of the instigators. There are two specialised kinds of overtures — those sent down under the Barrier Act, and those proposing changes in the Declaratory Articles, and these are dealt with at pages 358 and 359 respectively. In what follows it is the simple use of Overture that is discussed. Since it is most commonly to the Assembly that Overtures are addressed it is that case that we deal with hereunder, but any court may be approached by Overture and the procedure will be the same in each case.

Form of Overture — The document begins by stating who are its authors. It then goes on to set forth its premises in a series of paragraphs (un-numbered, though I think they might well be) each beginning with the word "Whereas", and it ends with the conclusion, "It is humbly overtured by .... that your Venerable Court" will do so-and-so. The Standing Orders of the Assembly require that an Overture must be accompanied by a proposed deliverance of which the opening paragraph is to be, "The General Assembly receive the overture." There is no comparable requirement in the lower courts. The same considerations apply to the question of receiving as are set forth above in the case of Petition. Increasingly Overtures end with the words about "doing further or otherwise" as appear in a Petition. I do not myself believe this to be either necessary or proper.

Presbytery to Assembly — The most popular use of Overture is as a means whereby a Presbytery can approach the Assembly on some topic of general interest to the Church. The proposal that such a subject should be raised in the Assembly will in most cases have originated with a member of Presbytery. There is no way (except Petition) whereby he can bring his ideas straight to the supreme court so he has to persuade the Presbytery to adopt his ideas and to frame, approve and lodge an Overture.

Presentation — When more than one overture is presented on the same or cognate subjects they will be grouped by the appropriate Committee before reaching the Assembly and it will be for the promoters to get together and to appoint one person to present the case. When the proposed deliverance can be seen as a counter-motion, amendment or addendum to the deliverance of a Committee deliverance it will be so treated. If it comes from a Presbytery it may be presented by a member of the Presbytery appointed for the purpose from the bar, or, if he is a Commissioner, from the floor, and in the latter case he may go on to move in terms of the proposed Deliverance.

From Assembly Commissioners — It is in order for any twelve Assembly commissioners to submit an Overture to the Assembly. This will be printed and dealt with as any other Overture, the twelve being responsible for the cost of the printing.

REFERENCE

In the olden days when Kirk Sessions were much exercised over matters of discipline it was not unusual for them to — in some cases they were required to — refer a case to the Presbytery, the charges being of a sufficiently serious nature. Any court may refer a matter to a superior court (but see Tyrrell Case hereunder) but the course is generally frowned upon, being seen as an attempt to evade responsibility, and in the past it has been not unknown for such cases to be sent back untouched to be disposed of in the court of first instance.

The crucial point was that the referring court either was unable for some reason to reach a judgment on the matter or was convinced that the issue was of such importance as to merit calling in the wisdom of the superior court. If the court of first instance is perfectly clear what its judgment ought to be then the proper line is for it to go on and pass that judgment, leaving it to the dissatisfied party to proceed along the regular route of appeal.

Stating the Reference — One very significant feature of reference is that members of the referring court retain their status in the higher court — that is to say, they are not at the bar. One who is a member of both courts may "state the reference" in the superior court and will do so from the floor. Such a statement should set forth clearly what the case is about and, more important, what are the reasons for it being referred. He must not be seen as presenting a case. The question is then put to the court, "Shall the reference be sustained?" If the answer be in the affirmative the court goes on to deal with the merits of the business as though it were the court of first instance. If not sustained the whole affair goes back to be disposed of by the referring court.

"The Tyrrell Case" — Around 1970 a case was referred to the Assembly by the Presbytery of Edinburgh which had been asked to agree that the Sacraments should be dispensed regularly by an Episcopal Minister from America who was acting as Assistant at St Giles'. Now this is a matter where it is declared that the decision of the Presbytery is to be final (p 153). When in the Presbytery after long debate the issue went to a vote a dead heat resulted. Rather than have a matter of such importance decided on his casting vote the Moderator suggested a reference to the General Assembly and this was moved, seconded and agreed. When the reference came to the Assembly the Procurator (Mr T P M'Donald) gave it as his opinion that the Reference was incompetent — the law put the responsibility for judgment squarely in the court of the Presbytery, and that body could not by reference evade that responsibility. The Procurator's opinion was accepted and the matter was depareted from. With the greatest of respect I do not think the advice was sound. The fact that finality of judgment is reserved to the Presbytery effectively prevents the dissatisfied litigant taking the matter further, but it does not in my view necessarily prevent the court itself *ex proprio motu* seeking the help of higher authority in a matter of some complexity and of no little importance to the Church as a whole. No-one could deny that an Assembly decision would have been of much more value than a Presbytery judgment reached on a casting vote. At the very least and conceding the Procurator's opinion, there was surely nothing to prevent the Assembly considering a matter of principle and reaching a decision thereon. With this advice the Presbytery could then have gone home and exercised its exclusive jurisdiction.

Reappraisal Cases — Section 6(b) of the Readjustment Act of 1984 (Act iv) provides that where a difference of opinion between the Presbytery and the Assembly Committee on a question of readjustment cannot be resolved the Presbytery may decide to refer the matter to the General Assembly. This seems a complete departure from accepted principles affecting reference insofar as the Presbytery instead of passing up an issue on which it has not reached a judgment is now referring something on which its mind is made up, firmly and clearly made up, the only trouble being that the Assembly Committee is convinced the Presbytery is wrong.

Nobody would contest that the Assembly is the body that should resolve this kind of situation — but is this the proper machinery?

The first case to arise under the Act came in 1985 and was far from satisfying. The reference was sustained and there was debate followed by two motions — the first that the Assembly recall the judgment of the Presbytery, and the second that the Assembly sustain the judgment of the Presbytery. These were motions highly proper to an appeal but quite out of place in a reference. Other considerations apart members of Presbytery, who had clearly become parties to the action were at liberty to vote. One wonders whether a more regular way of dealing with such a situation would not be a petition from the Presbytery craving the Assembly to instruct their Reappraisal Committee to concur in the judgment of the Presbytery. Since it is now accepted that Committees can go to the bar this would seem to ensure a proper confrontation of the opposing views with the congregtion ranged on whichever it thought the appropriate side.

MISCELLANEOUS

Reiewing its Own Decision — It is, I think, generally accepted in the courts of the Church that a decision once reached cannot be brought up for review until six months have elapsed. It is not, perhaps, so widely appreciated that there are matters on which a court cannot, of its own will, recall a judgment once delivered, that judgment having to stand until recalled by a higher court. When the matter is one of purely domestic concern — the size of a Presbytery Committeee, the hour of the regular meeting — then the matter lies wholly within the discretion of the court. But as soon as an outside party acquires an interest in virtue of the decision change can be effected only at best with consent of that party. In 1903 a case came to the civil courts from Auchterarder where the Presbytery had reviewed a judgment without consent of all possible parties and the Sheriff described the Presbytery's action as "incompetent on the face of it." It used to be possible to persuade the Synod to recall a Presbytery's judgment, but the Synod is no more. I do not think that a case has arisen since its demise.

Employment of Counsel — The Act of Union of 1929 provides — "Parties may appear by, or have the assistance of, counsel or agents in any process pending before the Presbytery or any higher court, unless such court shall otherwise determine. They shall not be entitled to have such assistance in any process depending before a Kirk Session except with the special permission of the Kirk Session. Any parties appearing by counsel or agents shall not be entitled to be heard also by themselves." It is further recommended that where such counsel or agents are engaged they should be members of the Church.

Nobile Officium — In virtue of being supreme court of the Church the General Assembly enjoys (as does the Court of Session in the civil sphere) a unique power known as the *nobile officium*. This is in effect a power to supply law where none exists — for a situation can arise which is quite simply not covered by legislation. It was said of this power by the late Sir Randal Philip when he was Procurator that "it is used to give an equitable remedy which the strict law would not give." It cannot be used to alter existing law or to enable the court to ignore existing law because it does not find it acceptable. It belongs, of course, exclusively to the General Assembly, and only very rarely indeed is recourse had to it.

Order of Debate etc — The whole field of debate in the courts, inlcluding the character of motions, the method of voting etc is dealt with in the chapter on the General Assembly (p 365).

Standing Orders — In the interest of keeping good order most courts have equipped themselves with a list of Standing Orders. It is usual practice to accept that in special circumstances these provisions may be "suspended", but only for the particular item of business, and a motion to suspend must be carried by a two-thirds majority of those voting. If it is desired at any time to change an item in the Standing Orders that may be done on a straight majority, but requires that Notice of Motion had been given. Where a court has no Order to cover a particular item it is generally held to be governed by the relevant order of the next superior court.

Privilege

Defamation is a slanderous attack upon the character or conduct of the person defamed. Scots law knows nothing of the distinction between slander (the spoken word) and libel (its written equivalent) — both alike constitute defamation. This is not normally a criminal offence but represents a civil wrong from which the victim is entitled to be protected and for which he may obtain an award of damages — not in Scotland intended to be punitive. Privilege is a defence against a charge of defamation and consists in the claim that the occasion when the words complained of were used was one where the offender had been bound, or was at least entitled, to speak frankly regarding the character and habits of the person in question. It is of two kinds — absolute and qualified. The former covers a limited number of cases, in connection with Parliament and with law courts principally. Qualified privilege, on the other hand, can be ineffective as a defence if the person maligned can prove that there was malice and want of probable cause.

I find it difficult to say exactly how the defence of privilege would apply within the Church courts, my difficulty arising to some extent from the fact that while a Presbytery, for example, sits as a court of the Church, enjoying all the powers and privileges of such a court, a great deal of the time and attention of today's Presbytery is devoted to domestic arrangements that have no "court" significance. I am sure that when a Presbytery is dealing with a libel members would enjoy the protection of absolute privilege in what they said in evidence or in comment. In other conditions, however, I would doubt very much whether any degree of privilege could be claimed. At the very least I would suggest that before making any statement to which exception could be taken one should be very clear that there was good ground *prima facie* for believing the allegation and that there could be no reason to imagine that one was motivated by malice. Except in libel actions the business of the Kirk can be advanced in the absence of defamatory statements — privilege or no privilege.

An interesting case came before the courts in 1863. A new Minister had just been inducted to a country parish. Clearly there had been some conflict about the choice and this had resulted in the resignation of the entire Kirk Session except the Session Clerk who was the local schoolmaster. Assessors were appointed and the Kirk Session made choice of three members to be ordained as Elders. The usual edict was duly read inviting "anyone having aught to object to in the life or doctrine of the said A, B, or C to repair to the meeting" — and the resigned Elders did just that in a body, bringing with them a widely subscribed paper attributing an illegitmate child to one of the three. All three nominees immediately withdrew, and so far as the Kirk was concerned that was that. The alleged father, however, raised an action of defamation against the group of objectors as joint wrong-doers. They naturally pleaded privilege — they were fulfilling a public duty. It was held that while that defence partially protected them in respect of their own appearing in answer to the edict it did not extend to cover their going around the parish spreading scandal and seeking signatures to a document. Very heavy damages were awarded against them.

My personal advice would certainly be that if at any time in a Kirk meeting you feel inclined to say something for which you think you might need to invoke privilege as your defence you should think again and say something else!

Chapter 11

THE KIRK SESSION

"ITS GOVERNMENT IS PRESBYTERIAN and is exercised through Kirk Sessions, Presbyteries, Provincial Synods and General Assemblies" — so runs the second of the Articles Declaratory of the Constitution of the Church of Scotland, thus confirming the Kirk Session clearly in its place as the base of the pyramid of Church Courts, a place accorded it by the fathers of the Scottish Reformation. (Acts v and vi 1992 abolished Synods and deleted from the Articles Declaratory the words "Provincial Synods", but this, of course, left undisturbed the position of the Kirk Session). Every Parish in Scotland is under the spiritual oversight of a Kirk Session, and since there is no corner of Scotland which is not within a parish there can be no-one living in this land who is not the spiritual responsibility of some Kirk Session. The National Church is at once a Presbyterian and a Parish Church, and the Kirk Session is the instrument of Presbyterian government within each parish.

In terms of Act viii 1952 a Services Kirk Session may be constituted in any unit of HM Forces. For full particulars see p 286 hereunder.

ITS MEMBERSHIP

The Kirk Session of a parish consists of its Minister (or Ministers) and Elders. Historically all alike are Elders, the Minister being the teaching or preaching Elder and the others the ruling Elders; but today, in popular usage at least, the term "elder" denotes exclusively the ruling variety. All alike are ordained, the Minister with, the Elders without, the laying on of hands. On occasion one hears the term "lay elder", but this, clearly, is a contradiction in terms.

Minister — There cannot be a meeting of Kirk Session without a Minister to preside as its Moderator. Normally he will be the Minister of the parish; during a vacancy or when the Minister has been granted leave of absence he will be a ministerial member of Presbytery appointed as

Interim Moderator; in the unavoidable absence of either of these another Minister may be authorised to act as Moderator *pro tempore*. In a collegiate charge both Ministers are members of Session and take turns at presiding. A retired Minister or a Minister engaged in non-parochial work may be associated with a Kirk Session, but so long as he retains his ministerial status he cannot be a member of it.

Elders — Being an Elder and being a member of Kirk Session are not the same thing. Ordination as an Elder confers the status of Elder, and this is retained for life or until the person has voluntarily relinquished or has been judicially deprived of it. To be a member of Session the Elder has to have been formally admitted. Moving to another charge does not carry any right to membership of the new Kirk Session. In the absence of a Moderator the Elders may meet as a group but they cannot constitute themselves a Kirk Session.

"Minister and Kirk Session" — It is not unusual in official documents to find this phrase, which is sometimes objected to on the ground that the Minister appears in it twice — "Kirk Session" of itself should be enough. It is true that the Minister appears twice, and this is as it should be, for he appears in two different capacities and the interests of the Minister *qua* Minister need not be identical with those of the Kirk Session. Indeed it would be easy to conceive a situation where the Minister would be bitterly opposed to something the Kirk Session was craving, and yet as Moderator he would have to sign the petition. In my view he would be entitled to speak against it in the higher court in his capacity as Minister. Where, then, an appeal or a petition stands in name of "Minister and Kirk Session" that means they are at one in promoting it, both being cited the Minister appears in both roles.

Assessors — The only way in which a Kirk Session can be increased in size is by it itself resolving to add to its number. Should then the membership of the Kirk Session of a regular charge fall below a *quorum* (in consequence, for instance, of a mass resignation) the Presbytery will appoint Ministers and Elders from neighbouring charges to act as Assessors to enable the Session to add to its number and so get itself regularly reconstituted. This having been done the Assessors report diligence to the Presbytery and get themselves discharged. It will be noted that in these circumstances Ministers do sit as Elders on a Kirk Session without endangering their ministerial status. In the early days of a Church

Extension charge the Kirk Session consists wholly of Assessors, being Elders from neighbouring Kirk Sessions, but once full status has been achieved immediate steps are taken to constitute a regular Kirk Session. According to an opinion given by the then Procurator, Sir William Chree, the Minister and Assessors must be taken as the Kirk Session for all purposes. Should anything occur that would bring such a Kirk Session to the bar of Presbytery or Assembly it would be the Assessors who along with the Minister would have to appear.

Self-Perpetuating — A Kirk Session keeps itself in being by from time to time adding to its number. It has a responsibility to see that its numbers are such that it does not fall below an adequate strength, but it is itself the judge of what that strength is. It is not a popularly elected body answerable to those who elected it, and even although a congregational meeting may be held to elect Elders (see hereunder) it is still for the Kirk Session to "make choice" of those elected, and the Kirk Session is not bound to accept any or all of them. Since the Session thus adds to its number a condition of stalemate will obviously be reached if the number is allowed to fall so low that a *quorum* cannot be formed. In such circumstances the Presbytery must intervene as indicated in the previous paragraph.

How Choosen

A Kirk Session having resolved to add to its number and having determined how many it wishes to add is faced with the question of how this is to be done. It may be done wholly, or more likely in part, by adding to the Session members of the congregation who are already Elders, having come from some other Kirk Session. There is no obligation upon the Kirk Session to include any such person, but he or she is available if willing. Or, of course, it may be done by ordaining suitable members of the congregation. When the time comes the latter will be ordained and admitted, the former being merely admitted, but otherwise the procedure is the same and it will be convenient to treat the two events as one.

Eligibility — Any person, male or female, eighteen years of age or over, whose name is on the Communion Roll and who is not under discipline is eligible to be chosen as an Elder. It was in 1966 (Act xxviii) that the Eldership was thrown open to women "on the same terms and conditions as men members of a congregation." In its report to the Assembly of 1991 the Board of Practice and Procedure presented a considerable argument in support of an opinion given by the Principal Clerk in 1987 and this received the approval of the Assembly. This agreed that there is no instruction upon Kirk Sessions to appoint women elders, but went on to declare that any decision to the effect that women will not be considered for the eldership is against the law and in breach of their ordination vows. It seems to me, however, that the condemnation could not embrace the case of a Kirk Session which after due consideration resolved "that as things are at present in this parish it would not be in the interest of the peace and unity of the congregation to add women to the Kirk Session." A resolution so phrased passes no judgment, hostile or otherwise, on the Act of Assembly but only seeks to assess the condition of feeling within the parish — a subject on which they are to be presumed to have intimate knowledge. Their defence would obviously be that so far from breaking their ordination vow to seek the peace and wellbeing of the congregation they were seeking to fulfil it!

In terms of Act x 1979 the minimum age for membership of Kirk Session was reduced from twenty-one to eighteen.

An eighteenth century Act requires the Elder to be "of good life and godly conversation, tender and circumspect in his walk, punctual in attendance on ordinances, strict in his observance of the Lord's Day, and keeping up the worship in his family; and one who will be careful of the flock, an example of sobriety, meekness, holiness."

There is nothing to prevent a paid servant of the Session (the Organist, for example) from being a member of the court, but there are practical considerations which may be thought to affect the advisability of this.

Methods of Choosing — There is a choice of three ways in which to select those who are to be Elders, and it is for the Kirk Session to decide which of these is to be followed.

(a) *Election by Congregation at Open Meeting* — Two Sundays' notice is given of the fact that the Kirk Session has resolved that (let us say) six persons should be added to its number and that towards this end a meeting of the congregation is to be held on a certain day, going on to give certification that "if the number nominated does not exceed those required they will be declared to be elected, subject to the judgment of the Kirk Session, and that if more than six are nominated a vote of the congregation will be taken by standing up or by voting papers as the meeting may determine." The chair at the meeting is taken by the

Moderator or by a Minister authorised by him in writing. All names proposed and seconded are written down by the Session Clerk. When six names have been proposed it is for the Moderator to put to the meeting the question whether they want to stop at that point or to go on and make further nominations. If the former is agreed the Clerk reads over the six names and these are declared to have been elected subject to the judgment of the Kirk Session. If further nominations are offered these also are recorded until it is clear no more are forthcoming. Let us say we now have ten. These ten names are read over and the Moderator puts the question whether the vote is to be taken by standing up or by the use of voting papers.

If it is decided to have an open vote tellers are appointed. The Moderator has then to explain that each person has six votes; and it would probably be wise to have the ten names read over again. The vote is then taken and the six who top the poll are declared elected subject to the judgment of the Kirk Session. In the event of a tie for the sixth place a straight vote is taken between the two (or more).

If, on the other hand, the meeting has favoured the use of voting papers the Moderator is to explain the procedure to be followed, after which the meeting will be closed. As soon as practicable the Kirk Session will arrange to have voting papers printed, setting forth the ten names (in alphabetical order) along with instructions that each voter has six crosses to award and that papers are to be returned to the church by a certain date. The Session has also to ensure that one of these papers is delivered to every member of the congregation. In due course it will be for the Moderator to count the votes in presence of the Session and the top six will be declared elected, subject to the judgment of the Session.

The Act speaks of "election to the office of the eldership" but what seems to be meant is "election to the exercise of the office of the eldership within this congregation" for otherwise it would not be in order to nominate anyone who had come from another congregation with the status of elder. From the point of view of sheer convenience there is much to be said in favour of closing once six names have been obtained. But that has the disadvantage of substituting as the criterion of choice speed of nomination rather than weight of popular support — and this can be unfortunate in the extreme. There seems little to commend, and a great deal to discourage, recourse to a ballot.

(b) *Election by Congregation by Signed Lists* — Pulpit intimation is given on two Sundays that the Kirk Session wishes to add, let it be six, to its number and that members are invited to prepare lists of names of up to six persons whom they consider suitable, to sign these and to hand them in at the Church or to the Session Clerk by a certain day. The Session then meets, counts the votes cast, and the top six are declared elected subject to the judgment of the Kirk Session.

There is a further provision which applies to this method that instead of, as in our example, asking for six nominations the Session asks for as near as may be one half nore than the number required (nine in our case), it being understood that the first six of these will be approached first, and if one or another declines the next in order will be approached, and so on. There is something to be said in favour of this. But if six are wanted and only four are willing what is to happen? Do they make do with four? Or hold another election? or what? It's hard to see why having asked for six the Session should not leave it at that, listing the names in order of merit (they would have far more than six) and persevering down the list till the required number of acceptances had been secured.

(c) *Resolution of Kirk Session* — The traditional method was that the Kirk Session not only resolved that it should add six to its number, it went on to determine who these six were to be. And this method is still available. It enjoys the great advantage that it allows the suitability of each candidate to be freely canvassed within the confidentiality of a Session meeting. And even if it is following this method there is no reason why the Session should not invite the congregation to submit lists of suggestions, so long as it is made clear that it is not a method of popular election.

It will have been noticed that in every case following upon the declaration of election there appears the phrase, "subject to the judgment of the Kirk Session". It is with the Kirk Session that the choice ultimately rests. If the first method be followed it will be extremely difficult not to accept all those elected, and only for the most cogent and compelling reasons should an exception be made.

A question may be asked as to whether special steps should be taken in a case where there are no women on the Session. In such a case, it seems to me, it is for the chairman to explain that it is now in order to have women on the Session and that the minimum age for either sex is now eighteen. It could be added that the General Assembly have urged that in such cases consideration be given to the appointment of women to the eldership. There must not be a vote taken as to whether or not to include women in their case. It would be quite out of order for a congregational meeting to resolve that the nomination of a woman (or of a person beween 18 and 21) would not be accepted, but it would be equally wrong for it to declare that there must be at least one woman (or one such younger person) appointed. The effect of the 1966 Act was to widen the field from which choice could be made, not to dictate how the right of choice might be exercised.

How Installed

The necessary number of people having now been selected and their adoption having been approved by the Kirk Session, it is for that body to take steps towards ordination and admission.

Consent — As a first step their consent has to be obtained. When a person has been elected at a congregational meeting his consent is to be presumed, though even here a visit will not be out of place. In the other cases it is usual for the Minister, accompanied by the Session Clerk or District Elder to call on the person elected and seek his consent. There is considerable advantage in visiting all of the nominees as nearly simultaneously as possible lest someone gets the impression of being a second choice, and this, of course, can be made difficult by those who require a long time "to turn it over in their mind." A letter sent simultaneously to all has advantages so long as instead of asking for a reply in writing it says that a visit is to be expected within the next few days.

Edict — Once a date has been fixed for the Service of Ordination and Admission an edict has to be served on two Sundays to the effect that if anyone has objection to the life or doctrine of any or all of those proposed this may be given in at a meeting of Kirk Session to be held not less than seven free days after the serving of the intimation, and certifying that if no such objection be given-in and substantiated the Kirk Session will proceed. The situation is exactly parallel to that of a Minister about to be inducted and reference should be made to this. (p ???) It should be noted that a "free day" is one falling between the day of reading the notice and the day of the event.

Service of Ordination and Admission — At this service those already Elders are to be admitted, others are to be ordained and admitted. The Session is constituted before the service and remains in session throughout. After a short narrative of proceedings, the Moderator, having read the Preamble, puts the prescribed questions, and the candidates sign the Formula. Thereupon the Moderator with prayer ordains first-timers and admits all, after which, followed by other members of Session, he gives the right hand of fellowship. The new members will then take their seats in the Kirk Session.

I was asked on one occasion whether in the case of a former Elder who had left the district but who had now returned and it was desired to re-enrol him on the Session — whether there had to be a full service in face of the congregation. It seemed to me that in these rather unusual circumstances the admission could take place at a Session meeting provided the questions were put and the Formula signed, but I was quite clear that edictal intimation was essential. The impression must not be given that someone has been admitted in a hole-and-corner fashion.

For How Long? — Membership of a Kirk Session is *ad vitam aut culpam*, but absence for a complete year from all meetings of Session without adequate reason known has the effect of terminating his membership of Session, though this does not affect his status as Elder. The new legislation imposing age-limits on members of Church Courts does not apply to the Kirk Session.

The suggestion was advanced by the Committee of Forty in 1979 that this pattern might be altered and appointments made for a period of five years with, possibly, a sabbatical year introduced, but this found little favour throughout the Kirk. Each Elder is subject to the discipline of his own Kirk Session which may suspend him from office. The fact that he may sit in Presbytery does not free him from the discipline of the Kirk Session, and if suspended by the Session he could not retain his seat in Presbytery. On moving to the membership of another congregation an Elder automatically ceases to be a member of his former Kirk Session.

Long Service Certificate — A suitable scroll bearing the crest of the Church of Scotland in colour and signed by the Moderator of Assembly is awarded to Elders who have given not less than thirty years' service. Application in name of the local Kirk Session should be made to the Principal Clerk of Assembly. It is usual to hand over such certificates in face of the congregation at Morning Worship.

Kirk Sessions in Units of H M Forces

A highly specialised kind of Kirk Session can be formed in a Scottish unit of H M Forces. In 1994 it was reported that there were five such Sessions enrolled on the Register of Kirk Sessions maintained by the

Committee on Chaplains to H M Forces. The legislation covering the position here is contained in Act viii 1952 which should be consulted for full details. Briefly the situation is that when it is desired to establish such a Kirk Session the Committee on Chaplains has to satisfy itself (a) that there is a demand to be met, (b) that there is a real prospect of such a Session continuing for some time, and (c) that the proposal has the approval of the Chaplain and the Commanding Officer concerned. The Session will consist of the Chaplain as Moderator with not fewer than two fully ordained Elders. Once established it may select, ordain and admit suitable persons as Elders, and, if necesssary, Assessors will be appointed to enable this to be done. Each such Kirk Session is to be associated with a Presbytery — if the unit have a depot in Scotland with the Presbytery in whose bounds he depot falls, failing which with the Presbytery of Edinburgh; but this will not affect the Presbytery membership of the Chaplain who is its Moderator.

ITS OFFICIALS

Moderator

There can be no valid meeting of Kirk Session unless the chair is occupied by an Ordained Minister as Moderator — of which there are three varieties.

(1) There is the Minister of the parish, and he is *Moderator ex officio.* Immediately following the induction of a Minister a certified intimation is given by the Presbytery Clerk to the Session Clerk, and this is recorded at the first meeting of Session thereafter (p 89) thus constituting the authority for the new Minister taking the chair. In a collegiate charge the Ministers act as chairman alternately or as may be arranged, the other meantime sitting and voting as a member of Session. An Associate Minister sits and votes as a member of Session but is not its Moderator. An Ordained Assistant has no place on the Session although he may be invited to attend (and has a seat in Presbytery). The Assembly have recommended that Deaconesses and Lay Missionaries (now Deacons) should be invited to be present at meetings of the Session of the charge in which they are working, but they have no voting rights. It may be, of course, that they are Elders, in which case they may be admitted to the Session in the regular way, if this is thought wise.

(2) There is the Ministerial member of Presbytery appointed by that body to preside over the Kirk Session during a vacancy or when the regular Moderator has, for any reason, been granted leave of absence,

and he is the *Moderator ad interim*. As such he enjoys all the powers and fulfils all the functions of the regular Moderator.

(3) For the conduct of a regular meeting any Ordained Minister of the Church may be authorised by the Moderator or Interim Moderator to preside over the Kirk Session as its *Moderator pro tempore*. The mandate must be in writing, must specify the time and place of the meeting and also the business to be transacted; and the fact has to be recorded in the minutes of the meeting (Act x 1933). Normally resort will be had to this provision for one specific purpose or in a case of illness or other emergency. On the occasion of the death of one of its active ministerial members the Presbytery meets at his Church on the occasion of the funeral for the transaction of necessary business.

Duties — It is the responsibility of the Moderator to convene meetings. He is to preside at all meetings, opening and closing them with prayer. He is to keep good order and is master of order. He puts issues to the vote and announces decisions. It is for him to ensure that proper records are kept, and he has to sign all minutes when they are approved. He has a casting vote only, but he may introduce business and may speak to any item of business so long as he does not propose a motion. He is as completely bound as any other member of the congregation by a decision taken by the Kirk Session, the distinction being that the Session will itself deal with the normal case of disobedience whereas if the offender is a Minister the matter must be referred to the Presbytery which may itself enjoin the Minister, and in the case of his continuing disobedience will deal appropriately with the affair.

Answerability — The Moderator is not answerable to the Kirk Session for the discharge of his duties in the chair or as Minister of the parish. Because of his unique position in the court it is difficult for the Session as such to approach the Presbytery in a case of discontent. The Elders, or a number of them, may, however, present a petition to the Presbytery if, for example, the Minister refuses to call meetings of Session, dissolves Session meetings against the will of the Elders, or seems to be neglectful of his parish duties. In all such matters the Minister is completely responsible to the Presbytery.

Session Clerk

Appointment and Tenure — The Kirk Session appoints a Clerk who holds office during its pleasure. On taking up office he takes the oath *de fideli* *administratione*. All records of the Session should be handed over to him. an inventory of them having been prepared, and he should sign a receipt for these — for his own protection if for no other reason. It used to be presumed the appointment was for life, but it is increasingly common for it to be made for a specific period of, say, five years. An eminently suitable person may accept on these terms who would not undertake a "life sentence." In the odd case and where a great deal of work is involved, a modest honorarium may be paid, though this is rarely done. It is in order, and may prove advantageous, to appoint as Clerk someone who is not a member of the court. As well as taking the oath *de fideli* such an "outsider" should give a solemn undertaking to observe the confidentiality of all Session business.

Duties — It is the duty of the Clerk to keep regular minutes and to engross these in a permanent record. On these being approved he signs them along with the Moderator (Act xv 1931) — if they are in loose leaf form they must be initialled on every sheet. He has to accept custody of Session documents entrusted to him, and it is he alone who can competently give extracts from Session records, though he may do so only with the authority of the court. When for any reason it becomes evident as the time for worship approaches that no Minister is to be forthcoming it is for the Session Clerk, whom failing the senior elder present, to lead, or to invite someone else to lead, the congregation in an act of devotion, the Clerk to report the circumstances to the Presbytery Clerk as soon as possible. In the absence of the regular Clerk at any time a Clerk *pro tempore* will be appointed and the oath *de fideli* administered. In the continuing absence of the Clerk it is the duty of the Moderator to keep the record, and this he will do and sign in his dual capacity as "Moderator and Clerk". This, however, is a most unsatisfactory state of affairs and should not be allowed to persist for longer than is absolutely unavoidable.

Kirk Session Treasurer

A Treasurer is appointed to look after funds which are the particular responsibility of the Kirk Session, generally a Poor or Benevolent Fund and bequest funds left in Session control. For historical reasons the Session used always to be in control (except in the former Free Church) of givings to "schemes". As the importance of the Mission and Aid Fund has developed in recent years this responsibility has passed to the financial court. The Treasurer holds office during the pleasure of the Session. The Kirk Treasurer, if he is an Elder, may also act as Kirk Session Treasurer, but if so he must be careful to render an accounting to the Session for funds within their control and to ensure that these are not included among the accounts to be submitted to the congregation for approval.

Roll Keeper

It is fairly common today for an Elder to be appointed Roll Keeper, his sole duty being to maintain the Commuion Roll. This can greatly relieve the burden carried by the Session Clerk though the responsibility must still lie with him.

Session Officer

Like other Church courts the Kirk Session should have an Officer to wait on its meetings and to execute its orders. He will normally be the Church Officer or beadle, and will hold office at the pleasure of the Session. He should be a member in full communion, or at least someone whom the Session would accept if he were to apply for membership. Suspension from congregational membership carries with it suspension from office.

ITS MEETINGS

Convening

Notice — Meetings are convened by the Moderator, and even although the calling is actuallly done by the Clerk this is so under authority of the Moderator. Meetings are normally called by pulpit intimation which, unless for the transaction of some very formal item must be "timeous", and that in my view means seven free days, though I imagine from one Sunday to the next would be acceptable. They may properly be convened by personal notice given to each member, and in the case where there are Assessors these are certainly entitled to such personal notice in supplement of the pulpit intimation. But whether personal or pulpit the notice must be timeous. From the point of view of efficiency there is much to be said for a notice accompanied by a print of the minutes and a copy of the proposed agenda being circulated — and in this day of word-processing this need not constitute a major exercise.

Regular Meeting — It is common practice for a rota of fixed meetings to be agreed — the second Tuesday of each month or what-have-you. Even so, a pulpit reminder would seem appropriate. There is a tendency to refer — erroneously — to such meetings as "statutory", a term properly applied to a meeting held in obedience to an order or statute imposed by a superior court. There is only one normal statutory meeting of Session, the one held within two months of the close of the General Assembly to appoint a Representative Elder to Presbytery. The correct name of the other meeting is a "regular meeting" or, if you will, a "monthly meeting".

Requisition — When so required in writing by not less than one-third of the Elders (at least five if there are more than nine) the Moderator must call a meeting within ten days (Basis of Union 1929). It is not clear whether the ten days refers to the calling or the holding of the meeting, though I should strongly favour the former. Provided that intimation has been given within ten days that a meeting is to be held on a date reasonably close it seems to me that all is in order.

If it appears to the Moderator that the requisition is to deal with an item of business which from the chair he would rule incompetent he is not obliged to call (1960 Sess 6). Should the Moderator refuse, or simply fail, to call a meeting the Elders concerned would be entitled to petition the Presbytery. Should the Moderator's ruling on competence be considered faulty they would, I imagine, have the same redress as would have been the case had the meeting been held and the ruling given then — that is to say, an appeal to Presbytery, though it might be safer to go by petition.

Restriction on Meeting — A Kirk Session cannot meet except in connection with the administration of the Sacraments or for urgent business at the time of an ordinary meeting of a superior court unless with permission of that court, except that if none of its members is a commissioner to the Assembly a Kirk Session may meet during the sittings thereof. The prohibition extends only to ordinary meetings of the superior court, so if, as often happens, the Presbytery appoints an *in hunc effectum* meeting for a time when a Kirk Session is accustomed to meet the latter body is not restricted.

Adjournment — A Kirk Session has power at any time to adjourn for further consideration of some piece of unfinished business. The time and place for the resumed meeting is fixed there and then, and unless it be for the same day intimation of it will be made in the usual way. If this is done the meeting need not be confined to completing the unfinished item but may deal with any piece of regular business.

Conduct of Business

Quorum — Irrespective of its size the quorum of a Kirk Session is three, of whom the Moderator is one.

Constitution — The law requires that every meeting of Kirk Session be "opened and closed with prayer," and the fact that this has been done should be recorded in the minute, though it is adequate to say that the meeting "was constituted." An extract from the minutes must, to be valid, testify that the court "met and was constituted". Practice varies as to the precise form which the opening devotions may take. The near universal custom is to close with the benediction.

In Private — The Kirk Session is the only Church court which regularly meets in private. At any time and for any reason the Session may itself resolve to meet as an open court, but unless this is done the utmost confidentiality should be observed in respect of all Session business. In the field of discipline when the character of men and women is involved the utmost discretion is clearly essential, but the condition of confidentiality is not confined to such cases. As the meetings are in private so also must be the minutes.

Approval of Minutes — The meeting having been constituted the first business is to approve all minutes not already approved and signed. Unless copies have been circulated, in which case they may be taken as read, they should be read over by the Clerk. If any serious adjustment has to be made the fact should be recorded in the contemporary minute, otherwise a marginal correction initialled by Moderator and Clerk suffices. Once approved the minutes are signed by Moderator and Clerk. On no account should they be signed in advance by either official, and no less emphatically they should not be left to be signed at some later date. The fact that Moderator or Clerk had not been present at the meeting in question is no barrier to their signing — they are not testifying to the accuracy of the minute but simply to the fact that it has been approved. For full particulars regarding the keeping of minutes see p 254.

Agenda — For practical reasons it is good to have an agenda prepared in advance and either circulated with the notice calling the meeting or handed out (or at least read over) at the opening of the meeting. Anyone who has business that he wishes raised is then invited to declare the same and to secure a place for it on the agenda. It should be made clear that once the agenda has been approved it will not be departed from. In this way when the final item on the billet has been disposed of the meeting is closed and that bugbear so often on an agenda "Any other competent business" should be omitted — for on that way of proceeding no other business is competent!

Standing Orders — A court is always at liberty to frame Standing Orders to regulate the conduct of its affairs, but it is not usual for a Kirk Session to do this. In these circumstances it is held to be bound by those of the next superior court — the Presbytery. One would expect these to be principally concerned with such matters as the character of motions, how to take the vote, how long must elapse before a decision may be reviewed, and the like.

ITS RECORDS

The Kirk Session is responsibe for maintaining, and keeping custody of, a variety of Church records. These have to be produced annually for inspection by the Presbytery. All records not currently in use which contain entries earlier than 1900 are, by order of the General Assembly, to be handed over to the Principal Clerk of Assembly for transmission by him to the Keeper of the Records of Scotland. The Assembly of 1985 (Repts, p 6) recommended that all records more than fifty years old should be so transmitted.

Kirk Session Minutes — The Session has to keep a record of its own proceedings which should also include a record of all congregational meetings held for ecclesiastical purposes. At some point within this volume (preferably at the begining or the end) the Formula should be written out and adequate space left so that it may be signed on every occasion of ordination and admission of Elders. It is also most useful to have the current delimitation of parish boundaries pasted in the cover of the volume — and that despite what was said earlier about "no pasting"!

Communion Roll — The Kirk Session has to keep a Roll of Communicant members of the congregation (Act vi 1938). The Assembly of 1934 stated (Reg 4) that there is no objection to a loose-leaf list of the communicants being kept by the Session for its own use, and the Assembly of 1985 agreed (Repts, p 6) that there is no objection to the use of computers for the keeping of rolls and records, but there must also be kept and produced at the annual inspection a bound volume containing a "consecutive list in alphabetical order" of the names of all members. It is clear that a list to which names have from time to time to be added cannot at once be consecutive and alphabetical. This requirement has in fact always been interpreted as meaning that the list should progress from A's to B's etc. It has always seemed to me that the ideal arrangement is that there should be a bound volume with names listed according to surname-initial to which new names would be added, and this would show how and when the person was admitted; and that the names of those departing would be deleted (but not obliterated) showing how and when the person left, and that there would be a cross-reference to a different loose-leaf, card-index, or computer system on which would be entered the record of addresses, attendances at communion — if this were desired, though Act iii 1991 declared that the keeping of such a record was no longer obligatory.

Baptismal Register — The Register of Baptisms will normally lie within the custody of the Minister who must be careful to enter therein the particulars of every baptism conducted within the parish either by himself or by another. It is, however, the responsibility of the Session to ensure that this is done. While it is not obligatory it is helpful if the Minister conducting a baptism enters somewhere on the Birth Certificate a signed statement as to when and where the child (or adult) had been baptized by him.

Supplementary Roll — The Kirk Session was required by Act vi 1938 to keep a roll of those former members whose membership had lapsed but who continued to live in the district. A Declaratory Act (vi) of 1961 makes clear that such persons are free to take communion should they so desire and that while they are not eligible to be appointed to any office in the congregation they are entitled if they so desire to have their names entered on the Electoral Register during a vacancy. This Roll does not have to be produced at the annual inspection.

Property Register — Where the Kirk Session is the body in charge of temporal affairs the responsibility for preparing and maintaining this volume lies wholly with it (Act xxi 1961), but even when the responsibility lies elsewhere it is the Kirk Session that has to ensure that the Register is being kept up-to-date. For fuller information regarding this register see Chapter on Property.

Register of Proclamation of Banns — With the termination of the practice of calling banns of marriage (Act iii 1978) this Register (Act xvi 1932) is not now required. If this has not already been done all earlier Registers should, through the Principal Clerk of Assembly, be lodged with the Keeper of the Records of Scotland.

Roll of Baptized Persons Not Communicants — A resolution of the Assembly of 1930 required that the Kirk Session maintain such a register but Act iii of 1977 relieved them of this duty, most Sessions having already relieved themselves of it!.

ITS BUSINESS

The Kirk Session is responsible for the spiritual oversight of its parish. Act xvii 1931 states, "It is the duty of the Kirk Session to maintain good order, to cause Acts of Assembly to be put into execution, to judge and determine causes, and to superintend the religious and moral condition of the parish." It will be convenient to look at the responsibilities of the Kirk Session as being directed (a) towards the people of the parish, (b) towards the services of the sanctuary, (c) towards the organisations of the congregation, and (d) towards the conduct of a vacancy.

(a) CARE OF THE PEOPLE

Traditionally, and still at least nominally, the Kirk Session has a responsibility towards all the people of the parish. Effectively to exercise such a concern became increasingly difficult from the mid-eighteenth century consequent upon the growth of independent denominations and on the break-up of the old parishes following on the massive population disturbances of the Industrial Revolution so that today, except in some rural areas, it is a fairly meaningless concept. More and more, therefore, the care of the Kirk Session is limited to the membership of the congregation and their families, the wider commitment being generally met by an occasional parish visitation and by the Minister making himself available to render assistance and comfort to all in the parish who are in need of his ministrations.

Elders' Districts

Congregations are generally divided into geographical Districts, an Elder being put in charge of each. At the lowest his duty involves delivering Communion Cards from time to time, but ideally he should concern himself deeply with the people entrusted to his care, particularly watching the development of the young and seeking to direct them towards church-membership, reporting to the Minister all cases that seem to call for his pastoral care, finding out and reporting to Session Clerk or Roll-Keeper the destination of those who have moved. The words "Gone Away" scribbled on the edge of a Communion Card is a remarkably unhelpful item of information. Each year the Assembly hears of a vast drop in numbers arising from members leaving without certificates of transference — 1586 reported last year, 1834 the year before. This could be greatly reduced were the Elders to keep closer track. Also, where the District falls within the area of the parish the District Elder has a special opportunity to keep himself, and his Minister, informed of all new arrivals.

Communion Roll

The keeping of the Communion Roll is governed by the provisions of Act vi 1938, Act i 1972, and Act iii 1977.

The Kirk Session is responsible for maintaining the Communion Roll, but it is responsible too for the activities of admitting and releasing members, activities of which the Roll is a reflection. It will add names of persons who have been admitted in any one of three ways — (a) by profession of faith, (b) by certificate of transference from another congregation, or (c) by special resolution; and it will remove names, also for one of three reasos — (d) because of death, (e) following on the issue of a certificate of transference, or (f) by resolution in exercise of power conferred in Section 4 of the 1938 Act — for manifesting insufficient interest in the life and witness of the congregation.

(a) *Admission by Profession* — The training of communicants is the business of the Minister (Act xvii 1971), but the Kirk Session has to judge of their suitability, has to hear their profession, and has to extend to each the right hand of fellowship. Communicants are received at a Service of Public Worship, which is preceded by a meeting of Session at which the candidates are presented by the Moderator who reports that he has had them under instruction, it being for the Session if they are satisfied that they have been baptized and that their life and character are in keeping with their proposed profession to resolve that they be now received. The court remains in session throughout the service and after the candidates have satisfactorily answered the questions the Elders (or a representative group of them) extend to them the right hand of fellowship. The Session Clerk is then instructed to add their names to the Communion Roll.

(b) *Admission by Certificate* — A certificate of transference consists of three parts — first the certificate proper testifying that AB leaves the congregation of X in full communion with the Church of Scotland; secondly a form of "receipt" to be returned to the issuing Kirk Session when the person has attached himself to another congregation; and thirdly an "advice-note" which where the address to which the recipient has gone is known should be sent without delay to the Minister of the parish concerned. Careful observance of these simple requirements can help greatly in keeping lapsing to a minimum. Receipt of such a certificate should be reported to the Kirk Session as soon as possible and the court should authorise the addition of the name to the Roll. Act iii of 1977 reduced from three years to a single year the period of validity of such a certificate, requiring that after the expiry of that period the Session should "examine the circumstances carefully" before accepting the name for addition to the Roll.

(c) *Admission by Resolution of Kirk Session* — When a person has already made profession of faith but for some reason has lapsed from membership and is desirous of making a fresh start it lies within the discretion of the Kirk Session to resolve that his name should be restored to the Roll. In terms of the 1977 Act a person presenting a certificate whose validity has expired is to be treated as falling into this caegory.

(d) *Removal by Death* — Such removals are regularly reported to the Kirk Session.

(e) *Removal by Certificate of Transference* — When application is made for such a certificate no effort should be spared to discover the new address and to despatch the advice-note to the parish minister. When it is known that a member is about to leave the district he should if possible be persuaded to take his certificate with him rather than "wait and see where I want to settle." Indeed the 1977 Act requires that such a certificate is to be issued in every case unless the person going "has expressed a definite desire to retain his connection and the Minister and Kirk Session are prepared to accept pastoral responsibility for him."

(f) *Removal by Resolution of Kirk Session* — At the annual revisal of the Communion Roll the Kirk Session is entitled to remove therefrom any who in its view are not showing sufficient interest or involvement in the life of the congregation. The original Act (of 1938) instanced absence from Communion for three years without reason known as "manifesting" such lack of interest (which seemed fair enough), but unfortunately the three-year rule came to be widely fixed upon and treated as the official yard-stick in a realm where accurate instruments are hard to come by. This was seen as undesirable and Act i 1972 removed the offending phrase. In the 1977 Act the general standard required is defined as "having shown sufficient interest or taken an adequate share in the worship, mission and service of the Church" and the person who has failed in this is first of all to have "the question raised with him personally" and, if no improvement follows, his name is to be removed the following year. No definition is offered of "sufficient" or "adequate". Drawing a clear line of demarcation is always difficult: here it is nearly impossible. The result is that with a view to keeping up numerical appearances many are "given the benefit of the doubt" where no shade of doubt really exists.

Annual Revisal of the Communion Roll — The Roll is to be made up as at 31st December in each year (Act vi 1931). What normally happens is that the Kirk Session meets towards the close of the year for this purpose. The Roll is carefully gone over and any name due for deletion in terms of paragraph (f) above having been removed it is attested as containing so many names as at that date. The fact of the revision and attestation is to be recorded in the Session minutes. The Act recommends that pulpit intimation should be made on two Sundays that this revision is to be undertaken, but I fear this is rarely if ever done, and it is difficult to see any useful purpose it would serve.

In a Vacancy — The Act of 1932 dealing with Vacancy Procedure made specific provision that in the early stages when the Electoral Register was in course of preparation the Communion Roll was to be "corrected (if necessary) by the Kirk Session as at that date" — that is, the occurrence of the vacancy. The new Act has no such provision, but if in preparing the Register obvious mistakes are found in the Roll steps should be taken to have these put right, and the fact reported to the Session This, however, is not the time to "purge the Roll" which should have been done the previous December at the annual revisal.

Supplementary Roll — Section 7 of the 1938 Act required that with a view to continued supervision the Kirk Session should keep a separate or Supplementary Roll on which was to be placed the names of those who had been removed from the Commnion Roll without a certificate of transference and who continued to reside in the parish or district. While the objective aimed at here is admirable the practical problems are formidable. In a large city parish it can be exceedingly difficult to keep track of the movements of those on the Roll proper with a view to continued supervision — how much more difficult with those on the Supplementary Roll. In a small country parish this need not be so, but in such a parish these folk are well enough known to the Minister without the need to have their names engrossed in a register!

Two points should be particularly noted about this Roll — first that a name should not appear on it unless the person is resident within the parish or district, and secondly that being on it confers very limited rights — the person may if he so desires come to Communion, he may be restored to the Roll by resolution, and his name may be added to the Electoral Register in a vacancy (Act vi 1951).

The Act also (Section 8) lays it upon Kirk Sessions in exercise of their pastoral supervision within the parish to take steps to ascertain, so far as possible, the names of those within the parish who have no connection with any Church. This would seem to be a doctrine of perfection, and, in any case, it is difficult to see how the cause of pastoral caring is advanced by ascertaining names.

Finally the Act declares that "access to the Lord's Table shall not be refused to any person who desires to communicate, provided such person has previously been admitted a member in full communion and is not under discipline by a court of the Church", also that the Kirk Session has a right to welcome to that Table a member of any Christian communion.

Minister's Name — There are Ministers who feel very stongly that their names should not appear on the Communion Roll since they are not subject to the discipline of the Kirk Session. I am perfectly satisfied that the Minister's name should appear. The Roll is a list of those entitled to take Communion not of those who are subject to Session discipline, and it would take more than having his name entered on a Communion Roll to deprive a Minister of his right to be tried only by his Presbytery.

Care of the Poor

Time was when care of the poor was one of the most important and onerous functions of a Kirk Session. In those distant days all collections taken in Church were for that object. The Church has long since been relieved of that obligation, and any work undertaken in the field is now in the nature of benevolence rather than of maintenance. Most, if not all, congregations continue to operate a Poor Fund, probably now called a Benevolent Fund, which is a survival from that older time and which today is usually more of an embarrassment than of a blessing. The responsibility for its administration lies with the Kirk Session which normally appoints the Minister its agent in distributing, but there should be a Session Treasurer to keep the books.

Perquisites for the Poor — An interesting survival from those earlier days are three statutory provisions assigned to the poor through the Kirk Session — (a) winnings on cards or dice, or winnings on horse racing, so far as they exceed three hundred merks (£5.56) in twenty-four hours; (b) fines for profaneness or for Sabbath profanation; and (c) every penalty and forfeiture under Day Poaching Act 1932. I do not imagine that prosecutions under the first two are instituted today, and in twenty years in a reasonably well-poached country parish I on only one occasion received the price of forfeited nets — not, apparently, very good nets at that! In case of any such windfall it should be noted that it is for the poor of the parish whether or not they are members of the congregation, and it should certainly not be lavished on a member of the congregation who lives outwith the parish.

Parish Trusts — When the Kirk Session holds property wholly or mainly for the benefit of the inhabitants of the parish or any of them "as such inhabitants", and when forty years have expired from the foundation of the trust, and when it is neither ecclesiastical nor educational, the Kirk Session may transfer it to the local authority or appoint three members to act on a Committee of Management of the property" (Local Government (Scotland) Act 1894). It is probably wise to do so.

Discipline — Along with the care of the poor the exercise of discipline within the parish constituted the main part of the work of the Kirk Session of an earlier generation. Today this whole field is left very much within the discretion of the Minister. There are, however, cases where the

Kirk Session as court of first instance finds itself involved in disciplinary action. Reference should be made to the chapter on Discipline at page 238.

Finance — The responsibilities of the Kirk Session in relation to all matters of finance are fully set forth in the chapter on the Congregation.

(b) PROVISION FOR WORSHIP

The Kirk Session has a large measure of responsibility in respect of the worship of the congregation — responsibility in fixing the services, in ensuring the comfort and convenience of the worshippers, in appointing an organist and church officer.

Services of Worship

"It belongs to the Kirk Session, in concurrence with the Minister, to regulate the hours of public worship and to fix the number of Church Services. The Kirk Session may appoint such occasional or special services as it judges desirable" (Act xvii 1931). Nothing is said in the Act as to what is to happen if the "concurrence" is not forthcoming. Suppose, to take a very extravagant example, the Kirk Session judged it desirable that a Special Servce be held on Maundy Thursday but the Minister expressed his conviction that his time that day could be otherwise used to greater advantage. What then? Clearly the Minister is in a strong position in that he can simply stay away and there will be no service. At the same time it has to be noted that this Act is particularly directed to defining the relative responsibilties of Minister and Kirk Session and it has taken the unexpected line of putting the initiative into the hands of the Session.

All matters affecting the actual conduct of public worship and the administering of the Sacraments lie outwith the control of the Kirk Session, being the prerogative of the Minister who, however, is acting as agent for the Presbytery which in the last analysis is the body responsible. Emphatically it is not true to say that the Minister is his own master in all matters connected with worship — he is the servant and executive of the Presbytery. "Matters entering into the actual performance of public worship, or the administering of ordinances, are the business of the Presbytery. In those things the Kirk Session has no authority ... . The executive of the Presbytery in such matters is the Minister." (Mair's Digest, p 126)

Consultation — Although the Elders have no authority in the matter of the conduct of worship they will usually have opinions on the subject, and these may well reflect those within the congregation as a whole. There is no reason why a Minister should not consult with his Session on any question concerning the conduct and content of the Service, and in particular with regard to any proposal for change in long-established patterns. It is often good that changes should be effected, it is always important that they be accepted with goodwill and understanding. Otherwise they are likely to fail in their objective of improving the service as a vehicle for the expression of the worship of the entire congregaton.

Unwelcome Innovations — In 1866 the General Assembly interpreted the relevant section of the 1592 Act of Parliament (which finally established Presbyterianism in Scotland) in fairly strong terms as will be found on page 152. Any member of a congregation is entitled to petition the Presbytery to take action in terms of this legislation.

Who May Conduct? — The law is perfectly clear that authority to conduct public worship can be conferred on only a limited group of people. This matter is dealt with fully at p 152.

Administration of the Sacraments

The administering of the Sacraments is basically a matter for the Minister, but the Kirk Session have an involvement.

The Lord's Supper — The Kirk Session appoints and intimates the time and place for the observance of the Lord's Supper and makes provision therefor. Act xxi 1956 states, "The Sacrament of the Lord's Supper shall be celebrated in Church at stated times. Exceptionally the Sacrament may be celebrated in Church or elsewhere at the discretion of a Minister. When the Sacrament is administered to the sick and infirm the fact is to be noted in the Communion Roll." The closing phrase presumably means that the person receiving "private communion" should be credited with an attendance, but since such attendances are no longer recorded this requirement would seem to fall. It would, however, be reasonable that in any record of the Communion in the Session minutes it should be stated that communion was also given to so many sick and infirm in their homes. The Elders assist the Minister in the distribution of the elements at Communion, but this they do as Elders and not corporately as a

Session, so the court need not be constituted for this purpose. The practice is based on tradition, not on constitution or on theology, but it is so long-established that it would seem unwise to discard it at any regular service. But at, say, a Woman's Guild Rededication Service there is everything to be said in favour of having the elements distributed by members of the Guild.

Children and Communion — It was reported to the Assembly in 1992 by the Committee on Returns to Overtures that an Overture anent Admission of Children to Communion had been approved by 30 Presbyteries, disapproved by 18 (1437 members to 1122) and an Act (xv) was passed accordingly. This begins by affirming that "the Lord's Table is open to any baptised person who loves the Lord and responds in faith to the invitation 'Take, eat'", and goes on to declare that a Kirk Session will normally require, in effect, that the baptised person shall have received instruction and be ready to make public profession of faith before being admitted to the Table. (It has been, I think, the *invariable*, not the "normal" practice of the Church that the person *has made*, not merely "has been ready to make" profession of faith. These differences are surely of considerable significance.)

The Act goes on in Section 3, "Notwithstanding the terms of section (2) and recognising the free discretion of the Kirk Session in this matter, where a Kirk Session is satisfied that baptised children are being nurtured within the life and worship of the Church and love the Lord and respond in faith to the invitation 'take, eat', it may admit such children to the Lord's Table, after pastorally overseeing the response of faith of such children to see when it is right for them to come to the Lord's Table. The names of such children shall be admitted to the Communion Roll of the congregation when they have made public profession of their faith."

The Act is said in the Report to be "permissive or enabling rather than mandatory" legislation in the sense that each Kirk Session is at liberty to reach its own decision as to whether or not it is going to avail itself of the option presented. It is interesting that the Working Party responsible for the Report consisted of eleven Ministers (six of them parish ministers) and one Elder. In a matter so intimately affecting what is the exclusive business of Kirk Sessions one might have expected a larger representation of Elders.

Communion Wine — Early in the present century a *quoad sacra* congregation in Barrhead departed completely from the use of fermented wine at Communion. A group of members appealed and the matter went through Presbytery and Synod till it reached the General Assembly which ordained that provision must be made to enable all who wished to do so to partake of communion in the ordinary elements of bread and wine according to the use and wont of the Church (1909, Sess 13). An attempt in the 'fifties to have this judgment recalled was unsuccessful. In 1971 a special commission of Assembly reported that it should be left to the conscience and judgment of individual Ministers to determine the nature of the wine suitable for use. The report went on to stress that the problem of the alcoholic in connection with participation in communion must be recognised as part of the pastoral concern of each individual Minister and that the variety of practice within the Church as a whole, and also within some congregations, meets the individual situation.

Communion Plate — Should a Kirk Session wish to sell some communion plate no longer in use it must apply for permission to do so to the General Assembly through the Board of Practice and Procedure (Reports 1975 pp 13-14).

Baptism — The Kirk Session "appoints and provides for" the administration of Baptism, which is to be administered to adults on profession of faith and promise of obediencce, and to children in terms of Act xvii 1963 (p 155). A certificate of baptism should be given by the Minister who should also endorse the Birth Certificate and enter the particulars in the Baptismal Register. In the case of chaplaincies and other non-parochial spheres of service it is especially important to ensure that any Baptism administered by such a Chaplain is recorded in the Baptismal Register of the parish where it occurred. Some Maternity Hospitals themselves maintain a Baptismal Register. Very recently approval was given to a congregation to instal within the Church a baptistry for adult baptism by immersion.

Appointments

Organist — The Organist, Precentor, or Leader of Praise is appointed and dismissed by the Kirk Session which has to satisfy itself as to the Christian character of the person appointed. The salary is the business of the financial court. In all matters of worship the Organist takes his instructions from the Minister (Act xvi 1931). Before an appointment is made the Kirk Session should prepare a statement covering all details of services, choir practices, access to the instrument (including access for teaching and for practice by pupils), fees for extra engagements, and other similar matters, and this should be clearly understood and accepted by the appointee, who should be furnished with a copy. Psalmody Committees and the like are purely advisory, responsibility for the whole field lies with the Minister or Kirk Session as the case may be.

A new complication has arisen affecting the organist's contract consequent upon the growing popularity for having videos recorded to immortalise wedding services. A special arrangement has to be made with the organist to cover his financial interest and note of this should be taken in that part of his contract dealing with fees for special services.

Church Officer — The Church Officer also is appointed and dismissed by the Kirk Session. He will act also, normally, as Session Officer. A contract of service should be drawn up setting forth clearly what are his duties and indicating very specifically from whom alone he is to take orders. The better the Officer the more he will resent a multiplicity of masters. Many congregations today are having to make-do with a variety of expedients in the shortage of Church Officers. Where an arrangement for part-time or voluntary service is being made steps must be taken to make certain that there is insurance to cover the possibility of industrial injury.

It is interesting that the term "beadle" which has been affectionately applied to this dignatory for many generations is of English origin, having its roots in the ancient trade guilds whence it was taken over by the vestries who applied it to their officer. Minutes of appointments in the old Scottish records show that the title in universal use was "Kirk Officer". Generally, of course, he was also Session Officer and not uncommonly too he was "the Minister's Man" with all that that implied. The term "beadle" may have offered a convenient way of knitting together the three strands.

Church Cleaning — Ultimately the responsibility for maintaining the place of worship in a condition of cleanliness and comfort rests upon the shoulders of the Kirk Session, but in most cases today it will be seen as the business of the financial court.

Use of Church Buildings

The situation here, which is a little complicated, may be set forth as follows — (1) the place of worship and other ecclesiastical buildings are at the disposal of the Minister (or Interim Moderator) for all purposes of his office; (2) the Minister can on his sole authority grant the use of the buildings for all purposes connected with the congregation and its organisations; (3) given the consent of the financial court the Minister can grant the use of the buildings for purposes of a religious, ecclesiastical or charitable nature not connected with the congregation; (4) neither the Kirk Session, Congregational Board, nor Deacons' Court can grant the use of the premises for any purpose whatever without consent of the Minister; (5) the Managers can grant the use of the buildings only with consent of both Minister and Kirk Session. It has to be added that there are congregations whose constitutions stipulate conditions for the use of buildings which are at variance with the above and in such a case the constitution will prevail. Two points have to be kept in mind — first that in any use that is to be made of the buildings their sacred character is to be kept in mind, and secondly that in any exercise of his powers in this field the Minister (or Interim Moderator) is answerable to the Presbytery.

Careful attention should be paid to the conditions affecting the insurance on the property, for these may attach restrictions to its use by other than Church organisations if the insurance cover is not to be affected.

Burial in Church — Burials in Church are forbidden in terms of a resolution of 1643. The decision of the Assembly in a case in 1955 (Sess 12) extended the prohibition to include the depositing of cremated remains within a Church.

Churchyard — The management of a churchyard no longer in use may be taken over by a Kirk Session, as may the custody and management of old ecclesiastical buildings within a churchyard which has itself been duly transferred to the local authority (Act Parliament 1935)

Kirk Bell — "To the Minister exclusively belongs the power of regulating the time and manner of ringing the bell of the Church in connection with ecclesiastical purposes (Mair, Digest)

(c) CONGREGATIONAL ORGANISATIONS

All societies and associations of members and adherents of the congregation are under supervision of the Kirk Session (Act xvii 1931) and the approval of the Session is a *sine qua non* for the establishment of any such organisation. It is usual for a Kirk Session to appoint from its own number a representative or representatives in respect of each of the organisations to keep in touch with them and to report from time to time on their activities and wellbeing.

Care of the Young — The care of the young should be the especial business of the Kirk Session whose duty it is to see that parents attend to the godly upbringing of their children. All Sunday Schools are under supervision of the Session, and the Minister, who is in charge of the instruction of the young (Act xvii 1931) is head of the Sunday School even where, as is customary, someone else acts as Superintendent. Care should be taken in the choice of teachers for whom training facilities should be provided. Help and advice in this field can readily be got in most Presbyteries through the agency of Sunday School Advisers appointed by the Assemly's Board of Education.

(d) VACANCY BUSINESS

On the occurrence of a vacancy the Kirk Session has the duty along with the Interim Moderator of making arrangements for the supply of the pulpit and for the preparation of the Electoral Register (p 73). Once a nominee has, or nominees have, been selected by the Vacancy Committee the Kirk Session assumes responsibility for the conduct of the election, for the preparation and signing of a Call, and for its prosecution before the Presbytery (Act v 1984).

(e) DISCIPLINE

This is a department of Kirk Session activity little known today. It is still on the agenda, however, and the following features should be noted. I quote from the Stair Memorial Encyclopaedia — "In cases of discipline involving elders, deacons, communicant members and baptised persons who are adherents the kirk session is the court of first instance (Act i 1929). When allegations of serious scandal are brought before the Kirk Session relating to any persons in the categories described the Kirk Session is bound to bring the matter to the attention of the Presbytery, which, in the absence of a confession appoints the Kirk Session to hold a proof. It is the function of the Presbytery and not of the Kirk Session to pass censure on those who have confessed, or who, by proof adduced before the Kirk Session have been found guilty of serious scandal (Act xi

1907). A Kirk Session is entitled to suspend the privileges of a person who is subject to, but repudiates, its discipline." I have to confess that in close on thirty years as a Presbytery Clerk I have never received a report in terms as above.

ITS RELATION WITH OTHER COURTS

With Other Kirk Sessions

No one Kirk Session has any authority or control over any other, and in the case of complaint (of intrusion into its parish, for example) approach must be made to the Presbytery to which all alike are subject in all of their proceedings. The Presbytery can at any time for reasons which to it seem good summon a meeting of a Kirk Session or of a congregation.

With the Presbytery

With certain very limited exceptions any matter coming regularly before a Kirk Session may be appealed to the Presbytery and thence to the General Assembly.

Quinquennial Visitation — On the quinquennial visitation of the congregation the visiting committee holds a separate meeting with the Kirk Session. For full particulars see Chapter on The Presbytery.

Visitation of Records — The Kirk Session Minute-book, Communion Roll, Baptismal Register, Minute-book of the Financial Court, and Property Register, along with a copy of the Annual Balance-Sheet duly audited, have to be produced at the annual visitation (or inspection) of records. All records prior to 1900 should have been put in custody of the Keeper of the Registers of Scotland to whom they are on permanent loan. They are available at any time for inspection and, on the occasion of a congregational exhibition or the like, may be "re-loaned" temporarily. For such a purpose approach should be made in the first place to the Presbytery Clerk.

Inventory of Property — The Kirk Session should prepare and maintain an inventory of all property, heritable and moveable, belonging to the congregation, showing in the former case where the titles are lodged. This should be methodically kept up-to-date, and particularly on the occurrence of a vacancy it should be carefully revised. On the death, demission or translation of a Minister all records and other property of the congregation held in custody of the Minister should be handed over to the Session for transmission in due course to his successor. At each time of handing-over a written receipt in some detail should be received and retained. All changes in matters of property must be notified at once to the Keeper of the Benefice Register of the Presbytery.

Representative Elder — Within two months of the close of the General Assembly each year every Kirk Session is to appoint a Representative Elder to Presbytery for the period 1st July to 30th June following. Normally he will be a *bona fide* Elder from its own ranks, but if it so wishes the Session may, with approval of Presbytery, appoint such an Elder from any other Session within the bounds. A form of commission is completed and this will be received and the Elder take his seat at any meeting of Presbytery, ordinary or otherwise, so long as it is after 1st July. After the expiry of the two months the Presbytery may itself make an appointment. In the case of a linked charge each of the components appoints a Representative Elder (Act ii 1977). In case of the death, resignation or disqualification of a Representative Elder the Kirk Session may at any subsequent meeting appoint someone to fill the vacant place.

With the General Assembly

The Kirk Session is not represented on the General Assembly and it has direct access to the supreme court only through Petition. Should the Session wish to raise in the Assembly an issue of general concern to the Church the course it has to follow is to petition the Presbytery asking that body to overture the Assembly, or, more simply, arrange that its own Minister or Representative Elder will move in the Presbytery for such an overture.

Representation — Elders to attend the General Assembly have to be commissioned by Presbyteries, but are not restricted to Presbytery Elders. Most Presbyteries operate a rota whereby each Kirk Session is invited, every fourth year, to nominate a *bona fide* acting elder who will in due course be commissioned by the Presbytery. (It would seem that the term *bona fide* as things are today would exclude only an Elder who was on the Roll as a Minister). It is for the Presbytery (not the Assembly as was once the case) to satisfy itself that all such commissioners are *bona fide* acting Elders.

Sent Down for Comment — From time to time matters are sent down from the Assembly to Presbyteries and Kirk Sessions for study and comment, and in such cases until 1991 copies of the relevant material were supplied in sufficient number to include members of Sessions. In that year (Repts 1991, p 3) the Assembly agreed that no longer would material be sent down sufficient to cover all members of Kirk Sessions but only copies for Minister and Session Clerk leaving it to local resources to produce copies for all. This sending down for comment is not to be confused in any way with Barrier Act procedure.

Referendum — There is no provision in the law or usage of the Church whereby any matter may go down for a vote of all members or of all Elders. A decision taken on the floor of the Assembly on the question of the admission of women to the Eldership resulted (in the 'thirties) in that question being sent down to be voted on in congregations. It seems to me highly questionable whether the legality of this can be upheld. A fundamental change of such magnitude in the way of determining the mind of the Church could not, as I see it, be put into operation until it had received Barrier Act approval. An attempt to repeat this procedure in 1966 was defeated. The simple fact is that even if such a referendum were declared to be both appropriate and legal there is no proper machinery in the Church that would allow such a vote to be taken in any fair or meaningful fashion.

With the Financial Court

While the body that manages the temporal affairs is not strictly a "court" in that it does not form part of the Presbyterian hierarchy of courts this may be the appropriate point at which to enter a note on its relationship with the Kirk Session.

Under the Model Constitution or where there is a Deacons' Court the Kirk Session is fully represented on the financial court and the danger of the two bodies disagreeing seriously is reduced to a minimum. Were such a situation to arise, however, the Kirk Session would be supreme.

The greatest danger of conflict arises from the large degree of freedom from Session control or representation enjoyed by the Managers under the old U P system, for they incline to see themselves as responsible only to the congregation. "Of course we're old UP's," they'll tell you triumphantly. Every UP constitution, however, includes towards the end, a clause declaring that "the constitutional right of the Kirk Session to intervene when in its judgment the welfare of the congregation demands it by calling a congregational meeting or otherwise is not in any way affected by what has gone before." The use of the word "constitutional" in defiance of the "constitution" is interesting — it clearly refers to the constitution of Presbyterianism and concedes that this must over-ride any congregational constitution.

Chapter 12

THE PRESBYTERY

THE PRESBYTERY WAS an almost accidental accretion to the structure of Presbyterian Church government. In its original conception Presbyterianism was to be a three-tier system, the Kirk Session being at the base of the pyramid, the General Assembly at its apex and the Provincial Synod sandwiched between the two. However, right from the days of the Reformation, there had been held regularly at local level group meetings designed to provide a forum where Ministers and people could meet for study and discussion of Scripture and to engage in prayer — a fraternal of sorts. And so, as the burden upon Synods increased, and as the position was aggravated by the difficulties created by distance, these intermediate bodies (which had come to be known as "The Exercises" or "The Weekly Exercises") were found to be a convenient instrument for easing that burden, so that by the time the Second Book of Discipline made its appearance in 1581 the Presbytery was recognised, being included as a fourth tier in the structure. The Presbytery had come to stay. The four-tier system was ratified in the famous Act of Parliament of 1592 (the Magna Carta of the Kirk) and it has been, of course, further ratified in the Articles Declaratory of 1921 where it is said of the Kirk that "its government is Presbyterian and is exercised through Kirk Sessions, Presbyteries, Provincial Synods and General Assemblies."

It is interesting to think that the "opening devotions" which characterise the start of every meeting of Presbytery are a survival, however dwarved in extent and importance, of the "exercises" of that earlier body.

Readjustment of Presbyteries — The General Assembly has power at any time to unite, disjoin or erect Presbyteries, or to alter their bounds so as to move a congregation from one Presbytery into a neighbouring one. This last exercise is generally designed to facilitate readjustment, and will be effected on petition from one of the Presbyteries affected, but it is also in order, and has been known to happen, for a congregation to crave that for some reason it should be moved into the bounds of a neighbouring Presbytery.

A hundred years ago there were in the Church of Scotland no fewer than eighty-four home Presbyteries (roughly double today's figure) and they included what seem to us such unlikely names as Penpont, Abertarf, Kincardine O'Neil, Weem — to mention only a few. In 1967 some uniting and readjusting of Presbyteries took place, but it was in 1976, following upon regionalisation of local government, that a major reshuffle was carried out, the idea being to make the bounds of a Presbytery so far as reasonable fall within one Region and conform with the bounds of Districts. This has had the effect of considerably simplifying, and probably strengthening, relations between the Church and local authorities — prior to the change Glasgow Presbytery, for instance, embraced schools belonging to no fewer than five separate Education Authorities, while the fate of its Church buildings was in the control of five different planning bodies.

There are at the time of writing forty-six home Presbyteries.

Overseas Presbyteries — In the early days of missionary activity the work in the various foreign fields was organised on a Presbyterial basis with congregations grouped in Presbyteries bearing such unlikely names as Bengal, Rajputana, the Gold Coast, Livingstonia, Jamaica, Jerusalem. In 1952 there were no fewer than sixteen such Overseas Presbyteries. The character of our missionary thrust has altered radically of recent years, the indigenous Churches are now independent communions, in many cases they have become involved in union with non-Presbyterian denominations, and the net result has been that the number of Overseas Presbyteries has steadily dwindled until by 1964 they had completely disappeared, with the single exception of Jerusalem (see hereunder).

Presbytery of England — At one time there were many congregations of the Church of Scotland scattered throughout England, and, true to pattern, they were grouped together into Presbyteries. By the 1930's the number was enormously reduced, and while they were still divided into three geographical groups they functioned as one Presbytery known as the Presbytery of the Synod of England. By 1950 the divisions had been forgotten and the Presbytery had become one simple unit, having dropped the "Synod" from its title but continuing to enjoy Synodical powers. The number of charges is today still further reduced and the congregations in Berwick and Carlisle have been transferred into the Presbyteries of Duns and of Annan and Eskdale respectively, so that now there are only nine charges in the Presbytery of England and of these two are in the Channel Islands (having been congregations of the Presbyterian Church of England which changed over in 1972, the time when that body became URC. The Presbytery, however, provides a focal point for a large contingent of Chaplains to the Forces (usually nearly a score) and others, so that its ministerial strength amounts to something like thirty-four.

For all ecclesiastical purposes the Presbytery enjoys all the rights, powers and duties of any Presbytery north of the Border. There are, however, obvious differences — two in particular. First of all, constitutionally a congregation of the Church of Scotland south of the Border does not enjoy the position *vis-a-vis* the State which obtains in the realm of Scotland. And secondly, on a territorial basis the Presbytery does not have bounds in any true sense of that term — it is rather a collection of gathered congregations located here and there in different parts of the country, their Kirk Sessions having spiritual oversight of those on their Communion Rolls, but nothing comparable to parish responsibility.

Presbytery of Europe — The Scot being the kind of gregarious animal history has shown him to be, it was inevitable that from an early day congregations of expatriate Scots should have been formed in many cities of Europe. It is interesting to realise that during the days of intense religious persecution under the Stuarts when Presbyterian ordination constituted a criminal offence many Scots ministers (of whom James Renwick was one) were ordained in our Scots Kirk in Rotterdam. In Holland alone at one time there were as many as eleven charges of the Church of Scotland. Since an area so vast as Europe was involved there had to be a number of Presbyteries to cope.

The situation today is governed by the terms of Act v 1978 (as amended by Act iv 1986, Act viii 1988 and Act vi 1989) which recognises the Presbytery of Europe as an Overseas Presbytery of the Church comprising charges at Amsterdam, Brussels, Budapest, Geneva, Gibraltar, Lausanne, Lisbon, Malta, Paris, Rome, Rotterdam — the "Sanctioned Charges". To this Presbytery, which meets twice a year in varying places is given "similar powers to those of Presbyteries in Scotland" and it is made responsible for the spiritual oversight and superintendence of the Sanctioned Charges — all subject to certain conditions fully set forth in the Act. It has the right to elect Commissioners to the General Assembly, to receive and vote on Barrier Act overtures and comment on these, and to have direct access to the General Assembly in the transmission of Overtures and Appeals. Allowance has always to be made for the particular and peculiar conditions existing in the local situation — that, for example, the body taking the place of the Kirk Session may be known by another name, that there may be constitutional relationships with the national Church of the country; and the appointment of Ministers is in the hands of the Board of World Mission, which is responsible for the oversight of their work. The Assembly of 1994 devoted a deal of care to details as to how this oversight was to be exercised (Reps 1994, p 153 ff).

Presbytery of Jerusalem — In terms of Act viii of 1980 very similar conditions to those affecting the Presbytery of Europe apply to the Presbytery of Jerusalem which is given specific "power to license and power to ordain medical and other lay missionaries when required to do so by the Board of World Mission." It appoints two Commissioners, a Minister and an Elder, to each Assembly, and while it does not have the right to make returns to Barrier Act Overtures it "may receive such Overtures, and all other documents sent down to Presbyteries for discussion and comment, and may transmit comment to the General Assembly." Though it has no status in the appointment of ministers and missionaries these come under its discipline. It is a very small Presbytery indeed, and has been continued as such largely in response to a plea that such status greatly strengthens the Church of Scotland in its relations with the Israeli authorities.

ITS MEMBERSHIP

True to the territorial conception of the Church of Scotland all home Presbyteries have geographical bounds and until 1990 they consisted exclusively of Ministers and Elders primarily from charges within their bounds. Thus all of the members had been ordained and had subscribed to the Church's position in matters of doctrine, worship, and government, since they had one and all signed the Formula. In 1970 when a new Act determining who were to be members of Presbytery was being framed the suggestion was advanced that Deaconesses should be included as a third class alongside Ministers and Elders. This was hotly contested on the ground, largely, that membership of Presbytery must be confined to those who had been ordained, and the proposal was departed from. It was not until 1990 that an Act of that year conferred seats in Presbytery on certain members of the Diaconate — as it had then become — to wit, those serving under a Department or with a Committee or Court of the Church, or in one of the appointments listed in Schedule II to the Act, or one who has retired from such a post on grounds of age or infirmity.

The situation regarding membership was regularised by Act ii of 1970 which contained provision for its terms to be revised quinquennially and which in fact has been the subject of no fewer than seven revisions. The most recent position is that of Act iii 1992 (already twice revised).

According to this a Presbytery consists of Ministers, Elders and Members of the Diaconate as follows :

1. Ministers

a) A Minister, or Collegiate Minister, or Assistant Minister, or Associate Minister, or Auxiliary Minister, or Community Minister, inducted, introduced, or assigned either for life or for a period of years to a charge within the bounds.

b) A Hospital Chaplain, a Chaplain to a University or College of Tertiary Education, a Prison Chaplain, an Industrial Chaplain, a School Chaplain serving full-time in a post within the bounds.

c) A Minister holding an appointment as a Professor, Lecturer, or Reader in the Faculty of Divinity of a Scottish University, or one teaching theological subjects or Biblical studies in a University in the United Kingdom — he may choose the Presbytery of his University or of his place of residence.

d) A Minister appointed to an overseas post who has not come under the direction and control of the indigenous Church — the Presbytery being that to which he belonged at the time of his appointment, or that which ordained him, or (if ordained overseas) of that which licensed him.

e) A Minister holding a commission as a Chaplain to HM Forces — the Presbytery being that within whose bounds he is serving, or, where there is no such Presbytery, that to which he belonged at the time of commissioning, or (if ordained for the post) that which ordained him.

f) A Minister acting full-time as a Teacher of or an Adviser in Religious Education in Scotland, or engaged full-time in Religious Broadcasting, or the holder of an executive post in an ecumenical body of which the Kirk is in full membership.

g) A Minister appointed to a post under a Court or Committee of the Church — he may choose between the Presbytery within whose bounds (1) he works, (2) he has an office, or (3) he has his congregational attachment.

h) A Minister holding one of the appointments listed in the Schedule to the Act — the Presbytery being that of the place of work or of residence as the person may choose.
i) A Minister who has successfully petitioned the General Assembly for a seat — the Presbytery being that specified by the Assembly, or if none was specified the Presbytery of his place of work or of residence as he may choose.
j) A Minister from any of the above groups who has retired on grounds of age or infirmity or to facilitate readujstment (unless in the latter case he has taken up full-time employment in the service of the Church) and in every case subject to an age-75 restriction — see below.

Transference of Presbytery — It used to be that for a Retired Minister to be transferred from one Presbytery to another (on moving house, for instance) he had to petition the Synod. Act vii of 1980 introduced a simplified procedure whereby the Minister required only to make written application to the Presbytery to which he wished to move, and in due course to lodge with it a Presbyterial Certificate, and his name was added to its Roll. The 1986 Act tidied up the situation by providing that any Minister who has a choice of Presbytery (as in the groups above) or who has retired may transfer to another Presbytery on lodging an application along with a Presbyterial Certificate and he will be admitted on renewing the vows of his ordination and signing the Formula.

Resignation of Seat — In terms of Act viii of 1980 a Retired Minister entitled to a seat in Presbytery may choose to resign that seat, which he does simply by making appliction to the Presbytery, and their decision is final. He remains, however, uder the direction and supervision of the Presytery which released him, and he is free to continue exercising the functions of the ministry.

"Age or Infirmity" — To qualify for retention of a seat in Presbytery demission of charge or resignation of appointment has to be on grounds of age or infirmity or to facilitate readjustment. At one time the phrase "age or infirmity" was connected with pensions (the Aged and Infirm Ministers' Fund) and meant being over seventy or holding a doctor's certificate to the effect that the holder was unfit for work and likely to remain so. Thus the person qualified for the benefits of the Fund. The Retirement Scheme now allows of one retiring before seventy on a reduced pension and many avail themselves. I incline to the view that today if a man retires from his charge and becomes a pensioner then so long as he does not undertake any full-time gainful employment he is to be regarded so far as membership of Presbytery is concerned as having retired on grounds of age or infirmity.

Restriction on Retired Members — Proposed new legislation anent Limitation of Right of Membership of Higher Courts of the Church (Overture II 1994) has considerably altered the situation. It provides that "ministers, elders and members of the diaconate shall cease to be members of Presbytery at the age of seventy-five years." It further provides that when a Minister or Member of the Diaconate intimates to the Presbytery his or her intention to retire a letter is to be sent "requesting him or her to submit in writing a declaration of intent to continue to attend Presbytery and to participate in its Committees, which declaration shall be lodged with the Clerk fourteen clear days before the meeting of Presbytery at which the retiral is to be considered." Further, the person granted the privilege of continuing membership is to renew the declaration every year in May. It is declared that the Act is not to be retrospective in its application.

2. Elders

If one is to sit in Presbytery as an Elder it is not enough to have the status of Elder, one must belong to a Kirk Session and hold a certificate that one is a *bona fide* acting Elder of a congregation witin the bounds. Elders are appointed as follows:

a) Each Kirk Session (whether linked or not), elects an Elder from its own ranks, or from another Session within the bounds, to represent it in the Presbytery. Two such Elders are appointed if there is a Collegiate Ministry, but not in the case of an Associate, an Auxiliary or an Ordained Assistant. Elders so appointed are *Representative Elders*.

b) The Presbytery itself selects out of its own Kirk Sessions one Elder to set against each Minister who is not an active Parish Minister or Collegiate Minister. These are *Additional Elders.* (There is no authority for the name but it is a convenient one).

c) In terms of Act v 1980, ratified by Act iii 1986 and Act iii 1992 , the Presbytery may appoint further Additional Elders to bring the total of these up to one-third of its congregations.

Age Restriction — The Act is quite peremptory in saying that an Elder "shall cease to be a member of Presbytery at seventy-five years of age", from which it would seem to follow that an Elder appointed within the age-limit is not to be allowed to finish the year of his commissioning. Presumably a new appointment would fall to be made. The wise policy might seem to be not to make an appointment of anyone over seventy-four.

Commissions — Elders' Commissions run from 1st July to 30th June in each year, and Kirk Sessions are enjoined to meet within two months of the close of the General Assembly for the purpose of electing these. There is, however, no reason why Kirk Sessions should not meet much earlier than this, and from the point of view of administrative convenience early elections are much to be desired.

Replacements — Should an Elder appointed to the Presbytery die, leave his Kirk Session, or be disqualified (by turning seventy-five or otherwise) then the Session which elected him its Representative Elder, or the Presbytery which appointed him an Additional Elder, may appoint another in his place. If the Kirk Session does not so appoint then the Presbytery has the right to make an appointment to fill the vacancy.

"The Parity Principle" — It was at the time of Union in 1929 that the principle of securing strict parity of numbers between Ministers and Elders in the courts of the Church (other than the Kirk Session) was first established. Regulations were devised to ensure that when the Roll of Presbytery was fully made up it would contain exactly the same number of Elders as it did of Ministers. This led to a difficulty when the idea of linking came to be widely adopted, for it meant that since there was only one Minister in a linked charge there could be only one Elder, and in consequence once a year a joint meeting of Kirk Sessions had to be held to make the choice. This was unfortunate, for it meant there were Kirk Sessions that had no direct link with Presbytery at Elder level. In 1977 the law was amended to allow of each congregation within the bounds appointing a Representative Elder; and then in 1980, at the instigation of the "Committee of Forty", power was given to Presbyteries to elect Additional Elders up to a maximum of one-third of the number of congregations within their bounds.

The parity principle has thus been completely abandonned. It has to be said that the parity was never as accurate as might have appeared, for although exactly the same number of places was available for Elders as for Ministers a few of the latter places were unfilled because of vacancies, and also a number of the senior Ministers were unlikely to be present with any great regularity. So that at any time had a show of relative strength been called for the Elders could have out-voted the Ministers. As things have now becomee they could hardly fail to do so — much too easily some might think. For in a Presbytery with many linkings the situation has been created where Elders outnumber Ministers to the exent of more than two to one. I cannot believe this was ever seriously intended.

3 The Diaconate

Members of the Diaconate engaged in the full-time service of the Church are entitled to sit in Presbyteries.

a) A Deacon or Deaconess appointed to a post under a Department or with a Committee or Court of the Church is so entitled.
b) A Deacon or Deaconess appointed to one of the offices designated in Schedule II to the Act — the Presbytery being that in which he or she serves.
c) A Deacon or Deaconess entitled as above who has retired on grounds of age or health shall continue his or her Presbytery membership, but subject to the restriction of age seventy-five and an undertaking to maintain interest in the work of the Presbytery (see under "Ministers" above).

"A Deacon or Deaconess who is a memer of Presbytery in terms of this Act shall not be eligible to be a member of a Kirk Session, but a Deacon or Deaconess working in a parish is entitled to be a corresponding member of the Kirk Session; any other Deacon or Deaconess, who is a member of Presbytery, may be associated in the practical work of the Kirk Session of the congregation of which he or she is a member."

Corresponding Members

"A Presbytery may itself elect Corresponding Members, who shall have the right to attend all meetings and to speak on any matter before the Presbytery, but shall not have the right to vote." This class of member — which has been a regular feature of the Assembly for many years — was first introduced to Presbyteries in terms of Act v 1980. The Act gives no guidance on who should have this status conferred upon them or how many of them there ought to be, beyond the requirement that Lay Missionaries and Deaconesses working within the bounds are to be Correspondents *ex officiis* — which is, of course, no longer relevant. It has also been recommended that the Presbyterial Council of the Woman's Guild (or Councils should there be more than one within the Presbytery) and the Diocesan Council of the Episcopal Church should be invited to appoint persons to act in this capacity. Further, the Presbytery may itself invite any member of another Presbytery present at its meeting to sit as a Corresponding Member. This will confer a right to speak which would not go with the more normal process of "associating" (see hereunder).

Members Associated

It is customary at a Presbytery meeting for ordination or induction or for the dedication of a building that Ministers and Elders present from other Presbyteries and also Ministers of other denominations whose orders are recognised by the Kirk are invited to be associated with the Presbytery for the business of that meeting. Since ordinary business is not being transacted on such an occasion the question of the powers of such Associates does not arise. All Ministers may join in the imposition of hands in ordination — (Mair, Digest of Church Law) says of ordination that it is "a sacred ordinance, in which Ministers, though not of the Presbytery, join." Oddly enough, on a strict interpretation the same is not true of giving the right hand of fellowship. Admission is a judicial act of the Presbytery and the law expressly connects the giving of the hand with admission — "it is the completion and overt sign of the judicial act of admission." I do not imagine anyone would be unduly troubled about this today!

Assessors

The General Assembly have power — rarely invoked today — to appoint Assessors to act with a Presbytery either for the conduct of some specific item of business or for the ordinary running of its affairs. I imagine that the "riding committee" so frequently appointed in the first half of the nineteenth century to carry through the induction of an unpopular presentee could be seen as an example of the former. A case of the latter kind occurred not very many years ago. The Presbytery of Islay had become so reduced in numbers that it was practically impossible for it to function and difficult even for it to meet, and so the Assembly appointed Assessors to sit with it until it was possible to have it united with two of its neighbours and thus form the Presbytery of Southern Argyll.

ITS OFFICIALS

The officials appointed by a Presbytery for the orderly conducting of its business are essentially those appointed by the courts generally. They are normally the following:

Moderator — It used to be that the doctrine of the equality of the ministry was taken so seriously that the custom was for each Presbytery to maintain a rota of Ministers on some basis of their own devising and from this each six months the person at the head of the list was chosen to act as Moderator for the next half-year. In 1944 Act xxi provided that the Moderator was to be a Minister chosen by free election on the nomination of the Business Committee and was to continue in office for at least twelve months, being eligible for re-election. In the absence of the Moderator the previous holder of the office, whom failing the senior Minister present, takes the chair. In the event of the death or translation of the Moderator his predecessor resumes the post until a fresh appointment can be made, but it is the Clerk upon whom devolves the powers in the matter of calling meetings. In fixing a meeting *in hunc effectum* the Presbytery may appoint a Minister to act thereat as Moderator *pro tempore*. The Moderator is responsible for calling a special meeting of the court. Otherwise the duties of the Moderator are those of a Moderator generally.

Clerk — The Presbytery appoints someone to act as its Clerk — generally, but not invariably, a Minister — even on occasion someone not a member of the court. For his services he is in receipt of a salary. In his absence a Clerk *pro tempore* is appointed, and no meeting of the court can competently be held without such an appointment being made, the oath *de fideli* administered, and these two facts recorded in the minute.

Treasurer — Most Presbyteries appoint a Treasurer to look after their funds, though it is not unknown for the Clerk to play a dual role. A layman may be, and very often is, appointed to this post. The oath *de fideli* is administered when he assumes office.

Officer — A layman, usually not a member of the court, is appointed Officer and will normally receive a modest salary. His most important function nowadays is to take charge of processions, seating arrangements, etc at special meetings.

Precentor — A member of the court with some musical acumen is usually appointed Precentor to "give the note" at the opening devotions, even if in some cases he does so with the aid of a piano and the whole verse supplants the note.

ITS MEETINGS

As well as having bounds a Presbytery has a "seat" — usually the principal town of its area — and it is here that all ordinary meetings are held, and it is often from this seat that it takes its title. As a consequence of the Union of 1929 the corresponding Presbyteries from the two sides, which usually covered substantially the same area but which ofen had different seats were merged and — as almost invariably happens in unions — they incorporated both names in their new title and met in the two places time about. For example, the Presbytery of Stirling and Dunblane met at both seats, as did the Presbytery of Haddington and Dunbar and others. The massive reorganisation of Presbyteries in 1976 tidied up a good deal of this, though the Presbytery of St Andrews meets alternately there and at Cupar. One novel feature today is that the chief town may be neglected in favour of a seat in what may seem an unlikely place. The Presbytery of Wigtown and Stranraer meets at Glenluce midway between, the Presbytery of Melrose and Peebles has chosen Innerleithen, the Presbytery of Buchan meets at Monquhitter. Availability of car-parking has ecclesiastical side-effects.

Regularity of Meetings — A Presbytery has to meet annually to fix a time when it will elect Assembly commissioners, and it has also to meet to do that, but, that apart, there are no rules governing when or how often a Presbytery must meet. In almost every case, however, Presbyteries meet more or less monthly, holding anything from seven to eleven ordinary meetings each year. For the convenience of Elders Presbyteries in the central areas meet in the evening, but in more scattered districts this is not practicable.

Meeting Outside Its Bounds — If for any reason a Presbytery wishes to meet at some place outwith its own bounds it can do so only with the special authority of the General Assembly. It is difficult to envisage why such a situation should arise unless a meeting were to be called during the sittings of the Assembly by order of that court and it was found convenient to meet in Edinburgh; but in such a case, one imagines, authority would be given in the judgment ordering the meeting.

TYPES OF MEETING

There are three — and only three — ways in which a Presbytery can meet — the ordinary meeting, the meeting *in hunc effectum*, and the meeting *pro re nata*.

Ordinary Meeting

An ordinary meeting of Presbytery is held for the transaction of all ordinary business, its place and date having been appointed before the previous ordinary meeting concluded, and it is open to the public.

Presbytery Lapsed — It is most important that the court should thus fix its next meeting, for, this having been done, when the last item on the agenda has been disposed of "the court adjourns to meet at .... on .... at ...." and the benediction is then pronounced. Thus either the court is in session or it stands adjourned. If by some oversight this has not been done then the Presbytery "lapses" and has to be "revived". Not fewer than three members have to requisition the Moderator to call a meeting *pro re nata* not sooner than ten and not later than fifteen days away, and at that meeting no business is to be transacted except that of fixing a time and place for the next ordinary meeting.

Meeting Forbidden — Unless with the special permission of the General Assembly a Presbytery is not to meet while the supreme court is in session.

Meeting in hunc effectum

When a specific item of business has to be transacted — such as the licensing of students, the induction of a Minister, the dedication of a building, or sometimes the receiving of a special report — it is usual to appoint a meeting specifically for that purpose. This is a meeting *in hunc effectum* and it has to be appointed by the Presbytery itself at an ordinary meeting, specifying time and place and the business to be dealt with. At such a meeting no other business may be taken in hand the solitary exception being that an Elder's commission may be received and sustained. It occasionally happens that after the Presbytery has duly appointed a meeting *in hunc effectum* there crops up an additional item which it would be convenient to dispose of at the same time. For instance, a meeting having been fixed for an induction it later transpires that a congregation has a call which it would be in everyone's interest to have sustained without delay. So long as the matter is arranged at an ordinary meeting there is nothing to prevent such an additional item being added to the agenda. It must have ordinary-meeting approval — it cannot be agreed at the meeting itself that the additional item will be taken.

Meeeting pro re nata

Should an item of urgent importance arise between ordinary meetings it is always within the power of the Moderator to call a meeting *pro re nata,* and when so requisitioned by three members of the court he is bound to do so or answer for his declining. In the event of the death of the Moderator his duties in this regard devolve upon the Clerk. The meeting has to be called by the Moderator and will begin by his narrating the circumstances which led to his doing so. If the meeting does not approve of the Moderator's conduct then of course it disbands and the item of business goes on to the agenda for next ordinary meeting. If the meeting approves of his conduct it will press on to deal with the particular item of business specified and with no other. At the first ordinary meeting thereafter the facts are reported and anyone so minded may complain that such a meeting should not have been held, and may even take his complaint to a superior court. All that can result from such a step, however, is a censure on the Moderator for his conduct, and probably on the Presbytery also for condoning it — it can in no way disturb the judgment reached at the meeting.

Funeral of a Minister — On the occasion of the death of the the Minister of a parish the Presbytery meets within his Church premises on the occasion of his funeral, and this properly is a meeting *pro re nata.* A public notice may be inserted in the press, but it is usually accepted nowadays that the Death notice giving particulars of the Funeral is sufficient to cover the Presbytery meeting. At that meeting, held immediately before the Funeral Service an Interim Moderator is appointed, arrangements are where appropriate made for the supply of the pulpit, and generally any urgent matters arising in consequence of the death are attended to. The conduct of the Funeral is in the hands of the Presbytery, that body standing, as it were, in the position of pastor to the pastor, though conference will of course be had with the family. The Presbytery does not meet as a court on the occasion of the funeral of any other of its members, Ministers or Elders, though doubtless members will wish to attend and may do so as a body if desired. In such a case the arrangements lie wholly within the discretion of the next-of-kin. It is not unknown for a Minister to have left instruction that there be no Presbytery Service associated with his funeral. Respect will be paid to his wish, but the Presbytery must nevertheless meet for the appointment of an Interim Moderator.

How Called — The meeting *pro re nata* must be called by the Moderator through the medium of a circular letter addressed to all the members setting forth clearly the business which it is proposed to transact and the reason for the urgency. In normal circumstances this will be sent out by the Clerk, but it must most certainly be over the signature of the Moderator. It may well be adequate for the Clerk to send it out over his own name provided he says, "I am instructed by the Moderator ...." It would be quite inept for him to say, "Notice is hereby given that a meeting *pro re nata* will be held at ....." and to add his own signature. The simplest and safest course is for him to begin, "I hereby call ....." and to close with the signature of the Moderator.

Meeting in Committee — The rush and pressures of an ordinary meeting can inhibit freedom of discussion, and so when some important issue has arisen or has been sent down from Assembly for discussion resort is sometimes had to meeting in committee (or in conference) under the chairmanship of the Moderator or of some other person appointed for the occasion. Cox says that at such a meeting "the ordinary rules of debate are understood to be suspended." It may well be that the rules will not be over-scrupulously observed, but on the other hand nothing but confusion can arise from throwing the rules to the wind. After all, they were designed to facilitate and not to impede discussion. No binding decision will be reached at such a meeting, but a deliverance can be framed and a minute prepared and this can be submitted to the next ordinary meeting which may be expected to be willing to adopt it.

THE CONDUCT OF ITS BUSINESS

Quorum — The quorum of a Presbytery — no matter what its size — is three, and of the three at least two must be Ministers, one of whom, of course, will be Moderator — it is a situation where his casting vote might be much in demand! Unless a quorum is present the meeting cannot be constituted.

In Public — The Presbytery is an open court, but it may resolve to meet in private when it deems it expedient so to do, and for certain items it is required so to meet — in dealing with a libel, in receiving a report on the quinquennial visitation of a congregation. The Presbytery being "an established judicatory of the land" it should recognise its public responsibility and meet in private for only the most compelling reasons. It is sometimes argued that on some important and delicate issue holding the meeting behind closed doors allows a wider freedom for discussion. On the other hand it can be said that the presence of reporters with pencils at the ready can impose a restraint and engender a sense of responsibility that are much to be desired. It is an offence for the press to report business which the Presbytery has resolved to deal with in private, and the editor could be in trouble in the civil courts and the member who 'leaked' the information could be in really serious trouble in the Church courts. The subject of "privilege" is dealt with at page 276

Constitution — The Presbytery is constituted with prayer, and this, I think, in every case means that the court engages in opening devotions which include, at least, praise, the reading of the Word, and prayer. At a special meeting the constituting will probably be by prayer alone. Being now in session the Presbytery will proceed to regularise the position of its membership, first of all by agreeing that the sederunt will be as taken on entering, then by sustaining Elders' commissions newly received, and finally by welcoming newcomers whose names have been added to the Roll and reporting on any who have left the Presbytery since last ordinary meeting. A Minister transferred from another Presbytery may be formally enrolled at this stage.

Minutes — The minutes are then submitted, adjusted if need be, approved by the meeting, and signed by Moderator and Clerk. For full details regarding minutes generally see page ???.

Tributes — It is usual at some point fairly early in the proceedings for the Moderator or some other person appointed for the purpose to read a tribute to any member who has died since last ordinary meeting. The fact that this has been done, but not necessarily the text, should be recorded in the minute.

Order of Business — In most, indeed I think in all, Presbyteries along with the notice reminding members of the meeting there will have been circulated an agenda. This should now be submitted as the proposed Order of Businsss, and any member who has any matter he wishes to raise which does not appear on the agenda is invited to say so — or remain for ever silent. A place will be found in the order for the additional item, or maybe he will be invited to give it as a Notice of Motion for next meeting. If additional business is treated in this way there is no need for that most dangerous item at the end, "Any Other Competent Business" — for the simple reason that there is no other business that can be competent.

Appointment of Next Meeting — It is usual — and quite natural — to await the end of the present meeting before appointing the date of the next one; but there is much to be said for disposing of this item fairly early on in the proceedings among the formal items. The court will still have to adjourn, but failure to do so formally will not be fatal to the existence of the Presbytery (see above p 325).

Committee Reports — To facilitate the discharge of its business and to ensure that important issues will be discussed fully and in detail Presbyteries nowadays do a great deal of their business through the medium of Committees which in most cases correspond in their remits fairly closely to the main Committees of Assembly, although *ad hoc* Committees are appointed as the need arises. At the same time Presbyteries are very jealous of their powers and only very rarely is any degree of authority delegated to a Committee. Normally the Committee is expected to consider each item with care and to bring forward a recommendation which the Presbytery may be prepared to adopt, or which, of course, it may want to amend and adjust, to send back for further consideration or even to reject out of hand. Dealing with the reports of its Committees occupies a large part of the time of the average Presbytery meeting of today.

Vacancy Business — This is another item likely to appear with some regularity on the average agenda, for the Presbytery has to deal with calls, translations, and demissions of Ministers. This subject is dealt with fully in an earlier chapter (ch 3). Generally such business is slumped together and dealt with under the title of Vacancy Business on an Order of the Day, for the convenience of those cited to appear.

Standing Orders — A Presbytery will usually have its own Standing Orders. In cases where it does not, or where a point emerges not covered in these, it is accepted that those of the next superior court obtain. For general rules covering Standing Orders see p 276.

In Writing — Any motion which is to be put to the Presbytery is to be handed to the Clerk in writing and, ideally, this should be done at the time when it is proposed. It has to be recognised, though, that in the heat of a debate this is rarely possible. Certainly before any issue is put to a vote the Clerk should be in a position to read out from a paper in his hand the precise terms of all motions, amendments etc.

Notice of Motion — If a member has strong views on some subject not before the court he may tender a Notice of Motion at an ordinary meeting, and a place will be found for this on the agenda for the following meeting. It is usually accepted, however, that if he hand his motion to the Clerk in time to be circulated with the papers this will be accepted as adequate notice. There are certain matters which may be taken only if advance notice has been given — the election of commissioners to the Assembly, voting on Barrier Act overtures, proposed amendments to the Standing Orders, are examples. These, of course, are not strictly Notices of Motion since no firm motion has been proposed but only public intimation that the items are to be taken, and in these cases inclusion in the billet is not enough — there must be a minute that it was agreed to have them dealt with. It is not uncommon in such cases that not only is it agreed the item will be dealt with but an Order of the Day is fixed for the purpose. In my opinion the proposer of a motion of which notice has been given is at liberty to make changes in the precise terms in the print so long as these are not so radical as to make it a completely different motion — they should qualify as amendments and not as counter-motions.

ITS RELATION WITH CONGREGATIONS

The famous Act of Parliament of 1592 which finally established the Presbyterian system in Scotland says that it belongs to the Presbytery to see that "the Word is purely preached within its bounds, the Sacraments rightly administered, and the discipline entertenyit." Obviously this will bring the Presbytery into very intimate relationship with all its congregations at many very different points in their life and work. Let us seek to examine these.

Vacancy

During the period when a cogregation is without a fixed Minister the Presbytery has a high degree of responsibility towards it. This it discharges in the first place by appointing one of its number to act as Interim Moderator with the duties of arranging for the supply of its pulpit, attending to the fulfilment of all necessary pastoral services, ensuring that proper steps are taken in the matter of the election of a Minister, and generally in supplying the want of a fixed Minister. The first step in the way of getting the vacancy filled is the preparation of an Electoral Register which when completed has to be submitted to the Presbytery for attestation. A Vacancy Committee having been appointed they take over the initiative.

Sustaining the Call — A Minister having been chosen, the election and call have to come to the Presbytery to be sustained. Today this is usually something of a formality, but it was not always so. Particularly in Churches of the Secessions Presbyteries argued long, earnestly, bitterly — and prayerfully — as to whether Mr XY should go to A or to B, both of which had presented him with a call, or whether in fact he should be allowed to leave C which wished to retain him, or maybe he should go to D where some member of Presbytery thinks he would be the perfect answer to prayer. In one case it is recorded that settling the competing claims for a Minister from a congregation in Glasgow and from another in Edinburgh was accomplished only after eight hours of debate.

As things are today the only question to which a Presbytery gives its mind has to do with the regularity of the procedure that has been followed. A Presbytery might well refuse to sustain a call because only one Sunday's notice had been given of the election arrangements, or because the appointee was not properly qualified, or because evidence was led that pressure had been brought to bear, or because the call was not adequatelyly signed; but not because in its view the man elected was quite unsuited to be Minister of that particular parish. I do not know of any law which determines what considerations are to weigh with a Presbytery when considering a call, but the *de facto* position is as I have indicated. An interesting situation could arise under the new vacancy procedure were the Presbytery Advisory Committee to report (as it is entitled to do) that in its view the Minister chosen was not suited to the needs of the parish. I am sure that such an issue lies within the competence of the Presbytery.

Induction — All that remains is for the Presbytery to induct the Minister. Time was when induction (which was then generally called "admission") was a kind of infeftment comparable to the sasines connected with the conveyance of land, and as a consequence of induction quite a number of material benefits vested in the Minister. Insofar as that had not already disappeared it came finally to an end with the Property and Endowments Act of 1925 which brought all the Church's assets completely within its own control. Induction, however, was still *ad vitam aut culpam* and so continued until 1972 when security of tenure in a parish was ordained to end at age seventy — and now (1994) it is all but certain that the age will become sixty-five.

In spite of these changes induction is still a most solemn act creating between Minister and people a unique relationship which cannot be broken by either side unilaterally nor even by mutual agreement. Only the Presbytery which forged the bond can break it, no matter what the reason may be. For full particulars regarding the results of induction see page 147. Incidentally it is interesting that although now it is established that age can bring tenure to an end the induction is still officially described as *ad vitam aut culpam*. To have achieved the age limit, it would appear is to be regarded as "culpable" within the meaning of the Act!

Demission — The principle is long-established that the Minister must apply to the Presbtyery for permission to demit his charge whatever the ground may be. Of recent years, however, two sets of circumstances have emerged where demission is automatic — permission is presumed to have been given. First of all there is the case referred to above of a man inducted to his parish subsequently to 1972 where it is provided in the Act that on attaining his seventieth birthday his ministry is to terminate as if he had resigned his charge and the Presbytery had fixed that date for his demission. Obviously he doesn't need to apply for permission to go! Secondly there is the case of the Minister retiring in the interests of readjustment, in which case it is taken that the acceptance by him, with the approval of the Presbytery, of the terms of the Basis of Readjustment is sufficient to effect the demission. The putting into operation of the readjustment releases such a Minister from his charge without any action being necessary on his part. It is important that the Presbytery should not allow the occasion to pass without public acknowledgment being made of the value of the ministries that have thus been terminated.

When a Minister approaches the Presbytery with a request to demit and that for no very obvious reason it is for the Presbytery to ensure that he is interviewed with a view to finding out whether there is some cause for the step in which as a court it ought to be taking a pastoral interest.

Translation — When a Presbytery has sustained a call to a Minister of a charge in another Presbytery it transmits the papers to that Presbytery whose Clerk arranges for the congregation concerned to be cited to the next meeting when a resolution will be reached whether or not to translate.

Ius Devolutum — The Presbytery has the responsibility of operating the *ius devolutum* — the law by which a time-limit is set during which a congregation may exercise its right to call a Minister. For full particulars see page 83.

Reappraisal

On the occurence of a vacancy in any charge the first problem that arises is that of reappraisal, or readjustment as it used to be called. This is a field where the Presbytery and the Assembly's Reappraisal Committee have a conjoint responsibility, and while initiative generally lies with the Presbytery decisions can become operative only with the concurrence of the Assembly Committee. The matter is the subject of a chapter at page 45.

Quinquennial Visitation

In terms of Acts of Assembly (1931, xii; 1975, i; and 1984, ii) a Presbytery is required to conduct a scheme of Quinquennial Visitation whereby each of its congregations receives a visit from representatives of the Presbsytery once during each five-year period. It has to be noted that this is not the same as a visit every fifth year. The scheme began in 1931 and the quinquennia are calculated from there. Suppose that we start from 1991. Each Presbytery is to list its congregations on a rota which will result in all of them having been visited by the end of 1994, the fifth year (1995) being left free to overtake any which may have been delayed because of, say, a vacancy, the illness of a Minister, a congregation's involvement in reappraisal negotiations, or other serious interruption of its ordinary way of life. It would be unfortunate, to say the least, to carry through a visitation at such a time.

Object — The Act is quite specific that "the object of the Visit is to strengthen the hands of the Minister, Kirk Session, Office-Bearers, and Members, to advise them should anything appear to be unsatisfactory in the state of the congregation or not in accordance with Church law and order, and in general to give counsel and encouragement as may be suitable to the circumstances of the case." It is not written into the Act, but from 1938 onwards the General Assembly has each year passed a Deliverance urging Presbyteries in carrying out the visitation "to keep particularly in view the promotion of the spiritual well-being of the congregation visited and the adequate sufficiency of the Congregational Agencies."

Visiting Team — A Team (until 1984 it had been a Committee) is appointed to carry out the Visit (it had been a Visitation) and it is declared desirable that it should consist of at least four and that the majority of these should be members of Presbytery. It is important that the Leader of the Team should be a person of experience. The Team meets separately with Minister, Kirk Session and Financial Court, and it may at its own discretion meet with members and office-bearers of groups and organisations within the congregation. The Leader takes the chair at all such meetings, but the Minister has the right to be present at all times. The Leader conducts public worship in the Church on a suitable Sunday, or, if found more convenient, he may address the congregation at a meeting on a week-day. The Minister should be present on this occasion (it is not to be "an exchange") and the Leader will convey to the congregation the greetings and good wishes of the Presbytery as well as offering any specific counsels which he may consider appropriate. This is an important element in the exercise and should not be treated lightly.

Basis for Discussion — A *pro forma* document was prepared in 1984 to take the place of the questionnaire that had previously been in use. It is emphasised that this is to be regarded as providing a basis for discussion and interview, and that its scope is neither exclusive nor exhaustive. It deals with the following subjects: Worship, Use and Deployment of Office-Bearers; Congregational Life; Christian Education; Mission; Christian Liberality; Fabric. What is in view is not so much to glean detailed information regarding this or that but to open up areas for discussion, to bring to the surface problems which are needing to be aired, and to create opportunities when it may be possible to lend encourgement or to offer counsel. The attitude of a witness can reveal so much more than his evidence, and the experienced and sensitive Leader will learn far more from the general atmosphere of the meeting than he will from the replies given to stereotyped questions. To assist them in all this the Presbytery Clerk is to provide the Team in advance with particulars of membership and financial statistics for the previous four years, with a copy of the previous report and with an indication of any planning policy affecting the congregation so far as that is known.

The Report — It is now for the visiting Team to prepare a full report of its findings and to pass this to the Superintendence Committee of the Presbytery which in turn will lodge a copy with the Kirk Session of the congregation visited, and when the Superintendence Committee submits its repoprt to the full court the Minister, Kirk Session, and any other party claiming an interest have a right to be heard. Not later than six months after the transmission of the Report to the Kirk Session the Superintendence Committee is to enquire how far the instructions have been, or are about to be, implemented, and it will report accordingly to the Presbytery. When any matter concerning the results of quinquennial visitation is to be before the Presbytery the court is required to meet in private.

Further Action — "In the event of the Presbytery finding itself unable to express satisfaction with the state of any congregation, it shall instruct the Superintendence Committee to make further enquiry and to endeavour to remedy what is deemed to be unsatisfactory, and the Presbytery may apply to the Board of Practice and Procedure for the appointment of an assessor or assessors from the members of any neighbouring Presbytery or Presbyteries, to act with the Superintendence Committee. If, after this further enquiry, the Presbytery finds that it is still unable to express satisfaction, it shall either proceed under Act i 1988, or submit a report to the General Assembly, through the Board of Practice and Procedure.

"It shall be the duty of each Presbytery, not later than the 31st day of March in each year, to prepare and transmit to the General Assembly, through the Board of Practice and Procedure, a return certifying that it has carried out the provisions of this Act." (Act vi 1992)

Weaknesses — That some such scheme as this is a necessity is, I am sure, beyond question. Nor can it be denied that, properly and sensitively executed, it can prove most helpful. Unfortunately it seems to be most beneficial in those congregations which are healthy and where problems are few. But all the schemes so far devised seem to have suffered from two weaknesses, and Teams should bear these in mind when paying their Visits. The first arises from the fact that there is a natural reluctance on the part of office-bearers to discuss their domestic troubles in presence of strangers, especially where these strangers represent "authority". Calling a Visitation a Visit and a Committee a Team may help, but it won't eradicate the feeling that these people are here to find fault. I remember an occasion when I knew that trouble of a serious kind was building up in a congregation that was due for a visit. I chose the Team with great care and briefed them fully. At the Session meeting the Leader did everything in his power to bring the trouble to the surface — quite without success. All was well: couldn't be better: just one big happy family. Or so they were assured, but within three months the whole thing blew up in a major scandal.

The other weakness is that while it is an excellently devised scheme for eliciting reports and passing them up the line it is in no position to offer the practical kind of help which in many cases the congregation is desperately needing. The buildings are in a state of utter disrepair and there are no funds; the organisations are falling apart and there is no leadership; Minister and office-bearers alike have lost heart; or perhaps relations between Minister and people have become sorely strained. What can a Report — or a Team — achieve in circumstances like these? An infusion of cash in one case, a change of ministry in another, would work wonders, but counsel and advice and filling-up schedules even if they are to be filed in the most influential cabinets is unlikely to have any beneficial effect.

Visitation of Records

The Presbytery is responsible for ensuring that records are properly kept and securely maintained by all its congregations. This duty it will normally discharge by annually appointing a time and a place or places where all records are to be produced for inspection and attestation. The volumes required are the minute-books of Kirk Session and of Financial Court, the Communion Roll, the Baptismal Register, the Property Register, and a copy of the duly audited Congregational Accounts. The Session Clerk is custodier of all congregational records and is therefore the person to be instructed to produce the books, but in case of his failure to do so a letter should be sent from the Presbytery Clerk to the Kirk Session through its Moderator instructing production. The result is to be reported to the Presbytery and a minute thereon transmitted to the General Assembly through the Board of Practice and Procedure not later than 31st March in each year.

Benefice Register — Act xiv of 1931 lays upon Presbyteries a most important duty, that of maintaining a Benefice Register. This is a book containing detailed information regarding the property of all its charges, particularly the heritable property (and where the titles are to be found), trust funds, endowments for whatever purpose, valuable furnishing and equipment, memorials, objects of historical interest. "Every Presbytery must keep and annually revise a Benefice Register containing information appertaining to every parish and chapel, regarding the stipend and emoluments attached to the living, ecclesiastical property, trust funds, bequests, donations, mortifications, or charities in which the Minister or Kirk Session, or trustees, or managers of *quoad sacra* parishes or chapels have an interest or any right of administration; all relative writs or registered copies thereof to be produced if possible, and an inventory of them entered in the register with the names of their custodiers. The Presbytery is responsible for the accuracy of the register and must therefore as far as possible verify information furnished to it." A certain amount of the foregoing is no longer relevant, but it is most important that there should be accurate information available regarding heritable property and trust funds and that this should include information about the custody of title-deeds and deeds of trust. The fact that this Register has been duly inspected is also to be transmitted to the Board of Practice and Procedure before 31st March in each year.

Keeping Up-to-date — One of the first duties of an Interim Moderator is to have prepared an inventory of all Church property that had been in the care of the Minister and to have this compared with the Presbytery Register. The new Minister is to have the items handed over to him in terms of the inventory. From the practical point of view the greatest difficulty in this realm lies in keeping the Register up-to-date, for congregations cannot be counted on to pass on information relating to additions and alterations. While I imagine most Presbyteries have a Benefice Register I wonder just how up-to-the-minute they all are. Which is regrettable considering how invaluable a trustworthy register can be.

"Unsatisfactory State"

It is never easy in language either ecclesiastical, theological or legal to define precisely what is meant by a "congregation in an unsatisfactory state". On the other hand no-one with any Church experience need have difficulty in recognising one when he meets it. I imagine such congregations have existed as long as has the Kirk itself — and probably will continue to do so for all our legislating.

The Act of 1960 — The first attempt since the Union of 1929 to tackle the problem in a systematic way was made in an Act of 1954 subsequently amended and updated in Act ii of 1960. The thinking behind this was that when things were sadly amiss within a congregation the responsibility for the unhappy state of affairs lay either with the Minister or with some individual person, or with some group of office-bearers or other members of the congregation. The Act set up machinery designed to locate and identify the source of the trouble and concluded by conferring power on the Presbytery to dissolve the pastoral tie if it were found that the unsatisfactory state was due wholly or substantially to faults personal to the Minister; or to remove an office-bearer from office, or issue to a member a Certificate of Transference if it were found that he or she was substantially to blame. Provision was made for the care of the Minister whose ministry had not been terminated even though his ministry in that particular parish had been brought to a close.

The Act of 1992 — What can only be described as an entirely new Act (i) was passed in 1992. I call this "entirely new" because it starts off from a totally different position — that of accepting the fact that through some measure of incompatibility to start with, followed probably by some stupid and petty conduct on both sides a condition has arisen within a congregation where the only hope for happiness and success in the future (for either Minister or congregation) lies in a new beginning in some other place in the one case and under a new Minister in the other. No attempt is made to apportion blame. The machinery which the Act sets up is of the most elaborate kind which I shall not attempt to reproduce here in any detail. Suffice to say that the first question is to determine whether the congregation is in fact in an unsatisfactory state, and the second question is whether it is likely to continue to be so unless the pastoral tie is dissolved, provison being made for evidence to the contrary being led by interested parties. The two questions are to be treated as quite separate and distinct. Ultimately the Presbytery may reach a judgment dissolving the pastoral tie, in which case it shall immediately suspend the Minister from office as Minister of the charge, but without prejudice to continued payment of stipend and occupancy of the manse, and it shall also appoint an Interim Moderator. Such suspension shall continue until the date appointed by the Presbytery for the dissolution of the pastoral tie, or until the case is settled on appeal.

Intimation that such a judgment has been reached shall be reported immediately to the Board of Practice and Procedure which shall arrange for a Minister from another Presbytery to be appointed to give pastoral advice and counsel to the Minister suspended.

The judgment shall also be reported by the Presbytery to the Department of Ministry along with a statement of all the circumstances known to it which ought to be in the view of the Church in dealing with the question of a maintenance allowance for the Minister so long as he has no other regular remuneration, and the Maintenace of the Ministry Committee shall report to the General Assembly and may make interim payments.

The Act does not apply in the case of the insanity of a Minister, which is dealt with at page 354, nor are its provisions to be pursued if it appears to involve to any serious extent the moral character or the doctrinal views of a Minister, Office-Bearer, or Elder.

"Changed Circumstances"

The Act anent Congregations in Changed Circumstances (Act v 1984) was designed to deal with the case, increasingly common at that time of urban renewal, when through no fault on anyone's part and due to circumstances wholly outwith the control of the Church the character of a parish had so drastically altered during an incumbency (had become what in Glasgow I used to call a "red blaes parish") as to raise very sharply the question whether the cause should be continued. In such a case it may be in the interest of the Minister, of the remanent bit of congregation, not to say of the Church as a whole that we should face up to reality and arrange for the cause to be terminated. In the ordinary way of things the Minister might be expected to receive a Call elsewhere and the Presbytery could then deal with the situation as a straightforward vacancy calling for reappraisal. But if the Church has been left standing in a sea of red blaes, its windows vandal-smashed, its vestibule decorated with pails catching drips from the roof, attended by a handful of elderly folk, there seems little hope that a Vacancy Committtee on tour is going to be favourably impressed! All very unfair, for it was not due to any fault of the Minister. Instances are not wanting in our cities today where what had been a reasonably healthy and bustling congregation in a densely populated area has in a matter of twenty years been reduced to a handful of old people meeting for worship in a heavily vandalised building. What meaning can you give to induction *ad vitam aut culpam* in circumstances such as these?

The Act provides that in a situation of this kind an enquiry is to be mounted by the Presbytery, and this may be initiated as a result of a report of quinquennial visitation, on the suggestion of a Presbytery Committee, on a written request by the Minister, or on a petition from the Kirk Session, office-bearers or members. If satisfied that the circumstances are as alleged the Committee is to prepare a report setting forth what are the changed circumstances, assessing how far they have adversely affected the life of the charge and how far they are likely to continue to do so, and making recommendations on what action the Presbytery should take.

Recommendation — Unless it be to the effect that no action be taken the recommendation of the Committee will take one of two forms, either that action be taken within powers already vested in the Presbytery, or that the changed circumstances are such that the continuance of the congregation as an indepedent unit can no longer be justified and that the Minister's tenure should be terminated to allow some appropriate form of readjustment to be implemented. When the report and recommendation are before the Presbytery all parties having an interest are to be cited and may appear and be heard at the bar, with the usual right of appeal.

Termination of Tenure — Where the recommendations involve the termination of a Minister's tenure the following provisions are made —

a) A Minister inducted before the passing of the Act is not affected unless he has given to the Presbytery Clerk written notice of his willingness to concur in any decision reached.
b) Provision is to be made for the maintenance of the Minister, and he is to be given an extract minute setting this forth in detail and showing

the concurrence of every interested body. For a period of two years he is to be paid the Minimum Stipend and given the use and occupancy of the manse (or payment in lieu) on the terms he had enjoyed during his incumbency. At the end of that period if the Minister is still unplaced the whole situation is to be reviewed by the Presbytery in consultation with the Maintenance of the Ministry Committee.

c) The Assembly's Committee on Parish Reappraisal must concur.

d) The Minister concerned is to have the same status as a Minister demitting his charge in the interest of readjustment.

It is a condition of the provision made under (b) that it shall terminate as soon as the Minister has obtained another charge, that he shall not accept gainful employment outwith the Church except with Presbytery consent, that if he obtains such employment the whole situation shall be reviewed by the Presbytery, and that so long as he is in receipt of maintenance he shall put himself at the service of the Church to perform without further payment the duties of locum, pulpit supply, assistant, as directed by the Maintenance of the Ministry Committee in any reasonable way, the Presbytery to be judge of what is "reasonable"; and all subject to the usual right of appeal.

There are two sad sights to be seen all too frequently in the Kirk today as a consequence of the enormous population movements that large-scale town-planning have brought. One is that of the Minister who went to a parish full of zeal and zest and with a vision of what could be done, but who has been overtaken by circumstances over which he had no control and who is now allowing himself to be carried along saying with a resigned shrug, "I suppose it'll see my time through." And the other is of the little group of maybe three devoted families who out of a misguided loyalty to the past are carrying the burden of a congregation which has served its day well but has nothing to contribute to this day and should no longer be there. They are denying themselves the joy and uplift that membership of a live congregation should be giving them — and all for nothing. It was with such things in view that the Act was passed. I doubt very much whether it has served any purpose in meeting either of these problems.

Care of Ecclesiastical Property

For the past quarter of a century the steady, relentless deterioration in the condition of the Church's fabric has been posing a problem of increasing urgency and terrifying gravity. A great deal of Church building dates from the period between 1830 and the turn of the century and is now from a hundred to a hundred and fifty years old. At that age the traditional Scottish structure of stone, timber and slates can be counted on to produce its problems. At the other end of the line the building programme undertaken to keep pace with the population migration of the immediate post-war years was all of it very strictly "built to a price" with all that that is now seen to imply. It has to be said that even congregations which have been highly responsible in other directions have tended to take their buildings for granted, assuming that so long as nothing was falling down all was well and would continue to be well, carrying out repairs when the need for these could no longer be ignored but not a moment before, and not an inch beyond what is absolutely essential. It is an unfortunate fact of life that expenditure on fabric can be put off till next year in the confidence that finances will be in better shape by then — which they rarely are. The bill, though, will be considerably higher. It is in this way that repair programmes of terrifying proportions are built up. The Church today is facing an outsize fabric programme if not indeed a major crisis.

The Act of 1979 — In 1961 a major Act was passed to grapple with the problem, this being followed by Acts of 1969 (xxvi), of 1977 (v), and of 1979 (ix), and although various amendments have subsequently been made this is still substantially the position.

The congregational authority responsible for the property is to set up a Fabric Committee that includes a person or persons with technical knowledge and experience (empowered if need be to co-opt such people), and this body has the duty of annually carrying out a thorough inspection of all Church property. It has to keep a Property Register in a form approved by the General Trustees and into this is to be entered full details of these inspections. The Register has also to contain a complete list of all ecclesiastical properties with full details of title and insurance and an inventory of all furnishings and equipment, as well as a record of all matters found at the annual inspection to be in need of attention and of the action taken thereanent.

At Presbytery level also a Fabric Committee is to be appointed with persons of knowledge and experience (who may be co-opted) and this body is to appoint an Insurance Sub-Committee available at all times to assist both the Presbytery and the congregations in all matters concerning insurance. Both Committee and Sub-Committee are to inspect with scrupulous care all Property Registers and to report thereon to the

Presbytery. The Insurance Sub-Committee may if deemed expedient confer with congregational authorities, giving advice and assistance in regard to appropriate types of insurance and the amount thereof.

At least once in the five-year period beginning 1st July 1987 and thereafter at intervals of not more than five years the Fabric Committee of the Presbytery is to instruct a professional survey of all property. The Presbytery has to approve the person appointed as Reporter and to give instruction in the following terms —

a) In regard to the inspection and report to be instructed in the five-year period beginning on 1st July 1987 and in the case of each alternate report thereafter, the Reporter shall be a person who is approved by the General Trustees: such a Report shall be known as a "Principal Report".
b) In regard to each inspection and report to be instructed, other than the Principal Reports, the Reporter shall be a person who is approved by the Presbytery; such a report shall be known as an "Interim Report".
c) At the request of Presbyteries and for good reason shown with respect to individual congregations, the General Trustees may reverse the sequence of Interim and Principal Reports laid down for the period beginning 1st July 1992 and 1st July 1997.

All properties should have been professionally inspected and reports submitted by 30th June 1992, yet in their report to the 1994 Assembly the General Trustees disclose that in 42 Presbyteries 1498 Property Registers out of 1552 had been examined out of which 67 had been found not to be satisfactory. In the same Presbsyteries the properties of 237 congregations had been inspected during the year to 30th June 1993 and there were still 65 cases in which professional reports had not been obtained.

In 1989 an amendment from the floor of the Assembly was carried providing that a second inspection should not be required after five years but only after ten. Two years later, however, the Assembly agreed to a restoration of the need for a five-year interim report, it having been pointed out that a conference of Presbytery Property Conveners had by a substantial majority favoured such a return to the original basis.

Paying the Bills — The professional report sets forth its findings on work necessary on the congregation's property under three heads — (a) work that is urgently needed and must at all costs be put in hand without delay; (b) repairs and improvements that are necessary and should be undertaken as soon as possible; and (c) work that will ultimately require to be done but that does not qualify under the heading of "urgent". It is for the congregational authority armed with this report to produce a fabric plan to cover the next few years, and, no less important, to devise a scheme whereby the work may be financed. Obviously new sources of income will have to be devised, for in the long run the bulk, if not all, of the cost will have to be met by the congregation.

Some help may be forthcoming. In the case of Listed Buildings there is a possibility worth exploring of getting a modest grant from the local authority, and if the Church has claims of historical interest then Historic Scotland may well come up with generous aid — though they seem to be permanently overspent. It's always worth while looking at the possibility of trust funds lending aid. Within the Church itself there is a Central Fabric Fund which the General Trustees have been trying, without much success, to boost. The capital of the Fund comes from determinations made under an Act of 1979 where congregations through the sale of property no longer needed have acquired a Fabric Fund beyond their requirements, and from an annual alloction from Mission and Service. In the year 1993 from this Fund a sum of £383,241 was given in grants — which may sound quite generous until it is recognised that it represented the answer to ninety-four pleas so that the average help given was under £5000 — a derisory figure in face of today's cost of building repairs.

The General Trustees also operate the *Consolidated Loan Fund* from which they are able to make loans to congregations faced with heavy fabric oncosts. These are given normally at an interest-rate of 7% (though on occasion this is radically reduced) and are expected to be repaid within seven years. This can be of great help to any comfortably off congregation. The problem is presented by those congregations that cannot possibly find the money to service such loans let alone repay them. They find themselves confronted with the unhappy choice of watching their property steadily deteriorate or of burdening themselves with a debt which they know in advance they can never hope to repay. In all such cases it is for the Presbytery to make a realistic assessment of the situation and to seek to assist in every way possible.

It is the fervent hope of the Trustees that once the enormous backlog of neglected repairs has been overtaken and a new awareness has been created in congregations that fabric is not to be taken for granted but that a systematic programme of maintenance must be pursued — it is hoped that the financial situation should be considerably eased in years to come.

Insurance — The adequate insurance of all Church property is also a matter of acute urgency. Here again is an outlay upon which it is tempting to try to effect savings. To the complaint, "We can't afford to insure," the complete answer is, "You can't afford not to." A difficulty arises in regard to the insurance of Churches in that in most cases it would be quite unrealistic, as well as financially catastrophic, to insure for the full replacement value of the building — if it were destroyed by fire it would never be replaced on any comparable scale. But insurance companies insist that unless full cover has been taken only partial compensation will be paid for any loss incurred however partial — if you are insured up to half the replacement value of your property you will be compensated to the extent of half of your actual loss. Special consideration may be given in respect of Churches because of the odd circumstances, and this is a realm where it is essential to have the best professional advice obtainable. And to pay particular attention to the small type.

Financial Matters

The Presbytery has an interest in congregational finance at three separate points — (a) it has to satisfy itself that proper accounts are being kept and that the finances are being properly administered; (b) it has to approve the arranagements in regard to the payment of stipend and the meeting of all other attendant ministerial outlays; and (c) it is concerned with the contribution made to Mission and Aid.

Annual Statement of Accounts — One of the documents which have to be produced at the Annual Visitation of Records (p 336) is a certified copy of the Annual Statement of Accounts. In the case of congregations operating under the Model Deed it is provided that "said accounts shall, after submission to, and approval by, the congregation, be laid before the Presbytery within one month thereafter, for examination and attestation to the effect that the accounts are correct and are in accordance with the terms of this constitution." No matter what the constitution under which the congregation operates it is for the Presbytery to satisfy itself that its funds are being properly administered.

A model type of accounting has been devised by the General Treasurer's Department and is commended for universal adoption throughout the Church. It would certainly be greatly convenient if this could be generally accepted, for the wide variety of different types of account-keeping can be most confusing. At the same time it has to be recognised that for our book-keeping at parish level throughout the Church we are dependent upon the goodwill of dedicated people who devote much time and care to this work and it is perhaps a small price to pay to accept the kind of accounting system to which they are accustomed. Accuracy matters more than method.

Costs of Ministry — The Presbytery is responsible for approving the Vacancy Schedule which sets forth the financial arrangements for the support by the congregation of their Minister, covering the matters of stipend, ministerial expenses, and aid given or received. Should circumstances change and the congregation be no longer able to implement these promises, or should they wish to increase the stipend, it is the Presbytery which has to apply for a Revision Schedule and to oversee the completion of it. It is also for the Presbytery to take all steps open to it to ensure that congregations meet all their obligations under these Schedules, and that they pay their share also towards the Retirement Scheme and the Housing and Loan Fund. It used to be that shortfalls in meeting Schedule obligations were simply written off. From now on the Committee proposes to accumulate these and take account of the total accumulation when considering future Vacancy and Revision Schedules (Repts 1994 p 308) — but see hereunder The Presbytery has the responsibility also for ensuring that a manse is provided which is adequate in the matter of size and condition, which is convenient in the matter of location, and which is maintained in a proper condition.

Mission and Aid — In the days when the Co-ordinated Appeal was first introduced (the early 'sixties) the Presbytery had a very important (and difficult) role to play in allocating among its congregations the grand total required of it as its share in the year's budget. Not only had it to determine fair allocations it had to take all possible steps to ensure that these were met. A new system is now being operated whereby the Committee on the Maintenance of the Ministry decides how much each congregation may be expected to contribute, the Presbytery being afforded an opportunity to comment in any case where the allocation seems unreasonable (up or down) so that an adjustment may be agreed. In earlier days the Presbytery had also to meet an item entitled Assembly Dues (later General Purposes Fund) representing the Presbytery's share of the administration costs of the Committees without Funds and in paying the costs of the Assembly itself — a much enhanced sum as a consequence of the Church's undertaking the payment of commissioners' expenses. This is now all included in the figure for Mission and Aid.

Shortfalls — In its Report to the Assembly of 1994 the Assembly Council had this to say by way of Instructions to Presbyteries: (Reports 1994, p 179)

3.9.1. Following any year in which a congregation has failed to pay in full its contributions to central funds, the Presbytery shall visit the cogregation to consider with the Financial Board the Congregtional Accounts, to encourge increased levels of giving, to make recommendations for action to achieve this, and to detail the further action that Presbytery will take if shortfalls continue or increase.

3.9.2. The further action shall include a determination that the first charge on the congregation's year-end credit balance shall be to repay any shortfalls it has in terms of its contributions to central funds. The Presbytery shall determine a level of expenditure of an abnormal or non-recurring nature which that congregation may not exceed until all accumulated shortfalls have been cleared. Where shortfalls continue or increase, Presbytery shall consider whether or not the congregation may be judged to be in an unsatisfactory state.

3.9.3. All shortfalls — any for the latest year and the accumulated total — shall be reported annually to the Presbytery Clerk by thc Committee on the Maintenance of the Ministry and the Board of Stewardship and Finance, and the figures shall be recorded in the Minutes of the Presbytery.

3.10.1. Accumulated shortfalls shall be met in full by the congregation(s) concerned before a further ministry is allowed. Shortfalls will not be written off either by the Committee on the Maintenance of the Ministry or the Board of Stewardship and Finance.

3.10.2. In a union of congregations, or in the dissolution of any congregation(s), the first charge on the free proceeds of the sale of any redundant buildings (subject to the titles thereof) and moveable assets shall be the clearing of accumulated shortfalls in contributions to central funds on the part of the congregation(s) whose building(s) or moveable assets are being sold. [This is now being reconsidered].

3.10.3. In a vacancy, a charge is not required to fund stipend, national insurance payments, contributions to the Insured Pension Fund and the cost of Council Tax on the manse. Money is, therefore, available to that extent to enable congregations with accumulated shortfalls to make speedy inroads into clearing these shortfalls.

Worship

The point has been made elsewhere (p 152) that the Presbytery is the body ultimately responsible for the worship of all its congregations and that it appoints parish Ministers its agents in this department; so that if anyone is dissatisfied with the way in which worship is being conducted in his congregation his first approach should be to his own Minister, and if no satisfaction is to be found there his remedy lies in a petition to the Presbytery. Reference is made to the subject of innovations in worship (p 151), to the question of who may conduct worship (p 152), and to the subject of authorisation for the celebration of the Sacraments (p 153).

Erection of a New Parish

It is part of the overall responsibility of the Presbytery for the religious weal within its bounds that it should take steps, where this seems necessry or expedient, for the creation of a new charge. In the initial stages it will be for the Presbytery to secure temporary accommodation where the new group of people may meet for worship, education and fellowship, and a house where their Minister may live. In due course the Presbytery has to find Assessor Elders to constitute a Provisional Kirk Session. It will be for the Assembly's Committee on Parish Reappraisal having agreed that a cause is necessary to confer with the Extension Projects Committee who have to make the appointment of a Minister while the Presbytery takes steps towards securing a site, having plans prepared and premises built; and in the end of the day it will be for the Assembly to erect the new charge, to disjoin a parish for it, and grant it a constitution. All along the way it is for the Presbytery to see that the necessary steps are being taken and finally to induct the Minister and to dedicate the buildings.

Evangelism

For long it was thought that evangelism was an affair in which Ministers and Kirk Sessions had a primary interest. The General Assembly of 1983, however, instructed their Mission Commitee "to prepare a coherent, long-term, Presbytery-centred programme for the evangelisation of Scotland." No longer was evangelism to be seen as parish-centred. In its report to the 1985 Assembly the Committee brought forward what they called a "Presbytery Development Process" which it believed to represent "the way forward for our time." The essential role of the Development Process is to be the emergence of "missionary parishes" and their continued reforming and renewal. So we are getting back to the parish. Presbyteries are to encourage leadership encouragement, sharing and support in the work of evangelism"; and they are to plan large gatherings for inspiration and witness — Festivals of Faith, Faith-Sharing Groups, Area Committees; and they are to link congregations with the natiooal resources for evangelism. And so we go on through four solid pages of the Blue Book.

By the following year (1986) it had been discovered that the National Strategy for Evangelism needed full-time prosecution through the Church via the Presbyteries and through the media. The past year had shown that urgent resource material cannot adequately be commissioned, serviced, produced and distributed by part-time Conveners, etc, and this had led to the appointment of a full-time Organiser for Evangelism. By the next year we learned that five Ministers had been taken out of parishes to become full-time Area Organisers for Evangelism working with and under the direction of the National Organiser. The most recent Report declares that the National Organiser is now housed at St Ninian's Crieff and co-ordinates the work of a team (now three) of Advisers in encourging and resourcing Presbyteries and congregations throughout Scotland in mission and evangelism.

Matters of Public Concern

I imagine every Presbytery has a Committee whose remit corresponds more or less with that of the Church and Nation Committee of the Assembly. It is right and fitting that the voice of the Church should be heard on matters of public concern, and where the issue is a local one it is fitting that the voice should be that of the Presbytery. It seems to me, however, that if the matter is one of general national concern the wise course for the Presbytery to pursue is either to overture the General Assembly or to get in touch with the Church and Nation Committee of Assembly to make sure it has the matter on its agenda. It would be unfortunate were the Church to be heard speaking with one voice in Edinburgh and with a different voice in Aberdeen. If on the other hand the matter is one primarily of local implication the most effective step the Presbytery can take can sometimes be to lend its weight and encouragement and know-how to the Kirk Session within whose parish the matter lies; for such a Kirk Session has, often, a *locus standi* not shared by the Presbytery.

General Oversight

The Presbytery has an overall responsibility for the spiritual wellbeing of all the parishes and people within its bounds, and while the rights and privileges of Kirk Sessions must be scrupulously observed the Presbytery does have a right as well as a duty to intervene by way of counsel and encouragement to office-bearers, or by calling a meeting of an entire congregation if in its view this is appropriate. The Presbytery must never be seen as an interfering busybody, but neither must it appear to adopt the role of a disinterested spectator of trouble and failure.

ITS RELATION WITH MINISTERS

Each Minister who is a member of a Presbytery is under the supervision and discipline of that Presbytery. If he is Minister of a parish then in respect of the discharge of his duties he is answerable to the Presbytery; if he holds a chaplaincy or other appointment under a Committee of the Church he is answerable to that Committee, if he is a Teacher of Religious Education in Schools he is answerable to his Education Committee. But in every case in respect of life and doctrine he is under control of the Presytery. Thus if a Teacher of Religious Education were to be instilling heretical doctrine into children the Presbytery would be powerless to deprive him of his post, but it could certainly deprive him of his status. The question of the responsibility of the Education Committee to guarantee proper teaching of the subject would be another matter to be pursued in another place.

I very vividly remember an occasion when disagreement arose between the Principal Clerk and the then Principal of Glasgow University regarding an appointment to a Chair in the Faculty of Divinity. In terms of the relevant Act such an appointment carries the right to a seat in Presbytery, but before taking his seat the Professor is required to reaffirm the vows of his ordination and to sign the Formula. The Principal strongly contested the right of the Church to lay down this condition on the ground that it constituted "imposing a test on my chair." This seems to me to arise from a confusion between the "chair" and the "seat". The Presbytery has no power (however much it may have the desire) to impose conditions upon appointments made within the Faculties of Divinity in our Universities, but it has, surely, the right to impose conditions upon anyone who is claiming a place within its own membership.

Auxiliary Ministry — The subject of the Auxiliary Ministry is dealt with at length at p 141. The Presbytery has the duty of recruiting candidates for this ministry, and in terms of the Act it was expected to do so only having regard to "the existing and anticipated demands of the charges within its bounds" though that restriction has now been adjusted to read "shall satisfy themselves that there is a reasonable expectation that spheres of service within their bounds where such Auxiliary Ministers could appropriately and usefully serve." (A verb seems to be missing.) Thc Presbytery is responsible for licensing, and in due course ordaining, candidates, and in this connection it has to take them on trials for licence. It is also the Presbytery which has to find and define a sphere to which it may assign the Auxiliary, making due arrangements for him to work under the supervision of a ministerial member of the court and approving of a kind of contract of service. Like any other Minister the Auxiliary is answerable to the Presbytery in all matters of life and doctrine.

Minister Without Charge — I have heard the view expressed that a Minister who is not a member of any Presbytery is not under the supervision of any Presbytery. This is quite false, and at this time when each year a sizeable number of Ministers because of age are going to fall, into this class it is well to recognise that this is so. So long as he retains his status as a Minister he continues to be answerable for his life and doctrine, and it is to the Presbytery that he has to give an accounting. The new legislation about ceasing to enjoy membership of Presbytery on retirement or at age seventy-five says nothing about which Presbytery (that of his residence or that of which he was last a member) has responsibility for him. I think it should probably be determined by his place of residence and that on moving to a new area he should be under obligation to advise the Clerk of that Presbytery into whose bounds he has moved. On the other hand it has to be said that a Minister who chooses to forego his right to sit in Presbytery in terms of Act viii 1980 (now Act ii 1992 para 10) remains under the care of the Presbytery which he left, no provision being made for his moving his residence.

When a Minister resigns a charge to take up some occupation completely outwith the scope of the Church — to teach French, to be a journalist, to practise law — he may elect to resign his status (see hereunder), but he is unlikely to do so, and unless he has done so he will be entitled to a Ministerial Certificate testifying to his status and character, and in the event of his moving he is to lodge this with the Clerk of the Presbytery into whose bounds he has moved and that within two months of his arrival. Presbyteries are expected to keep a list of

Ministers who, though members of other Presbyteries, are resident within their bounds.

Ministers in Limbo — An awkward situation could arise in the case of a Minister who had left the ministry of the Church of Scotland to take up a posting abroad which involved his coming under the discipline of an Overseas Church, and who having returned to Scotland is looking for a parish there. From the appropriate Committee he receives a Certificte of Eligibility without which he cannot be nominated in a vacancy. Possession of this does not, however, confer on him the status of a Minister of the Church of Scotland — for that he must await election and induction to a parish. In this interim period he is still to be presumed a Minister of the Oversesas Church of which he had taken farewell some months before and which is fairly certain to have written him off its books. Let it be that during this interim period he takes to preaching rank heresy or to indulging in drunken orgies who is to take action in the matter? It is in the interest of the man concerned no less than of the Church at large that any *fama* should be investigated, but there is no Presbytery in a position to take the matter into its concern and it is not for an Assembly Committee to do so. The situation seems less than satisfactory.

Ministerial Certificate — Act ii 1987 anent Ordination and Functions of the Ministry is very largely concerned with what up to that point had been called a Presbyterial Certificate but which was now to be known as a Ministerial Certificate. This tidied up the earlier legislation (Act i 1976) in a number of places, and in particular it removed the provision whereby a Minister who left the service of the Church under some kind of cloud could ostensibly leave on health grounds and choose not to make application for a Certificate. He needed have little difficulty in obtaining a medical certificate to the effect that he was in a state of nervous strain and would benefit from being relieved of the responsibilities of office; and no doubt both congregation and Presbytery would be happy to be relieved of the necessity of a messy libel action. After all he has not asked for a Certificate, so we can draw a discreet curtain over all that. But two years later — or better still from his point of view five years later — he could submit his request — he is feeling quite recovered now. Members of Presbytery with good memories might well be hesitant about granting, but it would be difficult at this stage to resurrect evidence of which there had been plenty at the time, and in any case to do so at this stage would seem vindictive. The new Act has done away with this provision.

The functions of the ministry are defined in the Act as (a) the conduct of public worship, (b) the administration of the Sacraments, and (c) the solemnisation of marriage. A Ministerial Certificate testifies in name of the Presbytery that its holder is a Minister of the Church of Scotland in good standing, authorised to exercise the functions of the ministry on an occasional basis, as a locum, in connection with an assistantship or similar office — all subject to the supervision of the Presbytery. The validity of the Certificate obtains up till 30th June subsequent to the date of issue in any year, after which it has to be renewed on application allowing two months' notice. The application is to be accompanied by details of present employment and of ministerial functions discharged since issue of the current Certificate. On moving to the bounds of another Presbytery the Certificate is to be exhibited to the Clerk thereof within two months of taking up residence, failing which it will lapse.

It is specifically provided in paras 8 (b) and (c) that "in the event of no application being received from a Minister who is entitled to apply the circumstances shall be considered by the Superintendence Committee and a report made to the Presbytery as to whether a Ministerial Certificate should be issued or withheld." If the latter the Minister concerned is to be informed of the contents of such report, and shall be notified of the meeting at which it is to be considered and is entitled to appear and to be heard thereat.

Demission of Status — Oddly enough the law makes no provision for a Minister voluntarily to relinquish his status, but it occasionally happens that someone wants to do so — if he wishes to stand for Parliament he must (p 169), or if he has completely lost his faith. In such a case he will intimate his intention to the Presbytery which will doubtless consult with him regarding his reasons, pointing out to him the gravity and irreversibility of the step he is contemplating. If he persists in his desire the Presbytery will accept his demission, declaring him to be no longer a Minister of the Church of Scotland. He will not, of course, be entitled to any kind of certificate but should receive an extract minute of demission. Should the Minister concerned be at the time under the shadow of any kind of *fama* care should be taken that the demission is not merely an evasion of deposition. Should a Minister have quite genuinely lost his faith then no obstacle should be put in the way of his demitting his charge if not yet his status, or perhaps being given a period of leave of absence in which to seek a new stability.

Discipline — As has been said above, all Ministers whether or not they are in charges are under the supervision of a Presbytery to which they are answerable for all matters of life and doctrine. The whole subject of discipline is dealt with at length at page 237.

Insanity of a Minister — In the case of a Minister inducted to his charge before June 1933 this matter was covered in the former Church of Scotland by what was known as "the Belhaven Act" and in the former United Free Church by an Act of their Assembly of 1904. As there are today no Ministers in charges where they have served since before 1929 the matter is of historic interest only and reference may be made to Cox or Mair.

Today the matter is governed by Act xvi of 1933 whose provisions shortly are as follow. When a Presbytery is satisfied on the strength of soul-and-conscience certificates from two independent doctors that the Minister of one of its charges is by reason of mental illness no longer fit to discharge his duties it is to appoint an Interim Moderator to the congregation concerned. If the incapacity looks to be of a temporary character leave of absence for a suitable period is to be granted. If it appears that no improvement is to be expected, or if after a year there is still no immediate prospect of recovery the Presbytery is to present the matter to the General Assembly (by way of Reference) which may dissolve the pastoral tie, and which if it does so will arrange that suitable provision is made for the Minister concerned — any such grants to be reviewable should he recover sufficiently to undertake ministerial or other duty of a remunerative nature.

ITS RELATION WITH STUDENTS AND PROBATIONERS

The responsibility for recruitment to the ministry lies with Presbyteries — a fact of which they are reminded from time to time by the Assembly. While the number of candidates continues reasonably adequate to meet the Church's pared-down needs it is a source of regret that few candidates are coming from the rural areas and very few indeed from the Highlands and Islands, which at one time so superbly filled so many pulpits. And while it is encouraging that so large a part of the intake is composed of people who have gained experience in other professions and occupations it would be good to see more young people coming in straight through school and university. It is true that recruitment is the business of the Presbytery, but it must be obvious that in the long run it is the Parish Minister who has to act as recruiting agent.

Full details regarding the nomination of students, the relation of candidates with Selection Schools etc are to be found at pp 111 ff. The Presbytery has the duty of exercising pastoral care over its students during their years in University, and in due time it has the duty of taking them on trials for licence and, once Exit Certificates are to hand, for arranging a Service of Licensing them as Probationers for the Holy Ministry. It has also the duty of sending to the Secretary of the Assembly's Probationers Committee a list of particulars of all persons so licensed.

In respect of life and doctrine it is to his Kirk Session that a student is answerable, after licence it is to the Presbytery which licensed him. A Student or Probationer moving to the bounds of another Presbytery is required to lodge a Certificate with the Clerk of the Presbytery to which he has gone.

ITS RELATION WITH THE DIACONATE AND WITH READERS

Deaconess or Deacon — A Deaconess or Deacon engaged in the full-time employment of the Church or in some other post entitling to a seat in Presbytery is for the discharge of the duties of her or his office answerable to the employing agency, but for matters of life and doctrtine to the Presbytery of which she or he is a member.

Readers — The recruitment and the continuing supervision of Readers are matters for the Presbytery, while for life and character they are under the discipline of their own Kirk Sessions.

ITS RELATION WITH OTHER COURTS

With Other Presbyteries

One Presbytery cannot review, or in any way interfere with, the business of any other Presbytery. If something has been done by a Presbytery of which its neighbour disapproves and in which it sees itself as having an interest it can make a friendly unofficial approach on the subject, but if that does not have the desired effect then it must petition the General Assembly to take action.

With the General Assembly

Apart from the fact that they have to put into execution all Acts and injunctions of the supreme court Presbyteries are related to that body principally in three ways — (1) they appoint commissioners who constitute the membership of the Assembly; (2) they may approach the Assembly by petition, overture or reference; and (3) they are expected to give an expression of opinion on any matter sent down to them and in particular on practically all proposed new legislation.

(1) Appointment of Commissioners

The Act of Union of 1929 ordained that the Assembly would consist exclusively of commissioners appointed by Presbyteries — up to one-fourth of their membership, Ministers and Elders in equal numbers. Some minor changes have subsequently been made, but today it is still subsantially true to say that the Assembly consists almost exlusively of commissioners appointed by Presbyteries. Such appointments are made at an ordinary meeting of the court, notice of this business having been given at its preceding meeting. I imagine that in respect of the Ministers to be appointed all Presbyteries work on some kind of rota, and that they also operate a rota of congregations whose Kirk Sessions are invited to make nomination of an Elder who would be happy to receive a commission. They are not, however, bound to do so, being free to appoint whom they will. And it is, of course, wrong to say that an Elder is *representing* the Kirk Session (or congregation) which nominated him. The Presbytery has to satisfy itself that all Elders whom it commissions are *bona fide* acting Elders. Since commissions have to reach the Principal Clerk by 31st March it is usual for Presbyteries to select commissioners at their March meeting.

Substitution — In the event of a person who had been commissioned subsequently withdrawing a substitute may be appointed to fill the place right up to the opening of the Assembly. A Minister given a commission by the Presbytery of A may still take it up even if by the time of the Assembly he has been translated and become a member of Presbytery B. Not only so, a Presbytery may grant a commission to a Minister whose translation to another Presbytery it has already sustained.

Ex-Moderators — In addition to the number of Commissioners to which it is entitled a Presbytery may, if it so resolves, appoint ex-Moderators of Assembly who are of its membership, and if it exercises this option it has also to appoint an extra Elder to offset such additional Minister. It is common, but not universal, practice for a Presbytery to find a place in its list of Commissioners for one who is Convener of an Assembly Committee. This has an obvious advantage from the Convener's point of view, though if it is not done he may be appointed by his Committee as a Corresponding Member.

The Commission — The actual terms of the Commission are of no little significance, making clear, as they do, that the persons are Commissioners and not delegates or representatives. They are appointed "commissioners to the next General Assembly indicted to meet at Edinburgh ...., willing them to repair thereto, and to attend all the diets of the same, and there to consult, vote, and determine in all matters that come before them, to the glory of God and the good of His Church, according to the Word of God, the Confession of Faith, and agreeable to the constitution of this Church, as they will be answerable; and that they report on their return therefrom." Should some very large-scale issue confront the Church one could conceive a situation arising comparable to that of the Ten Years' Conflict that preluded the Disruption when Presbyteries frequently had heated — indeed acrimonious — debates as to who should be appointed commissioners. You may not be able to instruct people how they are to vote, but you can be careful to choose people who will vote the right way!

Reporting Diligence — Most Presbyteries arrange that one, or perhaps two, of their Commissioners "report diligence" at the first ordinary meeting after the close of the Assembly.

2. Approach to the Assembly

There are three avenues along which a Presbytery may travel when it wishes to bring some matter to the attention of the General Assembly, these being petition, overture and reference and they are discussed very fully at pp 265 ff.

It should be added that the Presbytery may itself be brought to the Assembly in consequence of appeal or dissent and complaint against one of its judgments, and in such a case it will come as a respondent. The Presbytery will be at the bar — it should be represented by a duly appointed spokesman who will appear physically at the bar, but all of its commissioners will be affected to the extent of being prohibited from taking part in the proceedings or voting in the division.

3. Expression of Opinion

There are at least three different ways in which the Assembly may seek the opinion of Presbyteries on some issue.

For Consideration and Comment — It is increasingly common for the General Assembly to remit to Presbyteries for consideration and comment some proposal of interest and importance. In particular reports on ecumenical deliberations and on doctrinal issues seem invariably to be remitted in this way. This can prove exceedingly valuable, not only because of the worthwhile feedback to the responsible committee, but also because it results in the whole issue being aired, so that the final proposals, if and when they are formulated, do not come as a surprise. And certainly such discussion brings out suggestions much more useful and constructive than would ever be forthcoming from an Assembly debate no matter how inspired or inspiring.

Barrier Act — Before the Assembly can finally approve any legislation which is going to become "a binding rule and constitution to the Church" the proposal must, as it is usually expressed, "go down under the Barrier Act." The reference is to an Act passed in 1697 in a day when the Kirk was under heavy pressure from the Crown, an Act designed to secure breathing-space and opportunity for mature consideration before major changes could be introduced. It requires that before an Act of this degree of significance can be passed by the Assembly it must have been approved as an Overture and then sent down to Presbyteries for their judgment, and only if there is a majority of all of them (not just of those voting) in favour may the succeeding Assembly convert the Overture into a standing law of the Church — although even then it is not obliged to do so. What this amounts to is that Presbyteries are given a collective power of veto. See "Articles Declaratory" hereunder for special Barrier Act provisions.

Interim Act — At the same time that it resolves to send down the Overture to Presbyteries the Assembly may pass an Interim Act converting the Overture into law. It can be granted a place on the statute-book for at least a year until the returns are received. Should the returns be negative such an Act will have to be recalled and a very awkward situation could arise without invalidating what had been done. That is why the Assembly will pass an Interim Act only if it is very well assured that the proposal carries considerable support.

When the matter arrives at the Presbytery that court has to appoint a time when it will be dealt with and this is normally done by fixing an Order of the Day for the ordinary meeting immediately before the date when returns are to be in the hands of the Principal Clerk, or, if the issue is one likely to raise considerable controversy an *in hunc effectum* meeting may be called. After debate, if any, the question is put quite simply, Approve or Disapprove, and a vote is taken, the numbers voting being carefully recorded even when the decision is unanimous. It is in order for the Presbytery to transmit a Note commenting upon something in the proposal which is felt to be less than perfect, but it is important to recognise that the Note will have no effect upon the fate of the Overture. If the objection voiced in the Note is serious and basic then the Presbytery must Disapprove — it must not delude itself into thinking it is approving subject to something being done about the matter raised in the Note.

My own conviction is that the provision for the Note is unfortunate — it were better for Presbyteries to be presented with the stark choice. In 1979 three Overtures which had gone down under the Barrier Act each produced Approve by a majority, but a mass of comments, running to nine, five and eight pages of the Blue Book. As I see it, in a situation of that kind the whole affair should be withdrawn from the Barrier Act procedure and taken back by the Committee so that they may study the wealth of comment and criticisms offered and, where appropriate, for the Act to be amended and adjusted in the light of all this. It could then go down afresh in an amended form under true Barrier Act procedure. It would involve the loss of a year, but, as I have said on many occasions, good legislation is far more important than instant legislation.

The Act refers to "the more general opinion of the Church." This has been interpreted as meaning a majority of the Presbyteries of the Church irrespective of how many have made returns and irrespective of the relative size or state of the voting in each. The Presbytery of Jerusalem does not have a vote in these cases (p 316), which leaves a total of 48 Presbyteries. So that for an Overture to be carried at least twenty-five Presbyteries must have voted Approve.

Articles Declaratory — If it is proposed to make any change in the Articles Declaratory of the Constitution of the Church of Scotland in Matters Spiritual — a document enshrined in an Act of Parliament of 1921 — a highly specialised form of Barrier Act procedure is to be followed. Clearly these Articles represent the most important constitutional instruments of the Kirk, and any proposal to alter or amend one of them is a matter of grave moment. The first of the nine Articles sets forth the basic doctrinal position of the Church, and adherence to this, as interpreted by the Church, is declared to be essential to the Church's continuity and corporate life. This contains the unchangeable elements.

The other Articles are capable of being modified or added to provided the following procedure is followed. Any proposed change is to be framed as an Overture and submitted to the General Assembly. If it is approved on a straight vote there it is next to be sent down under Barrier Act procedure and Presbyteries are to indicate whether they Approve or Disapprove. At this stage there is some latitude and a Presbytery which was generally friendly disposed but had reservations would be justified in approving and sending its reservations in the form of a comment. If on this first tour the Overture has gained the support of two-thirds of the Presbyteries it may be revised and amended and the finished product will then be sent down the following year. This time there is no room for comment, the choice being the simple one of Approve or Disapprove. Again if more than two-thirds of the Presbyteries (at the time of writing thirty-three) approve then the matter is to be reported to next General Assembly which "may, if it deems it expedient, modify and add to these Articles in terms of the said Overture." This final Assembly approval is no mere formality though the Act for the Abolition of Provincial Synods was passed by the Assembly of 1992 without a hitch on a majority of 44 to 4. On the other hand in 1974 in what proved quite a dramatic division the Assembly resolved by 292 votes to 234 not to proceed meantime with changes proposed in the Declaratory Articles concerning the position of the Westminster Confession and the form of the Preamble, Questions and Formula used at Ordinations etc and that in spite of the fact that the proposal had in two succesive years been approved by two-thirds of the Presbyteries (46 out of 63 at the second time of asking).

If an Overture fail, the same or a similar one is not to be sent down until after an interval of at least five years. The issue has not been put to the test, but the opinion has been expressed that if one General Assembly declined to enact an overture which in its final form had received the requisite consent of Presbyteries a subsequent General Assembly could enact that same overture — that is to say it would be accepted that the necessary consents had already been secured. I would feel obliged to contest this. It seems to me that this elaborate machinery was designed to ensure that the Assembly could not enact legislation that was out of touch with the contemporary mind of the church as a whole — not with that mind as it had been ascertained five, ten, or even thirty years earlier.

AS A COURT OF REVIEW

The Presbytery is the body to which appeal has to be taken for the review of decisions of Kirk Sessions, of Congregations, of Congregational Boards, of Deacons' Courts and of Committees of Management.

Kirk Session Decisions — There is to my knowledge only one matter — the preparation of the Electoral Register in a vacancy — where the decision of a Kirk Session cannot be made the subject of appeal to the Presbytery. If the Session says you are not an adherent an adherent you are not! Should a member of a congregation appear on any other count at the bar of the Kirk Session and should he receive what he considers less than justice he is entitled to intimate an appeal (which he will subsequently lodge in writing) to the Presbytery. A member of the Session dissatisfied with a judgment of that court on any matter regularly before it is at liberty to dissent and complain to the Presbytery. And any member of a congregation who is at loggerheads with the Session on some issue, or who is ill-pleased with the Minister in respect of how he is fulfilling his duty, has a remedy in a petition to the Presbytery.

Congregational Decision — A member of a congregation who strongly disappoves of a decision reached at a congregational meeting — to sell the manse, to redecorate the church, to move the pulpit to the side or the organ to the gallery — has the right to approach the Presbytery by petition asking that the decision be recalled. To have any hope of success he would have to have a very strong case indeed on the merits (tantamount to showing that no reasonable congregation would have acted in this way) or he must be pleading irregularity in what is proposed or in the precedure — that, for instance, due notice of the meeting had not been given. There was a case in Glasgow where at the meeting of the congregation to elect a Vacancy Committee it had been agreed that the vote for the election would be by ballot, but the vacancy had dragged on for an unconscienable time and when at length a sole nominee had been found there seemed much unanimity and enthusiasm and it was thought to speed things up by having an open ballot the day the nominee preached. This was done and he was duly elected — or so it seemed. A disgruntled member petitioned the Presbytery pleading irregularity, and the Presbytery had no option but to recall the decision of the open meeting and order a ballot — which I am happy to add produced the same result. But short-cuts can prove dangerous routes, and, as so often happens, time was wasted instead of being saved. When I add that the occasion was the election of Revd Tom Allan to St George's Tron it will be agreed that no long-term injury was suffered!

Congregational Board Decisions — The Model Deed of 1965 (p 41) provides that "if any question shall arise with reference to the election of the Board or to the interpretation of any Article in this constitution, or to the legality of any particular exercise of the powers herein contained, it shall be competent to any person or body interested to apply by petition to the Presbytery to adjudicate upon the matter. It will be noted that the appeal is exclusively on questions of regularity and legality and not on merits. Finality of judgment in such an appeal is given to the Presbytery, except that the petitioner may within twenty-one days produce a certificate from the Procurator to the effect that the issue is one suitable for appeal to the superior courts, in which case the appeal will proceed as though it had been competently taken at the time when judgment was given.

Deacons' Court Decisions — The Act which in the former United Free Church dealt with the constitution and powers of the Deacons' Court stated clearly that there is no right of regular appeal or complaint to the Kirk Session or to any of the superior courts of the Church against a decision of the Deacons' Court. Their determinations are final when they keep within their province and obey the Acts of the General Assembly. Reasonably enough the Act goes on to confer power on an Elder or a member to petition the Presbytery when he is alleging that the province has been overstepped or the Acts breached. If satisfied that there has been irregularity the Presbytery may declare a judgment null and void and order the expunging of the minute — and against such a decision of Presbytery the Deacons' Court had a right of appeal to the Synod — now, presumably, to the Assembly. But what of the Deacon who does not approve of what the court is doing? What remedy lies to his hand? None is specifically set forth in the legislation. It is to be presumed that his wise course is to have his dissent recorded at the meeting of the Court and then, as a member of the congregation, to present a petition to the Presbytery.

Committee of Management Decisions — I cannot find any law on the subject of the redress available to a member of a former U P congregation dissatisfied with the actings of its Managers. The course would clearly be for him to raise his complaint at a congregational meeting which, if it agreed with him, would presumably instruct the Managers accordingly. And obviously if he is defeated here he can petition the Presbytery to review the decision of a congregational meeting. The other, and probably better, course for the member who thought the Managers had acted *ultra vires* or unwisely would be to seek the intervention of the Kirk Session by way of petition, and if they did not agree with him, then being at the bar of the Session he could appeal to the Presbytery. By either of these routes the disgruntled member could get his case to the Presbytery even if in either case it required two steps — I do not know of a more direct route.

Chapter 13

THE GENERAL ASSEMBLY

MAY I BEGIN with a word in parenthesis. As explained in the Preface I have fairly scrupulously but not invariably adhered to the convention whereby the Assembly is followed by a plural verb — or should it be "are followed"?

The Supreme Court

The General Assembly is the supreme court of the Church of Scotland, standing as it does at the apex of the conciliar pyramid. Judgments of Assembly on issues which are its proper concern are final and not subject to review, in even the highest civil court. In a case in 1936 (Ballantyne v Presbytery of Wigtown) the Lord Justice Clerk (Aitchison) says (Session Cases p 654), "the question must therefore be — Is the particular matter complained of ...... a matter which, on a reasonable construction, falls within the Declaratory Articles? If so the matter is at an end and neither the statute nor the common law, nor previous decision, whether upon statute or the common law, can avail to bring the matter within the jurisdiction of the civil authority." He went on in that case to refuse jurisdiction in reviewing the decision of a Presbytery which would not grant one of its congregations (Kirkmabreck) permission to call a Minister.

For the last three hundred years the Assembly has invariably met in Edinburgh (apart from a single session in 1988 held in Glasgow to mark the anniversary of the famous Assembly of 1638 which had met there), and since 1718 it has met some time in the middle of May — until the turn of the century on a Thursday, then from 1901 on a Tuesday through to the following Wednesday, while from 1978 it has convened on a Saturday, continuing through the next week and closing on the evening of the Friday. The reason for this last change was the idea that it would make it easier for working Elders to attend if the whole Assembly could be encompassed inside a calendar week. Certainly expense has been considerably curtailed by the change. The Assembly has met in various places in the capital — it was from St Andrew's Church in George Street, for example, that the disaffected but large minority marched out in 1843, and it was in a garage in Annandale Street that in 1929 the separated brethren met together again — the only building that could be found to accommodate the largest gathering ever held in Edinburgh, sixteen thousand in all. Latterly the Assembly invariably met in The Tolbooth Church. Since 1929 their meeting-place has been the Assembly Hall, a purpose-designed hall incorporated in the College built by the Free Church for the training of its students (now New College) on a site on the Mound running through to the Lawnmarket on which had stood the palace of Mary of Guise, the Queen Regent. The College premises have, since 1961 made over to the University of Edinburgh, but the ownership of the Assembly Hall and certain ancillary accommodation has been retained by the Church, which also has the right to the use of certain other parts of the premises when the Assembly is in session.

ITS MEMBERSHIP

The make-up of the Assembly has suffered many vicissitudes since first the Kirk met in General Assembly on 20th December 1560. Then it consisted of six Ministers and thirty-five others designated commissioners, of whom only two appear to have been Elders. The story of the early Assemblies is told in some detail in Cox (Ed VI p 197). The Act of Union of 1929 ordained that each Assembly was to consist of commissioners appointed by Presbyteries for that Assembly, being Ministers and Elders in equal numbers up to one-fourth of the complete roll of the Presbytery, the Ministers being members of the Presbytery and the Elders *bona fide* acting Elders of Kirk Sessions within the Church. This has continued practically unchanged, and the position until 1995 has been that each Presbytery elected one Minister and one Elder for every four, or part of four, ministerial places on its complete roll — to which had to be added certain other appointments as noted hereunder. The "complete roll" meant the list of all Ministers — in charges, in other appointments or retired — who held seats in the Presbytery, plus the number of vacant charges. Nothing was said in the Act as to when the Roll was to be made up, but the Standing Orders of Assembly declared it to be the Roll as at 31st December. Act iii 1992 (which *inter alia* conferred seats in

Presbyteries on members of the Diaconate in, and after retirement from, full-time service in appointments approved by the Church) made provision whereby such Deaconesses and Deacons were to be eligible to receive commissions to the General Assembly, one in four, or part of four, of the total on the Roll. A commissioner duly appointed by his Presbytery who has subsequently been translated to a different Presbytery may still fulfil his commission.

The Act of 1994 — Following upon the legislation designed to reduce the size of Presbyteries an Overture of the previous year received in 1994 Barrier Act approval whereby the General Assembly would consist of Commissioners appointed by Presbyteries — Ministers, one for every three or part of three on the complete roll; Elders, one for every Minister, and only Elders who are members of Kirk Sessions within the bounds may be appointed (the requirement about "*bona fide* active" has been dropped); and the Diaconate, one for every four or part of four, and again only those who are members of the appointing Presbytery. It seems to me that difficulty could arise regarding the interpretation of Para 2 (and to a lesser extent Para 6) of the Act which declares that "only Ministers who are members of the appointing Presbytery shall be eligible to hold commissions." It could well be argued that a Minister given a commission by Presbytery A when a member of that court could no longer "hold" that commission had he in the meantime been translated to Presbytery B — which would represent a departure from the present law on the subject.

Members Ex Officiis — Since 1956 there have been six members of Assembly who are not commissioners elected by Presbyteries — the Moderator (of the appointing year), the Moderator-Elect, the two Clerks, the Procurator, and the Solicitor of the Church. Act i of 1992 added to this the Convener and Vice-Convener of the Business Committee, thus making eight *ex officiis* members in all — the entire personnel of "the playpen". Before they acquired this status places had to be found for these officials among the commissioners appointed by Presbyteries, thus reducing the frequency with which others could attend.

Ex-Moderators — In terms of Act iv of 1969 Presbyteries are empowered to elect as commissioners ex-Moderators of Assembly who are on their Roll. Presbyteries are not obliged to do this, and if they do they are to elect also an Elder in addition to what their quota would otherwise have been.

Corresponding Members — These are not commissioners and have no voting rights, but they are entitled to attend all sessions of the Assembly and until 1994 they were free to speak on any matter before the court. A new Standing Order of that year restricted their speaking to "any matter affecting the interest of their Board or Committee" (Repts 1994, p 7). They fall into two classes — first Missionaries and Chaplains (whether Ministers or Elders) at home on ordinary leave; and, secondly, one person appointed by each of certain of the Standing Committees, the President of the Woman's Guild, and the Editor of "Life and Work" — all with a view to watching over the interests of their Departments and being able to answer questions and offer explanations when any matter arises which affects these Departments. It would seem that the new Standing Order will have the effect of reducing those in the former group to perpetual silence.

Delegates — These also have no rights in relation to, and are specifically barred from taking any part in, judicial causes, but otherwise they have a right to speak. They are appointed by denominations with which the Church of Scotland has close ties. Opportunity is afforded at the Sunday evening sederunt for a limited number of such Delegates on a rotational basis to address the Assembly and to bring greetings.

Visitors — Also in attendance, but with no rights either to vote or to speak, are Visitors, generally from overseas, duly accredited from their own Churches. Since 1969 the Roman Catholic hierarchy in Scotland have been asked to send an "Invited Visitor" and this they have consistently done.

Numbers — Inevitably the numerical strength of the Assembly varies slightly from one year to the next and has dwindled to a modest extent as the number of charges has declined. For some time the figure stood fairly steady at around the 1300 mark, but twenty-five years ago the number of commissioners alone was 1450. In 1985 the number entitled to attend was 1318, consisting of 1250 Commissioners, 25 Delegates, 11 Visitors, and 32 Corresponding Members. At the time of writing it remains a question just what figures the Assembly of 1995 will produce.

ITS OFFICIALS

The Moderator

The Assembly is presided over by a Moderator and the election of the new Moderator constitutes the first major item of the opening business. He has, of course, been nominated in the previous October. It is his business to preside, to take charge of the opening devotions, to keep good order, to refuse to accept motions that are offensive, irrelevant, or otherwise incompetent, and to sign documents in name of the Assembly. When it is not convenient for the Moderator to preside in person one of his predecessors, at his invitation, takes over in his stead.

Moderator's Chaplains — The Moderator chooses a Senior and a Junior Chaplain to attend upon him, to assist in the manifold affairs that have to be organised, with a particular responsibility for the more social aspects of his duties. For long the custom was that these were both Ministers but of recent years the choice has been extended to include Elders. I imagine they should be commissioners, but I know of no law on the subject.

Moderator's Residence — In 1973 as part of the celebration of the centenary of the foundation of their Trust the Baird Trustees, with consent of the General Assembly and in collaboration with the National Trust for Scotland, purchased, renovated, furnished, and endowed the two upper floors of the Georgian house at No 7 Charlotte Square in Edinburgh as an official residence for the Moderator throughout his year of office. Before that, Moderators generally functioned from their own homes with spells in an Edinburgh Hotel during Assembly time and on other appropriate occasions. It is now possible for the Moderator to have Charlotte Square as his base during the entire year, and this has the added convenience of being near 121 George Street where he has an office and secretarial assistance.

How Chosen — Time was when the Moderator was quite literally chosen by the Assembly at the start of its opening sederunt, but in view of the extent and complexity of his duties the Moderator of today must be given adequate warning, and so he is nominated by a Special Committee during the previous October. The precise constitution of this Committee has altered from time to time. At the time of writing it consists of the seven surviving most immediate past Moderators with an equal number of

Elders appointed by the Assembly, along with one representative (Minister or Elder) appointed by each Presbytery in the UK. The chair is taken by the most senior of the ex-Moderators prepared to act, and the Principal Clerk, being a member *ex officio*, acts as Secretary. The Committee meets on the third Tuesday in October, nominations will be accepted only of those known to be willing to accept office, and the choice is immediately made public. For a short time, as an experiment, nominations were invited from the Church at large, but this was seen to be building up into a system of candidature much to be deplored and was quickly departed from.

His Position — Once elected and installed the nominee becomes Moderator of the General Assembly of the Church of Scotland, and not, as is so frequently misrepresented in the media, "Moderator of the Church of Scotland." This latter term is not only inaccurate it is quite misleading, for the Moderator has, in fact, no relationship with the Church as such, but only with its Assembly of which he is Moderator, and, on a strict interpretation, his authority is wholly contained within the compass of the Assembly itself where he is complete master of order. I think even Moderators themselves sometimes forget this limitation. Now and again questions are raised regarding the exent of the Modertor's duties. In 1962 the Assembly adopted the report of a Special Committee appointed to look into this to the effect that "the Office, Functions, and Duties of the Moderator are as follows — (a) to preside over the General Assembly and to perform those duties as stated in the Standing Orders; (b) to visit Presbyteries according to the scheme of visitation sanctioned by the General Assembly; (c) to perform such duties as may be directed by the General Assembly, and to represent the Church of Scotland on historic and national occasions as they may arise; and (d) to undertake such other duties as he may choose during his term of office".

It must be obvious that the closing paragraph allows almost limitless freedom to the Moderator to act in any way he cares, but does not, of course, invest his actings with any authority other than his own. A report in 1979 drew attention to the fact that Moderators have on occasion "become involved in matters of public interest in ways which have not been authorised by the General Assembly and which would either have been disapproved by that body or would at least have aroused controversy if discussed there beforehand." This was noted, but no change was made in the position as it had been enunciated in 1962. So the position remains that the Moderator is not invested with power of any sort or degree beyond that of Chairman of the General Assembly. (That is not quite literally true, as I discovered during my year as Moderator — there is also the power that goes with being an Honorary Patron of the Magna Carta Trust!)

The situation, then, is in effect that it is left to the good sense of the Moderator to decide what engagements he will accept, what company he will keep, what views he will express — always on the understanding that nothing he does or says will have any binding effect upon the Church, and in the conviction that he wouldn't have been chosen as Moderator if he hadn'd had good sense! A part of the remit of the Board of Practice and Procedure is "to advise the Moderator anent his official duties if so required", and from time to time Moderators have availed themselves of this. When in 1961 the question arose as to whether the Moderator, who was to be in Rome on the business of the Kirk, should visit the Vatican a Special Committee was convened to advise him on what was then a highly controversial issue, but the decision had still to be his.

The Insignia of the Office — Immediately the new Moderator has been elected he is installed in office by a prayer and by the placing on his finger of a ring which he wears all through his year of office — a custom dating from as recently as 1911. Regarding this particular item it was agreed by the General Assembly of 1981 that "the wearing of a ring by the Moderator may have been influenced by the custom of other Churches, but it is tied to no interpretation of any such custom, nor is any ranking or ecclesiastical status indicated by the fact that it is an emerald stone that is set in the ring." The same Assembly were happy to agree that no steps should be taken to disturb the present position in regard to the wearing of the "Moderator's uniform" — to wit that it lies within the discretion of the Moderator whether and when he will wear the dress which has come to be associated with the office — black cut-away coat with breeches, black stockings, court shoes with silver buckles, and lace ruffles worn at the wrists and over the left lapel. In 1987 Dr Duncan Shaw completely departed from the traditional dress — without, be it said, any disastrous effects, but since then Moderators have conformed to custom except that black striped trousers have generally taken over from the breeches and black stockings.

Likewise the choice is left to the Moderator whether and to what extent he will use the official coat-of-arms on letter-heads and elsewhere. It was in 196? at the suggestion of the then Lord Lyon King of Arms that a standardised version of the burning bush symbol was prepared and registered with the Lyon Court (before that it had appeared in a wide variety of forms); but when this had been done it was pointed out that a rather more elaborate affair showing in heraldic terms and devices the relation beween the Moderator and the Kirk should be registered for use by the Moderator. Sight of the finished article (not helped by "Life and Work" printing it upside down) created something of a stir at the time and it has never been welcomed with any great enthusiasm — though it is generally used.

Financial arrangements are made to allow the Moderator to be given leave of absence for the "year" and for a short period before to allow for preparation, as well, of course, as for the covering of his various expenses.

In the matter of precedence the Moderator in Scotland ranks next to the Lord Chancellor of Great Britain and before the Prime Minister and the Dukes. During his year of office he is styled "Right Reverend" and thereafter as "Very Reverend".

The Clerks

There is a Principal Clerk and a Depute Clerk, both appointed by the General Assembly on the recommendation of the Board of Practice and Procedure, and both answerable to the General Assembly for the discharge of their duties. The Principal Clerk must be a Minister and until 1961 was invariably Minister of a parish; the Depute is generally a Minister, though a layman is eligible to fill the post.

Principal Clerk — Since 1961 the Principal Clerk has been *ex officio* Secretary of the General Administration Committee (now the Board of Practice and Procedure) and of the Business Committee of Assembly, he acts as Convener of the Commitee on Classifying Returns to Overtures, and as Secretary to the Moderator, to the Committee on the Nomination of the Moderator, to the Judicial Commission and to the Panel of Arbiters. His duties vis-a-vis the Assembly are to prepare the minutes and have them printed in the "Daily Papers", and to give extracts from the minutes. He acts generally as Clerk to the court, arranging for meetings, sending out papers, collecting schedules, sending down Overtures to Presbyteries and receiving returns. He is also available to advise the Moderator and the Assembly in relation to all matters affecting the conduct of the business of the court.

Depute Clerk — The Depute Ckerk, whose office is part-time, acts generally as assistant to the Principal Clerk, taking orders from him as to the allocation of their respective duties. He has no preferential claim to the office of Principal Clerk when that is vacant. He acts as minute-taker during the sessions of Assembly.

Clerk's Office — During the sittings of the General Assembly the Clerks maintain on the premises an office where someone is constantly on duty to deal with enquiries and where Notices of Motion may be lodged for printing in the "Daily Papers".

The Procurator

The Procurator is a Queen's Counsel appointed by the General Assembly on the commendation of the Board of Practice and Procedure. His duties were defined in 1969 in the following terms:

a) To attend all meetings of the General Assembly and of the Commission of Assembly.
b) To revise libels and other proceedings as required by Act of Assembly.
c) To be a member of the Board of Practice and Procedure and a General Trustee, but to attend only when matters are likely to arise requiring his advice.
d) To act as Senior Counsel for the Church in all matters of litigation.
e) To give Opinions on Memorials submitted by any of the courts.
f) To advise inferior courts by Note or through Consultation — but requests for such advice must be directed through the Principal Clerk.
g) He is not required to give advice in any form to Ministers or other members of courts or congregations.

In a day when the connection between the Kirk and the courts of the land was much closer than it is today the advice of the Procurator must have been quite indispensable on many matters coming regularly before the Assembly. He still advises on issues where the secular law has a particular relevance, but his advice on any matter which has a legal or procedural aspect is greatly valued. The Assembly are very jealous that this is "advice" and not "a ruling", and it must be sought only by the Moderator — though, of course, it is open to anyone to suggest to the Moderator that this is a matter on which he might seek the mind of the Procurator.

The Business Convener

One of the first things which every Assembly does is to appoint a Business Committee to supervise the arrangements for the orderly discharging of its business. Steps have to be taken in advance by the Board of Practice and Procedure to arrange an order for each of the days of the week, embracing all the business known to be arising; but from time to time adjustments have to be made as the exigencies of the situation demand, and it is for the Business Committee to advise on these. The Convener of the Business Committee, who occupies a seat at the table beside the Clerks, is often referred to as "the Leader of the House" (although the Assembly has otherwise resisted being called a "house"), and he gives guidance on the conduct of business, on how a vote should be taken, on whether the court should adjourn the sederunt or should continue with the business on hand, and on questions of order, and he is expected to be ready on call to unravel procedural knots with a nice mixture of firmness and good humour. A capable Business Convener can in a quiet and undemonstrative fashion contribute enormously to the efficient discharge of the Assembly's business. In all of this he has the help and advice of a Vice-Convener who sits opposite him at the table.

The Solicitor of the Church

In the pre-Union Church of Scotland all legal affairs were in the hands of the Solicitor, the Free Church had a Custodier of Titles, and the U P Church employed a Law Agent. The three offices were ultimately combined and the holder is now known simply as "the Solicitor". He is *ex officio* a commissioner to the General Assembly. His advice is sought principally on matters having to do with property — until 1979 in fact he had to direct through the Assembly all kinds of petitions affecting the sale of property, the disposal of proceeds and the passing of an Act.

The Law Department — In 1937 the General Assembly determined that a Law Department should be formed under a qualified Law Agent and with such clerical assistance as was necessary, and further that the work of the Department should include that of the General Trustees who, however, were to be entitled to employ and consult another solicitor as they might deem necessary. A Special Committee appointed in 1971 to look into the legal services of the Church reported satisfaction with the set-up, but added that in its view the Law Department would benefit from affiliation to a main Committee. So in 1981 it was resolved that for administrative purposes the Law Department was to be affiliated with the General Finance Committee. The following year the Assembly Council — which had been looking into the affairs of the General Finance Committee — reported its conclusion that "the administrative interests of the Law

Department are best served by creating access to the General Assembly as and when required through the Assembly Council itself", and although this never appears to have been approved as an Assembly deliverance it is to be presumed to represent the present official position — as it does the *de facto* position — of the Department.

The London Agent

The Assembly appoint a London Agent who is in receipt of a retainer and whose duties are defined as follows:

a) The daily perusal of the minutes of the House of Lords and the Votes and Proceedings of the House of Commons and attendances obtaining, and the perusal of all Public Bills introduced into Parliament in which the interests of the Church are directly or indirectly affected; writing with and forwarding to the Solicitor of the Church in Edinburgh all such Bills affecting Scotland, and also obtaining and forwarding to the Agent in Edinburgh any minutes or Reports laid before either House of Parliament dealing with Scottish ecclesiastical, educational and trust matters; waiting in ordinary routine cases upon a Government Department or any Member of Parliament in order to furnish information or explanation with reference to any matter affecting the Church in relation either to a Parliamentry Bill or to a question in either House.
b) To receive any deputation from the Church, and aid them in all their proceedings, including their attendance on Members of Parliament, Committees and Government Officials, but not including correspondence and attendance on Counsel.
c) Advising any Committee of the Church, through the Procurator or Solicitor of the Church, as to the general nature of proceedings required for carrying out any matter by the assistance of Parliament or otherwise.

The Precentor

In common with other courts the Assembly depend upon a Precentor to lead the praise in the opening devotions.

The Officer

The Assembly also appoint an Officer to wait on their proceedings and to execute their orders. He takes charge of processions, calls for Order at the beginning of each sederunt, and generally is of assistance to the Moderator's Chaplains, as well as looking after the catering arrangements for the Moderator's lunch parties.

The Lord High Commissioner

This may be a convenient point at which to say something about the position of the Lord High Commissioner, but it must be clearly understood that the Lord High Commissioner is not an "official" of the General Assembly — a suggestion that would be repudiated equally strongly by both Commissioner and Assembly. We are now for the second time enjoying the services of a lady in this office, and while I do not think any formal resolution has been reached on the subject the title is now accepted as "The Queen's Commissioner."

Roots of the Office — The office of the Sovereign's Commissioner may be said to be as old as the General Assembly itself, for it can in its essentials be traced back to the years immediately succeeding 1560, although it was twenty years later that it first took recognisable shape, and it was after the King had moved to London in 1603 that a Commissioner was regularly appointed. As far back as 1561 Maitland of Lethington had raised the question whether Assemblies could legally be held without consent of the Crown — "the question is whether the Queen allows such conventions?" It was to this question that Knox made his famous rejoinder — "Take from us the freedom of Assemblies, and take from us the Evangel; for without Assemblies how shall good order and unity in doctrine be kept?" Both the Regent Morton and King James VI would happily have done away with Assemblies altogether, and the King continued to claim the right to dictate at least when and where they should meet. This was bitterly contested by the Kirk which, however, had to concede His Majesty's right to know what was happening at these gatherings. So the compromise was struck of a Commissioner appointed by the Sovereign to attend and oversee — without the exent of his powers being too clearly defined.

It was in the reign of Charles I that things came to a crisis. At one point during the famous Glasgow Assembly of 1638 the King's Commissioner, the Marquis of Hamilton, solemnly in the King's name disbanded the Assembly and himself withdrew, followed by two Ministers and three Elders, the other 235 commissioners continuing in session, pressing on with the trial of the bishops, and sitting on to write the opening chapter of a sad and dismal story of religious persecution and civil warfare that Scotland could well have done without.

The Revolution Settlement of 1690 decided the question of "the intrinsic power of the Church" and did so in the Kirk's favour, but the position of the King's Commissioner was still, apparently, uncertain — we have the example of an Assembly suspending because the Commissioner was indisposed and unable to be present, and we have instances of the court pressing on with its business in the absence of the King's representative. In the famous Inverkeithing case of 1752 (which led to the deposition of Thomas Gillespie and ultimately to the formation of the Relief Church) the Presbytery of Dunfermline had refused to meet for the induction of an unwelcome presentee and the Assembly were debating what action ought to be taken. The Commissioner, the Earl of Leven, told the Assembly plainly it was time they were exerting their authority over the inferior courts. Whatever influence this intervention may have had that was in fact the view which the Assembly accepted and on which they acted. And apparently no-one told the Commissioner it was none of his business!

His Commission — As soon as the Moderator has been installed the Assembly turn their attention to the reception of the Queen's Representative. His Commission is handed to the Principal Clerk by the Purse-Bearer. It has attached to it the Crown Seal of Scotland, and it bears that the Queen authorises and appoints her Commissioner "to supply Our Presence and hold Our Place .... and to do all and everything ..... as we Ourselves might do if personally present." This is read to a standing Assembly and ordered to be recorded. The Commissioner also brings a Letter from Her Majesty wherein in less formal terms she expresses her concern for the Church and its work, renews her pledge to preserve and uphold its rights and privileges, and prays God's blessing on its forthcoming deliberations. This too is read to a standing Assembly and ordered to be recorded, and a committee is appointed to prepare an answer. The Lord High Commissioner is housed in the Palace of Holyroodhouse; in the matter of precedence he follows immediately behind the Dukes of Edinburgh and Rothesay and before the other members of the Royal Family; the Royal Banner (the lion rampant) is flown over the Palace throughout his stay; he is referred to as "Lord" and addressed as "Your Grace."

His Participation — There is no question today of the Commissioner seeking to interfere in the business of the court. On the opening day, after his Commission and the Royal Letter have been received, he is invited to address the court; on the closing day, in a short speech, he undertakes to report to Her Majesty that the Assembly have concluded their business and have appointed the date and place of the next General Assembly. All that on the business side. On the social side the Lord High Commissioner invites all commissioners with spouses to a Garden Party held in the grounds of Holyoodhouse on the afternoon of the opening Saturday, and throughout the week of the Assembly he entertains small groups to lunch and has dinner parties and receptions in the evenings.

The Purse-Bearer — In constant attendance on the Lord High Commisioner is his Purse-Bearer who, as a symbol of his office, carries over his left arm a magnificently embroidered velvet "purse". His office is an ongoing one, and he is responsible for all the organisation that lies behind the very heavy schedule of public and other engagements that Their Graces have to perform during their stay at the Palace.

ITS MEETINGS

The Assembly of today meet in the Assembly Hall on the Mound on a Saturday in the middle of May as fixed by the previous Assembly before they finally rose. It is important to recognise that the Assembly do not, as would an inferior court, adjourn to meet again next year, but having concluded their business they disband, having, before doing so, fixed time and place for the first meeting of next General Asssembly. Each year sees a different Assembly. The Assembly continues to meet from the Saturday morning till the following Friday evening. Each day represents a new sederunt, and sometimes there is more than one sederunt in a day. The Assembly may suspend their session for a limited period, merely resuming where they had left off when that period is over — each day around 1 o'clock they suspend for an hour in this way. When the business is concluded and the sederunt is at an end the Benediction is pronounced and the Assembly adjourn, to be reconstituted when they meet again.

Opening Devotions — Each sederunt is opened with praise, the reading of the Word and prayer. The ordering of this lies wholly within the domain of the Moderator, the only restriction being that the praise must be chosen from the Metrical Psalms or the Paraphrases, though recently hymns have been used at the opening of the Sunday evening session. The Word, which is read by one of the Clerks, is to-day in the version of the

New English Bible, though there is no rule on the subject. It has on occasion been suggested that hymns should be used, but this was defeated on a division; and on one occasion (I think in 1973) when an organ was to be employed in Assembly praise the instrument (specially overhauled and tuned for the occasion) simply refused to function! The message was taken and we continue to be given the note by the Precentor.

Saturday Morning — On the opening day, after the devotions, the Roll of Assembly having been laid on the table the Moderator says a brief word, concluding by nominating his successor. The new Moderator having been installed acknowledges the good wishes of the court and the Assembly go on to receive the Lord High's Commission and the Royal Letter and to hear the speech of the Lord High Commissioner. Since he is here in room of the Queen the Assembly stand for his address, though it is usual after the opening sentences that commissioners are invited to resume their seats. A number of formal items are then transacted and the Assembly suspend for fifteen minutes, to resume with the report of the Board of Practice and Procedure.

Saturday Evening — There is a Session at 6.30 at which some very important business is overtaken, generally the reports of the Assembly Council and of the Board of Stewardship and Finance.

Sunday — On Sunday morning a Service of Worship is held in St Giles' Cathedral. For Session III of the Assembly we return to the Hall at 6.30, though no formal business will be undertaken. An address is given by the newly-retired Moderator and this is followed by his successor welcoming Delegates and Visitors, three of the Delegates (on a rotational basis) being invited to address the court.

Holy Communion — It used to be that a Celebration of the Sacrament of the Lord's Supper was held in St Giles' Cathedral on Monday morning, but it was found that it was followed by a somewhat undignified rush back to the Hall to secure seats. Indeed to save the scramble an increasing number of Commissioners denied themselves attendance at the Communion Service in favour of the seat in the Hall. So in 1980 the experiment was tried of celebrating Communion in the actual Hall itself, and this was felt to be in every way a more acceptable pattern, so that it has been followed in every subsequent year.

Friday Evening — First the Assembly take the report of the Committee on Deceased Ministers. There is read out a list of the names of all Ministers, Deacons and Deaconesses who have died since last Assembly and prayer is led by the immediate past Moderator. Two Acts are then passed — the first empowering the Board of Practice and Procedure to summon meetings of the Commission as required (see hereunder) and the other appointing the time and place for the next Assembly.

Then there is a presentation to the Moderator (a) of retiring Professors, Missionaries, Chaplains and other Agents, (b) of persons newly appointed to such posts, and (c) of all parish ministers, deacons and deaconesses gone to their first charge in course of the past year. The question has been asked why immediately retired Parish Ministers should be omitted from group (a). I do not know the answer.

The Moderator then briefly addresses the court, to be followed by the Lord High Commissioner who closes his short speech with the words, "Right Reverend and Well-beloved, your labours are now at an end and I shall inform Her Majesty that, having concluded the business for which you were assembled you have passed an Act appointing the next meeting of the General Assembly to be held in Edinburgh on ....; and now in the Queen's name I bid you farewell" A verse of the National Anthem is sung. The Moderator then says to the Assembly, "Right Reverend and Right Honourable, in the Name of the Lord Jesus Christ, sole King and Head of the Church, I now dissolve this General Assembly and appoint the next General Assembly of the Church of Scotland to be held at Edinburgh upon ....." The Benediction is then pronounced and that particular Assembly has become a part of Church history.

I have never understood why the Lord High Commissioner should refer to the "next meeting of the General Assembly" when that is so patently wrong. Yet that is not only what he says, it is how it appears in the minute and presumably in his report to Her Majesty.

THE COMMISSION OF ASSEMBLY

From their earliest days Assemblies have been accustomed to remit matters to be disposed of by Commissioners. "With the single exception of legislation there would appear to be no power belonging to the General Assembly which has not been exercised by Commissioners" (Cox Ed VI, p 201) When Commissions are appointed the Assembly will set the bounds of their authority, and within these limits they are complete masters and act as though they were the Assembly itself. They report to the ensuing Assembly on how they have discharged their remit, but this is merely a recording of diligence and not a submission for approval or ratification. At the same time the Commission is accountable to the General Assembly and censurable by them for any thing done by it in excess of its powers.

Since Assemblies meet at such wide intervals it is good to have some body which may deal with any matter of urgency. So the Commission of Assembly came into being — a body appointed by each Assembly before they rose with instruction to meet in October and February "and oftener when and where they shall think fit and convenient." It consists of the whole membership of the Assembly. It used to include also one other person nominated by the Moderator, but this no longer obtains.

Powers of the Commission — The powers of the Commission of Assembly are defined in Act v of 1981 and are renewed each year, the Commission being appointed — immediately before the next General Assembly is appointed "in terms of Act v 1981." Their quorumn is as for the Assembly, see hereunder. Their powers are as follow:

a) to choose their own Moderator;
b) to dispose of any matter referred to them by or in virtue of any Act or Deliverance of the General Assembly;
c) to dispose of any matter affecting the general interests of the Church at home and abroad when the Church would be adversely affected by postponing consideration to the time of the next General Assembly;
d) to appoint representatives on behalf of the General Assembly when such appointments are required before next General Assembly;
e) to hear and dispose of all References, Dissents and Complaints, Appeals and Petitions brought from the lower courts or referred by the Committee on Unions and Readjustments, including all cases in which the General Assembly is the court of first instance, but excluding cases heard by the Judicial Commission in terms of Act xxii 1960, provided that cases requiring an Act of the General Assembly, and cases in which, in the opinion of the Commission, an important issue of principle is at stake, shall be referred by the Commission to the General Assembly; and all papers in cases brought before the Commission shall be printed and made available to members in the same manner as cases brought before the General Assembly;
f) to receive and consider Overtures proposing changes in the law or practice of the Church and to make representations thereon to the General Assembly; and

g) to appoint a representative or representatives to present any matter referred by the Commission to the General Assembly.

Meetings of the Commission — The position today is that the meetings of the Commission in October and February are to be held only at the instigation of the Board of Practice and Procedure, which may also on its own initiative, or on receipt of a request from any court, or on a requisition of a quorum of the Commission (that is, of the previous Assembly) call additional meetings. When in 1963 there was introduced the system of meeting the expenses of commissioners attendances at the Commission increased considerably — as, naturally, did the expense of holding it. Sometimes there was very little business, on occasion it looked as though considerable ingenuity had been required to frame an agenda. Hence the Act of 1981 since when the Commission have met very rarely indeed.

CONDUCT OF BUSINESSS

Quorum — The quorum of the General Assembly is thirty-one of whom at least sixteen must be Ministers. It is very many years since a count has had to be taken. There is no obligation on either Moderator or Clerk to be sure there is a quorum present. Any member may at any time draw the attention of the Moderator to the fact that in his view there is not a quorum present, and if he does so a count will be taken, and, if appropriate the sederunt will be suspended. As I see it this will have no effect on business transacted before the challenge was made, all of which should be held as regularly done. This view might seem to be contradicted by a decision of the General Assembly that proceedings taken by the Judicial Commission were inept because the number present at the outset of the meeting, while well above the quorum, was one short of the number which the Act required should be present when an appeal is begun. The fault was discovered only when the appeal was being prepared for the Assembly. This, however, was a special case where the Judicial Commission was operating in terms of an Act and where any deviation from these terms could vitiate the whole proceedings. Even at that I am not satisfied it was a sound decision and in any case I do not think it applies as a precedent for the situation where the Assembly has gone on unwittingly without a quorum, which is our present concern.

Standing Orders — The order of debate is governed by the Standing Orders, but the operation of these in regard to any particular item may be suspended in whole or in part on a motion to that effect supported by a two-thirds majority of those voting. Standing Orders may at any time be amended and that on a straight vote, but any proposal so to amend must take the form of an Overture and must have been the subject of at least two days' notice in print in the "Daily Papers".

Order of the Day — Any specific item on the agenda may appear as an Order of the Day for a particular time. The effect of this is that when the appointed hour is reached the business in hand is brought to a close, though a maximum over-run of thirty minutes may at the discretion of the Moderator be allowed for this, after which discussion is suspended. The Assembly then pass to the Order of the Day. Once this has been disposed of the Assembly return to their schedule at the point at which it had been interrupted. On a division in 1990 it was agreed by a majority that instead of saying the item is to be taken at the hour appointed it should read "not later than" the hour appointed. The would-be participant in an Order-of-the-Day item who arrived at the appointed time only to find he was too late might think (as does the writer) that the new form substitutes a pious hope for a guarantee.

Occasionally it happens that the day's programme gets badly out of hand, and in that event the Business Convener will usually intervene with a proposal that a certain item or group of items be held over to a later sederunt. If the Assembly agree to this the Business Convener will, the following morning, lay before the Assembly his Committee's proposals for the realignment of the agenda.

Point of Order — At any point in the course of a speech a commissioner may interrupt with a Call to Order, this representing a challenge to the propriety of what is being said from the point of view of competence, relevance or regularity — but not of veracity. On being so interrupted the speaker must resume his seat though he will normally be given an opportunity should he so desire of showing why he believes himself to be perfectly in order. No other member may speak to the point unless with the permission or at the request of the Moderator with whom the ultimate decision lies — though he may put it to a vote of the Assembly. It was recently agreed that a member challenging competence must be able to quote the number of the Standing Order which he claims is being contravened. I cannot believe this would be strictly enforced. If a speaker is out of order the urgent necessity is to have him stopped — hunting through the Standing Orders for the appropriate number can surely wait.

Further, the challege is that there is a breach of order, not necessarily of Standing Orders.

Character of Motions — All motions are regarded as falling into one of the following four categories, and the Moderator is the final judge as to which:

a) the *Original Motion;*
b) a *Counter-Motion*, being a motion contradictory or negative of the original motion or of a substantial part of it;
c) an *Amendment*, being a motion not substantially contradictory of the original motion or of a counter-motion, but designed to make alterations or additions to or deletions from it without defeating its main object; or
d) an *Amendment to an amendment* already moved.

It should be noted that the Assembly never accept a motion in the form of a "Direct Negative". If you are that way minded you simply vote Against the Motion or Counter-motion and you do so without having to "move" in the matter, though, naturally you may speak to your point.

Motions in groups (c) and (d) are disposed of first on a vote For or Against and may be so dealt with any time after they have been moved and seconded. A vote is then taken between or among the Motions in groups (a) and (b), continuing if need be by dropping out that with the fewest votes until one emerges with a clear majority of all the votes cast. A straight vote For or Against the winner has then to be taken. The same system operates in voting for appointments when there are more than two candidates.

Method of Voting — When a vote has to be taken the Moderator invites the members to stand in their places, first For then Against the amendments, or first For the Motion and then For the Counter-motion or Counter-motions, and he decides and declares which side has the majority. If he is in doubt, or if his decision is challenged, a vote is taken by Papers. Tellers are called up; the Moderator intimates which number of Paper is to be used (a packet of voting-papers having been issued to each commissioner along with the Blue Book etc); and once again he invites members to stand For or Against as the case may be. Papers are collected and counted by the Tellers, the totals are prepared by the Clerks, and the result is declared by the Moderator. In days before Papers were available the Tellers used simply to count those who were on their feet, and it was not unknown for a recount to be caled for. This, in fact, usually resulted in a re-vote, people voting who had abstained first time round, or even changing sides. It would still, I imagine, be in order to demand a recount of the Papers, but this has not so far occurred, and one may be forgiven for hoping it never will. Because of this difficulty of distinguishing a recount from a revote the appropriate Standing Order has been (in 1994) recast by the addition of the words in italics, "If the Moderator is not prepared to give an opinion on the result of a Vote by Standing, or if his opinion is challenged, *and whenever the Assembly are hearing a Case*, the Assembly shall proceed to take a vote by Papers." The phrasing is confusing, but I believe that what is intended is that in a Case no "trial" vote by Standing is to be taken at all — only a vote by papers will be in order.

Casting Vote — The Moderator has no deliberative but only a casting vote, and it is, I think, universally accepted in principle — though there is no binding obligation — that he should cast this in favour of the *status quo*. I can myself recollect only twice when the Moderator has had to exercise his casting vote — on the earlier occasion he ignored the custom and voted in favour of the creation of a new committee (the Advisory Board), and on the later occasion, which was a Readjustment appeal it was argued by some that the Moderator had not voted on the side of the *status quo*, though he himself was (and is) quite convinced that he had!

Dissent — Once a matter has been finally decided it is always open to any member to ask that his dissent be recorded. Since it is the General Assembly that is involved such a dissent cannot institute any process of appeal, the Assembly's decision being final. The member, however, may wish publicly to dissociate himself from what has been resolved. Others are entitled to "adhere to the dissent" and in that case their names will appear in the minute. Two points are to be noted — first that although one's ground of dissent may centre on, for example, some point of procedure against which one had protested at the time it is only when judgment has finally been pronounced that one may ask to have one's dissent recorded; and secondly that you can adhere to the dissent only at the time when it has been taken.

Protestation — At the final sederunt of the Assembly protestation may be taken that because of the failure of an appellant to pursue his case the judgment of an inferior court has now become final.

Special Commission — The Assembly may remit a cause to a Special Commission which they themselves have appointed. The powers of such a body arise from and are strictly limited by the Act or Deliverance appointing it. The Assembly may instruct such a Commission to report to the regular Commission of Assembly, authorising the latter body to deal with any question arising out of the said report.

Committee on Classifying Returns to Overtures — This body consists of the Clerks, the Procurator and the Solicitor, the Principal Clerk being Convener, and it meets on a date not less than four days before the Assembly opens, and it has to report not later than the third day of Assembly on Returns received to Overtures (whether Barrier Act Overtures or others) setting forth not only the numbers of Presbyteries voting but also the numbers voting within these Presbyteries.

ITS BUSINESS — LEGISLATION

The General Assembly is the supreme court of the Church in that it and it alone has power to pass laws that will be binding upon the whole Church and in that it alone can authoritatively declare what the law of the Church is on any subject and on how it is to be interpreted.

Law and Usage — In relation to our behaviour as citizens we are all of us subject to the rule of two different strands of law — first there is the common law, the rules that have never been written down but are universally accepted as binding, spoken of by Lord Stair as "our ancient and immemorial customs"; and, secondly, there is enacted law, mainly the statutes which Parliament produces with such persistent and terrifying regularity. Likewise in the Church there are two sources of law — there is that which comes from long-established usage and there is that which emanates from legislation. Both are equally binding, identical in force and effect. As an example of what is here in mind attention could be drawn to the fact that when in 1966 it was resolved by the Assembly after due Barrier Act procedure that women should be eligible for eldership on the same terms as men there was no Act that could be repealed or amended — it had just been accepted on all hands, and had always been so accepted, that only men became Elders. The same was true, of course, of the admission of women to the ministry. So that, legally speaking, women are Ministers and Elders by virtue of statute, men by virtue of immemorial usage.

The Assembly is the body which enacts statute law and declares what has the force of law as a result of long usage.

The Barrier Act — A most significant restriction on the legislative power of the Assembly is imposed by the Barrier Act of 1697 which requires that before the Assembly can pass any deliverance which is to constitute "a binding law and constitution upon the Church" it must first have sent it to Presbyteries as an Overture and have secured a majority of these in favour. The operation of the Act is set forth in detail at p 358, the point here at stake being that the Assembly is restricted in its function of law-making by a power of veto vested in Presbyteries. They cannot themselves make a law, but they can prevent the Assembly from doing so in any particular set of circumstances.

Other Acts — Not all Assembly Acts have to "go down to Presbyteries" — there are Acts erecting new parishes, Acts setting bounds for Presbyteries, Acts approving budgets for Mission and Aid, Acts adopting regulations for the administration of funds, Acts anent signing of deeds, etc. This kind of legislation originates in most cases with an Assembly Committee, appearing in the report of that Committee, the text of the proposed Act being presented as an Appendix. It is passed as a simple Deliverance on the report of the Committee concerned, and, once passed, it has the same force and effect as an Act having Barrier Act approval. Unless it itself specifies otherwise, an Act is to be taken as becoming effective immediately it is passed.

Declaratory Acts — Occasionally the Assembly pass a Declaratory Act, this being an Act which does not make law but declares what the law is on some subject. Usually such an Act is passed "for the avoidance of doubt." For example, Act iii of 1972 which introduced compulsory retiral for Ministers at age 70 stated that this wouild not in any way affect the existing rights of any Minister appointed to a charge before its passing. It was clear that a question would arise as to the position of a Minister admitted to Charge A before the passing of the Act and who in consequence of readjustment had after the effective date been introduced as Minister of Charge AB — had he sacrificed his rights *ad vitam aut culpam*? The Declaratory Act vi of 1975 did not confer this right, it merely made it clear beyond doubt that Miniser AB had not done so.

The Act enshrining the Declaratory Articles is properly a Declaratory Act, for, as it is at pains to point out, the Church-State relationship which it outlines is not created by, nor does it owe its existence to, the Act of 1921 — repeal that Act and the rights would still be there. The student of this particular aspect of the constitution of the Kirk is directed to Paragraph 1504 of the Stair Encyclopaedia where Lord Davidson deals at length with the ramifications of Ballantyne *v* Wigtown Presbytery (1936 Session Cases p 625).

Regulations — A great many of the administrative affairs of the Church are governed by Regulations approved by the General Assembly. Such Regulations will usually be found incorporated in Acts, but not necessarily so. They have, however, the same force and effect as Acts of Assembly.

Injunctions — There are times when in course of a Deliverance the Assembly go so far as to "instruct" or to "enjoin" that something be done or left undone, and failure to comply is a most serious affair constituting contempt. It seems to me that injunction should be resorted to to cope with an immediate and one-off situation — such as enjoining that returns be made by Presbyteries to a questionnaire, but that if what is in view is something that is to be a binding restriction on freedom it should more properly be made the subject of an Act. A section of a Deliverance in 1975 taken from a report on National Lotteries went on (more or less in passing) to "instruct all congregations to avoid recourse to lotteries, raffles, or other such means of raising funds for Christian purposes". Apart from the fact that Kirk Sessions rather than congregations might have been thought to be the proper bodies to be instructed, it seems unfortunate that something which is to be a binding rule upon the Church should be imposed in so comparatively informal and casual a fashion. Since the above was written the emergence of the National Lottery of 1995 has brought this whole subject very sharply into focus.

ITS BUSINESS — LITIGATION

The General Assembly is the supreme court of appeal in all matters of litigation — there is no higher ecclesiastical authority to which the disgruntled litigant can turn, and he cannot look for help to the civil courts for they have no jurisdiction. Further, there are only a very few matters which cannot be taken to the Assembly, the exceptions being those cases where finality of judgment has been specifically reserved to the Kirk Session, and to Presbyteries. The routes by which such cases may be brought to the Assembly are (a) Appeal, (b) Dissent and Complaint, (c) Petition, and (d) Reference — and these are dealt with in full at p 264 ff.

When the General Assembly turn their attention to a case the Standing Orders are very strictly observed. Before either party is heard the Clerk makes an announcement in these terms, "The Commissioners are reminded that justice demands that all pleadings at the bar should be heard by all those who vote in this case, and that their judgment should be made wholly on the basis of the pleadings." And then immediately before the vote is taken the Clerk further announces, "The Commissioners are reminded that only those who have heard all the pleadings at the bar are entitled to vote in this case." In view of all this it is clearly out of order for anyone to give Notice of Motion with regard to a case. And with a view to ensuring that no-one participates who has missed out on any part of the proceedings the doors are usually kept closed and anyone who leaves is not allowed re-admittance. Any audible expression of approval — or the opposite — by clapping, stamping or scraping of feet etc is very seriously frowned upon.

Nobile Officium — The General Assembly as supreme court have a power, as has the Court of Session, to deal with the *casus improvisus*, to make good the absence of law (p 276).

The Judicial Commission

It must be apparent that the General Assembly is a body ill-equipped to deal with cases, at least when they are of any complexity. A bench of thirteen hundreed judges is a difficult point from which to start. Beyond the minutes of inferior courts and *ex parte* statements from the contestants there is no printed material in the hands of members that they can study in advance (for a recent exception to this see "Answers" on p 267); there is no procedure for taking the testimony of witnesses; and the Assembly do not have limitless time to devote to any single case. Where you have a trial by libel, for example, many hours could be required, and indeed in an earlier day for the court to be sitting on into the not too small hours of the morning wrestling with a case was a not unusual occurrence.

In an attempt to help in this situation an Act (viii) was passed in 1940 creating an entirely new body, the Judicial Commission, which would have the duty of hearing and determining appeals coming up from the inferior courts affecting the character and conduct of Ministers (not when the matter centres upon doctrine) but which would have no jurisdiction to propose, determine or pronounce sentence or penalties. The Commission were to be masters of the facts but of nothing more. Clearly the idea was the admirable one of relieving the Assembly as such of the difficult and tedious business of staging a trial, but leaving with the Assembly the whole matter of deciding what should be done in the circumstances as these had been elecited by the Commission.

Reference is made elsewhere to Act xxi of 1960 anent Congregations in an Unsatisfactory State (p 338). Section 7 of that Act provides that the findings and final judgment of the Presbytery in a case where the pastoral tie had been dissolved "shall be subject to appeal or complaint only to the Judicial Commission of the General Assembly." The new Act (i,1988) likewise provides that "the procedure, Basis of Facts, and final judgment of the Presbytery shall be subject to appeal or dissent and complaint only to the Judicial Commission of the General Assembly." To cope with the new situation in 1960 a fresh Act (xxi) of that year was passed. The matter is now covered by Acts i and ii of 1988.

The Commission is to consist of forty-eight members appointed by the Assembly, retiring after four years and eligible for re-appointment only after a blank year, one member is appointed by the Assembly to be Chairman and one to be Vice-Chairman, and they serve for five years in these capacities. Any sixteen members will form a quorum, but no case is to begun unless twenty-four members are present. The Chairman has a casting vote only. The Procurator may not act on the Commission, but the Clerks of Assembly act as its Clerks.

The Commission is to hear appeals (1) against the decisions of inferior courts (including procedure, findings, final judgment and sentence — except that where sentence alone is involved the matter goes direct to the Assembly), and (2) against decisions of Presbyteries in all cases arising anent congregations in an unsatisfactory state.

Act xix of 1989 is to apply to appeals; at the commencement of the hearing the appellant may object to any member of the Commission taking part, showing cause, and the remaining Commissioners shall be judges of whether such complaint should be sustained; when deemed approprate witnesses are to be heard, being examined on oath, and upon conclusion of the hearing (which shall normally proceed *de die in diem* without interruption) the findings and final judgment of the Judicial

Commission are to be committed to writing, read over to the Commission and signed by the Chairman before the meeting is closed. This Report is to be transmitted to the General Assembly, but is not subject to review by that body whose sole responsibility is that of determining and passing an appropriate sentence or taking other appropriate action.

It seems to me that there will always be difficulty in libel cases and these will arise from the artificiality of striving to keep the facts of the case separate from the determination of the degree and character of the guilt involved and therefore of what represents an appropriate sentence. The Assembly are told that the party has been guilty of certain offences. A plea in mitigation — a far from impartial statement — has been offered. Inspired by this a member of Assembly immediately enquires for detail regarding some part of the story. He is told in effect that this is none of his business and he instantly complains as to how he is to determine sentence if he does not know the answer to his question. On the other hand he may be given an answer to his question and someone else follows up with a supplementary question, and before you know what is afoot the Assembly are engaged in a trial — this time a trial of the Judicial Commission on the rightness of their judgment! Now it is true that in the civil realm the jury are masters of the facts and decision on appropriate sentence lies with the judge; but the so-significant difference is that His Lordship has heard all the evidence and is conversant with the minutest detail of the case — he is not simply presented with a sheet of paper setting forth the facts as proved, as is the Assembly in similar circumstances. I well know how jealous are the Assembly of their right to have the last word in any case and of the member to take his case (all of it) to Caesar, but to me this is a realm where the Assembly have to delegate their power in its entirety or else accept the responsibility for conducting a trial with all that that entails — there is no satisfactory middle way.

ITS BUSINESS — ADMINISTRATION

This may be a convenient point at which to state that while it may not strictly be an administrative function of the General Assembly it is that court which has the responsibility for ensuring that adequate records are maintained by its own Standing Committees. This duty it discharges by calling for the production of all such records at Assembly time, and for arranging for these to be examined and attested by a group of sub-committees. Before the close of the Assembly an omnibus report is presented on the position.

The minutes of Assembly proceedings are presented each day from Tuesday onwards in the "Daily Papers" and are submitted for approval each morning at the outset of the day's business. Among the last things done by the Assembly is to appoint the Clerks "a committee to revise the minutes", those which have not yet appeared in print being taken as read and approved. To assist the Clerks in this task there is a "Verbatim Report" which has been taken by shorthand writers throughout the whole Assembly and which is finally extended and made available for reference at all times in the Clerks' Office at 121 George Street. It is hard to believe that there was a time when this report used to be printed in full and distributed to Commissioners, Presbytery Clerks, and others; but the years of war brought that to an end, and rising printing costs have ensured that it has never been — nor is ever likely to be — revived. Indeed at the time of writing it looks as though the verbatim report is about to be a museum piece — in its place we are to have a video film and a recorded sound-track! The main administrative functioning of the Assembly is represented in the Reports of its various Committees as these, page after page of them, are printed in the Blue Book year by year; and while all of that is properly part of the business of the General Assembly in the field of administration it is so very extensive, not to say complicated, as to demand a chapter to itself. So that the whole of what follows in the next chapter could be said to belong properly to this one.

Chapter 14

THE ASSEMBLY COMMITTEES

PRESBYTERIANISM AS A FORM of Church government was designed for the administration of an organisation the whole of whose activities were confined within its parishes, each of which was more or less self-contained and enjoyed a large measure of autonomy. Its initiatives almost all came from the perimeter, and its objective was that the ordinances of religion should be available to the people in every corner of Scotland completely free of any charge. For that purpose the design was both adequate and admirable.

Emergence of Committee System — It was in the latter half of the nineteenth century that the Church first began — not without many grave misgivings and much hesitation — to feel a sense of wider responsibility — for overseas mission, for example. This was something which had to be tackled by the Church as a whole, for obviously it could not be administered at parish level. The parishes had their part to play in furnishing the necessary funds, in creating interest, in maintaining enthusiasm, but the whole administration had to be centralised. And so the Assembly appointed a Committee of their own number to do this job, always under their own direction and control. With the passing of the years the number of such "outside" interests grew, with a consequent steady increase in the number of Committees. The Committee system had come to stay. The Year Book for 1950 records no fewer than sixty-five Committees all reporting directly to Assembly — twenty-five Standing and forty Special Committees.

Assembly Committees, however powerful they may sometimes appear, are all the creatures of the Assembly, and to that body they have all to report and from that body they have to take instruction. In all of these affairs the General Assembly are, of course, the court of first instance as well as the final court of appeal. Which can make things very awkward when a Presbytery is at variance with a Committee on some item, for in effect the Assembly when it comes to appeal is sitting as judge in its own cause.

Committee Reports — Each Committee submits to the Assembly each year a report the text of which is printed in the "Blue Book" that goes to all commissioners a fortnight or so in advance, and there is provision whereby a Supplementary Report may be submitted as a separate print, and no report will be received by the Assembly unless it is printed and in the hands of members. (Standing Orders express this in an odd way by saying "Verbal reports shall not be received" without telling us how they are to be expressed!) In its report the Committee explains and comments upon what it has been doing and what it is proposing to do, seeking Assembly approval for both. In the print the Report is preceded by a Proposed Deliverance, this being a series of numbered paragraphs covering each item of the Report and committing the Assembly, having "received" the whole report to "instruct" or "encourge" or "urge" or "approve" or whatever it may be, each item in turn.

It is not possible for the Assembly to change the terms of a report, though they may, of course, disapprove of it and even dissociate themselves from it. In that case they will amend the Deliverance in such a way as to reflect their attitude to what the report says. The report, after all, is a statement of what the Committee believed when it prepared it, and nothing the Assembly can do at a subsequent date can alter that. What usually happens if there is serious disapproval is that the Assembly sends the whole thing back to the Committee for further consideration and a revised report and recommendation.

COMMITTEE STRUCTURE

If on every occasion when a new need arises, or a fresh field opens up, an additional committee is created then clearly the time will come when the Assembly will have a plethora of committees. So from time to time the Assembly take a long hard look at the committee situation as it has come to be with a view to rationalising the structure, increasing its efficiency and reducing its cost. Major changes were effected following upon the activities of a special committee set up in the late 'forties under Professor John Baillie and given the ambitious task, "To Interpret God's Will in the Present Crisis." Then again in the early 'sixties, at a time when business consultants were increasingly being engaged by large firms and by local authorities to advise on organisation, a special committee under Dr William M'Nicol consulted such technical advisers (without finding them very helpful, the complexity of the system defied even their understanding) and came forward with a comprehensive programme of reorganisation. It was in 1971 that a Committee was appointed (known latterly as "the Committee of Forty") with the remit "to interpret for the Church the purpose towards which God is calling His People in Scotland, to investigate and assess the resources of the Church in persons and property for the fulfilment of this purpose, and to make recommendations for the reshaping of the life and structure of the Church." The researches of this Committee led in due course to a review carried out by the Assembly Council. Though the study began in 1981 it was three years later that a new structure began to operate. The principle envisaged was that of a series of Boards embracing all the various comittees, though in practice the material proved rather intractable in this regard and adjustments and deviations had to be made. In the final set-up, for example, the term "Board" was used in three different senses — (a) as the equivalent of Department (Board of World Mission and Unity), (b) to define a co-ordinating committee within a Department (Board of Ministry and Mission), and (c) to refer to a single uncomplicated Committee (Board of Practice and Procedure). The emergence in 1981 of the Assembly Council opened a new chapter in the story of re-organisation, and each year now we have the results and recommendations of that body's researches into some area of the Kirk's administration.

The position at the time of writing (1994) is briefly set out hereunder, though no guarantee is given that the account has completely caught up with things as they are or that the pattern will not have changed while the book is still in the hands of the printer!

ADMINISTRATION AND SPECIAL INTERESTS

The Commitees here grouped together form a quite irregular department in that they do not in any sense cohere to form a single unit, they have no common interest and no shared staff, there is no co-ordinating body within the Department, and each presents its own individual report to the Assembly. They are mainly committees each of which has a very important remit but one which will not fit neatly into a slot as part of a larger unit, and so they are gathered into a Department which is really not a Department so much as simply a "Collection".

Board of Practice and Procedure — This is the successor to the General Administration Committee and is still properly a Committee even though it is called a Board. Its function is well enough summarised in its old title — "General Administration". It has the following official remit —

a) To advise the General Assembly on Church Law and on Constitutional Law affecting the relationship between Church and State.
b) To advise and assist Committees of the General Assembly in the preparation of proposed legislation and on questions of interpretation.
c) To make all necessary arrangements for the General Assembly each year.
d) To advise the Moderator anent his official duties, if so required.
e) To be responsible to the General Assembly for the care and maintenance of all Assembly buildings and other property — but see hereunder p 398.
f) To compile the statistics of the Church, except Youth and Finance; and to supervise on behalf of the General Assembly all arrangements for the care of Church records, and for quinquennial visitations.
g) To act for the General Assembly in connection with proposals to sell surplus Communion Plate.
h) To attend to the general interests of the Church in matters which are not covered by the remit of any other committee; and to perform such other duties as may be assigned to it by Act or Deliverance of the General Assembly.

This Committee is always first to report to the General Assembly. The Principal Clerk is its Secretary and its Convener is, I think invariably, appointed Convener of the Business Committee of the General Assembly.

The Assembly Council — For many years it had been strongly felt in a number of quarters that there should be a body with an overall responsibility for committee business, accompanied by a measure of overriding authority; but on the other side committees were extremely jealous of their autonomy, claiming that they were answerable to the Assembly and to that court alone, and bitterly resisting the introduction of any intermediate body. Dr M'Nicol's Committee on the Review of Administration (referred to above) brought forward a proposal to establish a "Church Council" whose general purpose would be "to seek the greatest possible unity and effectiveness in the work and witness of the

Church as far as these are the direct responsibility of the General Assembly and their Committees." The detailed proposals were considered by Presbyteries which showed a distinct lack of enthusiasm while at the same time indicating a measure of agreement "that some form of co-ordinating body was essential." It was agreed that cconsideration of the problem be continued. This resulted in 1965 in the appearance of a fresh proposal for the reconsitution of the Advisory Board with both an advisory and a consultative function, and, thanks to the casting vote of the Moderator, this was approved. The Board's business generally was to be that of overseeing and co-ordinating the work of all the Committees, and in particular monitoring the engagement of ministerial staff. Indeed one of the most pressing reasons for introducing such a Board was anxiety about the tendency of the Committees to employ more and more Ministers, who at that time were in short supply, at the expense of the parishes. Considering that a good part of the membership of this Board consisted of the officials of the Committees whose activities it was to oversee and restrict it is not surprising that its progress was far from spectacular!

In 1981 in face of a good deal of bitter opposition the Assembly Council was appointed and the Advisory Board discharged. The Council's remit is set forth in Act vi of 1980 as amended by Act viii of 1981, and is as follows —

a) To establish a system of operating and servicing Boards as described in the Report, and to review periodically the structure by which the General Assembly delegates responsibility for those functions it determines shall be controlled centrally.
b) To keep under review the size and organisation of the staff at the Church Offices.
c) To establish a Management Committee to co-ordinate the work of the central organisation.
d) To appoint a Secretary to the Council, and to approve proposals for the appointment of secretaries and senior officials by the Boards.
e) To co-ordinate the policies of the Boards.
f) To advise the General Assembly on the relative importance of work in various fields.
g) To advise the General Assembly on those matters which can effectively be devolved from the central organisation to Presbyteries.
h) To check that resources, are or can be expected to be, available to support proposals before the General Assembly.
i) To evaluate the progress and effectiveness of the work of the Boards.

j) To deal with urgent issues arising between meetings of the General Assembly or Commission of Assembly, which do not fall within the remit of any Board, provided that

(1) It shall not be competent for the Council to take or authorise any action which is

(i) of such a nature that it would have been *ultra vires* of the Commission of Assembly; or

(ii) of a legislative or judicial nature; or

(iii) an order or instruction to any Court or Committee of the Church.

(2) Any action taken in terms of this clause shall be reported by the Council to the next meeting of the General Assembly or Commission of Assembly, whichever is the sooner.

In 1991 there was added to the tasks of the Assembly Council "All matters relating to Health and Safety at Work in the Church Offices, and the care, maintenance and amenity of the Church Offices, inlcluding the provision of service thereto and the allocation of accommodation among the various Boards and Committees of the Church." This had been the responsibility of the Board of Stewardship and Finance.

The General Trustees — This is very much the odd-man-out, for it is not an Assembly Committee in any strict sense but a body of trustees appointed in terms of an Act of Parliament and standing in a relationship to the Assembly comparable to that in which trustees stand to the beneficiaries under the trust.

Over the years since their emergence the various Committees of the Church had acquired considerable property of a heritable nature in the shape of offices, homes, hostels, dwelling-houses for secretaries, and so on, as well as trusts and other property bequeathed in terms of wills; and all these properties were held under a variety of deeds and by many different groups of trustees on many of which the same Assembly officials appeared *ex officiis*. It was generally recognised that only advantage could accrue from having a holding body in which all the property of the various Committees could be vested, with the result that in 1921 the General Trustees were created under the Church of Scotland (General Trustees) Order Confirmation Act of that year. In that original constitution they consisted of eleven Trustees, three of them Ministers, the others being all from the field of law. They were to report to the General Assembly when vacancies occurred in their ranks and the Assembly were given power to remove trustees from office, or to appoint trustees either as replacements or as additions. All had, and still have, to be either Ministers or Elders of the Church of Scotland.

When in preparation for the Union of 1929 it was envisaged that the Church would be taking into its own hand the various properties hitherto provided and maintained by the heritors in all the parishes of Scotland the General Trustees represented the obvious body into whose ownership to transfer these various assets. Accordingly the 1925 Property and Endowments Act provided that the General Trustees would hold a statutory title to Churches, Manses, Glebes, Burial Grounds and other heritable properties of which the heritors were divesting themselves. They were, however, no longer to be merely holding trustees, they had become administrative trustees. To them also was transferred the ownership of the heritable property of *quoad sacra* parishes. Burial grounds, the property of the heritors, were transferred to the Parish Council; those belonging to *quoad sacra* parishes were normally transfered to the General Trustees, but an Act of 1933 made provision whereby they could require the local authority to take over, and in most cases this has now been done. Where a Church was situated in a graveyard so taken over adequate right of access had to be provided. As the years have passed more and more of the Church's property has found its way into the hands of the General Trustees, while on the other side most of those properties originally transferred to the Trustees in 1921 have now been moved to the Church of Scotland Trust (see hereunder).

While in terms of the Act trustees are appointed by the Assembly this is not, as with other Committees, on the recommendation of the Nomination Committee but on that of the Trustees themselves, and appointments are not made for a period of years but until death, resignation or disqualification (ceasing to be a Minister or Elder of the Church of Scotland is such a disqualification, as, since 1995, is having passed one's seventy-fifth birthday). They elect their own Chairman and Vice-Chairman (who are in receipt of a small honorarium), and in terms of the Act they appoint a Secretary who is a solicitor. Each year they report to the Assembly, which in terms of the Act has power to make by-laws and regulations and these the Trustees are bound to observe.

They have to approve of any proposals for the sale or let of any property vested in them, and indeed any such transaction is carried out at their hand, and they make determinations regarding the disposal and use of proceeds; they operate a Central Fabric Fund and a Consolidated Loan Fund which make grants and loans respectively towards the cost of repairs to property vested in them; they hold moneys got from the sale of congregational property usually as fabric funds for the congregations concerned but see next paragraph (in the case of glebes it is the Consolidated Stipend Fund which benefits from the proceeds of such sales); they operate the Consolidated Stipend Endowment Fund which ingathers all teind stipend; they act as, in effect, factors for all glebes, regularly revising rents, trienially in the case of those held on full agricultural tenancies, collecting these and making them over to the Maintenance of the Ministry Committee; and they are responsible for the Church of Scotland Insurance Company Limited, a company wholly owned by the Church and whose profits are applied for Church purposes. Over and above these specific duties the General Trustees exercise a general supervision of all matters affecting the property of the Church — see Chapter on Property and Finance.

It seems likely that in the very near future changes will be made in regard to the use of the Special Funds created over the years through the sale of heritable property — in particular the Central Fabric Fund will deal with both grants and loans, and funds reserved exclusively for fabric or for stipend may be made available for more general purposes. But the above represents the present position.

Church of Scotland Trust — This trust was created by Act of Parliament in 1932 and further confirmed in 1948, 1958, and 1985. Heritable property of the United Free Church had latterly been vested in a body of general trustees of that Church, while, as was indicated earlier, the heritable property belonging to the Committees etc of the Church of Scotland had come to be vested in the General Trustees. All of this property was transferred into the name of the Church of Scotland Trust.

Since 1991 the Trust has been pursuing proposals for the future long-term administration of the properties, heritable and moveable, vested in it. The main objectives were —

a) to create a new statutory corporation (to be known as "Church of Scotland Investors Trust") with modern powers of administration, and to transfer to that body the whole investments currently held by the Trust; and
b) to transfer all the heritable properties in Scotland vested in the Trust to the Church of Scotland General Trustees to be held by them on the same basis as at present.

Appliction to Parliament was required to create a Statutory Order, and this proved a time-consuming exercise, but has now resulted in the appearance of the Church of Scotland (Properties and Investments) Order Confirmation Act 1994 setting up the Church of Scotland Trust and the Church of Scotland Investors Trust.

This latter Trust offers an investment service to congregations and committees of the Church. It operates three funds — a Deposit Fund suitable for short-term investment (repayable on demand); (b) a Growth Fund (previously known as the General Investment Fund) operating on a unitised basis; and (c) an Income Fund designed for long-term capital, also operating on a unitised basis.

Personnel Committee — This body, which was set set up in 1978, determines salaries, length of service and conditions generally for Secretaries and other members of the Office Staff and that without regard to their geographical place of service. It has no responsibility for the staff of the Board of Social Service but the staff of all other Boards — at St Ninian's, at St Colm's. at Badenoch, at Carberry etc are embraced. The Assembly of 1991 added a provision whereby annually in consultation with the Assembly Council it should agree the total salaries budget for the coming year for that section of staff for which it is the employing agency. It also carries oversight of the Cafe Lounge which functions within the Offices.

Board of Nomination to Church Chairs — This is a body constituted in terms of the Universities (Scotland) Act 1932 which provides that appointments to Chairs in the Faculties of Divinity of the Scottish Universities are to be made on the nomination of a board of nomination elected in equal numbers by the University and the General Assembly — provided such nomination is agreed to by two-thirds of the board. While the position today is that there are few Chairs to which appointments are being made but there are some Senior Lecturer posts to which appontments are made in terms as above. The Board is answerable to the Assembly for its actions and if it has approved an appointment which is not acceptable to the Assembly then it may as a Board be censured, but there is nothing the Assembly can do to overturn the appointment once made.

Nomination Committee — This a Committee of forty-four, twenty of them appointed by Presbyteries, whose duty it is to submit to the General

Assembly proposals of persons to serve on the Boards and Committees of the Church.

Board of Stewardship and Finance — Though now a Board this was established as a Department in 1983 on the recommendation of the Assembly Council after long exploration of possibilities and consultation with parties. It represents the fusion of two separate Committees, (a) the General Finance Committee which had been responsible for administering the financial affairs of the Church generally, for running the offices, for paying the expenses of those Committees which are not fund-raising, for meeting the expenses of the Assembly and their Commissions, and for paying the "membership fees" to ecumenical bodies; and (b) the Stewardship and Budget Committee which had been a product of the Co-ordinated Appeal and which took to do with budgeting for and funding what used to be called the "Schemes of the Church", with the added responsibility of encouraging the spirit of stewardship throughout the Church as a whole.

The outlays of the General Finance Committee had been charged to the General Purposes Fund, and had been met by collection through Presbyteries of what were called "Assembly dues", and what was in the long run simply a first charge on congregations. The income for the Stewardship Committee came mainly from congregational contributions to the Mission and Service Fund. Along with these two funds there now goes the cost of ministry, representing one all-inclusive assessment upon congregations under the name of "Mission and Aid Fund". The Board has a primary duty of promoting an understanding of Christian stewardship and in every practical way possible of assisting congregations and Presbsyteries in their efforts to foster and encourage such stewardship. The most recent expression of the remit of the Board is in these terms:

1 To promote teaching and understanding of Christian Stewardship throughout the Church. To provide programmes to assist congregations in visitng members, making known the work of the Church and promoting Christian giving. To help congregations through the service of its Field Staff in running conferences, advising office-bearers, and training visitors.

2 To prepare a Co-ordinated Budget for the costs of the Ministry and the Mission and Aid Fund and to submit it to the General Assembly each year for approval, together with a projected Financial Plan for the next four years.

3 To be responsible with the Ministry Department and Presbyteries for

allocating among congregations the Co-ordinated Budget approved by the General Assembly and to seek to ensure that congregations meet their obligations by transmitting regularly throughout the year to the General Treasusrer of the Church contributions towards their allocations.

4 To provide financial, administrative and accounting services for the General Assembly, the Boards and Commitees of the Church.

The Board has a duty to report annually to the General Assembly on the general financial position of the Church and has powers to examine the financial and statistical information of such Boards and Committees of the General Assembly as the Board may consider appropriate. The Board exercises control of the General Treasurer's Department and the Stewardship Department and maintains a close liaison with the Church of Scotland General Trustees and with the Church of Scotland Trust, which is serviced by officials of the Board.

Church and Nation Committee — This body, the presentation of whose report can be counted on to provide one of the debating highlights of the Assembly, operates through sub-committees on International Interests, Economic Interests, Social Interests, Scottish Interests, Church Interests, Mass Media. The function of the Committee was defined in the year of its inception 1919) as "to watch over developments of the national life in which moral and spiritual considerations specially arise, and to consider what action the Church may from time to time be advised to take to further the highest interests of the people." It would be hard to conceive a wider or a less specific remit, but the occasional attempt to restrict the scope of the Committee's activities has met with little success — as did a fairly recent attempt to bring its activities completely to a halt.

In answer to an instruction from the General Assembly of 1992 the Assembly Council "conducted a review of the Church and Nation Committee", presenting its report in 1994. This runs to seventeen pages of the Blue Book with a Deliverance containing no fewer than fourteen items and substantially confirming the policy presently being followed by the Committee and in particular continuing the remit in the precise terms of 1919 as quoted above. It is not without interest that in 1992, for example, out of fifty-seven deliverances advanced by the Committee while twenty-five were directed to urging H M Government to take fairly specific steps only ten could on the most generous interpretation be said to indicate "what steps the Church might be taking to further the highest interests of the people."

Panel on Doctrine — In 1959 two Overtures came to the Assembly from different Presbyteries, one anent Ordination to the Ministry and the other anent the Office of the Elder. Both were accepted. The practice had been in such cases to appoint an *ad hoc* commitee to deal with each such matter, but that year it was argued that it would be advantageous were there to be one standing committee to which such issues could be referred — it would avoid needless duplication in research, and even on occasion contradiction in conclusion. Following consideration by the General Administration Committee there was set up, the following year, a Panel on Doctrinal Matters with a remit which in 1976 at the Panel's request was adjusted as "the responsibilities" of the Panel, in the following terms —

a) To receive from the General Assembly remits on matters concerning doctrine and to make suitable arrangements for the fulfilling of them.
b) To draw the attention of the General Assembly to matters inside the Church of Scotland or elsewhere which might have significant doctrinal implications and which might affect members of the Church of Scotland, and to make representations to the General Assembly as to the action to be taken.
c) To be available for consultation by Committees of the General Assembly on any matter which might be of doctrinal significance.
d) To assist, on request, Committees of the General Assembly which are endeavouring to co-ordinate their work in similar doctrinal areas.
e) To communicate and consult on matters involving doctrine, in association with other interested Committees of the General Assembly, with bodies outside the Church of Scotland, such as the World Council of Churches and the World Alliance of Reformed Churches.
f) To inform the General Assembly if the expense of any of these undertakings be more than £100 a year, exclusive of travelling expenses, and to await the instructions of the Assembly.
g) To report each year to the General Assembly.

As from October 1994 this Panel shares, with the Panel on Worship and the Advisory Committee on Artistic Matters the services of a full-time Secretary.

Panel on Worship — Until the reorganisation of 1984 this was the Committee on Public Worship and Aids to Devotion, and it is responsible for the production of Ordinal and Service Books and for the occasional

Order of Service for special events. It might be said to hold a watching brief for the whole liturgical side of the life of the Church. See Note above re Secretary. See also p 150.

The Assembly of 1994 approved a statement regarding the remit of the Panel in these terms (Repts 1994, p 119) — "The Panel on Worship exists to witness to the importance of worship as a primary function of the Church. Through its several Committees it is responsible for the preparation of contemporary liturgies in English and Gaelic, the development of Church music and musicianship, and a deepening of personal and devotional life. The Panel co-operates with all other Boards of the Church on matters relating to public worship, and enables the musical education of Candidates for the Ministry."

The Woman's Guild — The aim of the Woman's Guild is to unite the women of the Church in the dedication of their lives to the Lord Jesus Christ through worship, fellowship and service. Membership is open to all women who accept this aim. It is organised in Branches and Young Women's Groups who meet by authority of the Kirk Sessions concerned. Branches and Groups meet together in Presbyterial Councils which send representatives to the Central Council, the decision-making body, which meets twice a year and which since 1964 has reported directly to the General Assembly. Prior to that the Report of the Woman's Guild appeared as a kind of insert in the Report of General Administration.

DEPARTMENT OF MINISTRY

The 1929 Basis and Plan of Union envisaged two Departments — a Church and Ministry Department embracing the work of (a) Maintenance of the Ministry, (b) Aged and Infirm Ministers' Fund and Pension Fund, and (c) Union of Congregations and Readjustment of Agencies; and a Home Department taking care of (a) Home Mission, (b) Church and Manse Building later to include Church Extension, and (c) Highlands and Islands. It was established on this pattern and so, with minor adjustments, it continued over a long period. In 1984, however, these two bodies were united to form the Department of Ministry and Mission. Practical difficulties were experienced in the operation of this body and the Assembly of 1989 agreed that as from 1st January 1990 there should again be two Departments, one of Ministry and the other of National Mission. To the former was given the remit of equipping and maintaining those engaged in the ministry, of taking pastoral care of them and their families, of overseeing their retirement, of taking oversight of Licentiates, and seeking to assist Probationers in search of a first charge and Ministers looking for a change of charge. The five Committees through which it functions are responsible to a Board which co-ordinates their work, approves their budgets and handles all matters relating to staffing etc.

Committee on the Maintenance of the Ministry — The responsibilities of this Committee are defined as —

a) To determine and declare the Minimum Stipend (see p 196 ff).
b) To advise the Church in matters relating to stipend levels and arrangements.
c) To deal with appropriate matters relating to endowments.
d) To deal with appropriate matters relating to allowances, expenses, loans, and the like for which those engaged in ministry in the Church and their families are, or may be, eligible.
e) The pastoral care of all in the Ministry insofar as centralised co-ordination and support are desired or required.
f) To advise the Church on particular topics relating to Ministry, such as study leave.
g) To administer the James M'Kechnie Bequest.

The Committee administers the Maintenance of the Ministry Fund which consists of stipend endowments, congregational payments towards stipend, legacies, gifts, and all other sources. Under an arrangement approved in 1981 the General Trustees are now responsible for the ingathering of all stipend endowments and investing these through the Church of Scotland Trust. The Committee in turn makes grants to assist poorer congregations which have accumulated some capital or come into some through a bequest to increase their stipend endowment (p 201). Until 1986 each self-supporting congregation contributed Aid to the Fund as agreed in their Vacancy Schedule, but since then this sum is included in the congregation's giving to the Mission and Aid Fund (p 22). The Committee is also responsible since 1991 for the payment of Centralised Travelling Expenses, for giving help towards the purchase of a car, and for providing funding to allow the Main Pension Fund to make payment of the Death-in-Service Grant presently fixed at the level of three times the Minimum Stipend, and for *ex gratia* payments to spouses of Ministers who die on or after attaining Normal Retiring Date or in retirement.

Probationers Committee — This used to be the Committee on Probationers and Transference and Admission of Ministers and it had four main areas of activity — (a) it accepted responsibility for probationers once their period of compulsory probation had been served until their settlement in a charge or appointment; (b) it operated a scheme to assist with the transference of ministers desiring a change of parish; (c) it was responsible for dealing with those from other denominations seeking admission to the ministry of the Kirk; and (d) it organised and was responsible for oversight of the arrangements for pulpit supply. In 1990 it was relieved of (c) and in 1993 of (b) (see Reps 1993 p 107). Now it is responsible for the care of probationers from the beginning of their probationary period and until their settlement.

Housing and Loan Fund — In 1965 the Assembly recommended the setting up of a Retired Ministers' House Fund "to help ministers .... to purchase houses and to make additional provision for ministers' widows." A widespread appeal was issued but met with a poor response. Maintenance of the Ministry had, however, made a grant of £25,000. Aged and Infirm Ministers' Fund had put up £40,000 and the Baird Trust had made a further generous promise. By 1969 £100,000 had been gathered, but by that time, of course, this was quite inadequate. Three years later the sum had risen to £181,000, administered by a Trust, and even at that loans were restricted to a maximum £2000 — a quite derisory figure in face of house values. By 1979 considerable progress had been made, the Trustees reporting that they were now able to advance up to £5000, that the capital fund stood at £600,000 and that they owned eleven houses for letting. The Assembly of 1978 approved the imposition of a levy of 2% of stipend on all congregations. In 1981 a donation of £100,000 was received from the Hugh Fraser Foundation. In 1983 it was possible to report that the capital fund had topped the million mark, that the Fund owned fifty-two houses, that the rate of interest was 4% for ministers, 1% for widows and that the maximum loan was now £10,000 — it had risen to £20,000 two years later.

The Trustees are at pains to point out that "in this whole field of housing and loan policy changes inevitably occur, and that with some frequency, so that the best advice that can be offered to anyone contemplating retirement and consequently having a housing problem, is that they should without delay make contact with the Secretariat of the Department of Ministry to discuss the whole affair in its many aspects."

The Retirement Scheme Committee — The Committee acts as administrator of three separate schemes and as Trustee also in the case of the latter two. All three are "exempt approved" for purposes of Income and Corporation Taxes. They are (a) The Church of Scotland Retirement and Death Benefits Scheme for Ministers and Missionaries, open to Ministers and non-ordained employees of the Board of World Mission; (b) The Church of Scotland Board of National Mission Retirement Benefits Scheme, open to non-ordained employees of the Church who are appointed by the Board of National Mission; and (c) The Church of Scotland Protected Rights Scheme, open to members of Schemes (a) and (b) and of the Church of Scotland Retirement Benefits Scheme, provided they are employed in the United Kingdom.

Diaconate Committee — As explained in another place (p 231), the Diaconate of today represents what is in effect a union effected in 1988 of what had been the Lay Missionaries and the Deaconesses of the Church (strictly, those Lay Missionaries who so wished became Deacons in a newly constituted Diaconate.) Deacons and Deaconesses are engaged in the service of the Church in works of a pastoral, evangelical, educational, and social nature, mainly in parishes but also with other Committees of the Church and with outside organisations as approved by the Committee. The responsibilities of the Committee are defined as —

a) The welfare of Deacons and Deaconesses.
b) The servicing of the Diaconate Council.
c) Conferring with other Committees where appropriate.
d) Keeping before the Church the opportunities offered by the Diaconate.
e) All policy affecting the Diaconate and its status.

Committee on Chaplains to H M Forces — This body is not a constituent Committee of the Ministry Department but an independent Committee associated with that Department. It is entrusted with the task of recruitment, appointment and subsequent care of Chaplains for the Regular, the Reserve and the Auxiliary Forces. Vacancies occur periodically and the Committee is happy to receive enquiries from all interested Ministers. It maintains a Register of all those who have been baptised and/or admitted to Communicant Membership by Service Chaplains (but complains that it is so rarely asked about entries therein). A tradition has developed over many years whereby the report of this

Committee is given in on an Order of the Day for the afternoon of the Thursday when all available chaplains are expected to be on parade in uniform in the West Gallery and when an Officer from one of the Services gives an address — though I understand this is beingc depaerted from.

DEPARTMENT OF NATIONAL MISSION

This Department was establishcd in January 1993 on the split-up of what had been Ministry and Mission and took over what essentially had been the work of the earlier Home Board with some adjustments the chief of which was the inclusion of Parish Reappraisal to replace what had been Unions and Re-adjustments under the Board of Ministry. The Department's remit is to plan and to resource the mission of the Chuch of Scotland in the home land. It works through a Board and five separate committees, the duty of the Board being twofold, to formulate overall policy and to prepare and implement the budget.

The Committee on Parish Reappraisal — This, the successor to the former Committee on Unions and Readjustments —

a) will see to the implementation and operation of Act iv 1984, the current Act anent Unions and Readjustments;
b) will be responsible for all matters coming from Presbyteries regarding vacancies;
c) will deal with proposals for the staffing needs of parishes, including ministers, deaconesses, deacons, lay missionaries and lay agents;
d) will undertake the work of the former sub-committee on New Forms of Parish Ministry;
e) will, in consultation with the Presbyteries concerned, and following detailed discussion with the Committee on Extension Projects, determine where new buildings will be erected;
f) will be available, when requested, to assist and advise Presbyteries in regard to their own forward and readjustment planning.

Under the banner of "New Forms of Parish Ministry" the Committee had in 1993 responsibility for thirteen Associate Ministers and eight Community Ministers (see pp 226 ff) as well as for students employed through the Summer Student Appointments Scheme.

The Committee on Extension Projects — This is the successor to the former Church Extension Committee, but confronted with a totally different set of problems from those with which the earlier body had to contend, and, consequently, with a totally different remit. In accordance with the overall policy of the Board, the Committee, without prejudice to any other body, such as the General Trustees, which has prior rights or jurisdiction,

a) will be responsible for the erection of those new buildings which the Committee on Parish Reappraisal, in consultation with the Presbyteries concerned, and following detailed discussion with the Committee on Extension Projects, has determined are required;
b) will be responsible for advising on and, within the limits of its budget, assisting with major problems and expenditure associated with ongoing necesssary maintenance of buildings where there are building debts outstanding on the part of the congregations concerned, or where the congregations concerned are not yet in full status;
c) will be responsible for the appointment of ministers to Church Extension Charges (p 94); and
d) will, where requested, provide arbiters to make choice of which building(s) are to be retained in a readjustment situation.

The Committee on Mission and Evangelism Resources — The remit of this Committee is:
a) to develop vision for the work of mission and evangelism in Scotland;
b) to encourage mission and evangelism in Presbyteries and parishes through congregations of the Church of Scotland by means of research, development and training;
c) to support the work of the National Adviser in Mission and Evangelism and all other Advisers;
d) to ensure that the Centres under the Committee's direction are serving the missionary and evangelistic purposes of the Church to best advanage; and
e) to support projects which are advancing mission and evangelism in key areas of life in Scotland.

There is a National Adviser based at St Ninian's Crieff (see hereunder) who co-ordinates the work of a team of Advisers in encouraging and resourcing Presbyteries and congregations throughout Scotland in mission and evangelism.

The Committee is responsible for three residential centres — (a) *Badenoch Christian Centre* at Kincraig on Speyside, opened in 1976, is designed to combine Christian mission with the enjoyment of the local outdoor pursuits. (b) *St Ninian's Centre, Crieff* established as long ago as 1958 in a former Church building in the town and extensively altered and greatly extended (it can now provide accommodation for up to ninety residents) directs its energies towards the training of personnel for the work of evangelism within the setting of the parish. (c) *Carberry Tower* is a mansion-house dating back to 1480, situated close to Carberry Hill where Mary Queen of Scots surrendered in 1567. It is used mainly as a conference centre. The property had been taken over in 1985 by the then Mission Committee from the Board of Education to whom it had been given in 1961 by the Elphinstone family. On economic grounds its future is very uncertain at the time of writing, a report and recommendation being expected at the 1995 Assembly.

Projects in a wide variety of fields are being run under the aegis of the Committee, principally these: (a) *The Netherbow and John Knox House* where the integrated facilities of the Netherbow Theatre and the John Knox House Museum provide an important cultural and visitor centre and an international point of enquiry for those concerned with the past, present, and future of the Kirk as well as playing its part in the life of historic central Edinburgh. (b) The *Society, Religion and Technology Project,* a vision "before its time" when a technologist was appointed in 1970. The Report for 1985 describes the project as having been "established out of the conviction that part of the life and witness of the Church is to discover and interpret the forces which are shaping the future of society. In the modern world science and technology are centrally important. From this point of departure the project explores the middle ground between theological and ethical assumptions on the one hand and the pressing problems of technology and social changes on the other. The Project functions as a think-tank, an open forum for policy debate and a resource for adult Christian education". It is under the care of a full-time Director of the Project, whose work is based at The Netherbow though he has no responsibility for the other work undertken there; *(c) Summer Missions* — Each year over six hundred volunteers take part in summer mission teams at various centres throughout Scotland. (d) *St Francis in the East Church House* — For more than thirty years the Committee has provided financial assistance for the activities of this Centre in Bridgeton, Glasgow, which provides club facilities for young and old who have little or no Church connection; (e) *Glasgow Lodging House Mission* is based in the Institute in East Campbell Street, Glasgow its object being to care for the thousands of homeless in Scotland's industrial capital. The Presbytery of Glasgow manages the mission and the Chaplain is a Deacon. (f) *Ethnic Community Work* — A Community Worker serves the ethnic community of Glasgow based on a project in Govanhill called "The Well". *Other Activities* — The Committee also supports Ministry to Deaf People, has an interest in the Compass Ski Club, encourages congregations to sponsor Playgroups and Mother and Toddler Groups, and places Chaplains at Butlins Holiday Centre, Ayr.

The Committee on Chaplaincies — In accordance with the overall policy of the Board this Committee is responsible for appropriate matters concerning Chaplains in hospitals, in industry, in prisons, and in universities.

It was under the National Health Act of 1947 that a scheme was introduced whereby Ministers are appointed as Chaplains in all hospitals in Scotland. There are seventeen full-time and over three hundred part-time *Hospital Chaplains* as well as five full-time Chaplain's Assistants. Appointments are made by the General Secretary of the Board as the "appointing authority" in terms of the Act, but the choice is made by the Presbytery of the bounds which is also responsible for the oversight of the Chaplains' work.

The aim of *Industrial Mission* claims to be threefold — (a) to provide pastoral care and witness to the Gospel for men and women in all branches of industry in their place of work, (b) to assess in the interest of the Gospel the nature of the influence which industry exerts both on individuals and on society, and (c) to promote the desire for just relationships and understanding at all levels of our industrial society. There are at present eight full-time Directors of Industrial Mission and over a hundred part-time Industrial Chaplains (see also p 173).

With one exception all *Prison Chaplainces* are part-time posts — there are thirty-eight Ministers so serving in nineteen institutions. Appointments are now made on the recommendation of the Joint Prison Chaplaincies Board (see herunder).

Many of our Scottish Universities and Colleges boast a *University Chaplain* who works full-time among students and staff and who takes charge of the Chapel services. In most cases the Chaplain is appointed and maintained by the university authorities, but in other cases financial aid is given by the Board. In an increasing number of cases the new Universities are served in this realm by a Parish Minister working part-time.

The Committee on Field Staff — In accordance with its overall policy, the Board since 1994 is to be responsible for its own budget as well as for Departmental matters relating to the selection, training, deployment, and pastoral support of the full-time Lay Agents of the Church; and will liase on behalf of the Department with the Diaconate Committee. All field staff work under the direction of this Committee.

The Iona Community Board — This body consists of members of the Community and Church representatives appointed by the Assembly. It meets twice yearly to hear accounts of the Community's work in Iona, on Mull and on the mainland, and to assist the Community's task of seeking "new ways to touch the hearts of all." Though independent from the Church the Board reports to the General Assembly each year and for this purpose it is regarded as falling within this Department.

Advisory Committee on Artistic Matters — This Committee is not part of the Department but is "associated" with it and reports to the Assembly under its banner. It was set up in 1934 to advise congregations and Presbyteries on the most appropriate way of carrying out renovations, alterations etc. It also advises on the installation of stained glass, tapestries, memorials, furniture and furnishings. Congregations are urged to seek the advice of the Committee at an early stage in any "alteration process", and in case of Churches dating before 1840 such consultation is mandatory. In recent years the Assembly has imposed additional duties upon the Committee — a) preparing reports on the architectural, historical and aesthetic merit of the buildings involved in questions of readjustment; b) verification of the propriety of repair and renovation work forming the basis of grant applications to the Historic Buildings Council for Scotland; c) establishing an Organ Sub-committee to offer advice on the maintenance and installation of pipe organs; d) setting up a Depository for surplus Church furnishings and furniture; and e) compiling a Register of Churches.

The Assembly of 1994 agreed on the recommendation of the Assembly Council that as from October 1994 a full-time Secretary should be appointed to serve this Committee as well as the Panels on Doctrine and on Worship, and when this happens (in 1995) the Committee will cease to be "associated" with the Department of National Mission.

Joint Prison Chaplaincies Board — The General Assembly of 1989 proposed and approved the setting up of this body to consist of seven representatives — from the Church of Scotland three, from the Roman Catholic Church two, and from the Scottish Episcopal Churches one, along with one from the Prison Department of the Scottish Home and Health Department. It is responsible for advising that Department regarding the appointment and terms of service of all Ministers and Priests acting as Chaplains in prisons. These duties had until then fallen to our own Prison Chaplains Committee, answerable to the General Assembly for all its actings. Clearly this new Board is completely free of Assembly control with the result that Assembly approval is no longer necessary for such appointments to be effective. I take it, though, that Presbytery approval would still be a *sine qua non* for any Church of Scotland Minister accepting such an appointment. It is provided that consultation with representatives of the Presbytery concerned is required before any chaplain is recommended for a second five-year stint, and this I take to mean that consultation will in every case take place with Presbytery before the end of the original five years to consider the possibility of renewal.

Consultative Committee on Church Properties — This is a body created by the Assembly of 1992. Presbyteries are not to approve repairs or improvements at buildings if the cost is in excess of a "Financial Limit" approved by the General Assembly (currently 15,000 inclusive of VAT and professional fees) unless it is satisfied either that the building is a necessary one, or that the work is necessary in the interest of safety or to preserve its value as a marketable asset. If the Presbytery is satisfied that these criteria have been met and wishes to give approval to the work proceeding it must refer the case to the Consultative Committee which may either concur or not. The ultimate decision, however, lies with the Presbytery.

BOARD OF SOCIAL RESPONSIBILITY

It was in the 1966 restructuring that the Committee on Social Service, the Committee on Moral Welfare (which included what had at one time been a very powerful Temperance Committee), and the Women's Committee on Social and Moral Welfare were brought together under one administration as the Department of Social and Moral Welfare, changing its name ten years later to that of Department of Social Responsibility. Changes recently effected in Committee structures have had little effect in this area except that the "Department" has become a "Board" and it has

moved its offices from George Street to Charis House, 47 Milton Road East, Edinburgh. Its aims have been defined as —
a) to secure in the Church informed opinion on contemporary social and ethical issues; b) to encourage balanced judgment on these issues and to press these judgments at all levels of influence; and c) to offer compassionate service through the varied activities which it operates, and to encourage and to enable increasing care work at the level of the parish. The "varied activities" referred to in (c) are divided under two heads of Community Services and Elderly Services. The former include Counselling and Support Centres, Dependency, HIV/AIDS, Epilepsy, General Supported Accommodation, Homelessness, Learning Disabilities, Mental Health, Offenders, Residential Schools; while the latter embraces forty-two residential homes for the elderly, four of which care specifically for those suffering from Alzheimer's Disease or Senile Dementia.

BOARD OF WORLD MISSION

It is difficult to dissociate the name of either of the main branches of the Church of Scotland from the idea of Foreign Mission to which they were so passionately attached. Thereby hangs a tale well worth the telling, but for our present purpose let us take up the story as recently as 1985 when a new body began to function under the title of World Mission and Unity being successor to the Overseas Council, itself a conglomorate of Foreign Mission, Jewish Mission, Continental Churches and Colonial Chuches, representing "World Mission" and the Inter-Church Relations Committee representing "Unity". These two bodies had been brought together at the time of the 1966 re-organisation as the Department of Overseas Mission and Inter-Church Relations, but had in fact continued to function as two completely independent bodies. From 1984 the attempt has been made for them really and not merely nominally to act as one, but with little success. The remit of the Board of World Mission was to enable the membership of the Church of Scotland at local, Presbytery and national levels, to experience and enjoy being part of the world-wide Church of Jesus Christ, sharing in the mission of God, as partners with other Churches in the work of seeking God's kingdom on earth.

It operated through ten Committees — (1) *Global*, dealing with relations with ecumenical bodies, co-ordination of specialist groups including Christian-Jewish consultations, working-party on racism, community of women and men, faith and order, dialogue with other faiths, theological education and ministry training, health and healing, and Latin-American concern; (2) *Local Involvement* — acting as a servicing committee on behalf of the other committees of the Board; (3) *Pesonnel* — taking to do with recruitment, selection and training of overseas staff, staff support and resettlement, and co-ordinating with World Exchange; (4) *Sub-Saharan Africa and the Carribean; (5) Middle East and North Africa* — both as the name implies; (6) *Asia*, covering relations with partner Churches in that continent; (7) *Europe*, having to do with the Presbytery of that name as well as with the Conference of European Churches; (8) *United Kingdom and Eire* — involving participation in ACTS (Action of Churches Together in Scotland) and CCBI (Council of Churches for Britain and Ireland), and relations with Anglicans, Baptists, Orthodox, Reformed, and Roman Catholics; (9) Finance; and (10) Executive — both as the names imply.

In 1993 the Assembly reviewed the work of the Board and resolved to split it into two bodies — the Board of World Mission and the Committee on Ecumenical Affairs. "The Board of World Mission continues with the work overseas and has Committees for sub-Saharan Africa, for Asia, for the Middle East and North Africa, for Caribbean, Central and South America, and a Europe Committee. It also has Local Involvement, Staffing, and Finance Committees. These indicate a slight reallocation in the area committees' work but a continuation of the committees as above or as already described. The work of the former United Kingdom and Eire Committee became a major part of the work of the Committee on Ecumenical Affairs. The working groups, which were made up of specialist groups reporting to the Global Committee continued in another form. The working party on Racism became part of the work of the Scottish Churches Agency for Racial Justice (SCARJ) the work of the Community of Women and Men is at the time of writing under review by the Assembly Council and will be the subject of report to the Assembly of 1995. Christian-Jewish Consultations are co-ordinated by Ecumenical Affairs. The Board of World Mission has representatives on most of these working groups."

It is through the Board that we maintain our connection with *Christian Aid*. This is an official relief and development agency of Churches in Britain and Ireland (including ourselves), in association with CCBI. Christian Aid's mandate is to challenge and enable us to fulfil our responsibility to the poor of the world. Half-a-million volunteers and collectors, some fifty Board and Committee members, and close on two hundred paid staff make this possible.

Committee on Ecumenical Affairs — As explained above, this is a new body that came into being on 1st January 1994 to enable the Church of Scotland at local, Presbytery and national levels, increasingly to maximise opportunities and resources for worship, witness and service together with other Churches and related organisations in this country, working wherever possible through existing Boards and Committees of the Church. In fulfilment of this remit the Committee is —

a) to be the body within the Kirk through which ecumenical instruments in Britain and Ireland relate;
b) to call together for planning, briefing and the exchanging of information the Church's representatives on WCC, ACTS, CCBI and the like;
c) to bring to the Assembly names of those who might serve on ACTS, CCBI and other ecumenical bodies;
d) to receive reports from Church representatives attending Assemblies or Synods of other Churches or ecumenical conferences or gatherings and to ensure that appropriate sections of such reports are passed on to Committees which have a concern;
e) to assist generally and report to the Assembly on local Ecumenical Projects and Parishes and to help where questions relating to the law and practice of the Church are involved; and
f) to be the Committee through which reports are submitted to the General Assembly from Groups appointed to take part on behalf of the Church in formal conversations and doctrinal dialogues with other Church and ecumenical bodies.

It is indeed sad that so much of the history of each of our Churches has been concerned with division and fraction, and it is cheering, therefore, that today there are so many forces working towards closer understanding and a deeper unity among denominations, and this largely through the activities of inter-Church organisations, of which there are many. One such body with which the Kirk has all along had the closest links is the *World Alliance of Reformed Churches*. This dates from 1875 and is oldest by far of such bodies. It began when twenty-one Presbyterian and Reformed Churches sent delegates to London where they constituted themselves "The Alliance of the Reformed Churches throughout the World Holding the Presbyterian System." In 1891 there had been established, also in London, the Inernational Congregational Council. At Nairobi in 1970 these two bodies voted themselves out of existence and united to form "The World Alliance of Reformed Churches (Presbyterian and Congregational)". The 1988 Report of the Alliance states, "The Churches in the Alliance differ greatly in size, ethos and organisation. Sadly, many of them are in an unhappy relationship with the State in their respective countries. Their witness to the Gospel brings them into conflict with their Governments; this is especially so in Korea, Taiwan, Souh Africa, Latin America and Islamic countries. The Alliance is a source of support to them in their sufferings, and for Churches in countries where there is no such repression it is a constant reminder that their loyalty is higher than national."

The Church of Scotland is a founder member of the *World Council of Churches* (WCC) formed at Amsterdam in 1948 by the fusion of the Faith and Order Movement (dating from 1927) and the Life and Work Movement (established in 1925). I have to confess that the Basis of this organisation, adoped in 1961 has always had me confused — it declares itself to be "a fellowship of Churches which confess the Lord Jesus Christ as God and Saviour according to the Scriptures, and therefore seek to fulfil their common calling to the glory of the one God, Father, Son, and Holy Spirit." It is the word "therefore" that has me puzzled. If it had said simply "and which seek to fulfil" that would seem to me a perfect description of the situation — or would be if it went on to define exactly what is the "common calling" referred to. Without that we are merely begging the question. And the interpolation of the "therefore" where there is no logical sequence seems merely an attempt to lend an air of logical certainty to something where it does not exist. So much for my own difficulty — which does not appear to be generally shared. The Council's more than three hundred member Churches are drawn from all continents and include all major traditions (except the Roman Catholic, though they now are taking an interest). In course of the nearly fifty years of its existence the rise in importance, prominence and indeed dominance of WCC has been meteoric so that it is now very much a force to be reckoned with in the affairs of its constituent Churches. Its extensive offices are in Geneva and its organisation there is indeed impressive.

Then there is the *Conference of European Churches*, a body with a most significant role to play at this time when we are still trying to accustom ourselves to the effects of the Single European Act of 1992. Founded at the time of the Cold War to assist in the work of reconciliation it is interesting that now it is facing the challenge of helping with the creation of a new order.

It was September 1990 that saw the emergence of the *Council of Churches for Britain and Ireland* (CCBI) and of *Action of Churches Together in Scotland* (ACTS) with sister organisations for Wales and for

England. CCBI holds a large Assembly every second year, Church Representive Meeting holds meetings two or three times a year, and a Steering Committee meets almost monthly. It has Commissions on a variety of topics. ACTS has a Central Council and three Commissions — on Unity, Faith and Order; on Mission, Evangelism and Education; and on Justice, Peace, Social and Moral Issues. It has five Committees — on Local and Regional Unity, on Communications, on Youth Action, on Women's Participation (entitled Network of Ecumical Women in Scotland), and on Scottish Churches' House.

DEPARTMENT OF EDUCATION

This consists of two Committees, the Committee on Education and the Committee on Education for the Ministry.

The Committee on Education — is the oldest continuing Committee of the General Assembly. It acts for the Assembly on all matters of education — in schools, colleges and universities. It participates in the work of the Scottish Joint Committee on Christian Education, endeavouring to foster co-operation between church and school. Towards this end it seeks to suppoprt those involved in religious education in schools, and especially School Chaplains. It has established useful and practical links with the Roman Catholic Church through its Education Commission, and it has a good record of liaison with the Educational Institute of Scotland and with the other unions in the educational field. It is the body generally approached by H M Government for submission of evidence on behalf of the Assembly.

The Committee on Education for the Ministry — The remit of this Committee covers both the regular full-time ministry and the Auxiliary Ministry.

The Committee is charged with the recruitment, selection and education of candidates for the ministry. It provides bursaries for those who are not eligible for SAAS (Student Awards Agency Scotland) awards, supervises the prescribed course of training and arranges the Probationary Period which candidates serve after the completion of their academic course. The Committee also interviews ordained Ministers who seek admission, or re-admission, to the ministry of the Church of Scotland by petition to the General Assembly, and it processes applications for Certificates of Eligibility.

"An Auxiliary Minister is a person who has been ordained for life to a ministry of Word and Sacrament exercisable under supervision on a part-time and non-stipendiary basis." All intending applicants must be communicant members of the Church of Scotland, must normally have been, over a recent period of not less than three years such communicant members, and must be recommended for this ministry by both the Minister and the Kirk Session of their congregation." The recruitment of candidates is declared to be a function of Presbyteries. A prospective candidate therefore makes approach in the first place to the Clerk of his Presbytery.

The matter is governed in terms of Act iii of 1987 as amended in 1989 and 1994 (see pp 141 ff).

BOARD OF PARISH EDUCATION

Why this Board should not be part of the Department of Education is a mystery for which the writer has been quite unable to find the solution.

It consists of Committees on (a) Leadership, Development and Training, (b) Curriculum Development and Production, and (c) St Colm's Education Centre and College, situated at 20 Inverleith Terrace, Edinburgh. Its remit is to oversee the development and delivery of an Education service for members of the Church of Scotland and to participate in the work of the Scottish Churches Open College. The Board is responsile too for the provision at St Colm's of training for Lay Agents for the Department of Mission, though training for overseas candidates of the Board of World Mission is now provided at Selly Oak. The eductional services provided cover a variety of areas and age groups and give scope for a wide range of delivery models. The areas currently catered for are — (a) Adult Education, (b) Youth and Young Adult Work, (c) Sunday School and Bible Class Work, and (d) Curriculum Development. The Board also maintains a Field Staff of five full-time personnel — A Curriculum Officer and Assistant, a Research and Development Officer in Special Educational Needs, a Glasgow Presbytery Youth Adviser, and a Warden of Stroove, the House at Skelmorlie.

BOARD OF COMMUNICATION

The Department of Publicity and Publication was created in 1965 and has continued with very little change under its new title of Board of

Communication. It has the remit *inter alia* "to keep before the Church the need for effective communication both within the Church and to the world .... and to provide for the Church of Scotland a professional service of publicity, publishing, bookselling (now departed from), and the production of the monthly magazine "Life and Work" and of the "Church of Scotland Year Book" a copy of which is now being distributed free of charge to all Miinisters in charges. It works through a number of channels —

1 *The Press Office* — providing a news and information service to press, radio and television.

2 *Publicity and Design Services* — concerned with the design and production of a wide range of literature, display materials and exhibitions. A mailing list is maintained to provide local magazine editors with suitable resource material.

3 *Pathway Productions* — producing and marketing audio-visual aids, videos, tape-slide sets and audio cassettes. Short training courses in television, radio and video are available.

4 *"Life and Work"* — the monthly magazine of the Church of Scotland designed to keep the membership informed about events in church life at home and abroad, to provide a forum for Christian opinion, and a facility for debating a variety of topics — and still boasting a circulation of well over eighty thousand. The Editor has complete control over the content of the magazine, though there is associated with him a consultative committee to whose "suggestions" he is "bound to give due consideration."

5 *The Saint Andrew Press* — which was created in 1954, largely as the result of the enormous success of Willie Barclay's Daily Study Bible series — has been responsible for a great number of publications many of which have contributed significantly to Christian literature. Not only has it functioned in the wider world of publication the press has provided publishing facilities for all the Departments and Boards of the Church. At this juncture the Press is confining its activities to the production of material ordered by the Church itself.

Until very recently the Board ran no fewer than eight Bookshops throughout the country. Financial considerations have led to these being made over to Wesley Owen Books and Music.

The Board also maintains a keen interest in the whole field of broadcasting and television, keeping in close touch with the Churches Advisory Committee for Local Broadcasting (CACLB) and the Association of Christians in Local Broadcasting (ACLB).

THE LAW DEPARTMENT

This is a Department in a different sense from those we have been dealing with hitherto, having neither Boards nor Committees — nor even Committee Members! It consists of the Solicitor of the Church and of the General Trustees (one person) and his Depute supported by three Assistants, all qualified Solicitors. Among them they contrive to provide the necessary advice and practical help of a legal nature required by all of the Departments and Boards of the Church as well as doing a great deal of work for congregations in matters of property.

The Church's principal legal adviser is, of course, the Procurator, but he is free of any connection with the Law Department, and can be approached only through the Principal Clerk.

GLOSSARY

I have tried so far as possible to avoid throughout the text the use of Latin tags, technical terms and the like, but this has not always been possible. In any case it is good to have a glossary available, and so I have compiled this fairly comprehensive one including in it terms which I do not think you will find in these pages but which are to be met with in common use in the field of Kirk law.

Ad vitam aut culpam — till life or fault
Apologia — justification
Apud acta — there and then in presence of the court
Attestation — the authenticating of a document by the signature of officials

Benefice — a living; what is provided for the Minister
Bona fide — in good faith

Ceteris paribus — other things being equal — not, as one often hears said, all things being equal
Citation — an order to appear at a court
Compear — appear in answer to a citation or in defence of an interest
Competent — accepted by law
Compus mentis — of sound mind
Conge d'elire — right of choice (of their own minister)
Contumacy — the offence of treating the court with contempt
Corpus delicti — the body of the offence
Cum nota — with a mark (or remark)

Decern — to find, to decree, to pass judgment
De die in diem — from one day to the next
De facto — the actual situation; as a matter of fact
De fideli (*administratione officii*) — the vow to perform an office faithfully
De jure — as of right
De novo — over again; afresh

Deposition — (1) judicial removal from an office: (2) a piece of evidence recorded on oath
Dictum (plural *dicta*) — a saying

Edict — a public intimation served by authority and attested as having been so served
Effeirs — belongs, pertains
Excambion — exchange, usually of one piece of land for another
Ex adverso — opposite
Ex gratia — a gift; from favour and not of right
Ex officio — in virtue of an office held
Ex parte — in favour of one party
Exit Certificate — a document testifying that a Candidate has successfully completed his training for the ministry
Expectant — a probationer looking for a call
Ex proprio motu — at one's own instigation
Extract — a passage from the minutes of a court, issued by the authorised official

Fama — a scandalous report
Fama clamosa — a widespread fama, a public scandal
Formula — a set form of words; used of the subscription to the Confession of Faith required of office-holders
Fiars (Fiars Prices) — the average price of various grains for each county judicially determined (for the calculation of stipend)
Funditus Nulus — absolutely void from start to finish

Glebe — a stretch of land usually adjoining the manse which is for the use of the minister during his incumbency

Hearsay — evidence at second hand
Heresy — divergence from the doctrine accepted by the Church

In causa — in the case
Infra — below
In hunc effectum — for this purpose only
In initialibus — in the preliminary pleas (of a case)
In retentis — held, used of documents not recorded but retained
Instanter — as of now; immediately
Inter alia — among other things
Interim — in the meantime; for the present
Interim Act — one in force for that year only
In toto — wholly

Inter vivos — between living persons
Ipsis factis et rebus — by the very facts and circumstances
Ipsisimis verbis — in those very words
Ipso facto — by the very fact or deed
Ish and entry — outlet and entry to property; right of access
Ius devolutum — a right which because it was not timeously exercised by those having it has devolved on another

Jurisdiction — the authority which entitles a court to entertain and to judge a cause

Libel — a formal indictment by which a Minister or Probationer is charged with misconduct or heresy
Locum tenens — temporary holder of an office: stand-in
Locus standi — official standing; the right to appear before a court

Minister emeritus — retired minister of .....
Ministerium vagum — a ministry at large
Modus operandi — way of doing a thing
Moiety — a proportion (usually of a stipend)
Mortis causa — following upon and consequent upon death
Munus publicum — a public office
Mutatis Mutandis — assuming all relevant consequent changes

Nec tamen consumebatur — yet it was not consumed — a reference to the burning bush, symbol of the Church of Scotland
Nobile officium — the power of a supreme court to make good the absence of law in a particular situation
Notour — notorious

Obiter dictum — a passing observation in a cause but not part of the judgment
Onus probandi — the responsibility to provide proof
Ordination — "the solemn setting apart of a person to some public Church office" (Ch Gov)
Overture — a call for legislation brought before a superior court

Pari passu — step by step; with equal pace
Per se — by itself; by himself or herself
"Playpen" — playful name for the enclosure in front of the Lord High Commissioner's gallery in the Assembly Hall reserved for the Moderator, the Clerks, the Procurator, the Convener and Vice-Convener of the Business Committee and the Solicitor of the Church

Preamble — Short statement of the Church's constitutional position read on formal occasions
Precognition — a preliminary statement taken from a witness but not on oath
Prescription — the eradication of a claim because it has not been timeously enforced
Prima facie — on the face of things
Primus inter pares — first among equals
Privilege — defence against action of defamation for statements made in good faith without malice, there being probable cause, in discharge of a public duty
Pro bono ecclesiae — for the good of the Church
Pro forma — an accepted way of presentation
Pro non scripto — treated as though it had not been written
Pro rata — proportionately
Pro re nata — for some unexpected and urgent item of business
Pro tempore — for the time-being

Quasi — as if; as it were
Quoad civilia — in respect of civil matters
Quoad omnia — in regard to all matters, sacred and civil
Quoad sacra — in respect of sacred (i e ecclesiastical) matters
Quoad ultra — in respect of all else
Quorum — the fixed minimum present to costitute a valid meeting
Quoad vide — which see
q v, a reference to some other part of the book

Reductio ad absurdum — the reduction of a claim because logically followed to its conclusion it leads to absurdity
Res gestae — things done; business transacted
Res noviter — some matter that has just emerged, having been unknown earlier in the proceedings
Respondent — the party replying to the appellant in a case

Sasine — The symbolic transference of earth or stone to mark the transfer of heritage — the event being recorded in the Register of Sasines.
Sederunt — "they sat"; those present at the meeting; sometimes applied to the meeting itself
Seriatim — in succession, one after the other
Serving — the technical term for the public reading of an edict or the delivering of a summons

Simpliciter — exactly as said, neither more nor less
Sine die — without limit of time
Sine mora — without delay
Sine qua non — absolutely essential
Singular successor — one who succeeds to property otherwise than by descent
Sist execution of sentence — in a case where sentence has been pronounced take no steps towards its execution because appeal has been taken or for other such reason
Sist parties — call parties to the bar
Sist procedure — to interrupt procedure temporarily
Slander — a defamatory statement made in malice
Spiritualia ("the spirituality") — the stipend of a living as distinguished from the *temporalia* (q v)
Sub judice — in process of being tried
Supra — above

Tanquam jure devoluto — see *ius devolutum* above
Temporalia — all the benefits of the charge apart from the stipend
Terminus ad quem — end towards which
Terminus ex quo — end from which

Ultra vires — beyond the legitimate power of the court

Vesting — the process whereby the property in some item of income passes to the new owner
Victual Stipend — the stipend expressed in terms of grain etc
Visitation of Records — examination and inspection of books by a superior court
Volte face — complete turn-about

GENERAL INDEX